CU00727584

THE YEARBOOK OF LANGLAND STUDIES

Editors
Alastair Bennett, Royal Holloway, University of London
Katharine Breen, Northwestern University
Eric Weiskott, Boston College

Editorial Assistants
Kaitlin Browne and Wenhan Zhang, Northwestern University

Editorial Board
Stephen A. Barney, Emeritus, University of California, Irvine
Michael Calabrese, California State University, Los Angeles
Andrew Cole, Princeton University
Rita Copeland, University of Pennsylvania
Isabel Davis, Birkbeck College, University of London
Andrew Galloway, Cornell University
Alexandra Gillespie, University of Toronto
Simon Horobin, Magdalen College, University of Oxford
Traugott Lawler, Emeritus, Yale University
Jill Mann, Emerita, University of Notre Dame
and Girton College, University of Cambridge
Linne R. Mooney, University of York
Ad Putter, University of Bristol
Elizabeth Robertson, University of Glasgow
Wendy Scase, University of Birmingham
D. Vance Smith, Princeton University
Thorlac Turville-Petre, Emeritus, University of Nottingham
Nicholas Watson, Harvard University
Nicolette Zeeman, King's College, University of Cambridge

The Yearbook of Langland Studies

34 (2020)

Edited by

ALASTAIR BENNETT, KATHARINE BREEN,
AND ERIC WEISKOTT

BREPOLS

YLS welcomes submissions dealing with *Piers Plowman* and related poetry and prose in the traditions of didactic and allegorical alliterative writing. Papers concerning the literary, historical, religious, intellectual, codicological, and critical contexts of these works are also invited. Submissions are doubleblind peer reviewed. In preparing their manuscripts for review, authors should avoid revealing their identity within the essay itself and follow the MHRA Style Guide (available at http://www.mhra. org.uk/Publications/Books/ StyleGuide/download.shtml). The editors are Alastair Bennett (Royal Holloway, University of London), Katharine Breen (Northwestern University), and Eric Weiskott (Boston College); please send submissions to yls.submissions@gmail.com.

Individual subscriptions are included in membership in the International *Piers Plowman* Society. To become a member, visit our website (www.piersplowman.org). Information on institutional subscriptions should be sought from Brepols Publishers (periodicals@ brepols.net). Back issues of volumes 1–19 may be ordered from Medieval Institute Publications, Western Michigan University, 1903 W. Michigan Avenue, Kalamazoo, MI 49008–5432 (http://www.wmich.edu/ medieval/mip/). Back issues starting with volume 20 can be acquired from Brepols. The complete run of *YLS*, from the first issue in 1987, is available online to those whose institutions subscribe to the e-journal through Brepols (see http://www.brepolsonline.net/loi/yls).

© 2020, Brepols Publishers n.v., Turnhout, Belgium.

All rights reserved. No part of this publication may be reproduced, stored in a retrieval system, or transmitted, in any form or by any means, electronic, mechanical, photocopying, recording, or otherwise without the prior permission of the publisher.

D/2020/0095/218
ISBN 978-2-503-58768-4
DOI 10.1484/J.YLS.5.121049

ISSN 0890-2917
eISSN 2031-0242

Printed in the EU on acid-free paper.

Table of Contents

List of Figures   7

Commentary   9

Soul-Making in *Piers Plowman*
Elizabeth ROBERTSON   11

Langland and Wales: Place, Identity, Borders
Helen PHILLIPS   57

Community, Charity, and Penetration: Langland's Queer Ecclesiology
Jamie TAYLOR   93

Personification, Action, and Economic Power in *Piers Plowman*
William RHODES   117

Convergent Variation and the Production of *Piers Plowman*
Lawrence WARNER   137

Teaching Reflection

**Langland, Milton, and the Weird Trees: Teaching and Learning
through *Piers Plowman* and *Paradise Lost***
Sarah TOLMIE   177

Notes

'Grace is a gras': Theological Uses of Metaphor in *Piers Plowman*
Jennifer SISK   203

**Contact between *Piers Plowman* and *The Prick of Conscience* in
Rawlinson Poetry 139**
Thomas KITTEL   211

Reviews

Historians on John Gower
(ed. by Stephen H. Rigby, with Siân Echard)
Stephanie L. BATKIE   223

*Richard Rolle's 'Melody of Love': A Study and Translation with Manuscript
and Musical Contexts*
(by Andrew Albin)
Timothy L. GLOVER   227

*The Penn Commentary on 'Piers Plowman': Volume 2: C Passūs 5–9; B
Passūs 5–7; A Passūs 5–8*
(by Ralph Hanna)
Kathryn KERBY-FULTON   230

The Politics of Middle English Parables: Fiction, Theology, and Social Practice
(by Mary Raschko)
Larry SCANLON   235

Approaches to Teaching Langland's 'Piers Plowman'
(ed. by Thomas A. Goodmann)
Jennifer L. SISK   239

Imagined Romes: The Ancient City and its Stories in Middle English Poetry
(by C. David Benson)
Zachary STONE   242

'Piers Plowman' and the Reinvention of Church Law in the Late Middle Ages
(by Arvind Thomas)
Jamie K. TAYLOR   246

Annual Bibliography, 2019
Chase PADUSNIAK   251

List of Figures

Figure 1. The soul, represented as a homunculus, leaves the body of a dying man, from a Carthusian miscellany, executed in Northern England in the second or third quarter of the fifteenth century. London, British Library, MS Additional 37049, fol. 19^r. © The British Library Board. 20

Figure 2. Soul being lifted up. Leaf from a Book of Hours with a prayer for the Dead and the beginning of Psalm 118, fourth quarter of the fourteenth century. London, British Library, MS Additional 71118F. © The British Library Board. 21

Figure 3. David playing the Cittern to his soul. Reproduced with kind permission from Stuttgart, Wuerttembergische Landesbibliothek, Cod. bibl. fol. 23, fol. 55^r. 24

Figure 4. Soul as castle: from a Carthusian miscellany, executed in the second or third quarter of the fifteenth century. London. British Library, MS Additional 37049, f. 71^r. © The British Library Board. 27

Figure 5. 'A dysputacion betwyx the saule & the body when it is past oute of the body', from a Carthusian miscellany, executed in Northern England in the second or third quarter of the fifteenth century. London, British Library, MS Additional 37049, fol. 82^r. © The British Library Board. 30

Figure 6. The parts of the soul. Cambridge, Cambridge University Library, MS Gg.1.1, fol. 490^v. Reproduced by kind permission of the Syndics of Cambridge University Library. 32

Figure 7. The Tree of Life, from a Carthusian miscellany, executed in Northern England in the second or third quarter of the fifteenth century. London, British Library, MS Additional 37049, fol. 25^r © The British Library Board. 38

Figure 8. Plowing with oxen, from the Luttrell Psalter, executed in England, c. 1320–40. London, British Library, MS Additional 42130, fol. 170^r. © The British Library Board. 41

Figure 9. Man sowing, from the Luttrell Psalter, executed in England, c. 1320–40. London, British Library, MS Additional 42130, fol. 170^v. © The British Library Board. 42

Figure 10. Harvesting, from the Luttrell Psalter, executed in England, c. 1320–40. London, British Library, MS Additional 42130, fol. 172^v. © The British Library Board. 43

Figure 11. Theoretical A>B Revision (Madrinkian's diagram). 139

Commentary

We write this commentary in May 2020 from our homes in Boston, Chicago, and London, either under lockdown due to COVID-19 or just beginning to emerge from it. Like many other academics, we are trying to combine caregiving and homeschooling with online teaching and scholarly publishing — not always successfully. One of us is the partner of a frontline healthcare worker. Another has been trying to cope with a family member's illness, at a time when much is uncertain and testing is not readily available. We recognize that other Langlandians face much more difficult situations: they are directly confronting life-threatening illness; they have been furloughed or terminated from their positions; they face extended isolation due to underlying health conditions; they are finishing up their studies at a time when the academic and non-academic job markets have almost ceased functioning.

Under these circumstances, the annual ritual of sending *YLS* to our publisher feels both less important and more important than usual. On the one hand, the publication of a scholarly journal devoted to *Piers Plowman* studies does not figure on any government's list of essential services. It will not feed the hungry, clothe the naked, or hasten the development of a vaccine. On the other hand, it represents the continuity of intellectual inquiry, and of the humanities' commitment to making sense of our world even as it changes. We very much hope that by the time this volume is published, in late winter or early spring 2021, we will again be teaching our students face to face and meeting with our colleagues to exchange ideas. Even without such in-person meetings, the essays in this volume participate in that dynamic of intellectual exchange and testify to the vibrancy of our field, despite the obstacles we are currently facing.

The first essay in *YLS* 34 recalls the last time Langlandians were able to meet in person, at the Seventh International *Piers Plowman* Society Conference, held at the University of Miami in April 2019. Elizabeth Robertson's keynote address, entitled 'Soulmaking in *Piers Plowman*', argues that the poem traces the process whereby Will comes to know himself as an embodied soul, simultaneously forming his own soul and developing increasingly sophisticated models of the soul as he proceeds. Later in the volume, Jamie Taylor's essay on Langland's queer ecclesiology, Jennifer Sisk's note on theological uses of metaphor, and Thomas Kittel's note on *Piers Plowman*'s influence on the version of the *Prick of Conscience* in MS Rawlinson poetry 139 likewise derive from work presented in Miami, and were enriched by the characteristic intellectual generosity of its question-and-answer periods. These essays' wide range of methodologies speaks to the productive breadth of approaches within Langland Studies.

Beyond the conference, Helen Phillips's study of Langland and Wales traces the poem's engagement with Wales and the Marches, connecting the dreamer's divided and equivocal self-presentation to a border mentality that looks on one hand towards the power centres of London and Westminster, and on the other towards a colonized hinterland. Will Rhodes's essay on Meed, Hunger, and Hawkyn carries on the work of *YLS* 33's cluster on personification, arguing that these prosopopoeia make economic relations visible, and thus subject to analysis and critique. Lawrence Warner responds to Michael Madrinkian's essay in *YLS* 32, arguing with George Kane and E. Talbot Donaldson, and *contra* Madrinkian, Ralph Hanna, and Sarah Wood, that convergent variation best accounts for agreements across *Piers Plowman*'s manuscript families.

Sarah Tolmie's contribution to the new category of 'Teaching Reflection' argues that *Piers Plowman* and Milton's *Paradise Lost* at once represent experiential learning and demand it from contemporary readers. Tolmie's interpretation complements Roberston's understanding of *Piers* as an enactment of self-formation, while at the same time expanding *YLS*'s remit to include the poem's role in twenty-first century pedagogy. Recognizing that the future of Langland Studies depends on compelling teaching, the editors invite additional submissions concerned with *Piers Plowman* in the classroom, ranging from reflections like Tolmie's to discussions of assignments and syllabi. Building on Tolmie's essay and recent publications such as Thomas Goodmann's *Approaches to Teaching Langland's 'Piers Plowman'* (reviewed in this volume), we hope to spark a more robust conversation about teaching Langland's poem.

Finally, the *YLS* editors ask you to join us in welcoming Chase Padusniak to the journal's editorial team. Beginning with this volume, Chase will be taking over from Alastair Bennett as editor of the Annual Bibliography. We thank Chase for the meticulous work he has already done, and for his broader spirit of service to the field.

Alastair Bennett
Katharine Breen
Eric Weiskott

ELIZABETH ROBERTSON

Soul-Making in *Piers Plowman*

▼ **KEYWORDS** soul, soul-making, will, Augustine, Aquinas, voluntarism, negative dialectics

▼ **ABSTRACT** *Piers Plowman* charts the protagonist Will's 'soul-making' (in a Keatsian sense). Through all his encounters, including those with images of the soul as a lady in a castle, a 'thing', a tree, and a plow, Will becomes 'informed', manifesting aspects of the soul described by Augustine and Aquinas, but ultimately as understood in voluntarist thought in which will predominates over reason. While the poem draws on the latest theological debates about the soul, including disputes concerning the autonomy and ethical demands of the conscience, it is the poetry itself — especially through its Adornian negative dialectical method — that most fully expresses the making of a soul governed by an ineffable will

This essay is dedicated to the memory of Sister Mary Clemente Davlin

On 21 April 1819, John Keats wrote a letter to his brother and sister-in-law in which he presented his alternative to the prevailing view of salvation: 'The common cognomen of this world among the misguided and the superstitious is "a vale of tears", from which we are to be redeemed by a certain arbitrary interposition of God and taken to Heaven — What a little circumscribe[d] straightened notion! Call the world if you Please "The vale of Soul-Making".'[1] The fourteenth-century poem, *Piers Plowman*, anticipates Keats's ideas about the place of the soul in the world, and presents, I argue, a history of the protagonist Will's soul-making. Critics have warned against identifying the 'I' of the poem with a single, consistently developing subject, asking us instead to consider the poem as proffering a number of subject positions made

---

1 Keats, 'Letter to George and Georgiana Keats', 21 April 1819, in *Letters*, II, 101–02.

Elizabeth Robertson (Elizabeth.Robertson@glasgow.ac.uk) is Professor and the Established Chair of English Language at the University of Glasgow and Professor Emerita at the University of Colorado.

The Yearbook of Langland Studies, 34 (2020), 11–56   BREPOLS ❧ PUBLISHERS   10.1484/J.YLS.5.121086

up of a variety of dialogic discourses.[2] But whomever we deem the protagonist of the poem to be, whether a person who in some form reflects the historical author of the poem named William Langland, as W. W. Skeat asserted, or a subject made up of a dialogic discourses, as David Lawton argued, it is crucial that we recognize that the speaking subject of the poem is not just a person, however complexly presented, but a person with a soul.[3]

Through the presentation of a series of instances of soul-making, the poem, I suggest, records the growth of a person with a soul named Will as he comes to understand the nature and function of the power of the soul within him. Over the course of the poem, Will develops consciousness of the powers of his soul, but above all, the power of his will, a faculty that has the potential to lead him to develop an ethical form of consciousness, that is, a conscience. *Piers Plowman* charts the making of Will's soul as it moves from its first glimmer of recognition of its value to a dynamic idea of its function in the messy world. *Piers Plowman* is England's *Divine Comedy*, but unlike Dante who progressively moves us from the world to heaven, Langland leaves us firmly in the world of everyday experience.[4] The poem, I argue, dramatizes both the desire for the transcendental finality of that 'arbitrary interposition' and the resistance to it that finds (if not for the protagonist of the poem, then for the reader) not salvation, but an ethically sound and consciously derived pursuit of value in the given world.

That *Piers Plowman* is a poem concerned with understanding the soul's powers has not gone unnoticed in Langland criticism. Most notably, Mary Carruthers and James Simpson show Langland's broad indebtedness to Augustinian and Thomistic thought in their comprehensive treatments of Will's cognitive and affective development.[5] The two primary faculties that were understood in the period to govern the soul, Reason and the Will, have also received in-depth detailed analysis in their own right. In a separate earlier study, Carruthers sketched the basic contours of the character of reason in action, that is, Conscience, in the poem, and Sarah Wood has more recently charted Langland's development of Conscience across the poem's A, B, and C versions.[6] The poem's representation of the ultimately indiscernible faculty of the Will, known primarily through its repeated failures, has been explored extensively in very different treatments by Nicolette Zeeman and John Bowers.[7] Masha Raskolnikov's far-ranging consideration of the gendered representation of the soul in Middle English poetry, including *Piers Plowman*, helps us understand the hermeneutic complexity of Langland's representation of the soul as abject in passus 15.[8] It is she who has

---

2   See Spearing, *Textual Subjectivity*, and Lawton, 'The Subject of *Piers Plowman*'.

3   See Skeat, *Vision of Piers Plowman*, II, pp. xxvii–xxxviii, and Lawton, 'The Subject of *Piers Plowman*'. Manly attributes the poem to five different authors in '*Piers the Plowman* and its Sequence', p. 1.

4   The comparison of Dante to Langland was made some time ago in Langland criticism. See for example, Calì, *Allegory and Vision*, and Boitani, *English Medieval Narrative*.

5   Carruthers, *The Search for St Truth*; Simpson, 'From Reason to Affective Knowledge' and *Introduction to the B-Text*.

6   Carruthers, 'The Character of Conscience', and Wood, *Conscience and Composition*.

7   Zeeman, *Discourse of Desire*; Bowers, *Crisis of Will*.

8   Raskolnikov, *Body against Soul*, pp. 168–96.

drawn our attention to the concern of those who compiled devotional writings with providing guidance for the health of the soul as indicated in titles such as this one found in the Vernon manuscript, a collection that includes a copy of *Piers Plowman*: 'Here bygynnen þe tytles off þe book þat is cald in latyn tonge salus a[n]i[m]e. and in englyhs tonge sowlehele'.[9] Relatively little attention, however, has been given to the soul itself as the driving force of the poem.

Drawing on these indispensable studies, I shall focus attention here on Langland's specific representation of the constitution of the soul as it grows to recognize its capacities through its experiences in day-to-day life. Keats concurs that the soul grows only through such interactions: he asks, 'how then are Souls to be made [...] but by the medium of a world like this ?[...] Do you not see how necessary a World of Pains and troubles is to school an Intelligence and make it a soul? A Place where the heart must feel and suffer in a thousand divers ways!'.[10] Keats explains that, '[salvation] is effected by three grand materials acting the one upon the other for a series of years — These three Materials are the *Intelligence*, the *human heart* (as distinguished from intelligence or Mind) and the *World* or *Elemental space* suited for the proper action of *Mind and Heart* on each other'.[11] As we shall see, Langland's map of the soul runs very close to Keats's. Langland, too, presents the soul's salvation as effected by the interactions over time between intelligence (what he calls Wit), the heart (what he calls Will), and the elemental space of the world. He presents a vision of an individual in relationship to the collectives of the labouring community and the Church when interacting with the elemental space of the earth through plowing, an activity that accrues meanings at both the literal and allegorical levels as the poem progresses.

Langland's conception of the soul differs from that of Keats in a number of significant ways, of course. Where Keats suggests the soul only comes into being through making, Will begins his journey with a soul, even though he has to 'make' it as he progresses. Furthermore, the journey of Will's soul, unlike that of Keats's soul, is inflected by a theology of grace, although what Langland's concept of that theology is remains controversial among critics.[12] Most noticeably Langland's idea of the soul is influenced by his absorption of and response to Augustine and Aquinas, whose views about the nature and function of the soul predominated in the period. He also, I shall show, engages voluntarist ideas about the soul in which the faculty of the will, the very name of the poem's protagonist, is given primacy over reason. Drawing on his knowledge of these commonly available theological

9   See folio 1ʳ of the Vernon manuscript in Doyle's edition (*Vernon Manuscript*, ed. by Doyle) and
    Raskolnikov's discussion in *Body against Soul*, pp. 1–30, esp. 6–10.
10 Keats, 'Letter to George and Georgiana Keats', 21 April 1819, in *Letters*, II, 102.
11 Keats, 'Letter to George and Georgiana Keats', 21 April 1819, in *Letters*, II, 102.
12 Most agree with Adams's view that Langland is sympathetic to what he calls the semi-Pelagianism of
    the voluntarists, although Aers challenges that view in 'Sacrament of the Altar'. See also Coleman's
    discussion of the voluntarist view in *'Piers Plowman' and the Moderni*. Grace plays a much more
    prominent role at the end of the poem than at the beginning. For a recent discussion of the theology
    of agency and grace, see Bugbee, *God's Patients*.

views of the soul, Langland, in sum, delineates Will's soul as constituted of the primary faculties of will and reason, but one in which will takes priority over reason. Voluntarist thought in which God is hidden (the *Deus absconditus*), his will unknowable because of his *potentia absoluta*, and the nature and power of the will in general ultimately indiscernible, is consonant with Langland's representation of the restlessness, uncertainties, and failures Will experiences throughout the poem in trying to learn how to save his soul.[13] In keeping with voluntarist developments of an essential Pauline proposition that the will is the locus of the self and moral worth, the poem shows, as Robert Pasnau has suggested, 'the human search for truth is not chiefly an intellectual one but a volitional one'.[14] Debates about the responsibility of the soul to prompt the individual to criticize the world around it, articulated especially forcefully by Ockham, have notable features in common with the end of the poem where the poem affirms the efficacy of the individual soul when guided by Conscience (who is in turn motivated by the Will) as a power for social and political critique. Langland engages these various theological positions not as a theologian, however, but as a poet, a position that allows him to test their resiliency in lived experience.

Langland's protagonist is initially less concerned with what the soul is than how he might save it, but he comes to realize that the first step to saving his soul involves becoming conscious of its powers. Everything in *Piers Plowman*, every encounter with a personified abstraction, every inner dream, outer dream, and moment in the waking world, every image, dialogue, and dramatic event, is an episode in Will's progressive understanding of both what it means to have a soul and the salvific potential of its powers. Instead of describing Will's journey in terms of progress, however, it is more accurate to consider its development within the framework of the medieval concept of *informatio*. Rather than grow, Will's soul becomes *informed*. According to medieval theology, *informatio* refers to the soul's acquisition of accidents which enhance its attempts to reach its ideal form; the substance of the soul itself never changes or grows, but instead every 'accident', that is, every thought or desire or even experience, informs the soul; when these thoughts or desires leave traces, they become habits or dispositions, which include intellectual habits (such as knowledge, wisdom, and

---

13   For these basic principles of voluntarism see Bonansea, *Man and his Approach to God*; Kent, *Virtues of the Will*; Courtenay, *Nominalism*; Oberman, *Theology* and *Harvest of Medieval Theology*; Coleman, '*Piers Plowman' and the Moderni*; and Pasnau, 'Voluntarism and the Self'.

14   Pasnau, 'Voluntarism and the Self', forthcoming. The foundational Pauline text is Romans 7.15–23, which Pasnau translates: 'For that which I do, I do not understand. For I do not do the good that I will, but the evil that I hate, that I do. If then I do that which I will against, I consent to the law, that it is good. So then it is not I who do it, but the sin that dwells within me. For I know that the good does not dwell within me, that is, within my flesh. For to will the good is present to me, but to achieve the good, that I do not find. For I do not do the good that I will, but the evil that I will against, this I do. But if I do that which I will against, then it is not I who do it, but the sin that dwells within me. Therefore I find a law, that while I am willing to do good, evil is present to me. For, with respect to the interior person, I am delighted with the law of God. But I see another law in my limbs, fighting against the law of my mind and imprisoning me in the law of sin that is in my limbs'.

understanding), moral habits (that is, virtues and vices) and theological habits (that is, faith, hope, and love).[15]

Such habits are ultimately actualizations of the powers of the soul. Because voluntarists understood the virtues to emerge from an autonomous will, they did not view the will as constrained by habit. Within a voluntarist frame, as Pasnau points out, 'moral goodness applies first and foremost not to our external actions, nor to our rational deliberations or to our acquired habits, but rather to the will's choices'.[16] Given the instability of Will's progress in the poem, the voluntarist understanding of habits seems more apt than the more determinative role granted to them by Aquinas.[17]

Will's soul is informed, I suggest, by his acquisition of knowledge, then by his procurement of moral habits through his development of Conscience, and finally by his attainment of the theological habits — faith, hope, and charity — especially the last, charity or love. Although critics such as C. David Benson, Lawton, A. C. Spearing, and Wood have rightly taught us to resist attributing a smooth narrative development to this unruly poem, we nonetheless can trace Will's acquisition of some habits or dispositions as his soul is informed.[18] The poem charts the soul's acquisition of information as it experiences suffering in the world and comes to realize the nature and the ethical responsibilities of its various powers. This is not at all to say that the poem presents Will's increasing withdrawal from this world and ascent to the realm of the spirit; on the contrary, Will stays firmly rooted in the world throughout.

The theological notion of information can help us resolve the critical puzzle that Will seems to progress at the same time that he seems not to change. Will's soul-making, although improved by its acquisition of accidents, nonetheless is both enriched and impeded by his continual return to the problems of embodiment posed by everyday life. Will's soul becomes informed in a spiral-like process — or perhaps more precisely in an episodic cyclical pattern like that of the liturgical year — in which he accrues accidents incrementally that leave significant traces on his soul,

---

15   The information of the soul ultimately stems from Aristotle's conception of the soul as a form and is articulated in Aquinas, *Summa theologiae*, trans. by Pasnau, 1a.75. See Pasnau's translation in *The Treatise on Human Nature*, pp. 10–13, and *Theories*, pp. 51–55. I am grateful to Pasnau for discussing with me the process by which the soul becomes informed. The first critic to consider information in terms of literary texts was Simpson in his important book *Sciences and the Self*, esp. pp. 7–10 and 168–72. His discussion points out the relationship between information and literary forms: 'a poem will take its own shape and style according to what faculty of the soul is being instructed' (p. 28). Simpson earlier correlated the genres of *Piers Plowman* with Will's development in *From Reason to Affective Knowledge*. I suggest Will's spiral-like development, governed by negative dialectics, is especially suited to the poem's emphasis on the primacy of the will over reason.

16   Pasnau, 'Voluntarism and the Self', forthcoming.

17   For a discussion of the movement of the virtues from reason to the will in voluntarism, see Kent, *Virtues of the Will*. For a discussion of varying views of habitus in the period, see Breen, *Imagining an English Reading Public*, pp. 43–79; especially p. 79, where she summarizes the voluntarist position: 'Scotus and Ockham break with Aquinas by locating all virtuous habitūs in the will itself, reasoning that the will alone is capable of choice, and thus of vice or virtue'.

18   Benson, *Piers Plowman*; Lawton, 'Subject'; Spearing, *Textual Subjectivities*; Wood, *Conscience and Composition*.

even though again and again he seems to have returned to almost exactly the same place.[19] Soul-making, then, is an immanent activity that never ceases in this world.

Will's soul-making occurs in encounters that Keats would call 'circumstances'. At the conclusion to his letter, Keats writes,

> I began by seeing how man was formed by circumstances — and what are circumstances? — but touchstones of his heart — ?and what are touchstones? — but proovings of his hearrt — and what are proovings of his heart but fortifiers or alterers of his nature? and what is his altered nature but his soul? And what was his soul before it came into the world and had These proovings and alterations and perfectionings? — An intelligence(s) — without Identity — and how is this Identity to be made? Through the medium of the Heart? And how is the heart to become this Medium but in a world of Circumstances?[20]

Keatsian circumstances in Langland are those daily experiences that contribute to the information of Will's soul. As Will acquires accidents, his soul nonetheless cannot settle in his apprehension of a solitary or a collective truth but instead, as it experiences the world in the body it inhabits, must repeatedly assess its place and ethical responsibilities within it.[21]

While Will's soul becomes informed through his interactions with a variety of allegorical personifications and persons he meets from day to day, it also does so through his encounters with allegorical representations of the soul itself in the form of images of it that impress upon him — or inform him with — its nature and function. *Piers Plowman* is perhaps more visual than it at first seems; as Benson has shown in his study of the poem and medieval English wall paintings, it is immersed in the pervasive visual culture of the time.[22] In this essay, I shall trace the growth of Will's discovery of the nature and powers of his soul in his interactions with four images — some that explicitly represent the soul and some that represent aspects of the soul: a lady within a castle, an allegorical figure of the soul called a 'thing', a tree, and a plow.[23] Each of these images brings to the fore aspects of the soul associated

---

19   Dante's *Commedia* also has a spiral-like structure but moves progressively from this world to heaven, whereas Langland's poem begins and ends in this world. Middleton importantly delineated the episodic structure of *Piers Plowman* in her essay 'Narration and the Invention of Experience'.

20   'Letter to George and Georgiana Keats', 21 April 1819, in *Letters*, II, 103–04.

21   See Strohm's brief but pointed discussion of this faculty as it appears in *Piers Plowman* as a forerunner of modernity's conception of conscience as a private and internal stand-alone phenomenon in *Conscience*, pp. 14–16. For a discussion of the chief virtues of the will as charity and justice, see Pasnau, 'Voluntarism and the Self', forthcoming.

22   Benson, '*Piers Plowman* and Parish Wall Paintings'.

23   In this essay, I shall be focusing attention almost exclusively on the B text, even though Langland's change of the speaker who introduces the vision of the Tree of Charity from Anima in B to Liberum Arbitrium in C is important to his developing idea of how the soul functions and hence to an enriched concept for Will to grasp. Since *liberum arbitrium* was understood as a capacity we possess in virtue of both will and reason, the change might be said to provide a more balanced vision of the relationship between will and reason at this point in the poem than we have in the B text, where the dream within a dream seems to place emphasis on the activities of the will. The import of this change

respectively with Augustine, Aquinas, voluntarism, and Jerome, and as I move from image to image, I will outline the major elements of those theological positions.

By focusing on these images, I shall show how Will learns a particularly Langlandian theology of the soul. Through his engagement with the first of these images, the castle of passus 9, Will, as we shall see, learns a basic Augustinian lesson that he has a soul within that needs protection from the dangerous intrusions of the world upon it, an image that focuses Will's attention inward. Through his subsequent meeting with the soul itself as a thing called Anima in passus 15, Will learns a basic Thomistic precept that despite its status within, the soul only has meaning through its outward actions in the world; the soul manifests itself in performance. His encounter with the Tree of Charity in passus 16, an implicit image of the soul that brings to the fore more voluntarist concepts of the soul, turns him at once inward and outward by showing him the place of charity at the centre of the human being and the power of its action outwards to love. When he subsequently witnesses the plow in passus 19, working literally to cultivate the land and allegorically to cultivate souls, Will discovers the power of a soul inflected with Jerome's notion of its structure, guided by grace and united with others to form a collective, the Church. The ending of the poem does not abandon the voluntarist concerns raised in the earlier passus, however, and the poem concludes with a primary focus on conscience as guided by the will. The culminating image of the plow takes us back to the plow we saw in passus 6, which Piers uses to plow the half-acre, and brings to the fore yet another dimension of soul-making: writing, an activity commonly linked to plowing in the period.

As we shall see, however, the poem does not end with that vision of collective strength conveyed by the image of the plow, but instead returns us to the quest of the still inquiring soul frustrated in its search for truth. While the images of the soul Will encounters inform him about aspects of his soul, his understanding of those powers is continually negated as each vision dissolves and is replaced by further encounters in the world. Indeed, these repeated negations go hand in hand with what seems to be weakness of will in our protagonist, Will. Bowers argues that Will's principal sin is *acedia*, a failure of will. Zeeman, in contrast, sees Will's misdirection as an aspect of Langland's particular form of 'voluntarism', which she describes as 'dark and supremely optimistic'.[24] I understand Will's irregular progress — or rather his step-by-step (passus-by-passus) acquisition of information — as his growing recognition not only that he has a soul, but also that he has a soul dominated by the will, which repeatedly prompts him to make and remake it. For Langland, then, soul-making involves a growing consciousness of the soul's powers — and especially the power and resilience of the will — even as those powers are repeatedly shown to be inadequate in the face of experience. As I suggest in my concluding discussion of the poem's final passus, despite the seeming negation of the lessons taught by the powerful images of the soul, the soul's faculties are nonetheless shown to be resilient even as the poem approaches its seemingly apocalyptic ending.

---

for Langland's purposes vis-à-vis the place of the will in the C text as a whole awaits a fuller treatment beyond the scope of this essay. For a discussion of the distinction between free will and free choice (*liberum arbitrium*), see Kent, *Virtues of the Will*, pp. 98–110.

24 Zeeman, *Discourse of Desire*, p. 21.

A form of negation that leads to self-knowledge is fundamental to the poem's methods. Will's experiences of frustration, failure, and renewed hope as he seeks to understand his soul reflect what D. Vance Smith has described as the poem's negative theology.[25] As Smith writes, 'We ought to embrace the poem as a failure, as a poem that not only engenders negativity but that is deeply formed by negation'.[26] In Hegelian terms, such experiences of negation are, as Smith points out, fundamental to the 'energy of thought, of the pure I'; he cites Heidegger, 'a negation of a negation is nothing less than the "essence of spirit"'.[27] Will approaches an understanding of his spirit, his soul, through his experiences of such negative dialectics.[28] That the purpose of this dialectics is to focus social and political critique suggests that an Adornian as much as an Hegelian dialectics is at work in the poem.

Although negative dialectics are clearly fundamental to the poem's methods, Smith's proposition that the poem is self-negating or apophatic in a mystical sense seems unconvincing. Fundamental to the poem's dialectical method is an oscillation between the self and the world, and the world continually comes into focus for Will as the source of new knowledge; in the apophatic, both the self and the world ultimately disappear as the contemplative unites with God. In my view, Langland is too concerned with the exigencies of daily life — most urgently hunger and thirst — to be described as apophatic. Even as the information Will gains in his journey leads him to a more expansive understanding of his own soul and to the development of his own conscience, it also continually points him to the ways in which the soul is made, unmade, and made again through its encounters with the world, or more specifically what Adorno would call the 'social antagonisms' of the world: from legal corruption and the problems of maintenance, to labour unrest and famine, to the inadequacies of institutional learning, and finally to the corruption within aristocratic households reliant on confessors and within the Church itself.[29] Given his concern with social critique and his eschewal of the transcendence sought by both Hegel and apophatic medieval mystics, Adorno in his form of negative dialectics more aptly points to the social critique that is a fundamental part of Will's soul-making.

What Is the Soul?

That the agent Will has the capacity for soul-making is made clear in his first encounter with Holy Church when he asks, 'how I may saue my soule'? (B.1.84).[30] This opening

---

25 Smith, 'Negative Langland'.

26 Smith, 'Negative Langland', p. 39.

27 Smith, 'Negative Langland', p. 41.

28 Aers, in 'Piers Plowman' and Christian Allegory, was one of the earliest critics to discuss the poem in terms of its dialectical method, a method he investigates in detail in Beyond Reformation?, pp. 161–73. Zeeman in her Discourse of Desire and in a forthcoming book also explores the negative dialectical methods of the poem.

29 Wood discusses in detail the problems of maintenance both in the lord's retinue and in large land-owning households in Conscience and Composition. Aers discusses labour unrest in Community, Gender and Individual Identity, pp, 20–72. For Adorno, see 'On Lyric Poetry in Society', p. 45.

30 All quotations refer to Schmidt's parallel-text edition.

scene awakens in Will a desire to know what his soul is and how he can save it; it might be described as Will's *confirmation*, for it presents a formal interaction in which Will kneels ('courbed on my knees') before Holy Church (B.1.79). Holy Church reminds him of his earlier baptism when she says

> 'þow oughtest me to knowe.
> I vnderfeng þee first and þe feiþ tauȝte.
> Thow brouȝtest me borwes (that is, pledges at baptism) my biddyng to fulfille,
> And to louen me leelly þe while þi lif dureþ.' (B.1.75–78)

What then does the scene present but Will's coming to consciousness of the presence of a soul within him and his need to take responsibility for it, his recognition that he has within him what Jerome and Thomas called synderesis and what Bonaventure defined as 'the spark of the soul' — that is, a disposition to do good?[31]

Will's question 'how may I save my soul?' presupposes that he knows what the soul is. The idea that a person has a soul generated numerous questions in the medieval period. What is the soul made of? Where is it located? What are the powers of the soul and how do they interact with the powers of the body? Which entity has control over the person, body or soul or both? What is the soul's nature when separated from the body at death? Is the soul gendered? The answers that theologians, philosophers, and artists provided to these questions shape Langland's representation of Will's soul. The prevalent premodern view of the soul was that it took the shape of a homunculus as shown in a typical image from British Library MS Additional 37049 of the soul leaving the body (fig. 1) and in the image of a soul being lifted up from a fourteenth-century English Book of Hours (fig. 2). Another prominent image of the soul especially in the early modern period is of the soul as a *tabula rasa*, an image taken from Aristotle.[32]

Langland shows no particular concern for the soul's appearance, or indeed its makeup after death, but, as we shall see, he is interested in the constitution of the soul and its location, gender, and powers and many of the answers he finds are

---

31 See Potts's discussion of each of these authors and selected translations of texts in *Conscience*: on Jerome, pp. 1–11 and pp. 79–80; on Aquinas, pp. 45–60 and pp. 122–26; and on Bonaventure, pp. 32–45 and pp. 110–21. See also Hort, *'Piers Plowman' and Contemporary Religious Thought*, on synderesis, pp. 71–76, and on the 'spark of the soul', p. 74. Wood, *Conscience and Composition*, summarizes: 'Bonaventure and other Franciscan writers defined conscience as an act of judgement directed towards behavior, synderesis as the bias of the will towards the good. Aquinas described synderesis as a disposition of the practical reason by which theoretical principles are known, and conscience as an actualization, the application of knowledge of principles to particular cases' (p. 2). See also her summary of critical opinions about the Dominican versus Franciscan emphases in the poem itself, p. 3. In Langland's representation here we seem to see a spark of what later will become Conscience for Will. Notice, however, that Langland does not draw on the imagery of the spark.

32 I learned of the prevalence of the image of the soul as a tablet in early modern art in a talk given at the University of Glasgow by Tommaso Ranfagni on 16 January 2020: 'Representing the Soul in the Renaissance: The Iconographic Theme of "Tabula Rasa"'. The idea of the image is discussed in Aristotle's *De anima*, ed. by Barnes, 429a.18 ff. and the analogy is made in 430a.1. Although the *tabula rasa* is well suited to the representation of the idea of the soul's acquisition of information, the images rarely show signs of the soul's acquisition of information such as might be conveyed by writing on the tablet.

Figure 1. The soul, represented as a homunculus, leaves the body of a dying man, from a Carthusian miscellany, executed in Northern England in the second or third quarter of the fifteenth century. London, British Library, MS Additional 37049, fol. 19ʳ. © The British Library Board.

Figure 2. Soul being lifted up. Leaf from a Book of Hours with a prayer for the Dead and the beginning of Psalm 118, fourth quarter of the fourteenth century. London, British Library, MS Additional 71118F. © The British Library Board.

consonant with those given in contemporary theological discussions and debates. As Greta Hort explained long ago, Langland is a profoundly theological poet rather than a devotional or even a religious one.[33] In order to appreciate Langland's poetry of soul-making, we need therefore to become aware of his sophisticated knowledge of the developing theology of the soul. This does not mean, however, that we can

---

33   Hort, *'Piers Plowman' and Contemporary Religious Thought*, pp. 15–16.

reduce that poetry to these theological precepts; indeed, it is through poetry that Langland variously engages, resolves, or exposes the contradictions in theology that emerge in the midst of lived experience.

As I mentioned above, Will's encounters with images of the soul teach him aspects of the three dominant theological models of the soul current in the period in which Langland wrote: an Augustinian soul, a Thomistic soul, and a voluntarist soul. Even as we are exposed to images of the soul that highlight different theological strands concerning its nature, it is important to take note of the fact that each image contains within it elements of the other strands, that is, Will's soul is whole at all times even though he comes to realize sequentially different aspects of its powers.[34] The medieval theological models of the structure of the soul that influence Langland's representation of it can be epitomized in these phrases: 1) The Body is the Prison of the Soul (Augustine); 2) The Soul is the Form of the Body (Aquinas); 3) The Will is the Ruler of the Soul (Ockham). Foucault responded to these ideas of the soul with his own well-known formulation: 4) The Soul is the Prison of the Body.[35]

To address the last of these first: we might concur with Foucault that the soul often serves regulatory and repressive functions, but in *Piers Plowman*, I suggest, the soul, far from imprisoning the body, expands its reach. The medieval idea of the soul has not only spiritual but also material consequences for the individual, and does indeed regulate the individual by placing a person firmly in space and time — for example, it organizes a person's year around the liturgical calendar, marks quotidian temporality with bells, and grants the person a place in a graveyard associated with a parish. But, as we shall see, the powers of the soul that Langland demonstrates — particularly conscience and the drives of the will — also provide a means to expand time and space by guiding the person to embrace, organize, and critique the social, political, and material world he or she inhabits. Furthermore, rather than repress desire, the soul in Langland enables desire for the good and channels and directs it to its fulfilment in love. Where Foucault focuses his attention on the repressive power of the Church as an institution, Langland dramatizes the soul in the midst of a 'social antagonism', in its simultaneous dependence on and fragile independence from the institution.

---

34 Minnis, for example, demonstrates how aspects of the poem that seem particularly voluntarist can actually be attributed to Aquinas and 'passages which look nominalist turn out to be capable of less radical readings, and/or to have been placed in a dialectical framework which does not allow them the last word' ('Looking for a Sign', p. 177). While in this essay I argue for a voluntarist emphasis in the poem, there is no doubt that Langland's theology weaves together many different theological strands at once and is ultimately distinctly his own.

35 For Augustine, see *Soliloquies*, ed. by Rotelle and trans. by Paffenroth; for Aquinas, see *Summa theologiae*, 1a.75; for Foucault, see *Discipline and Punish*, p. 30; for Ockham, see Adams, 'Ockham on Will, Nature, and Morality'.

The Body Is the Prison of the Soul

Let us consider first Will's first encounter with the image of the soul as a castle, an image that expresses predominantly an Augustinian understanding of the soul epitomized in the phrase, 'the body is the prison of the soul'.[36] In contrast to Foucault, who sees the soul as holding the body back from realizing its pleasures, Augustine sees the body as the primary force hindering the soul's ascent to the realm of the spirit. Before turning to the image, let me summarize the contours of Augustine's definition of the soul. To Augustine, the person is a body/soul composite in which the soul takes primacy over the body. He sets out a definition of the soul that persists throughout the Middle Ages and that answers most of the questions about the soul I listed earlier. He defines the soul as an incorporeal, wholly incorruptible, and immortal substance located everywhere in the body which survives death in the form of what was called a *separated* soul.

Augustine establishes these attributes of the soul in his *Soliloquies*, a text highly distinctive among philosophical writings in that it is the first to present a dialogue made up of parts of the self; the dialogue is between Augustine and a part of himself presented as an interlocutor, Reason.[37] It is unusual for the inner self to be split in this way in philosophical discourses — though such a self-division is represented in the image provided in this essay of David playing the lyre for his own soul (fig. 3). The *Soliloquies* is perhaps, as Zeeman also observes, a more important source for Langland's representation of Will's journey than has been fully recognized.[38] Although other texts such as the *Psychomachia* and *Sawles Warde* also present allegories of the soul in which different faculties of the soul debate with one another, *Piers Plowman*, like the *Soliloquies*, places an inquiring protagonist at the centre of the narrative who seeks to find out about the nature of his soul.[39]

Augustine's emphasis on the soul's desire to escape the body draws on Plato's understanding of the soul as an entity enclosed and constrained by the body and thus blames the body as the source of sin. Adopting a trinitarian notion of the soul as made up of will, understanding, and memory, Augustine in his *Confessions* describes the difficulties he faced in abandoning the habit of lust and focusing his soul on God as a struggle between two wills, one carnal and one spiritual. This Neoplatonic model of the body as the prison of the soul predominates in early medieval literary representations.

---

36 Hort, *'Piers Plowman' and Contemporary Religious Thought*, p. 93, points out how the model of the soul provided in passus 9 is influenced by Thomistic thought; however, its image of a soul within to be guarded from the onslaughts of the flesh is Augustinian in its emphasis. For a discussion of Foucault's problematic understanding of the Middle Ages, see Lochrie, 'Desiring Foucault'.

37 Augustine, *Soliloquies*, ed. by Rotelle and trans. by Paffenroth.

38 Zeeman, *Discourse of Desire*, pp. 97–99.

39 For a discussion of these allegorical models for *Piers*, see Raskolnikov, *Body against Soul*, pp. 31–69. Boethius's *Consolation of Philosophy* similarly presents the person in debate with an entity that might be considered an aspect of himself, but Lady Philosophy is not presented as an interior faculty. In these works, parts of the self debate with one another.

Figure 3. David playing the Cittern to his soul. Reproduced with kind permission from Stuttgart, Wuerttembergische Landesbibliothek, Cod. bibl. fol. 23, fol. 55ʳ.

Typical of such representations is the Anglo-Saxon poem known as 'Soul and Body II' in which the soul passionately castigates the body for drawing them both into sin and damnation, as indicated in this excerpt:

Eardode ic þe in innan.   No ic þe of meahte,
flæsce bifongen,   ond me firenlustas
þine geþrungon.   þæt me Þuhte ful oft
þæt wære þritig   þusend wintra
to þinum deaðdæge.   Hwæt, ic uncres gedales bad
earfoðlice.   Nis nu se ende to god!
Wære þu þe wiste wlonc   ond wines sæd,
þrymful þunedest,   ond ic ofþyrsted wæs
godes lichoman,   gæstes drinces.
þær þu þonne hogode   her on life,
þenden ic þe in worulde   wunian sceolde,
þæt þu wære þurh flæsc   ond þurh firenlustas
stronge gestyred   ond gestaþelad þurh mec,
ond ic wæs gæst on þe   from gode sended,
næfre þu me swa heardra   helle wita
ned gearwode   þurh þinra neoda lust.
Scealt þu nu hwæþre minra gescenta   scome þrowian.[40]

(I dwelt within you. I never could exist without you,
enclosed in flesh, and your criminal desires
crushed me. It very often seemed to me
that there would be thirty thousand
winters until your death-day. Ever I begged
miserably for our parting.
Indeed that end has not turned out too well!
'You were proud at your feast and sated with wine,
prominent, majestic, and I thirsted
for God's body, for the drink of souls.
You were never mindful in those moments, here in this life,
since I had to dwell with you in the world,
so that you were guided eagerly by your flesh
and your criminal desires, and strengthened by me,
and I was the ghost sent within you by God —
you never preserved me from the compulsion,
from the torments of hell so harsh by your lust for pleasure.
'You must suffer the shame of my ruination'.)

---

40 'Soul and Body II', ed. by Krapp and Dobbie, ll. 30–46, pp. 175–76. Translation from 'Soul and Body I', ll. 36–49, trans. by Hostetter. (Hostetter translates the Vercelli Book's 'Soul and Body I', which corresponds up until the final section to the Exeter Book's 'Soul and Body II').

In keeping with Augustinian ideas about the body and soul, only the soul has a voice in this poem and it longs to flee the body in which it is imprisoned.

Will encounters such a Neoplatonic model in passus 9 when Wit shows him an image of the soul as a courtly lady protected in a castle of flesh. As in Augustine's conception, the soul here is envisaged as enclosed in a container and in need of protection from the intrusion of desires of the flesh. We might think of this castle in terms of the well-known image of the Castle of Truth from Bodleian Library MS Douce 104.

> 'Sire Dowel dwelleþ', quod Wit, 'noȝt a day hennes
> In a castel þat Kynde made of foure kynnes þynges.
> Of erþe and eyr is it maad, medled togideres,
> Wiþ wynde and wiþ water wittily enioyned.
> Kynde haþ closed þerinne craftily wiþalle
> A lemman that he loueþ lik to hymselvue.
> *Anima* she hatte; [to hir haþ enuye]
> A proud prikere of Fraunce, *Princeps huius mundi*,
> And wolde wynne hire awey wiþ wiles and he myȝte'. (B.9.1–9)

I have written elsewhere about the gender of the soul in this passage in passus 15, and have considered a variety of its details; here, I will focus only on those aspects that reveal Langland's use of the image as a step in Will's understanding of the constitution of his own soul.[41] Clearly, the idea that the soul needs vigilant protection is reinforced by its gendered representation as a precious treasure within a highly defended castle. This image recalls those such as the castle of the soul in *Sawles Warde*, in which the castle is governed by Wit but potentially led to ruin by Will, his unruly Wife, and the Christ-Knight allegory of the *Ancrene Wisse* in which Christ fights on behalf of a lady in a castle under assault by the Devil.[42] The image is common in the period, as in the image of the soul as a castle (fig. 4).

Drawing on pervasive Aristotelian notions of the feminine as inherently passive, the poet presents the soul, called Anima, as female. Kynde places her within the castle and shields her from the active assault by the devil. Described only with passive verbs — she 'is called' Anima; she 'is loved and protected by' Kynde; she 'is envied by' the devil — we never see her performing an action. Will learns that the primary feature of the soul is that it is a precious treasure deep within that requires protection from the continual assault of the Devil. He has yet to learn, however, that the soul's actions are as important as its preciousness.

Will is introduced here to a prominent faculty of his soul, a form of reason called Inwit, and in this emphasis on reason and in his description of the senses as powers

---

41 The analysis of this passage as well as of the image of the soul in passus 15 draws on my differently focused and more extensive analysis of the gender implications of these passages in 'Souls that Matter'.

42 For the Christ-Knight allegory, see *Ancrene Wisse*, ed. by Tolkien, pp. 198–99. For *Sawles Warde*, see *The Katherine Group*, ed. by Huber and Robertson.

Figure 4. Soul as castle: from a Carthusian miscellany, executed in the second or third quarter of the fifteenth century. London. British Library, MS Additional 37049, f. 71ʳ. © The British Library Board.

of the soul, Langland brings to the fore ideas of the soul's constitution consonant with Thomistic rather than Augustinian thought. It is perhaps not surprising that the ruling knight of the castle should be Sir Inwit, since the vision of the castle is provided by Wit.

> 'Ac the Constable of þat castel, þat kepeþ [hem alle],
> Is a wis knyȝt wiþal le— Sire Inwit he hatte,
> And haþ fyve faire sones bi his firste wyue:
> Sire Se-wel, and Sey-wel, and Sire Here-wel þe hende
> Sire Werch-wel-wiþ-þyn-hand, a wiȝt man of strengþe,
> And Sire Godefray Go-wel — grete lordes [alle].
> Thise fyue ben set to saue þis lady *Anima*
> Til Kynde come or sende to kepe hir hymselue'. (B.9.17–24)

It is not entirely clear what *inwit* means. First used in English in the thirteenth-century *Ancrene Wisse* and appearing later in the fourteenth-century title *The Ayenbite of Inwit*, the word, according to Hort, might simply refer to the *sensus communis*, but Randolph Quirk argues that *inwit* means here Conscience.[43] He writes, 'the *agens* aspect of *intellectus* in Thomist terms. [...] is concerned with the apprehension of truth [...] with the distinction between true and false, good and evil — hence its [inwit's] functions can come near to, and be confused with, those of conscience'.[44] Tracing the shift in diction from the word *inwit* to conscience, R. D. Eaton argues that the term suggests a concept closely linked to the self, perhaps self-awareness, self-consciousness, or moral awareness, that, over time, shifts in meaning to refer to a concept of moral authority increasingly detached from the self, called *conscience*. Langland uses the word *conscience*, then, during a period when 'a fundamental shift was taking place in the conceptualisation of conscience and its social realization'.[45] Eaton explains further that, as *inwit* comes to be 'assigned a more precise psychological role [...] *inwit* is represented metaphorically as a defensive agency that negotiates the boundary between the self and the outer world, controlling what goes in and out'.[46] *Inwit* here seems to represent an inner mental faculty that simply registers data as it enters the soul. *Conscience* becomes of increasing importance to Will, but, at this point in the poem, this narrower form of conscience, *inwit*, rather than being presented as enabling the soul to process and put data into action, is presented as static, as merely a porter who protects the soul from encounters with the outside world.

---

43   Hort, *'Piers Plowman' and Contemporary Religious Thought*, p. 95; Quirk, 'Langland's Use', pp. 185–87; the *Ancrene Wisse* introduces the word *inwit* as an alternative for conscience: 'ure ahne conscience, þ[et] is ure inwit', p. 157 in Tolkien's edition of MS CCCC 402, but the OED, s. v. *inwit*, points to other early usages of the word that seem to focus on mental activity or reason alone. See also Millett's note on the word in her edition, note to 5.9, p. 207.

44   Quirk, 'Langland's Use', p. 187.

45   Eaton, 'From "Inwit" to "Conscience"', p. 424.

46   Eaton, 'From "Inwit" to "Conscience"', p. 428.

This image of the soul reveals the powerful but limited notion of the soul that Will at this stage of the poem comprehends. At this stage of his journey, Will is able to understand only that his soul is deep within himself, that it needs protection from the intrusions of the world and the devil, and that it is governed by a relatively passive form of reason. Will's immersion in the courtly convention that a woman is a prized object to be immured in a highly defended castle blocks his ability to see that the soul is not an object but rather a subject. That is, he has yet to realize that the soul is not only precious and something to be loved but also something from which love emanates and whose powers must be actively engaged. It takes a more shocking encounter to shake Will/us out of a complacent understanding of the nature of the soul as a passive entity within and to learn its active powers.

The Soul Is the Form of the Body

Langland's understanding of the soul is similar not only to that of Augustine but also, and more fully as the poem unfolds, to that of Aquinas whose ideas about the soul are expressed in his extensive commentary on Aristotle's *De anima*. Aquinas introduces Aristotle's definition of the soul as the 'actuality of the first kind of a natural body having life potentially in it', and his assertion that the 'soul is the form of the body'.[47] The latter formulation in which soul and body are understood to be inseparable from one another suggests that the body and soul are in a dynamic dialectic with one another and furthermore that there is no clear boundary between one entity and another. In contrast to Augustine's model in which the soul is unwillingly contained by the body, which restrains its spiritual impulses, the Aristotelian Thomistic soul is realized in the body. Aristotle's ineffable statement that 'the soul is the form of the body' has important consequences for literary representations of the soul that present debates between the soul and body in which each bears equal responsibility for the fate of the person. For example, in the Middle English soul/body debate poem 'Als I lay in a Winteris Night', the body responds to the soul's accusations that it has brought them both to ruin by proclaiming that it should have done a better job of regulating the body: 'þou berst þe blame & y go quite, | þou scholdest fram schame ous have yschilt'.[48] The idea that the body and soul debate equally with one another is conveyed in an image of the soul in conversation with the body provided in this essay taken from the heavily illustrated fifteenth-century Carthusian miscellany, Additional MS 37049; the raised hands of the body and the soul indicate that they are both speaking (fig. 5).[49]

---

47 Aquinas, *Summa theologiae*, 1a.75 and 1a.76, trans. by Pasnau, p. 3 and p. 23. See also Aristotle, *De anima*, ed. by Barnes, 2.1, 412a, ll. 27–28, pp. 656 and 413b, l. 4, p. 657.

48 'Als I Lay in a winteris nyt', ed. by Conlee, ll. 183–84.

49 That this gesture indicates speech is reinforced by the accompanying poem, which recounts the debate of the body and the skeleton and which is accompanied by additional images; when the debate ends, the skeleton drops its formerly raised hand. For a discussion of this poem, see Robertson, 'Kissing'.

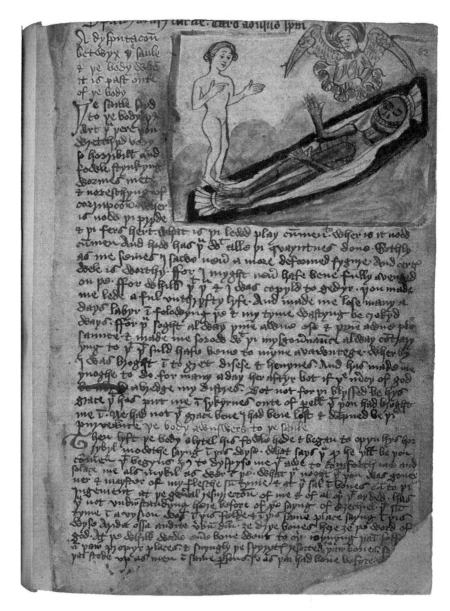

Figure 5. 'A dysputacion betwyx the saule & the body when it is past oute of the body', from a Carthusian miscellany, executed in Northern England in the second or third quarter of the fifteenth century. London, British Library, MS Additional 37049, fol. 82ʳ. © The British Library Board.

That the soul and body are inextricably intertwined profoundly shapes Langland's representation of the soul, for every spiritual impulse in the poem is entwined with the impulses of the body. Indeed, it becomes difficult to determine where the body ends and where the soul begins. This is nowhere more evident than in Langland's representation of Need, where the spiritual impulse to seek the truth continually reverts to the pressing problem of the individual's and the society's need for food. As Jill Mann has so carefully demonstrated, food — how and what we eat — is a recurrent site in the poem for the investigation of the ever-shifting border between the material and the spiritual.[50]

In addition to adopting the generative concept of the soul as the form of the body, Aquinas also follows Aristotle's more lucid and accessible delineation of the powers or faculties of the soul. In what is known as faculty psychology (a term emerging from the meaning of *facere*, to do, as Raskolnikov points out), Aquinas explains that the soul performs both appetitive and cognitive activities emanating from its two major faculties, will and intellect.[51] That the soul was made up of parts is shown in an early fourteenth-century image in which the imagination, memory, and other mental powers are located in the head (fig. 6). In Aquinas's view of the soul, reason takes primacy over the will, understood as an appetite or power that inclines or moves the person to action. Will is made up of both choice — Liberum Arbitrium in C.16 — and enjoyment, that is, delight in having obtained what was sought. The remainder of the faculties, given different names at different times, includes the internal and external senses and the sensual appetitive aspects of the soul, that is, the concupiscible and irascible appetites. The inner senses, all of which mediate between the outer senses and reason, include some that Will meets elsewhere in allegorical form, such as Imaginatif.[52]

Although the soul Langland presents in passus 15 outlines this familiar faculty psychology, Langland radically defamiliarizes this model of the soul in his paradoxical representation of the soul as a *thing* with no tongue or teeth, which nonetheless speaks. Will tells us he was rocked to sleep by Reason:

> Til I sei3, as it sorcerie were, a sotil þyng wiþalle —
> Oon wiþouten tonge and teeþ, tolde me whider I sholde
> And wherof I cam and of what kynde. (B.15.12–14)

In contrast to the familiar image of the soul as a castle, this peculiar image, produced as if by magic, registers, as we shall see, the radical transformation of the idea of the soul from a static entity governed by hierarchically arranged powers hidden

---

50 See Mann's superb discussion of this dialectic in 'Eating and Drinking' and 'The Nature of Need'.
51 Raskolnikov, *Body against Soul*, p. 14.
52 For a lucid and illuminating discussion of the faculty of imagination in *Piers*, see Karnes, pp. 179–206. Karnes distinguishes her argument from that of Simpson by arguing that Will's encounter with Imaginatif teaches him to harmonize experience and doctrine (p. 182 n. 11). In my own argument, the faculty of Will, rather than cognition, takes on an increasingly prominent role as the poem progresses, a faculty that, like affect as described by Simpson, is especially amenable to poetic rather than theological exploration.

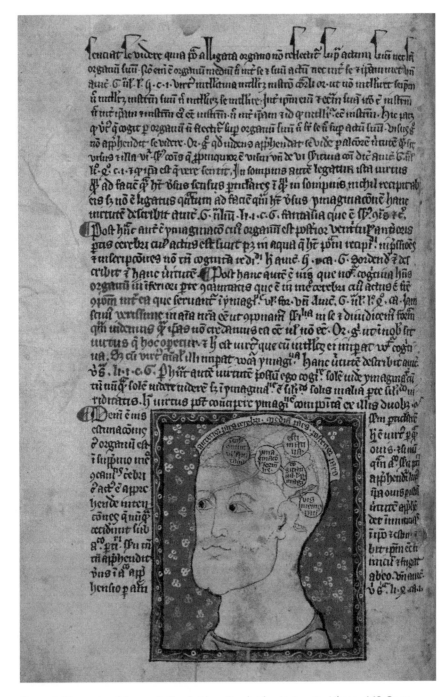

Figure 6. The parts of the soul. Cambridge, Cambridge University Library, MS Gg.1.1, fol. 490ᵛ. Reproduced by kind permission of the Syndics of Cambridge University Library.

from the world to one that is dynamic, non-hierarchical, and fully immersed in the world. The poetry then shifts from a description of a weird creature to that creature's presentation of an unexpectedly restrained and systematic inventory of his faculties:

> 'The whiles I quykke þe cors', quod he, 'called am I *Anima*;
> And whan I wilne and wolde, *Animus* ich hatte;
> And for þat I kan and knowe, called am I *mens*, "Þou3te";
> And whan I make mone to God, *Memoria* is my name;
> And whan I deme domes and do as truþe techeþ,
> Thanne is *Racio* my ri3te name, "Reson", on Englissh;
> And whan I feele þat folk telleþ, my firste name is *Sensus*
> And þat is wit and wisdom, þe welle of alle craftes;
> And whan I chalange or chalange noght, chepe or refuse,
> Thanne am I Conscience ycalled, Goddes clerk and his notarie;
> And when I loue leelly Oure Lord and alle oþere,
> Thanne is "Lele Loue", my name and in Latyn *Amor*;
> And whan I flee fro the flessh and forsake þe careyne,
> Thanne am I spirit spechelees — and *Spiritus* þanne ich hatte.
> Austyn and Ysodorus, eiþer of hem boþe,
> Nempnede me þus to name — now þow my3t chese
> How thou coueitist to calle me, now þou knowest alle my names'. (B.15.23–39)

The soul then recapitulates this naming sequence in Latin: 'Anima pro diuersis accionibus diuersa nomina sortitur; dum viuificat corpus, Anima est; dum vult, Animus est, etc.' (B.15.39a).[53]

Langland's use of Latin and English in this passage makes the static list of the faculties dynamic by replacing forms of the verb 'to be' with active verbs and by specifying an agent for the action. When the creature describes itself in Latin, its attributes are designated as permanent states of being; for example, the soul states, 'dum viuificat corpus Anima est' and 'dum vult, *Animus* est', but when it describes those attributes in English they manifest actions performed by an embodied first-person individual: 'whan I wilne and wolde, *Animus* ich hatte'.[54] Langland here associates the activity of the will with *animus*, a word often used to designate the mind alone; following the author of *De spiritu et anima*, Langland here calls that part of the soul associated with the mind *mens* rather than *animus*.[55] *Spiritus* is a

---

53 It is worth noting that Langland's seemingly authoritative summary is not a transcription of the Latin of *De spiritu et anima*, but rather his own version in Latin.

54 For a more detailed discussion of the interplay between Latin and English in this passage, see my 'Souls that Matter', pp. 178–79.

55 In late medieval philosophy, the relationship between mind and body was conceived as one between soul and body, even though there was a consideration of actions we usually associate with the mind alone such as thinking, called *mens* here. It is Descartes who can be singled out as the person who made the shift from soul to mind. He expressly says that he prefers the latter word, because he wants to limit the soul to the powers of the *rational* soul. He doesn't believe in animal souls, let alone

word referring to the soul after it has left the body. Langland here concentrates his attention on the powers of the soul as they function within the body. In contrast to the soul of passus 9, this embodied English soul performs actions in daily life. Theological principles gain meaning, then, as the individual enters what Keats called the elemental space of the world.

What appears to be a static list is transformed into a dramatic biography of an agential soul, from birth, when a person is informed with a soul called *anima*, to the manifestation of its most important faculties, to death when it leaves the body and is simply known as *spiritus*. The form of the passage as a paratactic list in which no one power is more important than another reinforces the idea that the soul accumulates rather than develops traces of the habits it acquires. In addition, it reinforces its vision of the protean character of the soul as it shifts and changes according to its embodied experiences. Although no one faculty takes precedence over another in this passage, the emphasis in the English on embodied action brings out the inherent meaning of faculty psychology that the soul's powers exist only as they are performed. That such a list occurs relatively late in the poem suggests that a level of self-consciousness is necessary even before such a list is conceivable.

While this section of the poem follows well-known Thomistic descriptions of the soul's faculties, Langland's specific sources for this passage are Isidore of Seville's seventh-century *Etymologies* and the twelfth-century pseudo-Augustinian *De spiritu et anima*.[56] Isidore tells us the soul is one entity, which we can rightly think of as having parts only inasmuch as we use different terms for the soul 'according to the effect of its causes'.[57] The later voluntarists return to and develop this Isidorean proposition:

---

plant souls, and since that leaves only the rational soul, it's more apt to refer to it as the mind, which had always been another way of referring to the rational parts of the soul — viz., intellect and will (Pasnau, personal correspondence).

56   Isidore's Latin says, 'Pro efficientiis enim causarum diversa nomina sortita est anima [...] Dum ergo vivificat corpus, anima est: dum vult, animus est: dum scit, mens est: dum recolit, memoria est: dum rectum iudicat, ratio est: dum spirat, spiritus est: dum aliquid sentit, sensus est. Nam inde animus sensus dicitur pro his quae sentit, unde et sententia nomen accepit' (Different terms have been allotted to the soul according to the effects of its causes [...] Therefore it is soul when it enlivens the body, will when it wills, mind when it knows, memory (memoria) when it recollects, reason (ratio) when it judges correctly, spirit when it breathes forth, sense (sensus) when it senses something). The Latin text is taken from the online edition based on *Etymologiae*, ed. by Lindsay, 11.1. 12–13 <https://www.thelatinlibrary.com/isidore/11.shtml> [accessed 1 July 2020]. The translation is from *Etymologies*, trans. by Barney and others, p. 231. Note that they translate 'dum vult, animus est' as 'will when it wills'. This presumably reflects Isidore's intention, but it is odd that he uses the word *animus* here instead of *voluntas*, and the author of *De spiritu et anima* follows Isidore in this odd usage: 'Anima nominatur totus homo interior [...] Dum ergo vivificat corpus, anima est: dum vult, animus est: dum scit, mens est: dum recolit, memoria est: dum rectum iudicat, ratio est: dum spirat, spiritus est: dum aliquid sentit, sensus est' (the soul is the name given to the whole inner human being [...] While it gives life to the body, it is soul. While it wills, it is animus, while it knows, it is mind, while it remembers, it is memory, while it judges, it is reason, while it contemplates, it is spirit, while it senses, it is sense) (ed. by Migne, col. 803).

57   Isidore, *Etymologiae*, ed. by Lindsay, 11.12; *Etymologies*, trans. by Barney and others, p. 231.

the emphasis on the faculties as mere names rather than as really distinct parts becomes of paramount significance to Ockham, who stresses that there is merely a conceptual distinction between the soul and its powers — in his view, while one can speak of a will and intellect, the soul is simple, with no distinct parts.[58] Langland's representation of the soul here reflects the idea of a simple soul although that very simplicity is made strange in Langland's presentation of the soul as a thing with no tongue or teeth.

Langland significantly adds to his sources, both in English and in his Latin summary, the faculty of conscience, although in his version it serves a relatively minor function. Conscience is presented as one who challenges or bargains ('chepe'), using language that Wood points out is associated with day-to-day legal or mercantile practice, that is, diction associated with the soul as it acts in the world.[59] Later in the poem, Conscience will accrue more complex meanings. In his developing representation of Conscience, Langland shows features in common with Aquinas, who defines it, following Origen, as 'the correcting and guiding spirit associated with the soul, by which it is separated from bad things and adheres to good things [...] we judge through our knowledge that something should or should not be done [...] And in this way conscience is said either to excuse or to accuse or torment [...] all of these result from an actual application of knowledge to the things that we do'.[60]

It is part of Will's soul-making that he learns to let conscience be his guide. Conscience comes and goes in the poem, but the activities associated with it of excusing, accusing, and tormenting permeate the poem. In keeping with Aquinas, who argues that the character Conscience develops as it is informed, we see this character expand from a purely rational faculty unguided by grace (as Carruthers points out), to a faculty at work in the marketplace, to one that takes centre stage as it guides the will to witness Christ's suffering, the foundation of the Church, and the rise of Antichrist. We also see, however, that it is fallible — just as Aquinas had said it could be — as it succumbs to Friar Flatterer at the end of the poem.

Like Piers Plowman, the character Conscience appears and disappears in the poem, and given that Will observes him act in various contexts from the law court to the Church, Conscience can be said to function as a principle in the world not unlike Reason, whom John Alford persuasively argues is not meant to indicate the reason of any particular person but rather an idea of reason as an absolute moral principle. Conscience is presented as a principle whose strengths and limitations Will needs to come to know. But just as reason is not only a principle in the world but also an aspect of Will's soul, so the character Conscience, too, in the dialectics

58 See Pasnau's discussion of the simple soul of the voluntarists in 'Voluntarism and the Self', forthcoming.

59 Wood, *Conscience and Composition*, p. 4.

60 Aquinas, *Summa theologiae*, 1a.79.13, trans. by Pasnau, pp. 103–105.

that are characteristic of the poem's methods, is as much a faculty within Will as one in action in the world without.[61]

Langland adds not only conscience to the list of faculties in the Latin sources, but also and most significantly, Amor, an act of the will.[62] In his version of the faculties, then, Langland highlights the two faculties of the soul that become of paramount importance as the poem develops: conscience and love. By harnessing conscience as its guide, the will can even more powerfully enact its characteristic powers: to love, to enjoy, and to choose. By giving a privileged role to conscience, a form of practical reason, rather than to reason alone, Langland creates out of prevailing ideas about the soul an embodied vision of the soul whose faculties emerge as they perform socially meaningful actions in daily life.

But before he can fully understand the nature of conscience, Will must learn, first, that the will's primary activity is to love, and, second, that he has to search for both faculties, conscience and will, deep within himself.

The Will Is the Ruler of the Soul

Through his engagement with the much critically analysed image of the Tree of Charity, Will discovers that the soul within him, made in the trinitarian image of God, is ruled ultimately by the will in the form of love.[63] In this image and in the image of the soul as plow to follow, Langland shifts attention from one element to another in what is a metonymic chain — that is, from the tree to the ground to the apple on the tree, and later, from the plow to the ground to the harvest. Unlike the castle and the thing, the Tree of Charity is not explicitly an image of the soul per se, but implicitly it conveys the essence of the soul as a force for love (also called *caritas* or charity) that is located deep within the individual but also emanates outwards beyond itself and into the world.[64] As we shall see, this image conveys a voluntarist understanding of the soul in which the will, the source of

---

61   Alford, 'Idea of Reason', pp. 199–216.

62   Wittig observes these additions but underestimates their importance as an anticipation of Langland's development of each of these faculties as the poem progresses. He writes, 'one might simply suggest that Langland adapts a traditional list of names and powers of the soul without attempting to present a rigid faculty psychology. In the spirit of this tradition he can add Amor and Conscientia in to emphasize the roles of charity and disciplined judgment, and sharpen the role of free choice in C by adding Liberum arbitrium to the list'. See Wittig, '*Piers Plowman* B', p. 213 n. 9.

63   Particularly illuminating analyses of this image are those by Salter, *Piers Plowman*, pp. 73–76, and Simpson, *Introduction*, pp. 186–99. Salter and Pearsall discuss the allegory of the Tree of Charity as diagrammatic and static in their introduction to their edition of excerpts from the C-text of *Piers Plowman*: 'Introduction', pp. 14–16; Aers in '*Piers Plowman' and Allegory*, pp. 77–109, provides a particularly extensive and sensitive analysis of the passage.

64   Will asks about the nature of charity at the same moment in the poem when he first names himself. This is an ironic moment in that he does not realize that his identity is not as much revealed by his name as by the charity that is within him and which he must enact, a fact he learns through an encounter with yet another image of the soul as a tree.

love, predominates over reason. This section of the poem, then, is in keeping with voluntarist definitions of the soul, which can be epitomized as 'Will is the Ruler of the Soul'. Voluntarist theologians such as William de la Mare, Peter Olivi, Gonsavus of Spain, Duns Scotus, and Ockham all argue for the predominance of will over reason.[65] Voluntarist propositions include the following ones, as summarized by Bonnie Kent: 'the claims that beatitude or happiness consists more in an activity of the will than in an activity of intellect, that man's freedom derives more from his will than his rationality, that the will is free to act against the intellect's judgment, and that the will, not the intellect, commands the body and the other powers of the soul'.[66] Will's contemplation of the image furthers his soul-making, as we shall see, by teaching him that his soul is not only the simple strange entity that must perform various acts, including thinking and judging, that he learned about during his encounter with the soul as thing, but is also a substance that is both nourished by and nourishes others through the primary activity of the will: love.

Anima explains the meaning of charity — synonymous with the word *love* — through his powerful image of charity as a tree. The tree recalls the many kinds of tree images readily available in the period, from trees of virtue to trees of life, including the image in British Library, MS Additional 37049 that presents charity as a leaf on a tree of life (fig. 7). Each of these images provide visual guides to moral development in terms of vegetal growth. Anima describes the tree as if he were looking at just such an image:

> 'It is a ful trie tree', quod he, 'trewely to telle.
> Mercy is þe more þerof; þe myddul stok is ruþe;
> The leues ben lele wordes, þe lawe of Holy Chirche;
> The blosmes beþ buxom speche and benigne lokynge;
> Pacience hatte þe pure tree, and pore symple of herte,
> And so þoru3 God and goode men groweþ the fruyt Charite'. (B.16.4–9)

Told first in the outer dream that charity is the Church, Will must enter a dream within a dream, even further from ordinary consciousness, to realize that charity is also the most significant aspect of his inner self and the primary activity of the will. Anima explains:

> 'It [Charity] groweþ in a gardyn', quod he, 'that God made hymselue;
> Amyddes mannes body þe more is of þat stokke.
> Herte highte þe herber þat it inne groweþ,
> And *Liberum Arbitrium* haþ þe lond to ferme,
> Vnder Piers the Plowman to piken it and to weden it'.
> 'Piers þe Plowman!' quod I þo, and al for pure joye
> That I herde nempne his name anoon I swowned after. (B.16.13–19)

---

65 See Kent's discussion of the development of voluntarist thought, *Virtues of the Will*, pp. 94–149.
66 Kent, *Virtues of the Will*, p. 96.

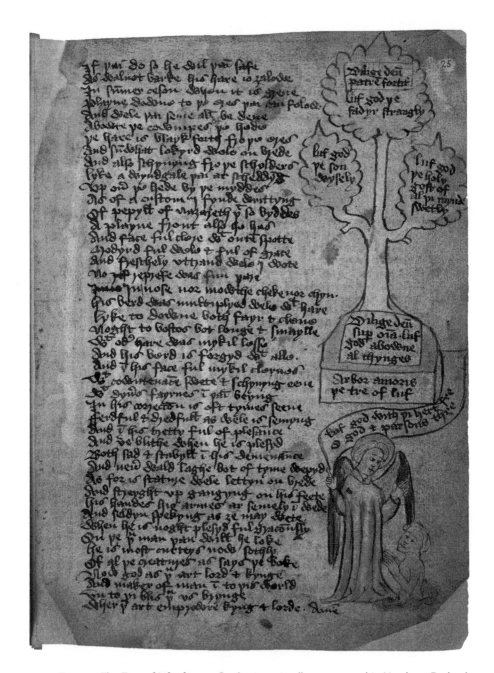

Figure 7. The Tree of Life, from a Carthusian miscellany, executed in Northern England in the second or third quarter of the fifteenth century. London, British Library, MS Additional 37049, fol. 25ʳ © The British Library Board.

Piers's name precipitates Will's entry into a different state of perception. Anima had, in fact, told Will earlier that Piers could grant him deeper perception of the will:

> 'Clerkes haue no knowing […] but by werkes and by wordes.
> Ac Piers þe Plowman parceyueþ moore deppe
> That is þe wille.' (B.15.198–200)

Will is told to gaze on the tree intently:

> Piers þe Plowman […]
> […] bad me toten on þe tree, on top and on roote.
> Wiþ þre piles was it vnderpiȝt — I parceyued it soone. (B.16.21–23)

The alliterative stress on the word 'toten' in the line signals the intense state of absorption in the image that Will must enter into in order to apprehend what is impossible to comprehend, a total cosmic vision, one from the top of the tree to the root, and one that encompasses all of human history.

As numerous critics have observed, Anima's initial tree image is transformed into a moving image, which unfolds before Will over time.[67] Will first engages in a dialogue with Piers, who explains how the trinitarian props of the tree protect it from forces that threaten its growth, from wicked winds and worms of fleshly sin to the more grievous forces of the devil that attack the root itself. Engaging directly with the practices of fruit cultivation, including staking the tree and carefully preparing and weeding the ground beneath it, the image shows Will how the tree grows over time as it first produces fragile blossoms and then plump and tempting apples. Not only does the tree suggest that the soul is an entity within but it also points outwards since it produces fruit the devil wishes to possess and that Will himself wishes to eat. Told that the fruit is under the special care of Liberum Arbitrium, Will, as he becomes a participant in this scene, comes for the first time to perceive the motivating power of the will within his own soul. As Zeeman writes, 'In the vision of a Tree of Charity that grows in the human heart, the seeker of *Piers Plowman* gets a sudden sight of the spiritual potential of the soul. When he asks to 'taste' the apples of the tree he expresses a desire to comprehend and absorb this vision in every way, spiritually, "inwardly", even physically'.[68] The temporal scheme of Will's own biography as he comes to desire the apple is mapped on to the larger temporal scheme of salvation history as the drama evokes the temptation of Adam and Eve and the devil's acquisition of the souls, which in turn prompts Will's desire to learn more about the nature of God's love for humanity.

Powerfully invigorating an image common to Christian iconography, Langland simultaneously situates Will within the Christian collective, invites him to witness Christian history, and teaches him not only that his own soul is made in the image of God but also that he needs to learn how to love through witnessing God's suffering

---

67 See especially discussions of the image by Aers, *'Piers Plowman' and Christian Allegory*, pp. 77–109, and Simpson, 'Introduction', pp. 86–99.

68 Zeeman, *Discourse of Desire*, p. 2.

as well as the salvation made possible through it.[69] Langland's interest in elucidating the soul's primary activity to love is precisely what Sister Mary Clemente Davlin sought to illuminate in her writings on *Piers Plowman*.[70]

Soul as Plow and the Fallibility of Conscience

The image of a fruit tree cultivated by Piers anticipates the final image of the soul in the poem, one that takes us right back to the poem's beginning: the soul as plow. In passus 19, in a Pentecostal vision filtered through Conscience, Grace gives to Piers a plow as a weapon with which to fight Antichrist and gives him oxen to draw the plow:

> Grace gaf Piers a teeme — foure grete oxen.
> That oon was Luk, a large beest and a lowe chered,
> And Mark, and Mathew þe þridde — myghty beestes boþe;
> And ioyned to hem oon Iohan, moost gentil of alle. (B.19.264–67)

The plow has various significations from a literal tool of agricultural labour to an allegorical instrument for the cultivation of the soul, but the discussion of the four evangelists in connection to this entity might also recall Jerome's explanation of the structure of the soul itself in his commentary on Ezekiel, in which he parses the four beasts associated with the four evangelists as follows: 'Most people interpret the man, the lion and the Ox as the rational and appetitive parts of the soul [...] And they posit a fourth part which is above and beyond these three which the Greeks call *synteresin*: that spark of conscience [...] by which we discern that we sin [...] this is the eagle, which is not mixed up with the other three, but corrects them when they go wrong.'[71] Thus, the plow with its oxen at one level signifies the soul itself marshalling all its powers to engage in both literal and metaphorical plowing. Given the fact that Langland focuses attention not simply on the oxen, but specifically on the cultivation the plow enacts, that is, the cultivation of souls, Langland's oxen-led plow in passus 19 stands not only for the individual soul, but also for one in the community of souls that makes up the Church.

Passus 19 of the poem presents an extended metaphor of plowing, then sowing and then harvesting, as aspects of the Church's role in the cultivation of souls. These fundamental agricultural activities are beautifully illustrated in the images from the Luttrell Psalter (figs 8–10).[72] As Stephen Barney and Carl Schmidt have explained with reference to hundreds of agricultural images in the Bible, plowing was understood allegorically as 'the preaching of the gospel [through what Barney tells us was known as the "plowshares of the tongue"] through which the "earth" of

---

69 For a discussion of the soul's shape as an historical phenomenon see Simpson, *Introduction*, pp. 167–245.

70 See Davlin's brilliant exposition of Langland's playful use of language in his demonstration of the nature of charity in *The Game of Hevene* as well as her analysis of vocabulary concerned with motion towards God in *The Place of God in 'Piers Plowman'*.

71 Potts, *Conscience in Medieval Philosophy*, p. 79.

72 For a superb analysis of these images see Camille, *Mirror in Parchment*.

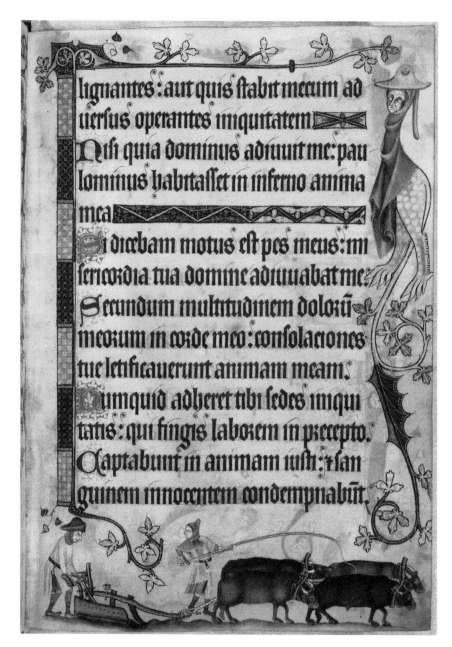

Figure 8. Plowing with oxen, from the Luttrell Psalter, executed in England, *c.* 1320–40. London, British Library, MS Additional 42130, fol. 170ʳ. © The British Library Board.

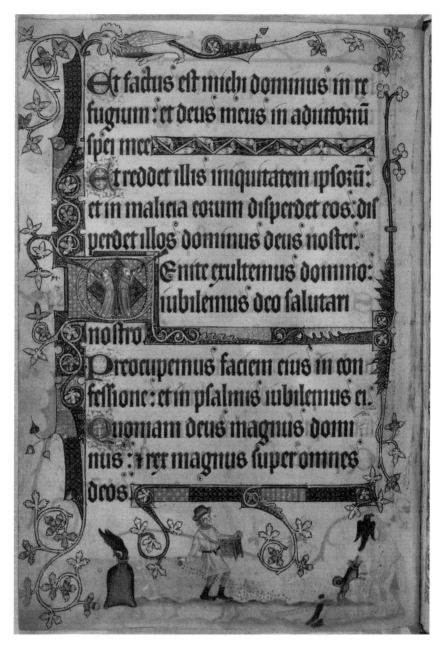

Figure 9. Man sowing, from the Luttrell Psalter, executed in England, c. 1320–40. London, British Library, MS Additional 42130, fol. 170ᵛ. © The British Library Board.

Figure 10. Harvesting, from the Luttrell Psalter, executed in England, *c.* 1320–40. London, British Library, MS Additional 42130, fol. 172ᵛ. © The British Library Board.

human hearts is prepared to receive the "seeds" of the virtues'.[73] Salter and Pearsall describe the presentation of the plow as a 'diagrammatic allegory [...] [that] lacks in evocative power'.[74] Yet the image becomes richer when it is considered not only in terms of its biblical references, but also in terms of the layers of meaning it accrues as agricultural images accumulate in the poem from the Plant of Peace in passus 1 to the plowing of the half-acre to the Tree of Charity.

The plow of passus 19 clearly recalls the plow we encounter in the Visio, and both the earlier and later plows interweave literal and allegorical significations, although in different ways. David Aers argues that Langland 'deprives' the Visio's plow of its allegorical signification, so that the plow only gains meaning after Will has experienced Christ's suffering.[75] As he writes, 'the Incarnation, life of Jesus, Passion, Resurrection and *Harrowing* of hell and Ascension, followed by the Pentecostal gifts, release the allegorical potential of the agricultural images'.[76] Although Will does not yet see the allegorical signification of the Visio's plow, I suggest that it is as *available* in the earlier image as it is in the later one. Similarly, even though the later image seems to emphasize its allegorical meaning, its literal meanings are just as important. The cardinal virtues, for example, are explained in literal and allegorical terms: Temperance, for example, avoids spiced meat and fine cloth; fortitude will keep a person from illness. In this climactic vision, as Aers points out in a later study, 'the acquired cardinal virtues enable someone to flourish as a human being and achieve an end proportionate to created nature [...] Characteristic of Langland's theology of grace, humans are passive receivers of divine gifts beyond comprehension or merit *and also* active agents'.[77] Grace's gifts include the clerical, commercial, manorial, and contemplative crafts, that is, activities to do with everyday labour.

The fair field full of folk has become a fair field full of souls in need of cultivation. Will's soul now embraces the perspectives of the individual, the historical, and the collective. His understanding of the soul has expanded from a recognition of the need to act, to an appreciation, through his witnessing of Christ's suffering, of the need to act with love, and finally to an acknowledgment of the power of acting in concert with others in the formation of a well-functioning and integrated society of souls under the guidance of the Church.

The Resilience of the Will

Arriving at passus 20, we seem to have returned to a Thomistic view of the soul that Will learned about earlier in that a form of reason, Conscience, guides the soul. Yet the will as it emanates in love is not subordinate to this form of reason. Although the

---

73   Barney, 'Plowshare of the Tongue' and the notes to B.19 in Schmidt's edition, p. 708.
74   Salter and Pearsall, 'Introduction', p. 15.
75   Aers uses this word frequently throughout his analysis of the plow image in *'Piers Plowman' and Allegory*, pp. 109–31; see especially, pp. 118, 124, 130.
76   Aers, *'Piers Plowman' and Allegory*, p. 113.
77   Aers, *Beyond Reformation?*, p. 33.

entire last vision is dominated by Conscience, and he is the final character we see in the poem as he sets off on his pilgrimage, Kynde reminds Will before he enters the Barn of Unity that it is his will that should predominate in his soul-making activities: "'Counseilleþ me, Kynde", quod I, "what craft be best to lerne?" | "Lerne to loue", quod Kynde, "and leef alle oþere"' (B.20.207–08). Love, or charity, is one of the primary virtues of the will, not of reason. In recounting the breakdown of the smoothly functioning Barn of Unity, this passus returns us again to the energies of the voluntarist soul, one in which the stumbling but motivating faculty of the will takes charge, for it is ultimately the force of his will that overcomes Conscience's fallibility in having succumbed to Friar Flatterer and which leads him away from the barn of corruption and out into the world again. Such energies, then, become available to Will who witnesses here the force of the will as it redirects Conscience away from the corrupt institution.

The concluding lines of the poem are obscure, for we do not know where Will is located: Is he still inside the Barn of Unity and simply witnesses Conscience's departure? Is he among the company of fools who do not follow the devil? Or at the moment he wakes up (the very last line of passus 20) is his own conscience awakened? The poem concludes:

'By Crist!' quod Conscience þo, 'I wole bicome a pilgrym,
And walken as wide as þe world lasteþ,
To seken Piers þe Plowman, þat Pryde myghte destruye,
And þat freres hadde a fyndyng, þat for nede flateren
And countrepledeþ me, Conscience. Now Kynde me avenge,
And sende me hap and heele, til I haue Piers þe Plowman!'
And siþþe he gradde after Grace, til I gan awake. (B.20.381–87)

Are Conscience's cry for grace and Will's subsequent awakening a sign that Will has finally recognized his dependence on grace (recalling a late Augustinian emphasis on the inadequacy of human efforts), or does this passage simply signal the renewal of a search for grace that has always been in progress? Does the fact that the last word of the poem is 'awake' signal the beginning of yet another waking episode to follow, or does it suggest Will's achievement of a significant new level of consciousness? Conscience recognizes his dependence on grace; the degree to which Will understands his need for it is obscure. Regardless of Will's place either within or without the Barn of Unity and of the degree to which Conscience's pilgrimage to some extent signifies Will's own, we have returned to the beginning of the poem, where the narrator — like Conscience, who announces that he will 'walken as wide as the world lasteth' — searches 'wyde in the worlde' (B.20.382; B.1.4). Just as soul-making for Keats involves immersing oneself in the immanence of the world, so the ending of Langland's poem directs the dreamer Will's and our attention outward to seek salvation 'wyde' in the world. There is no reason to view this conclusion as an end. Indeed, we have learned to expect infinite oscillations between ends and beginnings through the negative dialectics of the poem but, spiral-like, Will here returns to a beginning that is shaped by his experiences of the world ('circumstances') in which he has acquired accidents, that is, if not moral habits, at least predispositions towards them.

The ending of the poem makes clear the fallibility of conscience, a revelation that yet again suggests Langland's engagement with voluntarist thought. Although Aquinas discussed the fallibility of conscience, Aers, in his groundbreaking book *Beyond Reformation?*, demonstrates significant commonalities between Langland's vision of the failure of the Church in passus 19 and Ockham's affirmation of evangelical freedom in his account of the individual's responsibility to speak the truth in the face of institutional, even ecclesiastical, corruption. Ockham's position emerges from his consideration of a long-standing discussion of the predicament of friars told that they must submit their will to a superior *unless* it contradicts their soul's health.[78] Ockham's emphasis on the obligation of the individual to speak out against corruption, as Aers has shown, 'clashes sharply with the hierocratic ideal of comprehensive direction of man's spiritual life from above'.[79] As Takashi Shogimen explains, Ockham's vindication of the right of any Catholic to dissent from a heretical pope has implications for the place of the layman, even a layman such as Langland's protagonist Will, in pursuit of knowledge, for 'Ockham makes clear that ultimately any individual Christian can take such radical action. Should all the experts in theology, the pope and the cardinals teach that the Christian faith is false, an "illiterate" individual who has the correct knowledge of faith could act as judge over them'.[80] Ockham's position, however, is not as individualistic as it might seem. As Shogimen writes, 'this is not to say that Ockham is a preacher of rebellious anarchism. On the contrary, his programme of radical action is anchored in a renewed vision of the Christian community where the authority of an individual's conscience is ensured and the individual's commitment to the common good is enshrined'.[81] Ockham's assurance that the Christian community can be renewed by the assertion of an individual's conscience helps us to see beyond the seemingly apocalyptic ending of the poem.

In the concluding passus, then, Langland seems to be dramatizing the far-reaching effects of political theories like that of Ockham on his representation of the status of the soul within a corrupt institution. It is possible that Langland knew not only Ockham's political commentaries but also his discussions of the will, and indeed the works of a number of voluntarists. But given how little we know about Langland's education, we can only for the moment point to commonalities between Langland's thought and that of the voluntarists, which itself has only begun to be studied. Voluntarism has many guises, as Kent has explained, and is associated with the thought of numerous theologians who vary greatly in their consideration of the nature and function of the will.[82] Just as the poem is not simply Augustinian or Thomistic, so it would also be a mistake to deem it simply voluntarist. Nonetheless, the poem's engagement with a number of issues like those found in voluntarist commentaries deserves further careful scrutiny.

---

78   The history of the debate is summarized in Shogimen, *Ockham and Political Discourse*, pp. 123–31.

79   Aers, *Beyond Reformation?*, p. 31.

80   Shogimen, *Ockham and Political Discourse*, p. 144.

81   Shogimen, *Ockham and Political Discourse*, p. 153.

82   Kent surveys the varieties of voluntarist thought in the period in the introduction to *Virtues of the Will*, pp. 1–38.

Among the issues worth pursuing further are those raised by critics such as Janet Coleman who proposed some time ago that the poem demonstrates its embrace of the voluntarist principle of the widely read Dominican Robert Holcot that 'facientibus quod in se est Deus non denegat gratiam' (to those who do what is in them God does not deny grace).[83] In his more recent book, *Salvation and Sin*, Aers argues that such an emphasis conflicts with the Christocentrism of the poem; yet his discussion elsewhere of the presence of absence in the poem is in keeping with voluntarist discussions of God's hiddenness (for example, of the *Deus absconditus*).[84] Langland, however, seems less interested in exploring voluntarists' inquiries into the nature of an arbitrary and indiscernible God than in their assertion of the resilience and autonomy of the individual will (taken up by voluntarists following Scotus) as well as their acknowledgment of the frustrations experienced by the viator who cannot know whether or not he is saved. That the protagonist of the poem is named Will points us towards a voluntarist focus in the poem.

We might, in addition, explore the particularly voluntarist emphasis of the poem's eschewal of the soul's mystical union with God. As Heiko Oberman explains, for many voluntarists 'intuitive knowledge of God is strictly the prerogative of the *beati*, the members of the Church Triumphant'.[85] It is consonant with voluntarism that Will reaches no final or secure vision of God. Langland does not end his poem with the triumphant Eucharistic celebration of union with God that we experience at the end of passus 18; indeed, Will falls asleep in the middle of the Easter Mass. (Will's falling asleep cuts two ways, however — on the one hand, it is a sign of his spiritual failure; on the other, it allows him to perceive more deeply.) Yet, as Aers has argued in his discussion of the sacrament of the altar, the elusiveness of the Real Presence does not mean that Langland does not believe in it.[86] Will's search for union accords with a different kind of affective mysticism possible in voluntarism, one, as Oberman explains, that involves 'the outreach of the soul to a union with God through the desire of love, which resides not in the intellective but in the affective power of the soul and has not the *verum* but the *bonum* as its object'.[87] This kind of affective desire to do well in the world drives Will in *Piers Plowman*, but the ending affirms the power of the will to propel the individual to channel that desire.

It is difficult not to see the conclusion of the poem as profoundly apocalyptic with its representation of the rise of Antichrist and the corruption of the Church and all its officials. Yet, even though, as both Bowers and Zeeman have shown, the poem charts one moment after another of the failures of the will, it also affirms its

---

83   Coleman, *'Piers Plowman' and the Moderni*, p. 24.
84   See Aers, *Salvation and Sin*, pp. 83–131; for his studies of the presence and absence of Christ in the poem, see *Sanctifying Signs*, pp. 29–51, and *Beyond Reformation?*, passim.
85   Oberman, *Harvest of Medieval Theology*, p. 329.
86   As he writes in *Sanctifying Signs*, p. 32, 'to discern the body of Christ in *Piers Plowman* we will have to follow a complex dialectic of absence and presence, a dialectic which is inseparable from Langland's representation of the mystical body of Christ, the Church'.
87   Oberman, *Harvest of Medieval Theology*, p. 331.

resilience.[88] Expressing a radical scepticism and resisting the impulse towards finality or closure, the poem emphasizes not the end of the quest, but its renewal. Langland emphasizes that aspect of the will that take prominence in voluntarist thought: its freedom. As the forerunner to voluntarism Peter Olivi wrote, 'nothing is as beloved and as dear to us as freedom and power of our own will'.[89] Will's soul-making seems consonant with the ways in which voluntarists 'treat the will as an autonomous object that may or may not follow the advice of the intellect, or the dispositions ingrained through past action'.[90] As Aers points out, though, Langland repeatedly rejects the speculation of the friars. In my view, he articulates a dialectics in which he rejects the speculation of the friars at the same time that he embraces the autonomy and resilience of the will they affirm.[91] In sum, soul-making for Langland involves a continual reaffirmation of the ineffable force of the will as it engages the elemental space of the world.

Writing Poetry as Soul-Making

In the spirit of Will's defence of his poetry or 'makynge' (B.12.16) as play ('gaudia' in B.12.23), and therefore as especially well suited to the ineffable and changeable soul he represents and to the freedom of the will that defines that soul, I conclude now by turning to three medieval riddles that reveal another vital aspect of soul-making associated with plowing that is implicit throughout *Piers Plowman*: writing. These riddles are, of course, in a distinctly different mode from that of Langland's poem, but his delight in riddling wordplay is precisely what Davlin brought our attention to in the poem, and Langland would certainly have been aware of the plow's association with writing from classical times.[92] Here are Tatwine and Eusebius's eighth-century riddles. Tatwine's:

---

88   Such a renewal of the will is in keeping with both voluntarism and Augustinian theology; Zeeman points out that as Augustine and Gregory argue 'the soul's experiences of itself as tempted and at risk enables it to apprehend its own nature and its relation to God: the experience of failure and loss is often connected to the renewal of spiritual desire', *Discourse of Desire*, p. 30.

89   Olivi, *De perfectione evangelica*, q. 5. Cited in Pasnau, 'Voluntarism and the Self', forthcoming.

90   Pasnau, 'Voluntarism and the Self', forthcoming.

91   For Aers's repeated references to Langland's dismissal of the speculation of the friars, see his *Beyond Reformation?*, passim.

92   Davlin, '*Game of Hevene*'. John H. Henkel tells us that Isidore of Seville was the first to draw an etymological link between plowing and writing, but also gave evidence that it was known in the first century. Isidore claimed the ancients used to write as they plowed (in a kind of writing from left to right and then alternately from right to left called *boustrophedon*, from the Greek for ox-turning) and that rustics 'to this day' call furrows 'verses' (*Etymologiae*, ed. by Lindsay, 6.14). Virgil uses the association of the plow with writing especially in his *Georgics*. See Henkel, 'Plowing as a Metaphor for Poetic Composition', and his *Writing Poems on Trees*. There is another eighth-century late Latin or early vernacular Italian version of this riddle called the *Veronese Riddle*: 'se pareba boves | alba pratalia araba | et albo versorio teneba | et negro semen seminaba', paraphrased as 'he held the oxen in front of him with | white lawns | and had a white plow | and a black seed sowed'; see <https://it.m.wikipedia.org/wiki/Indovinello_veronese> [accessed 1 July 2020]. My thanks to Stefano Milonia for drawing my attention to it.

Effferus exuviis populator me spoliavit
Vitalis pariter flatus spiramina dempsit
In planum me iterum campum sed verterat auctor
Frugiferos cultor sulcos mox irrigat undis,
Omnigenum nardi messem mea prata rependunt
Qua sanis victum et Izesis praestabo medelam.

(A fierce robber ripped off my hide
Plundered the breath-pores of my skin.
I was shaped by an artist and author
Into a flat field. Furrowed and wet,
I yield strange fruit. My meadows bloom
Food for the healthy, health for the sick.)[93]

And Eusebius:

Antea per nos vox resonabat verba nequaquam,
Distincta sine numc voce edere verba solumus;
Candida sed cum arva lustramur milibus atris;
Viva nihil loquimur, responsum mortua famur.

(Once silent, voiceless, wordless, dumb —
Now voiceless, silent, bearing words we come,
White fields crossed by myriad black tracks:
Alive we are dumb — dead, answer back.)[94]

These two riddles about parchment together tell of the transformation of the once three-dimensional animal into a two-dimensional surface, which when unfolded becomes three-dimensional again — a fertile meadow — marked by the furrows made by the scribe's pen. Like the Tree of Charity, the plowed field then produces 'fruit'. The authors draw on a common metaphor of verse as the furrow made by a plow: just as a farmer turns his plow to make furrows in the field, so the poet produces lines of poems, the black tracks, that turn at the end of the lines, that is, verse. A more compressed form of these themes can be found in a traditional Scottish Gaelic saying:

Talamh geal
Is treabhadh dubh
Is tu ga chur
Le d'inntinn

(White land and black ploughing
and you do it with your mind)[95]

---

93 *Anglo-Latin Satirical Poets*, ed. by Wright, p. 526; translation from Williamson, *Feast of Creatures*, p. 178.
94 Cited in *Say What I Am Called*, ed. by Bitterli, p. 183; translation from Williamson, *Feast of Creatures*, p. 178.
95 Kathleen Reddy of the University of Glasgow introduced me to this riddle, which is commonly available on the Internet as a Scottish Gaelic proverb. See, for example, the last entry on this website: <http://www.bbc.co.uk/scotland/alba/tbh/beulchainnt/pages/index.shtml?page=toimhseachain>

Drawing on the image of writing as the production of black lines on a white surface, this riddle emphasizes the power of the mind — or what in the Middle Ages would be called the soul — that drives the body in the production of writing. Just as a plowman guides the plow, so the mind or soul pushes the pen across the page, producing words that take on a life of their own — the fruit that emerges in the plowed field — expressions of the soul that transcend death. Just as Langland's plow is both structured like a soul and engaged in the activity of the cultivation of the soul, so the plow in these three riddles is guided by the soul/mind to produce the 'strange fruit' of verse.

William Langland, if not the character Will himself, is engaged in an activity of writing commonly associated with plowing in the period. That Will himself was understood as a writer is asserted, as I mentioned above, in B.12, when Imaginatif scolds him for writing verse when he could say prayers: 'þow medlest þee with makynge — and my3test go seye þi Sauter' (B.12.16). Furthermore, in the C text when Will is interrogated by Reason about his laziness, he is accused of writing rather than performing proper work. Lamenting his life of idleness, he comments 'For Y made of tho men as resoun me tauhte', which E. Talbot Donaldson translates as, 'For I wrote rhymes of those men as Reason taught me'; Derek Pearsall glosses, 'made' as 'composed verses about' (C.5.5).[96] In his introduction to a collection of essays co-edited with Kathryn Kerby-Fulton, *Written Work: Langland, Labor, and Authorship*, Steven Justice writes that 'Anne Middleton suggests [...] that Langland imagined and presented his writing as *work* analogous to agricultural labour, a notion that would seem to imply that the text not merely is the result of, but is in some sense constituted by, the history of the poet's activity'.[97]

Langland's particular mode of poetry — personification allegory — heightens the soul-making capacities of his verse by animating language: he gives words like Conscience, Reason, Need, and Hunger souls which allow them to speak and interact with the world.[98] We have seen how the dialectical method of the poem suits the uncertain development of the will in the poem. The change of genre as the poem progresses, as Simpson has shown, marks the poem's shift from reason (one consonant with a Thomistic intellectualist model of the soul) to the affective (one consonant with a voluntarist one).[99] We have also seen how Will's encounters with images of the soul and its faculties have progressively informed him, that is have made him progressively conscious of what it means to be a person with a soul. This consciousness, furthermore, has taught him the primary activity of the soul should be to love and to seek love, a primary activity of the will.

Poetry, with its arational, non-verbal dimensions (what recent poets have called its non-semantic elements, such as rhythm, metre, line length, and sound) is particularly well suited to an exploration of the ineffability and unpredictability of

---

[accessed 1 July 2020].

96   See *Piers Plowman*, ed. by Donaldson, Appendix, l. 5, and *Piers Plowman*, ed. by Pearsall, C.5.5, p. 104.

97   Paraphrased in Justice, 'Introduction', p. 2; see Middleton, 'Acts of Vagrancy', pp. 208–17.

98   I am grateful to Kate Crassons for suggesting this further link between the soul and writing in the very form of the poem.

99   Simpson, *Introduction* and 'From Reason to Affective Knowledge'.

the soul in which the will predominates.[100] Even the alliterative line itself seems apt for the earthly-focused soul-making Langland presents. Langland's long line, saturated with alliteration, is inherently thick, and thus apt for the image of the furrow that Isidore tells us 'rustics' called verse; just as the soil resists the plow that turns it over, so the four-beat alliterative long line with its variable alliterative patterns mimics the uncertain progress of the will as it slows reading down.[101] Furthermore, the slow reading the line requires helps make the reader conscious of the poet's craft.

What does writing do but bring us to consciousness of ourselves, of our place in the world, and of the world itself, precisely what Will learns as he is informed in the poem? Furthermore, in Langland's vision — and it is significant that the first part of the poem (passus 1 through 7) is called a vision — writing brings us to a particular form of consciousness, one guided by conscience; that is, for Langland writing is both an ethical act and a means to impart ethics to others. Will's process of becoming informed, then, has taken him from an understanding of his own divinely inspired nature out into the world, where he has witnessed a supreme act of love and has learned that this is the primary act his soul must perform. And then he has learned that his actions in the world, even acts of love, must be guided by conscience. He moves in a cyclical negative dialectical process of soul-making that will continually recur just as the episodes of Christ's life continually recur in the liturgical year, even as he himself moves forward in a teleological process from life to death.

But, of course, it takes the reader to reanimate the once living words of the author/scribe when he or she infuses those words with his or her own breath. Not only does the act of writing and rewriting cultivate the field of the page for Langland and cultivate in us that primary act of the soul, conscience, but we also, as readers, engage in our own soul-making as we read and reread this magnificent poem.[102]

---

100 For a paradigmatic essay on the non-semantic elements of poetry, see McCaffery, 'Writing as a General Economy', pp. 201–21.

101 See n. 92.

102 This essay was originally delivered as a plenary at the *International Piers Plowman Society Meeting* in Miami, Florida on 4 April 2019. I thank Emily Steiner, Fiona Somerset, and Tom Goodmann for the kind invitation to speak and the *YLS* editors, especially Katharine Breen, for their helpful editorial comments on this expanded version. It could never have been written without the thorough and generous philosophical guidance of Robert Pasnau and the intellectual direction and encouragement of James Simpson in person and in his published work. I am also grateful to Nicolette Zeeman for a timely and engaging conversation about my proposed paper and for her discerning comments on my revised draft; to Adrian Streete and Rita Copeland for positive feedback on the plenary version of the paper; to Kate Crassons, David Benson, and Jeremy Smith for their careful and challenging readings; to David Aers for kindly reading the essay at a late stage; and to Paul Strohm for a discerning reading of a late version. Andrew Prescott kindly pointed me to numerous images of the soul. Georgina Wilde, Mark Amsler, and Kristin Morrison also made valuable suggestions for revision. R. W. Hanning, Jennifer Jahner, Alastair Minnis, and Derek Pearsall gave positive responses to the penultimate version of the essay. Marjorie Levinson responded brilliantly to the essay's engagement with negative dialectics and set out questions well worth further consideration in a longer study. I also thank Ralph Hanna for his far-ranging and challenging responses to the talk version of this essay. I would also like to thank the loyal attendees of the University of Glasgow *Piers Plowman* Reading Group: Samuel Cocker, Sophie Conaghan-Sexon, Johanna Green, Pamela King, Diane Scott, Fraser

Works Cited

Primary Sources

Als I Lay in a winteris nyt: A Debate between the Body and the Soul, in *Middle English Debate Poetry: A Critical Anthology*, ed. by John W. Conlee (East Lansing: Colleagues Press, 1991), pp. 20–49

Ancrene Wisse: The English Text of the 'Ancrene Riwle', Corpus Christi College MS 402, ed. by J. R. R. Tolkien, EETS o.s. 249 (London: Oxford University Press, 1962)

Ancrene Wisse: A Corrected Edition of the Text in Cambridge, Corpus Christi College MS 402 with Variants from Other Manuscripts, ed. by Bella Millett, EETS 325, 2 vols (Oxford: Oxford University Press, 2005)

The Anglo-Latin Satirical Poets and Epigrammatists of the Twelfth Century, ed. by Thomas Wright (London: Longman, 1872)

Augustine of Hippo, *Confessions*, trans. by R. S. Coffin (London: Penguin, 1961)

——, *The Soliloquies: Augustine's Inner Dialogue*, ed. by John E. Rotelle, trans. and notes by Kim Paffenroth, intro. by Boniface Ramsey (Hyde Park, NY: New City Press, 2000)

Aquinas, Thomas, *Summa theologiæ*, trans. by L. Shapcote (New York: Benzinger, 1947–48) <http://www.newadvent.org/summa/> [accessed 1 July 2020]

——, *The Treatise on Human Nature: 'Summa theologiae' 1a 75–89*, trans. by Robert Pasnau (Indianapolis: Hackett, 2002)

——, *Summa theologiæ: Latin Text and English Translation, Introductions, Notes, Appendices and Glossaries*, XVII, ed. and trans. by Thomas Gilby (Cambridge: Cambridge University Press, 2006)

Aristotle, *De anima*, in *The Complete Works of Aristotle: The Revised Oxford Translation*, ed. by Jonathan Barnes, 2 vols (Princeton: Princeton University Press, 1984), I, 641–69

Boethius, *The Consolation of Philosophy*, trans. by Richard Green (Indianapolis: Bobbs-Merrill, 1962)

De spiritu et anima, in *Patrologiae cursus completus: series latina*, ed. by Jacques-Paul Migne, 221 vols (Paris, 1844–64), XL (1845), cols 779–832

Isidore of Seville, *Etymologiae*, in *Isidori Hispalensis episcopi Etymologiarum sive originum libri XX*, ed. by W. M. Lindsay, 2 vols (Oxford: Oxford University Press, 1911), available online at <https://www.thelatinlibrary.com/isidore/11.shtml> [accessed 1 July 2020]

——, *The 'Etymologies' of Isidore of Seville*, trans. by Stephen A. Barney and others, with the collaboration of Muriel Hall (Cambridge: Cambridge University Press, 2006)

Jerome, *Commentary on Ezekiel 1.7*, in *Conscience in Medieval Philosophy*, ed. and trans. by Timothy Potts (Cambridge: Cambridge University Press, 1980), pp. 79–80

Keats, John, *The Letters of John Keats, 1814–1821*, ed. by Hyder Edward Rollins, 2 vols (Cambridge, MA: Harvard University Press, 1958)

Dallachy, Kristin Morrison, Lynn Verschuren, and the late, brilliant Desmond O'Brien. Above all, I am grateful to Jeffrey Robinson for his continual support during the production of this essay and for his illuminating insights into the nature of poetry.

Langland, William, *The Vision of William Concerning Piers the Plowman*, ed. by Walter W. Skeat (Oxford: Oxford University Press, 1886)

——, *Piers Plowman: An Edition of the C-Text*, ed. by Derek Pearsall (Berkeley: University of California Press, 1978)

——, *Piers Plowman: An Alliterative Verse Translation*, trans. by E. Talbot Donaldson (New York: Norton, 1990)

——, *Piers Plowman: A Parallel-Text Edition of the A, B, C and Z Versions*, ed. by A. V. C. Schmidt, 2 vols (London: Longman, 1995)

Sawles Warde, in *The Katherine Group (MS Bodley 34)*, ed. by Emily Rebekah Huber and Elizabeth Robertson (Kalamazoo: Medieval Institute Publications, 2016), pp. 249–66

'Say What I am Called': The Old English Riddles of the Exeter Book & the Anglo-Latin Riddle Tradition, ed. by Dieter Bitterli (Toronto: Toronto University Press, 2009)

'Soul and Body I', trans. by Aaron Hostetter, for the Anglo-Saxon Narrative Poetry Project <https://anglosaxonpoetry.camden.rutgers.edu/soul-body/> [accessed 1 July 2020]

'Soul and Body II', in *The Exeter Book*, ed. by George Philip Krapp and Elliot Van Kirk Dobbie (New York: Columbia University Press, 1956), pp. 174–78

The Vernon Manuscript: A Facsimile of Bodleian Library MS. Eng. poet.a.1, ed. by A. I. Doyle (Cambridge: Brewer, 2009)

Secondary Sources

Adams, Marilyn McCord, 'Ockham on Will, Nature and Morality', in *The Cambridge Companion to Ockham*, ed. by P. V. Spade (Cambridge: Cambridge University Press, 1999), pp. 245–72

Adams, Robert, '*Piers Plowman* and Langland's Semi-Pelagianism', *Traditio*, 39 (1983), 327–418

——, 'Langland's Theology', in *A Companion to 'Piers Plowman'*, ed. by John Alford and Anne Middleton (Berkeley: University of California Press, 1988), pp. 87–114

Adorno, Theodor W., 'On Lyric Poetry and Society', in *Notes to Literature*, I, ed. by Rolf Tiedemann and trans. by Sherry Weber Nicholsen (New York: Columbia University Press, 1991), pp. 37–54

Aers, David, *'Piers Plowman' and Christian Allegory* (London: Edward Arnold, 1975)

——, *Community, Gender and Individual Identity in English Writing: 1360–1430* (London: Routledge, 1988)

——, *Sanctifying Signs: Making Christian Tradition in Late Medieval England* (Notre Dame: University of Notre Dame Press, 2004), pp. 29–52

——, *Salvation and Sin: Augustine, Langland, and Fourteenth-Century Theology* (Notre Dame: University of Notre Dame Press, 2009)

——, *Beyond Reformation?: An Essay on William Langland's 'Piers Plowman' and the End of Constantinian Christianity* (Notre Dame: University of Notre Dame Press, 2015)

Alford, John A., 'The Idea of Reason in *Piers Plowman*', in *Medieval English Studies Presented to George Kane*, ed. by Edward Donald Kennedy, Ronald Waldron, and Joseph S. Wittig (Cambridge: Brewer, 1988), pp. 199–216

Barney, Stephen, 'The Plowshare of the Tongue: The Progress of a Symbol from the Bible to *Piers Plowman*', *Mediaeval Studies*, 35 (1973), 261–93

Benson, C. David, '*Piers Plowman* and Parish Wall Paintings', *Yearbook of Langland Studies*, 11 (1997), 1–38

——, *Public 'Piers Plowman': Modern Scholarship and Late Medieval English Culture* (University Park: Penn State University Press, 2003)

Boitani, Pietro, *English Medieval Narrative in the Thirteenth and Fourteenth Centuries* (Cambridge: Cambridge University Press, 1982)

Bonansea, Bernardino, *Man and his Approach to God in John Duns Scotus* (Lanham: University Press of America, 1983)

Bowers, John, *The Crisis of Will in 'Piers Plowman'* (Washington, DC: The Catholic University of America Press, 1986)

Breen, Katharine H., *Imagining an English Reading Public, 1150–1400* (Cambridge: Cambridge University Press, 2010)

Bugbee, John, *God's Patients: Chaucer, Agency, and the Nature of Laws* (Notre Dame: Notre Dame University Press, 2019)

Calì, Pietro, *Allegory and Vision in Dante and Langland* (Cork: Cork University Press, 1971)

Camille, Michael, *Mirror in Parchment: The Luttrell Psalter and the Making of Medieval England* (Chicago: Chicago University Press, 1998)

Carruthers, Mary (as Mary C. Schroeder), 'The Character of Conscience in *Piers Plowman*', *Studies in Philology*, 67 (1970), 13–30

Carruthers, Mary, *The Search for St Truth: A Study of Meaning in 'Piers Plowman'* (Evanston: Northwestern University Press, 1973)

Coleman, Janet, '*Piers Plowman' and the Moderni* (Rome: Edizioni di Storia e Litteratura, 1981)

Courtenay, William, 'Nominalism and Late Medieval Religion', in *The Pursuit of Holiness in Late Medieval and Renaissance Religion*, ed. by Heiko Oberman and Charles Trinkhus (Leiden: Brill, 1974), pp. 26–59

Davlin, Mary Clemente, '*A Game of Hevene': Word Play and the Meaning of 'Piers Plowman' B* (Cambridge: Brewer, 1989)

——, *The Place of God in 'Piers Plowman' and Art* (Aldershot: Ashgate, 2001)

Eaton, R. D., 'From "Inwit" to "Conscience" in Late Middle English Literature', *Neuphilologische Mitteilungen*, 105 (2004): 423–35

Foucault, Michel, *Discipline and Punish: The Birth of the Prison*, trans. by Alan Sheridan (London: Penguin, 1979)

Henkel, John H., 'Plowing as a Metaphor for Poetic Composition in Vergil's *Georgics*', presented at the 2009 meeting of The Classical Association of the Middle West and South, available at <https://camws.org/meeting/2009/program/abstracts/08E5. Henkel.pdf> [accessed 1 July 2020]

——, 'Writing Poems on Trees: Genre and Metapoetics in Vergil's *Eclogues* and *Georgics*' (unpublished doctoral dissertation, University of North Carolina, 2019)

Hort, Greta, '*Piers Plowman' and Contemporary Religious Thought* (London: Society for Promoting Christian Knowledge, 1938)

Hostetter, Aaron, Anglo-Saxon Narrative Poetry Project <https://anglosaxonpoetry. camden.rutgers.edu/> [accessed 1 July 2020]

Justice, Steven, 'Introduction: Authorial Work and Literary Ideology', in *Written Work: Langland, Labor and Authorship*, ed. by Justice and Kathryn Kerby-Fulton (Philadelphia: University of Pennsylvania Press, 1997), pp. 1–12

Kane, George, *'Piers Plowman': The Evidence for Authorship* (London: Bloomsbury, 1965)

Karnes, Michelle, *Imagination, Meditation and Cognition in the Middle Ages* (Chicago: University of Chicago Press, 2011)

Kent, Bonnie, *The Virtues of the Will: The Transformation of Ethics in the Late Thirteenth Century* (Washington, DC: The Catholic University Press of America, 1995)

Lawton, David, 'The Subject of *Piers Plowman*', *Yearbook of Langland Studies*, 1 (1987), 1–30

Lochrie, Karma, 'Desiring Foucault', *Journal of Medieval and Early Modern Studies*, 27 (1997), 3–16

Manly, J. M., '*Piers the Ploughman* and its Sequence', in *The Cambridge History of English Literature*, 11: *The End of the Middle Ages*, ed. by A. W. Ward and A. R. Waller II (Cambridge: Cambridge University Press, 2008), pp. 1–42

Mann, Jill, 'Eating and Drinking in *Piers Plowman*', *Essays and Studies*, 32 (1979), 26–43

——, 'The Nature of Need Revisited', *Yearbook of Langland Studies*, 18 (2004), 3–39

McCaffrey, Steve, 'Writing as a General Economy', in *North of Intention: Critical Writings, 1973–1986* (New York: Roof Books, 2000), pp. 201–21

Middleton, Anne, 'Acts of Vagrancy: The C Version "Autobiography" and the Statute of 1388', in *Written Work: Langland, Labor and Authorship*, ed. by Stephen Justice and Kathryn Kerby-Fulton (Philadelphia: University of Pennsylvania Press, 1997), pp. 208–317

——, 'Narration and the Invention of Experience: Episodic Form in *Piers Plowman*', in *The Wisdom of Poetry: Essays in Early English Literature in Honor of Morton W. Bloomfield*, ed. by Larry D. Benson and Siegfried Wenzel (Kalamazoo: Medieval Institute Publications, 1982)

Minnis, Alastair, 'Looking for a Sign: The Quest for Nominalism in Chaucer and Langland', in *Essays on Ricardian Literature in Honour of J. A. Burrow*, ed. by A. J. Minnis, Charlotte C. Morse, and Thorlac Turville-Petre (Oxford: Clarendon, 1997), pp. 142–78

Oberman, Heiko, 'Some Notes on the Theology of Nominalism, with Attention to its Relation to the Renaissance', *Harvard Theological Review*, 53 (1960), 47–76

——, *The Harvest of Medieval Theology: Gabriel Biel and Late Medieval Nominalism* (New York: Labyrinth, 1963)

——, 'Fourteenth-Century Religious Thought: A Premature Profile', *Speculum*, 53 (1978), 80–93

Pasnau, Robert, *Theories of Cognition in the Later Middle Ages* (Cambridge: Cambridge University Press, 1997)

——, 'Voluntarism and the Self in *Piers Plowman*', in *Gender, Poetry and the Form of Thought in Later Medieval Literature: Essays in Honor of Elizabeth Robertson*, ed. by Jennifer Jahner and Ingrid Nelson (Bethlehem, PA: Lehigh University Press, forthcoming)

Pattison, George, *A Rhetorics of the Word: A Philosophy of Christian Life*, pt 2 (Oxford: Oxford University Press, 2019)

Potts, Timothy C., ed., *Conscience in Medieval Philosophy* (Cambridge: Cambridge University Press, 1980; repr. 2002)

Quirk, Randolph, 'Langland's Use of "Kind Wit" and "Inwit"', *Journal of English and Germanic Philology*, 52 (1953), 182–88

Ranfagni, Tommaso, 'Representing the Soul in the Renaissance: The Iconographic Theme of "Tabula Rasa"', lecture delivered at the University of Glasgow on 16 January 2020

Raskolnikov, Masha, *Body against Soul: Gender and Sowlehele in Middle English Allegory* (Columbus: Ohio State University Press, 2009)

Robertson, Elizabeth, 'Souls that Matter: The Gendering of the Soul in *Piers Plowman*', in *Mindful Spirit in Late Medieval Literature: Essays in Honor of Elizabeth D. Kirk*, ed. by Bonnie Wheeler (New York: Palgrave Macmillan, 2006), pp. 165–86

———, 'Kissing the Worm: Sex and Gender in the Afterlife and the Poetic Posthuman in the Late Middle English *The Disputation betwyx the Body and the Worms*', in *From Beasts to Souls: Gender and Embodiment in Medieval Europe*, ed. by E. Jane Burns and Peggy McCracken (Notre Dame: University of Notre Dame Press, 2013), pp. 121–56

Salter, Elizabeth, *'Piers Plowman': An Introduction* (Oxford: Blackwell, 1963)

Salter, Elizabeth, and Derek Pearsall, 'Introduction', in *Piers Plowman*, ed. by Elizabeth Salter and Derek Pearsall (Evanston: Northwestern University Press, 1969), pp. 1–58

Shogimen, Takashi, *Ockham and Political Discourse in the Late Middle Ages* (Cambridge: Cambridge University Press, 2007)

Simpson, James, 'From Reason to Affective Knowledge: Modes of Thought and Poetic Form in *Piers Plowman*', *Medium Aevum*, 55 (1986), 1–23

———, *'Piers Plowman': An Introduction to the B-Text* (London: Longman, 1990)

———, *Sciences and the Self in Medieval Poetry: Alan of Lille's 'Anticlaudianus' and John Gower's 'Confessio amantis'* (Cambridge: Cambridge University Press, 1995)

Smith, D. Vance, 'Negative Langland', *Yearbook of Langland Studies*, 23 (2009), 33–60

Spearing, A. C., *Textual Subjectivity: The Encoding of Subjectivity in Medieval Narratives and Lyric* (Oxford: Oxford University Press, 2005)

Strohm, Paul, *Conscience: A Very Short Introduction* (Oxford: Oxford University Press, 2011)

Williamson, Craig, *A Feast of Creatures* (Philadelphia: University of Pennsylvania Press, 1982)

Wittig, Joseph S., '*Piers Plowman* B, Passus IX–XII: Elements in Design of the Inward Journey', *Traditio*, 28 (1972), 211–80

Wood, Sarah, *Conscience and the Composition of 'Piers Plowman'* (Oxford: Oxford University Press, 2012)

Zeeman, Nicolette, *'Piers Plowman' and the Medieval Discourse of Desire* (Cambridge: Cambridge University Press, 2006)

HELEN PHILLIPS

Langland and Wales

*Place, Identity, Borders**

▼ **KEYWORDS** History of Wales, medieval Marches, borders, London, Marcher lordships, Chester, Malvern Hills, penitence, the Cross, topography, identity, class, colonialization, Jews, boundary theories, theft, minstrels, Seven Deadly Sins, satire.

▼ **ABSTRACT** Langland's Welsh allusions witness to a significant presence in *Piers Plowman*, albeit one largely submerged from first sight. The poem's depictions of Wales and the Welsh, generally disparaging, are products of the historical and contemporary conditions and outlooks of the Welsh and English Marcher region, and represent a symbiotic relationship with these. Unlike most of Langland's isolated individual geographical allusions, the Welsh and Marches references represent constellations of ideas and associations which contribute to core themes and recurrent patterns, especially those of opposition, mirroring, and marginality. The most obvious are the images of London and Westminster and dualities constructed in relation to these, and the divided and equivocal self-presentation of the narrator. Other themes influenced by the Welsh and Marcher presence in the text include those of penitence, the Cross, minstrels, social class, and the figures of the robber and the wanderer. Langland's presentation of Wales and the Marches and their bearing on such elements, together with his handling of place and identity, geography and theological symbolism derived from local topography, are examined through theoretical perspectives of colonialism, borders, and ethnic difference.

*   I am very grateful to Helen Fulton who read and generously commented on an earlier version of this essay, and to the editors and anonymous readers of the *Yearbook of Langland Studies* for their helpful suggestions; errors are entirely my responsibility.

Helen Phillips (phillipshe@cardiff.ac.uk) is Professor Emerita in the School of English, Communication and Philosophy at Cardiff University.

The Yearbook of Langland Studies, 34 (2020), 57–92   BREPOLS ❦ PUBLISHERS   10.1484/J.YLS.5.121087

Across the A, B, and C versions of *Piers Plowman*, Langland makes four references to Wales and Welsh things or people:

'Gryffyth þe Walshe', sitting among the customers with disreputable or criminal lifestyles in the tavern Glutton patronises, A.5.167; B.5.317; C.6.372;
Ȝeuan the 'Walschman', with a lifetime of robbing other people, who now repents and swears to make restitution, C.6.308–10;
Avarice/'Couetyse' himself, a personification that Langland presents predominantly in terms of theft and deceptions, wearing a 'Walsshe', a tabard of Welsh wool so threadbare that lice reject wandering on it, A.5.107–13; B.5.186–95; C.6.196–205;
The description of both 'Engelond and Walis' as 'Al […] heþynesse' at the time of Augustine's conversion of the English, B.15.442–46.[1]

Langland presents what is Welsh as disreputable, dishonest, or both.
He also refers to places in the English–Welsh Marches:

the opening naming of the Malvern Hills, A.Prol.5; B.Prol.5; C.Prol.6; and further references at A.8.142, B.7.129, C.9.295; also B.Prol.215–16, C.Prol.163–64; and C.5.110;
'rymes of Robyn Hood and Randolf Erl of Chestre', B.5.396; C.7.11
the 'Roode of Chestre', A.5.233; B.5.460.[2]

These Welsh and Marches references and their backgrounds contribute to Langland's geographical vision, his imagined Britain and England, and to characteristic structures of his satire and spirituality. Numerically few within a massive poem, the allusions prove illuminating and significant, especially when examined in their contexts, which yield further historical and cultural meanings. These are not just isolated names but constellations of associated ideas, implications, and discourses, and as such they engage with major networks of ideas and themes in *Piers Plowman*. The themes include the figure of the thief, repentance, devotion to the Rood, corruption and moral integrity, social class, legitimate and illegitimate minstrelsy, poverty, wandering, and unsettled identity.

There is a likely connection between disparaging images of the Welsh and the background in the English–Welsh Marches which is suggested by aspects of *Piers Plowman*, which include, besides the above allusions, the linguistic and codicological links with the English–Welsh borders, evident in many texts and manuscripts, especially of the C version. These denote a distinctive area within Britain, its identity marked by being a large border territory between England and the principality of Wales, by its mixed population and its medieval lordships' high degree of independence. Within Langland's poem the most significant effects of such a connection are not

---

1   All quotations from the poem are taken from *'Piers Plowman': A Parallel-Text Edition of the A, B, C, and Z Versions*, ed. by Schmidt.

2   Kaske, '*Piers Plowman* and Local Iconography', suggested another local link, between Langland's image of two greedy sows, B.5.341; C.6.397, and a carving in Little Malvern Priory. Two pigs feeding from one pot was perhaps proverbial. That would fit with 'The Two Pigs' used as a pub name. I can find the phrase recorded recently only for two pubs, but both located in the western area of central England, Cheltenham (Gloucestershire) and Corsham (Wiltshire) — pleasing but statistically insignificant.

simply straightforward signs from a probable literal background. The creative effects are above all the generation of repetitive, often uneasy, patterns, of both opposition and reciprocity, a border-like consciousness of division and of encounter with and mirroring of the Other. The two categories of references listed above, to Wales and the Marches, speak of a symbiotic relation, a symbiosis created out of a complex and contested history and present, including the relations of colonizer and colonized. Wales was England's first colony. Belittlement of the colonized is a symptom of colonialism. Such a relationship and pattern of response underlies attitudes to the Welsh in Langland's writing and engages with other dualities and preoccupations.

One example is the way in which Wales and the Marches, particularly through the association of the Malvern Hills with the narrator and his early visions, construct a duality with the world of London: a small but significant counter to the fact that, in Emily Steiner's words, predominately the poet's 'gaze is trained on London and its vicinity'.[3] In one very direct duality, A.Prol.84–89; B.Prol.211–16; C.Prol.158–64, an allusion back to the western rustic Malvern Hills location provides a platform from which to direct an attack against privileged corruption in the distant world of London — when Malverns mist mocks London silk.

Such an environment as that of the medieval Marches and Wales, with two ethnicities, combined with legal inequality and entrenched colonialist strategies of ethnic disparagement, enters into the poem's preoccupation with social status too. The association sometimes manifests itself in typically Langlandian parallels. The narrator's assertion of his own superior status above manual workers (C.5.12–69) has a parallel in the discourses of low class and wildness hovering around Langland's Welsh allusions (e.g., A.5.107–13, B.5.186–95, C.6.196–205; cf. B.15.459–60). Then there is a further parallel in Langland's contrast of *gentil* Christians gaining superior status over *cherle* Jews, a nation once noble but now legally subordinated to Christians. The passage, at B.19.26–50; C.20.26–50, about the advent of Christianity, takes the form of a narrative about a defeated people, their status reduced to servitude, and a reversal of power with one regime supplanting and subjugating another. The exposition employs vocabulary of a 'conquerour' defending his 'conquest' over the Jewish nation: the imagery of Christ's Crucifixion as a victory is here extended into and entangled with these discourses of a defeated nation and of overturned social status.[4] The narrative and vocabulary mirror a familiar narrative used about the conquest and subjugation of the Britons by the English and their 'degeneration' into the Welsh, a subordinated people marked by low status, wildness, and barbarousness, after once possessing the whole kingdom.[5]

---

3 Steiner, *Reading 'Piers Plowman'*, p. 19, examines Langland's England as a complex construction. See also Barron, 'William Langland'.

4 B.19.34-50; C.20.34-50.

5 The *locus classicus* for this degeneration from *nobilitas* appears in closing sections of book 12 of Geoffrey of Monmouth's *Historia regum Britanniae*. See Geoffrey of Monmouth, *The History of the Kings of Britain*, ed. by Reeve, trans. by Wright, pp. 145–47. See also Faletra, 'Narrating the Matter of Britain'. On the presentation of Jewish loss of inheritance and status see Goldstein, '"Why calle ye hym Crist?"'.

A parallel between the Welsh and the Jews had appeared in writings from Gildas and Bede on.[6] The slanting of the narrative about British/Welsh subjugation, in these and later writers, varied with the period and whether it was being used by the Welsh or against them. This political mythology which explained, and in English eyes justified, subordination, together with the regulations that made the Welsh of Langland's period second-class inhabitants in their own country and the English border areas, makes it unsurprising that social status in these places could be a complex matter. And, indeed, Helen Fulton points to evidence for social anxiety and ambivalence in environments where contrasts in status and ethnic difference coincided, creating a variety of apprehensive or equivocal attitudes to social status and hierarchies for both the Welsh and English, while 'the resident English asserted their difference by calling for sanctions against the unruly Welsh that would reinvigorate their colonial power'.[7]

Patterns of contrast often carry structural and thematic importance in *Piers Plowman*.[8] The Malvern Hills, London, and the Welsh are not just instances of isolated naming like many of the poem's geographical allusions: each is a network of associations and they also interact variously with each other, not least in contrastive judgements. Thus, following the spiritual revelation on the Malvern Hills, a negative gaze is directed against a prosperous and successful world centred in London, and also against the Welsh (massively in the first case, a tiny handful of references in the other). Such a Janus-like satiric gaze parallels the Malverns' own geographical position, a vantage-point looking down on landscapes below to either side, towards the west and ultimately Wales and towards the east and the rest of England. It also resembles the Marches' geopolitical situation more generally: looking both ways, they formed the western margin of England extending away on their east and England's interface with Wales to their west.

Satire attached to geographical identity is a favourite Langlandian device, and geography is a central element in the speaker's identity. His self-presentation in C passus 5 is disruptive and 'awkward', as Hanna observes, because he identifies himself with two locations, naming them separately and announcing his dual residence: 'opelond' and London.[9] Yet this locational duality, with that profound creative connectivity of which Langland is master, contributes to other significant dualities in the poem as well as the impression of doubleness and unsettled, unsingle, positioning that marks its speaker.

Neither the double locations nor other multiple and equivocal presentations of the speaker are a flaw. Writing about the subject of *Piers Plowman*, David Lawton characterizes its subjective consciousness as essentially (i.e., not merely contingently)

---

6 Mulligan, 'Moses, Taliesin and the Welsh Chosen People', includes a useful historical outline at pp. 86–96.

7 Fulton, 'Class and Nation', pp. 200–04 (quotation at p. 201); see also Davies, *The Revolt of Owain Glyn Dŵr*, p. 283.

8 On Langland's structuring through repeated isomorphic patterns, see Phillips, 'Structure and Consolation'.

9 Hanna, *Penn Commentary*, II, 6.

fragmentary, multiple, and dialogic. He also, interestingly in view of this essay's argument, characterizes it as a 'marginal subject':

> The subject of *Piers Plowman* is resolutely marginal — by whatever definition of marginality one might apply, social, religious, intellectual, economic, except gender: a wanderer from place to place (or position to position), a hermit out of order, a would-be clerk without a place or probably a degree, and in a broader sense 'without degree', one who lives among 'lollares' but is not one, and so on.[10]

Without trying to press too narrowly a literal biographical hypothesis, it is illuminating to consider this marginal and non-unitary subject consciousness in relation to the border, and the divisions, contested history and inequalities of the two ethnic groups in Wales and the Marches. Both locations present him discordantly linked with dishonest and disreputable lifestyles: he is on the Malvern Hills and like a hermit unholy of works, living in London but among 'lollares of Londone and lewede ermytes' (C.5.4). His first identification with London, in C.5.1–4, comes attached to a lengthy contesting of his personal status and lifestyle by Reason (C.5.11–104), who disputes his right to a life without labour and undercuts his personal position, judging it as 'lollarne lyf, þat lytel is preysed' (C.5.31). This C passage gifts the speaker simultaneously with a second residence and dialogic demolition of his moral and class standing. Alongside the identification through place, it uses, more interrogatively, identification through profession. Where he lives, C.5.1–4, is presented in tension with what employment he lives by (see especially C.5.26–52). An alliterative lexicon centred on *life* is defining identity variously in this passage — as residence, as class and profession, as means of livelihood (*byleue, lyflode*, ll. 21, 29, 45), and as contrasted judgements on the life he might adopt: 'lyif þat is louable' to God and the soul (103) or life 'lytel ylet by', 'þat lytel is preysed' (3, 31).

Amid this destructive interrogation comes the dreamer's abrupt announcement that he lives in two places: 'And so Y leue yn London and opelond bothe' (C.5.44), where it seems reasonable to assume, but not certain, that *opelond* equates to the region containing the Malvern Hills. Another contrast here between youth and adulthood, alongside other dualities (two locations, two concepts of legitimate work, two social classes, two judgements on his style of living) might suggest a youthful period in the Marches. *Opelond* speculatively might be the nurturing environment that bestowed upon him that superior, clerical status.

Turning for a moment to the possible clues for a background for the author, the note identifying Willielm de Langlond as the son of Stacy de Rockayle, a 'generosus' (i.e., *gentil*) tenant holding lands belonging to the Despenser family, is found in a manuscript, Trinity College Dublin MS 212, which forms part of an intricate network of manuscript links and political, geographical, dynastic, and clerical connections that witnesses to the worlds of Welsh–English religious culture and Marcher dynastic power of the Welsh–English borders, and witnesses also to how such connections might indicate possible shared backgrounds for some parts of the poem's readerships

---

10 Lawton, 'The Subject of *Piers Plowman*', p. 26.

as well as its author. Trinity College Dublin MS 212 contains a C text of *Piers Plowman*, whose language is, like many C texts, West Midlands, mapped by *LALME* to south-west Worcestershire.[11] The note itself is written on the same page and in apparently the same hand as a small set of annals that are related in content to a south Wales religious house, probably Abergavenny Benedictine Priory. They particularly record Welsh rebellions and Welsh leaders and the deaths of Marcher lords.[12] As Ryan Perry shows, this manuscript, mainly a religious miscellany, and its contents may derive from and reflect the household piety of the *familia* of Isabella Despenser, second wife of Richard Beauchamp, Lord of Abergavenny.[13]

What, then, were the Marches, their relationships with Wales, the place of the Welsh in them?[14] This paper focuses on the English–Welsh borders but 'Marches' also denoted south Wales territories subject to Norman invasions followed by a history of shifting lordships, alliances, and conflicts, between Welsh and Norman/English lords. Marcher lordships in the fourteenth century extended as far west into eastern Wales as Denbigh, Builth, Brecon, and Glamorgan, as well as through south Wales to Pembroke.[15] The English border areas and eastern and south-east Wales comprise a broad swathe of land from Chester in the north to the Severn estuary in the south. Its medieval inhabitants were familiar with two ethnicities, two languages, two levels of citizenship, complex relationships between two systems of law, and domination by one ethnic group over another, particularly after Edward I's 1284 Statute of Wales claimed feudal overlordship over all Wales. William I and William II's policy of allowing Norman lords to undertake invasions into Wales had produced quasi-independent Marcher lordships, notably the Mortimer, Despenser, and De Bohun dynasties, and earls of Chester, together with many castles and well-defended walled and castled towns. The Marches, distinctive in legal, commercial, and lordship structures, amounted virtually to a third quasi-buffer state between England and Wales.[16] Frequently the power and aggression of the Despensers (especially during the early fourteenth century) and Mortimers (throughout the fourteenth and fifteenth centuries) rivalled the authority of the Crown in Westminster. The earls of Chester,

---

11 The *Piers* text in this manuscript probably shared an exemplar with the 'Clopton' *Piers* text in London University, Senate House Library, MS Sterling V.17; the source for its annals was probably an Abergavenny Priory chronicle. Ryan Perry, 'The Clopton Manuscript and the Beauchamp Affinity', shows intricate links between Beauchamp and Despenser households, their affinities, and related religious houses.

12 Brooks, 'The *Piers Plowman* Manuscripts in Trinity College Dublin', esp. pp. 44–53, gives the annals' content.

13 Perry, 'The Clopton Manuscript', pp. 150–53. Isabel would become a considerable patron of the arts, among other things commissioning Lydgate's translation of *Fifteen Joys of Our Lady*. See also Adams, *Langland and the Rokele Family*.

14 Lieberman, *The March of Wales, 1067–1300*, provides a succinct introduction, pp. 1–14. See further Davies, *First English Empire*; Rowley, *The Welsh Border*; Meecham-Jones, 'Where Was Wales?'; Young, *Constructing 'England' in the Fourteenth Century*; Lieberman, *The Medieval March of Wales*; Dolmans, 'Locating the Border'.

15 See Lieberman, *The Medieval March of Wales*, pp. 1–22, and map, p. 3.

16 Lieberman, *The Medieval March of Wales*, pp. 2–7.

including the three powerful Ranulfs, ruled a palatinate: the king's writ, Westminster government, did not operate in it until the reigning monarch became earl of Chester in the late medieval period. Matthew Lampitt's recent study of society and writing in the Marches powerfully shows, drawing on the social theory of the network, both the tensions and also the complex coherences of the multi-ethnic, multilingual world of the Welsh Marches, a political and cultural entity unique in British history.[17]

R. R. Davies outlines the 'suspicion, even fear of Englishmen for the Welsh' in the Marches: 'they were not to be trusted [...] The March was disconcertingly different, an area where one could credibly locate tales of Gog and Magog but not an area which an Englishman could visit without trepidation'.[18] John Davies records the fear-fuelled declarations of English burghers of Denbigh and several other Welsh towns in the mid-1340s, who protested to the English government that the Welsh were constantly liable to attack and that their aim was to exterminate English people completely from Wales.[19] The degree of independence that Marcher lords could exercise contributed greatly to the propensity to lawlessness in the Marches, especially from the Crown's point of view. Though the fourteenth century brought more peaceful conditions, despite such brutal disruptions as those caused by the Despenser War, 1321–22, English landowners and burghers remained nervous and self-protective. Welsh–English military conflict returned with the start of the fifteenth century. Rees Davies says that in the fourteenth century, 'a veneer of stability concealed deep-lying disaffection and resentment', and by 1345 the Black Prince 'was being warned that "The Welsh have never been so disposed [...] to rise against their liege lord [Edward III] and to conquer the land from him"'.[20] Landowners possessed resented powers to harness the services of Welshmen as soldiers and demesne workers.[21] Hugh Despenser the elder and his son, as the *Vita Edwardi Secundi* records, were widely loathed for their brutality and exploitation, especially by the Welsh in Despenser lands.[22]

By the fourteenth century many Welsh people lived in towns in the English border areas.[23] They 'had severely limited rights in any of the medieval towns whose markets they frequented, whether in Wales or England'.[24] English fear created urban defensive strategies such as banning Welshmen from Chester between sunset and sunrise, and the 1400–01 Parliament decree, which gave expression in law to English aggression and to a sense of ethnic divide that had long been present, and made statements about the 'ancient hatred and suspicion of the Welsh toward the English' and the great difference between the English and Welsh. It banned any Welshman or husband of a Welsh woman from holding any office, for example as a burgess, in Welsh

---

17 Lampitt, 'Networking the Marches'.
18 Davies, *Lordship and Society*, pp. 2–3.
19 Davies, *History of Wales*, pp. 179–78.
20 Davies, *First English Empire*, pp. 185–86.
21 Davies, *First English Empire*, pp. 78–81.
22 *Vita Edwardi Secundi*, ed. by Denholm-Young, rev. edn by Childs, pp. 110–11, 113, 140.
23 Griffiths, 'Who Were the Townsfolk of Wales?', pp. 9–18.
24 McKenna, 'The City of Chester', p. 27.

or English borders towns, holding property in towns of the Marches, or carrying a weapon on roads; no one of full English blood could be arrested on the word of a Welshman or tried by any but a jury of unmixed English blood.[25] Marcher society was uniquely complicated within Britain: a complicated environment in which to be raised. Griffiths observes that the easy permeability of the English–Welsh border, compared with the more challenging geography separating Ireland and Scotland from England, created a fear of 'reverse colonization' that underlay such regulations as those excluding Welshmen from overnight habitation in some English towns.[26] It is important to remember that the Marcher lordships over-rode the border. And there were Welsh communities in many border areas of England. As an instance at the feet of the Malvern Hills, medieval Herefordshire, whose boundary starts along the top of the Malverns ridge looking westwards, still had areas with strong Welsh and Welsh-speaking communities, customs, and culture.[27] Langland's Welsh allusions are not expressions of hostility against an overseas foreign power but reflexes of long-ingrained belittlement and apprehension towards a familiar Other: people walking the same streets in communities possibly familiar in his youth or later. The language of denigration frequent in English allusions to the Welsh goes deeper than satire, snobbery, or jokes: its political instrumentality is illustrated by the fact that it is a staple of English/Norman historical accounts and official documents: 'In the March', Robin Frome says,

> English domination of the higher offices [...] was a perpetual reminder that this was a conquered country. English administrative documents were peppered with stereotyped references to the unreliability and moral shortcomings of the Welsh.[28]

Great Malvern Priory's position as a subservient cell to Westminster Abbey might possibly provide a factual background for the narrator's locations of the Malverns and London, and the scenes of Westminster and city life. A Malvern/London background has been conjectured for the author of twenty-four early fifteenth-century poems in Digby MS 102, because of their language and contents; the author may even have been a Chancery clerk originally from Great Malvern Priory.[29] Referring, seemingly, at times to political events, within broader religious concerns, these interesting poems nevertheless throw into relief the extraordinary originality of the structures of ideas created out of the duality of the contemporary socio-political world of London and the Malvern Hills by Langland — far beyond anything directly attributable to a literal Great Malvern–Westminster Benedictine link.

---

25 Davies, *The Revolt of Owain Glyn Dŵr*, pp. 287–92. Davies points to earlier English agitation in the fourteenth century for such restrictive laws, pp. 71–72; it hardened 'ethnic barriers' and an 'orthodoxy' long-established though to some extent disregarded: 'no parliamentary statute was as crudely racist', p. 287.

26 Griffiths, 'Crossing the Frontiers', pp. 211–25, p. 212.

27 For the intermittent local debate about returning it to Wales see 'Herefordshire in Wales?'.

28 Frome, 'Kingdoms and Dominions at Peace and War', pp. 175–76.

29 Verheij, 'New Light on the Author'. *Digby Poems*, ed. by Barr, pp. 73–74, however, suggests the Benedictine house at Gloucester.

The Malvern Hills, running north to south, only moderately high but with some fairly steep slopes, offer long-distance views on a clear day, looking on one side towards Worcestershire and on the other westwards to Herefordshire, the Black Mountains, and Wales. Though not literally a national boundary, the place conveys a sense of geographical division. Theories of borders and identity, and of 'boundary maintenance', developed during the last fifty years in relation to psychology as well as to history and studies of race and culture, prove illuminating to the examination of how *Piers Plowman* handles personal and national identity.[30] Lieberman characterizes medieval Marches attitudes to the Welsh as typical of borderlands internationally: thinking of one's land as a border country is a state of mind, positive or negative.[31] Barth seminally described identification of oneself and the group one belongs to through 'boundary maintenance', the root of negative ethnic stereotyping.[32]

Marches is used in this paper not just as a synonym for the West Midlands. It is a term that denotes power as well as geography: the power of a very distinctive oligarchy over a distinctive region and society, and it connotes the history of an area as a border, with features of society, culture, and arguably mindsets and prejudices, shaped by this.

Place and (Double) Identity. London and Malvern Hills Allusions

Identification through place is a recurrent device of *Piers Plowman*. Sister Mary Clemente Davlin has shown how profoundly place and space pervade Langland's imagery, thinking, and writing.[33] Individual places and their socio-political and economic dimensions are frequently named: real-life place names (Westminster, Normandy, the Arches, etc.), plus allegorical place names (the 'erldom of Envy', londe of Longynge, etc.) and place names for satire (the reeve of Rutland, Clarice of Cock's Lane, etc.). Langland's satirical jibes against the Welsh, in tandem with the Marches background discernible in the text, seem to bear out a theory about traditions of disparaging geographical communities, that these frequently express a mindset generated by the self-identity of 'another place', a more powerful or sophisticated adjacent territory, a line of interpretation examined further later.[34]

Besides the polarization of London and the West, the poem makes other uses of directional dualities: contrasted compass points, right and left, and the sun's changing positions. Like the Malvern Hills, these contribute theological symbolism, especially about salvation versus damnation. This is not the place for detailed examination

---

30 See especially Barth, *Ethnic Groups and Boundaries*; also Stallybrass and White, *Politics and Poetics of Transgression*.
31 Lieberman, *The March of Wales, 1067–1300*, pp. 91–103.
32 Barth, *Ethnic Groups and Boundaries*.
33 Davlin, *The Place of God*. See also Elliott, 'Langland's Country'.
34 Benbrough-Jackson, *Cardiganshire and the Cardi*, outlines the theory in specific relationship to geographical insults.

but, for example, passus 2 starts with Holy Church instructing the narrator, after the revelations about salvation lying in Truth, which was first seen in the east, to look towards the left, in order to see 'the false'. The passus 1 section that starts with Lucifer's Fall correctly locates his Fall in the north (which points up the singularity of the C Prologue's location of evil in the west, discussed below), then proceeds in C.1.106–32 to a north–south contrast related to the sun in the south, to Christ sitting on the right hand of God, i.e., the 'contrarie' to Lucifer's northern 'lefte' side (112), and the separation of the saved and damned at Judgement, when the saved will 'wende [...] Estward til heuene', C.1.129–32.[35] C's particularly elaborated version of this passage negotiates these directional contrasts and their theological potentialities intricately. C's directional eschatology here in passus 1 looks back to the east–west division introduced in the C Prologue's initial Malvern Hills vision and, with its echoes of the Athanasian Creed, also looks forward to the Pardon.

The C Prologue turned the Malverns ridge's real-life east–west vistas into a divider between good and evil:

Estward Y beheld aftir þe sonne
And say a tour, as Y trowed: Treuthe was thereynne.
Westward Y waytede in a while aftir
And seigh a depe dale: Deth, as Y leue,
Woned in tho wones, and wikkede spiritus. (C.Prol.14–18)

There were some traditions associating the West with evil, in Latin writings from Augustine onwards and vernacular texts that include *Ancrene Wisse* and *Dives and Pauper* (1405–10). They often associate the west *inter alia* with Christ's death and the east with the Resurrection.[36] Langland's A and B Prologues had a wholly eastward-looking and vertical schema for the eschatological contrast.[37] C's use of the east–west, horizontal, contrasts of the actual geographical location is one of several possible pointers suggesting closer creative engagement with the Marches region, perhaps, at the time of C's composition.

The Malvern Hills references are also structural. Their first naming and the later one in A.8.129; B.7.142; C.9.295 function like the typical framing devices familiar in dream vision tradition, and that use of the place name near to transitions between dream and waking appears additionally at C.5.110 (they could also be seen as features

---

35 'Lefte' (C.1.112), in view of C's complex directional exposition here, seems likely to be a correct reading, preferred by Schmidt, rather than the scribes' cautious 'north'.

36 Honorius Augustodunensis explains ecclesiastical east–west symbolism in several works, including *Gemma animae*, ed. by Migne, col. 575B ('De situ orationis'), where the sun symbolizes Christ as Sun of Righteousness and turning east to pray symbolizes the Resurrection, 'when we see the Sun, that we saw seemed to die in the west, rise again with so much glory in the east'. A story linking the west to devils appears in *Ancrene Wisse*, 1.4, ed. by Millett, p. 925. *Dives and Pauper*, 1.16, ed. by Barnum, I, 113–17, offers several symbolisms; its editor, Barnum, notes the *Glossa ordinaria* twelfth-century commentary says Christ died as the sun declined for our sins, which had caused us to fall away from the divine light, II, 39–41.

37 On the vertical symbolism see Davlin, *The Place of God*, pp. 54–63.

that separate the Visio from the Vita). The narrator's careful labelling in C.5.110 of the 'furste' dream as located on 'Maluerne Hulles' is an insistent tying of that seminal vision to the West that is introduced into the very passus that announces the narrator's identification with another place, London. The Malvern Hills appear associated with the moral authority of the early dreams (above all through their revelations about salvation, damnation, and worldly corruption), just as their geography matches symbolically some forms the first vision takes (see above). 'Opelond' in C.5.44, which we might assume means this western area, is certainly a word whose associations match that moral authority. 'Opelond' meant 'countryside' contrasted with city, a rusticity distanced from a powerful and fashionable centre, as well as the literal sense 'upland'.[38]

In C.5.44 'opelond' is in conjunction and quasi-alliteration with 'London': 'And so Y leue yn London and opelond bothe'. *So* does nothing to veil the oddness of this interjection. The next lines appear to harness the values of 'opelond' by appropriating the imagery of the labourer, a figure to which Reason has just accorded higher value, to the narrator's clerical profession. The 'lomes þat Y labore with', says the narrator, are prayers (C.5.45).

We see, early on, the Malverns' literal upland become an elevated platform for viewing heaven's revelations and a moral high ground for clear and superior perception, looking down upon corruption, often located in London or Westminster. *Jack Upland*, although probably written some years later than *Piers Plowman* C, may witness even so to an existing tradition of the 'opelond' man's potential as a yardstick of probity and judgement against worldly corruption.

The contrast between the Malverns and London made in A.Prol.84–89; B.Prol.211–16; C.Prol.159–64 employs such a trope. It begins as a London court scene (and sergeants of law worked in London courts), with prosperous lawyers visualized as hovering in a miasma of fluttering silk hoods, an image that looks forward to the equally hovering, obfuscating, and silent upland mists that will mock and expose their venality. That abrupt repositioning back to 'Maluerne hulles', and a humble workaday familiarity with those uplands and their mists, implicitly possessed by both speaker and audience, takes a localized *opelond* standpoint for its shrewd, peasant-like put-down of top London lawyers. (The mists on the Malverns, well known and attractive to artists and photographers, are possibly attributable to the contrast locals are convinced exists between the warmer, drier, eastern- and England-facing, slopes and the colder, wetter, western- and Wales-facing, slopes of this north–south range.) These provincial rural (i.e., *opelond*) uplands are an ethical binary, not just a distanced geographical contrast vis-à-vis London and its world of power, fashion, and corruption. The narrator's own *opelond*ish rough clothing, hunger, poverty, and resemblance to one of the Malverns' usual rural wandering inhabitants, its sheep, align him with a lifestyle lacking prosperity on these western hillsides and with spiritually authoritative simplicities.

After the spiritual splendour and moral discernment vouchsafed there, his situation on waking from his dream 'meteles and moneyles on Maluerne Hulles',

---

38   *MED*, s.v. 'uplond'; *OED*, s.vv. 'upland'; 'unplandish'.

acquires a para-Franciscan simplicity, a holy poverty that is a prerequisite for the gift of revelation. Such a relationship to spiritual privilege in this bare location is enhanced if 'meteles', meaning 'foodless' (A.8.142; B.7.129, C.9.295), suggests also 'meteles', meaning 'dream', repeated twice in the next two lines. Returning to Lawton's illuminating analysis of the 'resolutely marginal' narrator, which Lawton also relates to his negative 'outsider' role in multiple forms of powerlessness, we might in this instance see a positive value for marginality. Another critic who voices a spiritually positive reading of the narrator's border-like positioning is Bloomfield, who sketched an analogous spiritual positioning when he wrote 'Will is the bridge [...] between the soul and the world'.[39]

London, as locus of luxury and materialism, is once again set in contrast with these moral if moneyless *opelond* attitudes in C.16. The equivalent B.15 passage contained the line 'I have lyued in londe', quod I, 'my name is Longe Wille', 152 (with the apparent fragmented personal name, *will, long, lond*), adding that he has nevertheless never found charity.[40] C's variant locates the absence of charity specifically in London:

> Ich haue yleued in Londone monye longe ʒeres
> And fonde I neuere, in faith, as freres hit precheth,
> Charite [...] (C.16.286–88)

London with its lack of charity is then in contrast with the following lengthy portrait of charity, which foregrounds generosity but also includes contentment with poverty, with simplicities like a 'goun of a gray russet', running around in 'raggede clothes' and caring nothing for rents and riches, C.16.298, 316, 349.[41] Here Langland endows Pauline charity with some *opelond* values which are also characteristics of the narrator. Similarly C's narrator desires to find charity even if it means him wandering and begging his food (C.16.336), which recalls his wandering and 'meteles and moneyles' state on the Malvern Hills.

The narrator is told to seek Piers Plowman. Piers, of course, is an embodiment of those *opelond* attributes that constitute moral authority, in contrast to Meed and London corruptions.[42] Langland's Piers may be connected with the idealization of the plowman in a famous poem by his Welsh contemporary Iolo Goch (*c.* 1325–*c.* 1402).[43] Though Iolo might have known *Piers Plowman*, the more likely explanation is that both authors were aware of ideas concerned with social order and religious faith, which included admiration for the contribution made by the faithful peasant.[44]

---

39   Bloomfield, '*Piers Plowman' as a Fourteenth-Century Apocalypse*, p. 19.
40   On the centrality and complexities of self-naming in the text see Middleton, 'William Langland's "Kynde Name"' and Simpson, 'The Power of Impropriety'.
41   See Godden, 'Plowmen and Hermits', for the dichotomous complexities of Langland's employment of the trope of poor clothing, with the argument that poverty is linked to penitence in the poem.
42   There are many images of rural sin and many rural topographical terms in the narrator's travels and observations but, as Elliott observes, London and the Malvern Hills are the only places visualized with circumstantial detail: 'The Langland Country', esp. p. 229.
43   Iolo Goch, *Gwaith*, ed. by Johnston, pp. 123–24. See Davies, 'Plowman, Patrons and Poets'.
44   See Dyer, '*Piers Plowman* and Plowmen'; Johnston, 'Iolo Goch and the English'.

In view of the multiple meanings Langland draws from the geographical position of the Malvern Hills, does the duality the C Prologue introduces, its east–west contrast which locates evil spirits and death to the ridge's west, also carry an insult towards what lies literally to the west of the Malvern ridge: Wales? Or does the theological gravity carried by the east–west compass directions here and the learned traditions, make an anti-Welsh jibe unlikely? Is the image like or unlike the anti-Wirral slur in *Sir Gawain and the Green Knight*, ll. 701–02 (which incidentally also portrays bordering areas of Wales and England)?[45] That seems a joke, an in-joke with serious local political basis, for audiences familiar with that area of the north Marches that includes Chester, Cheshire, and the lands of Dieulacres Abbey. Note, however, Langland's readiness to insert a jibe about northerners, in an equally serious theological context (C.1.114–16).

Welsh Allusions

Elsewhere in *Piers Plowman*, what is Welsh certainly seems to be presented negatively. Gryffyth's labelling as 'Walshe' is presented as if equivalent to the reprehensible or disgusting livelihoods of his companions: ratcatcher, street-raker, prostitute, hangman, pickpocket, and so on, concluding:

> Dawe þe Dikere, with a dosoyne harlotes
> Of portours and of pikeporses and of pilede toth-draweres,
> A rybibour, and a ratoner, a rakeare and his knaue,
> A ropere and a redyngkynge, and Rose þe Disshere,
> Godefray þe Garlek-monger and Gryffyth þe Walshe.
> (C.6.368–72; cf. A.5.164–67; B.5.314–17)

Here are twelve types of *harlot*, i.e., 'rogue', with Gryffyth the Welsh the twelfth. A specifically Welsh name, Gryffyth, reinforces the national designation.[46] Perhaps fortuitous but worth noting: did Langland's associative mode of composition link 'Garlek-monger' (variant 'of Garlekhiþe') with the stereotypical national leeks here?

The next figure designated Welsh, in C.6.308–29, is the first of a sequence of robbers' names: 'ȝeuan' the 'Walschman', Robert the 'ruyflare', Dismas the thief on Calvary, and *Latro* ('Robber'), Lucifer's aunt. Nationality is again underlined by another Welsh name, Ieuan. A and B depicted an unnamed repentant thief (A.5.229–32; B.5.455–60). C makes him a

> Walschman, was wonderly sory,
> Hyhte ȝeuan-ȝelde-aȝeyn-yf-Y-so-moche-haue-
> Al-þat-Y-wickedly-wan-sithen-Y-witte-hadde. (C.6.308–10)

---

45 *Sir Gawain and the Green Knight*, ed. by Tolkien and Gordon, rev. by Davis, p. 22.

46 Manuscript variant 'Griffin' was 'an anglicized and latinized version', perhaps created 'by Anglo-Norman and English clerks […] familiar with […] the mythical bird'; Morgan and Morgan, *Welsh Surnames*, pp. 102, 104. Some scribes don't recognize the name and substitute 'Geffrey'.

Langland labels the life-long thief emphatically as Welsh. Yet he morphs in the same sentence and within his name into a different figure: the repentant thief. That is a figure that will recur in relation to Langland's handling of the Crucifixion and the Cross (see below). Hanna points to the complexities in Langland's presentation of robbery.[47] Though Ieuan, and his A and B unnamed equivalent, exemplify restitution, what we have in C is also one of the most familiar insults against the Welsh — they are thieves.

It was long established. The rhyme 'Taffy was a Welshman' is not recorded before the eighteenth century but the insult itself dates back to the period of Norman colonialism.[48] Statements by Gerald of Wales and Walter Map (a Herefordshire man) about the Welsh as thieves are well known. Both present theft as habitual among the Welsh as a people.[49] Dafydd ap Gwilym (c. 1315–c. 1350) mocks at suspicious uncouth Englishmen in a tavern who, hearing the Welshman moving about at night, are frightened for their packs and warn each other,

'Mae Cymro, taer gyffro twyll,
Yn rhodio yma'n rhydwyll;
Lleidr yw ef, os goddefwn,
'Mogelwch, cedwch rhag hwn'.

(There's a Welshman, fierce deceitful commotion, roaming around here, most cunningly; he's a thief, if we allow it, watch out, keep clear of him)[50]

In such discourse the senses of *thief* and *subversive* or *traitor* often merge, as a reflection of Edward I's claim to feudal lordship over all of Wales. Ranulph Higden, monk of St Werburgh's, Chester, records in the *Polychronicon* an Englishman's parody of the epitaph for Llwywelyn ap Gruffydd, last Prince of Wales, executed by Edward I: the

---

47 Hanna, 'Robert the Ruyflere'.
48 'Taffy was a Welshman, Taffy was a thief. Taffy came to my house and stole a piece of beef. I went to Taffy's house, Taffy wasn't home. Taffy went to my house and stole a marrow bone. I went to Taffy's house, Taffy was in bed, I took the marrow bone and hit him on the head'. There are many variations, including Taffy hit with a poker or other things. It was particularly popular in the English–Welsh border counties, sometimes sung with a Welshman effigy on St David's Day, Opie and Opie, *Oxford Dictionary of Nursery Rhymes*, pp. 401–02. *Welsh*, 'renege on a financial agreement', is only recorded from mid-nineteenth century in *OED*. In unpublished materials from a lecture that formed the basis for her 'Playing the Plowman', Middleton pointed to 1401–02 legislation aimed at banning 'minstrels, rhymers and wasters' from performing at *cymorthau* (gatherings for raising money); cited by Hanna, *Penn Commentary*, II, 137–38. However, this 1401–02 ban is in the panic-reaction anti-Welsh legislation following the Glyn Dŵr Rising; see Davies, *The Revolt of Owain Glyn Dŵr*, pp. 281–92. The thinking behind the ban was political: minstrels were considered 'probably correctly as the chief fomenters of sedition'; Davies, *The Revolt of Owain Glyn Dŵr*, p. 285. The donations were probably for Welsh military preparations.
49 Gerald, *Itinerarium* and *Descriptio*, 2.2, ed. by Brewer, Dimmock, and Warner, pp. 206–07; Map, *De nugis Curialium*, ed. and trans. by James, rev. edn by Brooke and Mynors, pp. 190–91, 196–97; see also Marsden, 'Competing Interpretations'. Jusserand, *Piers Plowman*, pp. 23–25, mentions fourteenth-century parliamentary petitions asking for restitution for alleged Welsh cattle thieving.
50 Dafydd ap Gwilym, 'Trafferth mewn Tafarn', in *Cerddi*, ed. by Johnston and others, pp. 302–03. See <www.dafyddapgwilym.net/eng>, poem 73, for text with Johnston's translation.

insults substituted for the epitaph's honorific clauses, include 'Robber and oppressor of true men'. The parody was still being recalled in the late fifteenth century.[51]

'Ȝeuan' surely plays on English *ieuen/ȝeven*, 'to give', matching his allegorical surname 'ȝelde-aȝeyn' — and the theme of restitution.[52] However, the older form of the Welsh names derived from Johannes, and apparently commonest in Langland's day, was *Ieuan/Iwan*, without medial f/v, though evidence for the sound change that produced *Ifan*, with f/v, starts to appear by Edward I's reign (the surname Evans emerges from the 1500s). Langland therefore needed to intend pronunciation with f/v; otherwise wordplay on English *ȝeven* could only be visual.[53] Since Ieuan was and is still a common Welsh first name, we should not jump to concluding the name of this Welshman actually *is* 'Yeven', English 'give'. At first appearance the figure introduced is not 'Mr Giving' but Welshman Ieuan — i.e., implicitly Taffy the thief — one who has gained wealth wickedly all his adult life. 'Walschman' here, like other names that follow, '*Latro*', and 'Robert', functions as a generic term for 'thief'.

Contrition and restitution are recurrent themes more than once taking the form of the thief offered the chance of accessing salvation, for example, in Robert's tears, A.5.235–49; B.5.462–73; C6.315–27. The penitent thief is one of Langland's polar opposites, a joining of bad and good: C.6.308–14, contains both identities in one complex sentence and one name: Ieuan is presented on a cusp — a figure on a moral border.

The next thief associated with Wales is Covetise himself. His introduction is in terms of low social class, unfree status, vermin, and poverty. His beard resembles 'bondemannes bacoun' and he wears a Welsh wool tabard. Bacon was a poor person's food and tabards were associated with peasants.[54] His hat is full of lice. Welsh people's lack of equal rights and the narrative of degradation to low social status and barbarousness (above) are perhaps present in the juxtaposing of Welsh wool with signals of servile status.

Degradation is gleefully elaborated in the 'Walch', a habitat repelling even his lice, A.5.113, B.5.195, C.5.205, rendered more pauperish by being torn and twelve years old, B 5.193, C.5.203. In fact, by the fourteenth-century Wales and the Marches were producing woollens of prized quality, with wool a major industry of the whole borders area, aided by the massive spread there of fulling mills. By 1373 the de Bohun estates in Wales and the Marches produced 18,500 fleeces, commanding high post-Black Death prices. Ethnic insults, however, are typically formulaic and long-established: back in the thirteenth century the predominant product, called simply 'Welsh cloth', was coarse (and this still constituted a large part of the cloth produced in Wales right on through the early modern period). Cloth of the finest grade needed to be

---

51 Marx, 'Middle English Texts and Welsh Contexts', pp. 21–22.

52 See Johnson, '*Reddere* and Refrain'.

53 Morgan and Morgan, *Welsh Surnames*, pp. 130–38; the third variant, *John* or *Siôn*, entered Welsh nomenclature following the Norman Conquest.

54 *MED*, s.v. 'tabard(e' n.(1), (a); a tabard also marks Chaucer's Plowman's peasant status in the General Prologue to *The Canterbury Tales*, 1.389.

imported from England in the thirteenth century but by the mid-fourteenth century high-quality woollens were being exported from Wales.[55]

We saw Langland using the same trope, associating members of another supplanted people, the Jews, with the status of bondmen, in B.19.34–37, C.21.34–37. They become 'lowe cherles [...] vnder tribut and taillage as tikes and cherles' (B.19.35–37), inferior to Christians who have been raised to being franklins, free men, 'gentil men wiþ Iesu' (B.19.39). If, as argued earlier, Langland visualized this social bondage in terms of the familiar narrative of the subjugation of the Welsh, that would strengthen a suggestion by Andrew Breeze that Langland's terms for serfdom here may include in *tike* an Anglicized form of Welsh *taeog*, meaning bondman of the lowest kind. It had a specific local sense, denoting, as Breeze observes, a type of bondman status worse than that of the unfree in England: the Welsh bondman in the Marches suffered a more brutal form of servitude, since his lord could buy or sell him.[56] The Welsh word would be well known to anyone with a background in the Welsh Marches and familiar with feudal and legal structures there. As Langland multiplies the insults through this thesaurus of serfdom, *tikes*, meaning 'dogs', though possible, fits less well than would an (admittedly putative) locally familiar Welsh loan which also meant 'cherles'.

The C-text passage naming the 'Walschman [...] Hyhte ȝeuan' alongside the other thieves is placed immediately after Covetise's confession and Repentance's command that he make restitution. A and B place their string of allusions to thieves after Sloth's confession. It seems as if the desperately penitent thieves form a subsection, within the Sins section, focused on hope for absolution. Did C place this Welsh thief first in this penitent-thief coda positioned at the end of Covetise's confession, rather than following A and B in positioning the thieves after Sloth's confession, in the same way that the Welsh wool tabard had appeared at the beginning of Covetise's confession — because of the strong identification of Welshmen as thieves?

If a Welshman came to mind when Langland envisaged Covetise, the embodiment of dishonesty, then does that other Welsh stereotype, as historically degraded bondman, underlie the poverty and bondman associations in Covetise's opening description? Otherwise hard to explain, this initial caricature of extreme poverty and decrepitude jars with the often substantial businesspeople later making up most of Covetise's composite personification of the sin of theft.

Covetise's puzzling name, 'Heruy', may be another anti-Celtic slur or signal theft or poverty, or all three. It possibly reflects the, originally Norman, anti-Breton prejudice, engendered out of the targeting of a poorer, ethnically, and linguistically distinct geographical neighbour. Anti-Breton prejudice appears when Langland makes Waster a Breton and 'braggere', A.7.141, 16; B.6.154, 176; C.8.153, 173, insubordinate when given orders, then punished by starvation. *Hervé* entered British nomenclature with the Norman invasions, a Celtic name still popular with Bretons today, after the sixth-century Breton saint St Hervé, the blind son of a Welsh bard who became a

55 Harriss, *Shaping the Nation*, p. 258; Gummer, *Scourging Angel*, p. 391.
56 Breeze, '"Tikes" at *Piers Plowman* B.XIX.37'.

hermit, bard, and abbot, patron saint of bards, minstrels, and the visually impaired.[57] Another example of national identity bolstered through 'boundary maintenance', denigration of Bretons had been an element in 'Normanitas', the forceful promotion of Norman identity.[58] Langland's usage might derive from the tradition's afterlife planted in the Marches and Wales during the Norman invasions, and the establishment of Breton families there.[59] Bretons, Welsh, Scots, and Irish were denigrated via the same stereotypes: wild and barbarous (i.e., naturally and therefore deservedly subjugated), rustic, backward in civilized advancements, dishonest, and deficient in faith. Langland describes a 'mansed [cursed/excommunicated] preest, was of þe march of Irlonde', as an adherent of Covetise, and mercenary and drunken, accompanied by sixty others who use the kind of oath that wound Christ's body: 'inparfite preestes and prelates', B.20.221–29; C.22.222–29.

Covetise may be called 'Heruy' because, like 'Robert' — and, one might add, 'Welshman' — this name connoted 'thief'.[60] Harvy Hafter (Harvy the Hefter, i.e., 'the Lifter') is a thief in John Skelton's *Bowge of Court* and *Why Come Ye Nat to Court?* Either Skelton knew 'Harvy' as a still-current byword for robber or picked up the name and that implication from Langland — or both. This part of the *Bowge* borrows extensively from Langland's depiction of the Seven Sins.[61]

Possibly Langland himself associated 'Heruy' with that caricatured poverty that he evoked in his description of Covetise. Covetise's combination of poverty, rusticity, and money-grubbing exemplifies a cluster of insults familiar to social anthropology, typically produced by an 'other place', a wealthier and more upwardly mobile neighbouring territory — against Bretons by Normans, against Aberdonians by people in Edinburgh and Glasgow, against medieval Norfolkians by the successful world of the south-east midlands and London; and within Wales against 'Cardis' from rural Ceredigion/Cardiganshire.[62]

It is possible that 'Heruy' connoted such prejudices, meaning that the name matches with the pauperish 'Walch' tabard that Covetise wears.[63] Wright's *English*

---

57 Baring-Gould, *Lives of the Saints*, VI, 239–46.

58 Thomas, *The English and the Normans*, pp. 39, 40–41, and notes.

59 See Keats-Rohan, 'The Bretons and Normans of England'. For a high-profile early example, Hervé le Breton was the, very unpopular, first non-Welsh bishop of Bangor, appointed in 1192 by William Rufus.

60 Is 'sire Heruy', like 'Syre Glotoun', A.5.186; B.5.336; C.6.392, and 'Syre Resoun', C.5.53, a usage that signals a generic term?

61 Skelton, *The Bowge of Court*, ll. 138, 190–93, 231–315, 344–41; and Skelton, *Why Come Ye Not to Court?* l. 97, in *Complete English Poems*, ed. by Scattergood.

62 See Benbrough-Jackson, *Cardiganshire and the Cardi*. The anti-Norfolk jokes in B.5.224 and 235 are a good example: mockery of the unsophisticated 'left-behinds' of a region whose neighbours are the more successful areas of the south-east midlands, southern East Anglia and London; the 'other place' in the case of 224's clichéd form of Norfolk dialect is also linguistic: the south-east midlands dialect. Unlike the anti-Welsh belittlement, which it in these ways resembles, this remains wholly English interregional denigration and it has no ramifications in themes and structures further within the text.

63 Duby, *France in the Middle Ages*, p. 23, traces a sense of threat from Bretons, and their concomitant stereotyping as savage, back to Frankish defensive fear after Bretons' resistance to Carolingian aggression.

Dialect Dictionary has an entry for *hervy*, drawn from John Jamieson's 1808 *Etymological Dictionary of the Scottish Language*. There it is an adjective meaning 'Mean, having the appearance of poverty', recorded from Angus. This apparent survival in Scotland suggests at one time a widespread familiarity with the term in Britain (though Jamieson's record does not report the sense 'thief' which was clearly present for Skelton and possibly for Langland).[64]

Langland's fourth belittling Welsh allusion concerns a lack of faith rather than honesty, denying to the Welsh their history of Christian faith for centuries before the English were converted:

> Al was heþynesse som tyme Engelond and Walis,
> Til Gregory garte clerkes to go here and preche.
> Austyn at Canterbury cristnede þe kyng þere,
> And þoruʒ miracles, as men mow rede, al þat marche he tornede
> To Crist and to Cristendom, and cros to honoure. (B.15.442–46)

Langland's first line above voices a history of England extended to Wales, without admitting differentiation: that imperialistic verbal unification 'Englond and Walis', that still regularly signals erasure of differentiation for Wales in English historians' and modern media discourse.

The passage exemplifies what Simon Meecham-Jones identifies as an 'erasure of Wales' in medieval English culture. He comments: 'It is hard to imagine that Langland, as a Malvern man, did not have some ideological intent to account for this historically absurd representation of familiar events'. This form of erasure is symptomatic of colonialist defensiveness, disparagement, and denial, and 'In Langland's vision of universal history there is no place for Wales to exist, except through its relationship with England'.[65] In B.15.442–46, Anima says that 'men mow rede' accounts of the conversions, as if what is said here has learned textual authority. Yet chronicles from Bede on, including Geoffrey of Monmouth's *Historia* and vernacular histories like the Prose *Brut*, record — and Langland must have known — that Wales had been Christian centuries before Augustine arrived to convert Saxon Kent.[66] He would surely know of the Welsh saints whose lives appeared in legendaries that included John of Tynemouth's *Sanctilogium Angliae, Walliae, Scotiae et Hiberniae* (*c.* 1366?) and collections derived from it.[67] Bede praises the quality of Christianity among the Britons after their conversion in 156 and the glory they won through their faith under persecution in the third century.[68] Chaucer correctly observes that, after the Anglo-Saxon invasions, 'To Walys fledde

64 Wright, *English Dialect Dictionary, H–L*, p. 148. The *Scottish National Dictionary* says 'origin unknown'; what is suggested here may supply that origin.
65 Meecham-Jones, 'Where Was Wales?', p. 30. See also Steiner, *Reading 'Piers Plowman'*, pp. 161–62 on Langland's 'Englishing of Universal History'.
66 See Geoffrey of Monmouth, *History of the Kings of Britain*, ed. by Reeve, trans. by Wright, p. 47; *The Oldest Anglo-Norman Prose 'Brut' Chronicle*, ed. and trans. by Marvin, pp. 114–17.
67 See Görlach, 'Introduction' to *The Kalendre of the Newe Legende of Englande*, pp. 7–12, 28–23.
68 Bede, *Ecclesiastical History*, ed. and trans. by Colgrave and Mynors, 4.7, I, 24–29.

the christynytee' of Britain (*Man of Law's Tale*, 2.544–46). Marsden comments that twelfth-century writers including William of Malmesbury, Henry of Huntingdon, William of Newburgh, Ralph Diceto, and Roger of Howden, are 'symptomatic of a process of national redefinition in England following the Norman Conquest' and consequently share Gerald's identification of the Welsh as 'politically unstable, violent, pastoral and not properly Christian'.[69] From the time of the Norman kings, English ecclesiastical authorities frequently imposed non-Welsh bishops and priests on the Welsh church, and its structures and practices grew closer to those in England and the rest of Western Europe, including the introduction of Benedictine and Cistercian religious houses. Madeleine Gray shows, however, that neither the creation of the March and an English–Welsh border nor the pace and extent of Welsh acceptance of Gregorian reforms were precise processes.[70] At the Reformation, Protestant reformers including Tyndale claimed that the traditions of the Celtic church before Augustine preserved a faith uncontaminated by Rome.[71] Langland's phrasing when he says that Augustine, sent by Gregory, turned 'al þat marche' to 'Crist *and to Cristendom*' (my emphasis) perhaps envisions conversion to European 'cristendom' as integration into a true faith.[72] Tensions and fears remained: Archbishop Pecham urged reparations to churches and burgesses in Wales harmed by Edward I's invasion. John Davies says that Pecham despised the Welsh as a people and that his concern was to try to encourage Welsh clergy's allegiance, because some priests and monks 'excited the people by glorifying the ancestry of the Welsh' — reminders of their ancient rule over all Britain — with ambitions and prophecies aimed at recovering independence.[73]

Langland's references to 'miracles' (B.15.445, 448) suggests he knew narratives about the conversion by writers including Bede who mention miracles. Interestingly, Bede's account links miracles to a condemnation of the Welsh church of Augustine's era as heretics. He recounts a series of events after Augustine heals a blind man where the British bishops fail, presented as a competition about which sort of Christianity is superior. Bede represents the British bishops as confessing that Augustine's is the 'true way of righteousness' but wanting to discuss things further at a conference. Angered by Augustine's arrogance when they met, they refused to alter their practices (or preach to the pagan English) and Bede calls Æthelfrith's subsequent defeat of Britons and massacre of their bishops at Chester the heretics' punishment.[74]

69 Marsden, 'Competing Interpretations', p. 319.
70 Gray, 'Saints on the Edge', pp. 89–90.
71 See Williams, 'Some Protestant Views of the Early British Church'.
72 See Davies's discussion of the subjugation of the Welsh church's structures to Canterbury, *Age of Conquest*, pp. 179–85. On potential threats represented by Rome to Canterbury's control of the church in Wales, Lieberman argues the apparent paradox that the 'Europeanization' of England during the High Middle Ages was 'inextricably entangled in the attempts at Anglicization of Wales', *The March of Wales, 1067–1300*, pp. 98–99.
73 Davies, *History of Wales*, p. 169.
74 Bede, *Ecclesiastical History*, ed. and trans. by Colgrave and Mynors, 2.2, I, 135–43.

March and Boundary

'Miracles' was perhaps the alliterative trigger for 'marche' at B.15.445, an intriguing word-choice when collocated with 'Walis'. *March* primarily meant 'border', often the Welsh–English border areas.[75] It can also mean generally 'territory'. Meecham-Jones comments 'Maybe his perception of lawlessness in his native March inspired an ironic wordplay in the reference to an earlier "marche" being turned to Christ'.[76] The passage moves on to savagery and barbarousness, and an assertion that wild peoples need to be ruled by other superior nations, common elements in anti-Welsh propaganda. Lawlessness and 'rebellion' are entrenched in Norman and English historians' representation of Welsh resistance against English invasions and imposition of lordship.[77] And lawlessness is Langland's next topic: defining 'heþynesse' correctly as from *heath*, he characterizes unconverted peoples in general as wild: 'As in wilde wildernesse wexeþ wilde bestes, | Rude and vnresonable, rennynge wiþouten keperes' (B.15.459–60). Such a jump from the unconverted, misapplied to the Christian early Welsh, to 'wilde' animal-like barbarians in 'wilde' wilderness, requiring controllers, is common colonialist rhetoric discernible in several Norman and English writers. Subjugating barbarians became a trope of developing English national identity. William of Malmesbury employs a distinction between 'civilized' and 'barbarian' to define an idea of England that includes identifying Celtic peoples as barbarous, living in wildernesses.[78] Fourteenth-century examples include the language of *Vita Edwardi Secundi*, which describes the earl of Hereford's retinue as 'defended by a mob of Welshmen, wild and from the woods', commenting that the Welsh and Irish races, *genera*, 'are easily raised to rebellion […] and curse the lordship of the English', and the Welsh 'frequently rebel'.[79]

   March appears twice more: used for Ireland, C.22.221–27, as homeland of the disgraceful Irish priests, and in the term 'this marches' in C.10.138 where a garrisoned castle is built. C.10's allegorical scene in 'this marches', of castle-building to defend against an ever-present alien-nation threat, recalls the real-life English–Welsh Marches landscape filled with castles and strongly fortified towns. By 1215 Wales and the Marches contained around four hundred castles in contrast to around three there in 1066.[80] The Chester monk Higden and his translator Trevisa, having said that it is unsurprising the Welsh are not stable or peaceable and, having been expelled from

---

75   *MED*, s.v. 'march(e)'.

76   Meecham-Jones, 'Where Was Wales?', p. 30.

77   Faletra, 'Narrating the Matter of Britain', argues that the twelfth-century burgeoning of history writing itself actively supported the Norman enterprise of colonizing Wales and the Welsh borders.

78   See William of Malmesbury, *Gesta regum Anglorum*, ed. and trans. by Thomson and Winterbottom, pp. 348; 216–17, 606–07; Gillingham, *The English in the Twelfth Century*, pp. 3–18, 93–109; Fenton, *Gender, Nation and Conquest*, pp. 90–91. Gillingham sees William as at the start of English imperialist, as opposed to merely hostile, attitudes towards Celtic people: *The English in the Twelfth Century*, pp. 3–18.

79   *Vita Edwardi Secundi*, ed. by Denholm-Young, rev. edn by Childs, pp. 32, 61, 69. Trevisa, translating Higden, calls the lifestyles of the Welsh 'bestial', and attributes any improvements over time to their growing association with English people; Waldron, 'Trevisa's Translation', pp. 112–13.

80   Lieberman, *The March of Wales, 1067–1300*, p. 15; Davies, *Age of Conquest*, pp. 89–92, 280–81, 360.

their land, want to expel their expellers, state that they have been frustrated in this aim because 'Buþ castels ybuld fol strong' (castles have been built, very strong).[81] The castle built in 'this marches' in B.9, and C.10 is Kynde's fortification surrounding Anima, to defend her against her enemy, under the protection of 'Sire Dowel, duk of this marches' (B.9.11, C.10.138). In this title for Dowel, who is imagined in the character of a grand chivalric lord, there may be an echo of the title bestowed on Roger Mortimer in 1328, 'Earl of March'. Sire Dowel, like a Marcher aristocrat, has a constable and 'grete lordes' in his household retinue, B.9.11–22, C.10.138–48. Both political and psychological perceptions of the experience of a border appear to be present in this passage's imagery of a fortification of the bodily senses built to enclose Anima, the living spirit, with an aristocratic protector and retinue. Langland's allegorical correlation in this symbolic scene between bodily boundaries and a border territory, 'this marches', fortified against an ethnically distinct enemy is a classic manifestation of anthropological 'boundary maintenance' in its combination of psychology, a sense of the body and the Other.[82] Langland gives Anima's enemy, the devil, an ethnic label, 'A proude Prikere of Fraunce'. Yet the actual French enemies of Langland's day were across the Channel, nothing similar to the fears of an ever-present threat from an enemy in the same countryside that is being evoked here in 'this marches'. Fear and control of such an enemy, the Welsh, had produced the real-life castle-building in the Marches and Wales. Langland's use of *march* for Ireland, and in a context of insults against Irish clergy, suggests again that he associated it with territories where English colonialist incursion encountered resistance from Celtic-speaking peoples, against whom racist stereotypes were one of the weapons of control and self-assertion.

The term also appears in Langland's scathing use of it in the related verb 'marchen', meaning to meet at a boundary, when talking about the commercialization of the friars' spiritual duties: 'hire moneie and marchaundiȝe marchen togidere', B.Prol.63, C.Prol.61 ('marchaundiȝe' is ironically spiritual services like prayers treated as saleable commodities). *Marchen* has the sense of two powers and operations meeting and coinciding along a geographical boundary; they form a joint organization like a March (*marchen* 'advance against' might also have an associative presence here: an image of friars purposefully advancing on their targets).[83] Langland's relatively frequent use of *march* may reflect the familiarity, of a man with a background in the region, with both the historical association of *march* with Norman and English imperialist aggressions and the increasingly strong formal recognition of the Marcher lordships as a distinctive political region during the thirteenth and fourteenth centuries, with the title earl of March just one of the indicators of that crystallization of that sense of the Marches as an entity.[84]

---

81 Waldron, 'Trevisa's Translation', p. 109.
82 See on bodily boundary maintenance Stallybrass and White, *Politics and Poetics of Transgression*, p. 25.
83 *MED marchen* v.(1); cf. also *marchen* v. (2), but there the quotations are fifteenth century.
84 Lieberman, *The Medieval March of Wales*, pp. 5–22 traces and analyses both the varied senses, in Latin, English, and French, and the changing and inconsistent applications of *march* and *Marchia Wallie* especially between the twelfth- and early fourteenth-century senses, and also the growing political recognition of the term and the region as a political entity in late medieval England and Wales.

Claire Weeda has explored evidence that 'boundary' outlooks can be exacerbated in ethnically mixed communities, applying the finding to medieval ethnic mockery in twelfth-century Paris.[85] If demographical melting-pot milieus fostered such satire, London and the Marches were two locations whose inhabitants were familiar with mixed ethnicities and migrants from other places. If these two environments lay in the background of the mind creating the poem, then that might be a further factor informing its penchant for satire linked to geographical origins, including the negative representation of Welsh people.

Mobility, wandering, is one of the narrator's attributes, something associated with the Malvern Hills, right at the beginning of the poem. Naming the Malvern Hills as the location of a dream vision is unusual, as Andrew Galloway observed: dream visions rarely begin with naming a place.[86] What is frequent, however, is a preliminary trope of the narrator going forth, *chanson d'aventure*-style. In dream visions that movement is typically into a garden or other enclosed, upper-class, place, or sometimes going hunting (again aristocratic), while a common location for revelation is a grand building: a palace, castle, or temple. To site a dreamer on a lone western hillside is singular. Associated motifs, appropriate to that lone hillside, of wandering and the narrator's duplicitous sheep's-wool garb, tie this particular place to attributes that will recur in the narrator's self-presentation throughout the poem.[87]

While his own comical wool wrappings have an *in malo* mirroring in the anti-Welsh associations of the figure of Covetise, this image of the narrator as an unfixed traveller was also often associated with the Welshman for English people. The type of lower-class Welshman familiar in London and southern and midlands England, before the Tudor influx of the Welsh into London's residential population, was the drover, constantly moving across country bringing fresh meat to the shambles and butchers of London and other towns. Langland's image of Gryffyth perhaps conjured up such an itinerant, another mirror of the narrator as wanderer and also idler. The tavern customers of Glutton's confession all have jobs that are casual and/or involve periods of idleness or waiting for employment. A drover's work necessitated mobility, periods of slackness and periods far from home spent in inns, commemorated in the inn title 'Drovers' Arms' in many parts of Wales, Scotland, and England along their routes.[88] Moreover, Dafydd ap Gwilym's lines quoted above show how readily any travelling Welshman, in a tavern — whether a drover or well-born poet — might be regarded with suspicion by English eyes.

---

85 Weeda, 'Ethnic Stereotyping in Twelfth-Century Paris'.

86 Galloway, *Penn Commentary*, i, 35.

87 See O'Neill, 'Counting Sheep', and Galloway's excellent analysis, *Penn Commentary*, i, 26–29.

88 See Bonser, *The Drovers*, p. 26. One drovers' route included a stretch across Linley Green to Malvern; see Moore-Colyer, *Welsh Cattle Drovers*, p. 156.

A Submerged Presence

A distinctive region is a presence in the poem, with importance and influence extending widely through the text, albeit not wholly visible at first sight. This presence is a world of regional familiarities, drawn from Wales, the Marches, and English perceptions of the Welsh, shaped historically by colonialization and a complex border area.

It is a distinctly localized familiarity that Langland's specific references to Wales and the Marches represent. With 'Maluerne Hilles', Langland introduces his poem to his readers with a place not widely known outside its region, and the Rood of Chester and Ranulf earl of Chester both had fame and popularity but it was an intense regional fame and popularity. Other local familiarities present in the text range from mist on the Malverns and accurate Welsh names to the poem's style of habitual and unmarked anti-Welsh perceptions and colonialist narratives.[89]

The poem's negative images of Welshness, an ethnic identity, correlates historically with the growth of a more ethnically exclusive sense of English identity that developed from the thirteenth century onwards.[90] This development was also a factor encouraging the lordships extending from south Wales up through the Anglo-Welsh borders to claim their distinctive rights and exemptions as powers and administrations ruling *Marchia Walliae*, the March of Wales.[91] The granting to Roger Mortimer of the title 'earl of March' emblematizes recognition of a region with individual separate status within Britain and the distinctive powers of the Marcher lordships. Indeed, Lieberman argues that it was the dominance of the Marcher aristocratic families that, above all, heightened increasing late medieval consciousness of the March as a distinctive place: 'a territory under the command of a select group of border lords'.[92] These contemporary facts strengthen the cases I have already made for believing that when Langland at several points employs the term *march*, it is never just in the most general sense of 'territory' but carries also something of the high profile, and currency in his own period of *March* and *Marches*, with their specific implications of a region that was also a boundary territory and/or an interface with an ethnically distinct, potentially hostile, other nation.

Countering an earlier view that national identity did not exist in the Middle Ages, historians who include R. R. Davies, Robin Frome, and David Green have argued, rather, for a strengthening of its development in the fourteenth century, stimulated by English claims to France, and reflected in English attitudes to Wales, Scotland, and Ireland.[93] At the same time, regional consciousness was growing more prominent, including the contribution of regional cultural and literary consciousness, as Barratt

---

89 Note also words that were used in the Marches region but apparently not very common outside it (e.g., 'bache', 'valay', 'speke', 'toft' (hill), 'fisk' (probably a Welsh loan)); Elliott points to copyists' occasional apparent puzzlement and some words' removal from the B text and their return in C, 'The Langland Country', pp. 238–42.

90 Davies, 'The English State and the "Celtic" Peoples'.

91 Lieberman, *The Medieval March, 1067–1300*, pp. 244–45.

92 Lieberman, *The Medieval March, 1067–1300*, pp. 56–57, 218.

93 See for an overview Green, 'National Identities and the Hundred Years War', p. 116.

has demonstrated, looking particularly at the case of the Welsh and Marcher regions centred on Chester.[94] Chester like Shrewsbury was a gateway to Wales, logistically, economically, and militarily. The border with Wales begins just beyond the city's western edge; its economy and its rulers' policies were inherently involved with Wales as much as England. Symptomatic of this substantial coherence between English and Welsh, reverence for the Rood of Chester was deeply embedded in Wales and in Welsh writing, while the real-life career of Ranulf III of Chester showed him often prioritizing relations, hostile or positive, with Welsh rulers, even if necessary over the requirements of the English king (Ranulf's erstwhile closeness to Welsh leaders on occasion probably decided Henry III finally in 1237 to annex the earldom to the Crown).[95]

Langland's two Chester allusions, both of them iconic regional cultural references, to the earldom and the Rood, also relate to some of his poem's most recurrent themes. Interest in the figure of the thief perhaps prompted Langland's introduction of Robin Hood, outlaw and thief (Robin only gradually developed a high-minded [and high-born] character, starting seriously in the late sixteenth century, and only patchily then until the nineteenth century), among Sloth's faults. Ranulf may have seemed a fitting associated hero because Ranulf III (earl of Chester 1181–1232) appears in the legends about the Shropshire outlaw Fouke le Fitz Waryn.[96] Ranulf's obvious link with wider themes in the poem, however, lies in the subject of minstrelsy and the recurrent distinction between good and bad minstrelsy. Sloth's beloved 'rymes' in B.5.396, C.5.11 are exemplifying the wrong type of minstrelsy. There is a mirroring in Imaginatif's accusation against the narrator 'þow medlest þee wiþ makynge — and myȝtest go sey þi Sauter', B.12.16.

A major story about Ranulf, earl of Chester revolved round minstrels. In 1216, Ranulf III was saved during an otherwise disastrous campaign against the Welsh, when his army fled into Rhuddlan Castle, was holed up by Llywelyn's army, and only escaped when the constable of Chester sent out an apparently substantial army. The story is that it was full of minstrels and shoemakers from Chester making a tremendous noise, causing the Welsh to retreat. This was the founding myth of another famed local cultural reference, the annual Chester Minstrels' Court, held on St John the Baptist's Day, and centred on St John's Church — Chester's most ancient church, where the Holy Rood was and where the annual Passion Play, forerunner of the Chester Cycle, was performed also at Midsummer, the time of Chester Midsummer Fair. Did Langland know, as most people in the Marches and Wales would do, of both St John's Holy Rood and the minstrels' festival and religious drama linked to St John's, as well as stories to do with Earl Ranulf? The court's function was in part competitions and performance, in part to license approved, professional minstrels (the same concern to maintain high professional standards was the core of Welsh *eisteddfodau*, held since the twelfth century, with French *puys* another more distant

94 Barratt, *Against All England*.
95 Husain, *Cheshire under the Norman Earls*, p. 111.
96 Burgess, 'I kan rymes'; Price, 'Welsh Outlaws'.

analogue). St Werburgh's, which possessed the right to hold the Midsummer Fair, was a Benedictine abbey, well endowed by the earls of Chester. Was Langland familiar with Chester's cultural and intellectual riches through Benedictine connections?

As Glyn Burgess decisively showed, 'rymes' about Ranulf III certainly existed.[97] John Spence presents further evidence from British Library MS Cotton Otho B.III. Virtually obliterated by the fire at Ashburnham House that destroyed or damaged many books in the Cotton collection and a later fire, this manuscript contained a Latin chronicle (probably from the library of St Werburgh's, a source for the *Annales Cestriensi* written there in the second half of the thirteenth century) and verses 'de gestis Ranulphi, comitis de Cestria' (about the deeds of Ranulph, earl of Chester). Spence presents reasons to think this was about the siege and the famous minstrels saving the earl.[98] The verses may perhaps have been a Latin version of a popular tale familiar in English or French: for sophisticated clerics to transpose entertaining vernacular material into a Latin composition was not uncommon: an example is the adventurous and humorous Arthurian romance *De Ortu Waluuanii*, by Ranulph Higden. Another Ranulf III story had links with Dieulacres Abbey, re-founded by him: the Abbey's hounds barked so loudly that Ranulf was released from Hell.[99] Ranulf's quasi-legendary status appears too in Thomas Chestre's *Launfal*, mostly located in Caerleon (though 'Caerleon' was also a name for Chester), whose hero defeats a constable of Caerleon, 'Walssche knyghtes', and the earl of Chester (469–80), regional exploits and allusions absent from the French *lai*.[100]

Their regional popularity may be precisely why rhymes about Ranulf have left relatively little evidence. In contrast, stories of Robin Hood, Guy of Warwick, and Bevis of Hampton continued to be produced and popular until the late early modern period, well attested in printed quartos, ballads, even chapbooks. Guy and Bevis, though originally local heroes like Ranulf, gained wider English popularity, and became subjects of substantial written narratives, with some dynastic patronage. Ranulf's fame as the hero of popular 'rymes' (as opposed to appearances in chronicles) may have remained both more oral and more regional; moreover, the dynasty died out in the mid-thirteenth century. Robin, Guy, and Bevis's England-wide currency made them promising investments for early printers to publish.[101] To cite Robin, often yoked with Guy and/or Bevis, became a late medieval and early modern cliché of moralists' complaints about popular literature, something perhaps already current in Langland's time, though the extant early examples are later: *Dives and Pauper*, c. 1405–10 and the *Dialogue of a Fool and a Wise Man*, c. 1400.[102] In citing tales of 'Randolf, Erl of Chestre'

---

97   Burgess, 'I kan rymes'.
98   Spence, 'A Lost Manuscript', pp. 4–7.
99   Burgess, 'I kan rymes', p. 66.
100 Burgess, 'I kan rymes', pp. 59–60; Chestre, *Launfal*, ed. by Laskaya and Salisbury, ll. 433–92.
101 Phillips, 'Reformist Polemics'; Richmond, *The Legend of Guy of Warwick*; Fellowes and Djordjević, eds, *Sir Bevis of Hampton*. Ranulf's occasional appearance in some Elizabethan plays and poetry is likely to represent early modern antiquarian inspirations, and in Anthony Munday's *John a Kent and John a Cumber* reflects very specific personal Welsh connections.
102 Phillips, 'Reformist Polemics'.

as if they are self-evidentially popular, Langland perhaps reveals assumptions that are themselves restricted to a world of specifically regional familiarities.

Langland's other Chester reference is to its Holy Rood, which was widely revered and a site of pilgrimage in the Marches and Wales. Walsingham, Canterbury, and Bromholm were far more familiar in England in general and easily accessible from London and the prosperous south-east midlands. Richard Davies labels Walsingham and Canterbury England's 'establishment' shrines.[103] Again, Langland cites something whose celebrity is intense but intense within a particular region, in introducing the 'Roode of Chestre'.

Familiarity with the Marches and Wales may have a link with the poem's emphasis on veneration of a rood: the repeated focus in the text on the Cross and on parishioners', penitents', and converts' veneration of the Cross, with references to devotion to physical, painted or carved, roods. See C.5.105–08; C.20.473–79; C.21.200–01; A.5.145, B.5.227; and Wrath's failure to perform such devotions sincerely (A.5.103–16, B.5.85–97). Repentant Robert the Robber looks on '*Reddite*', implicitly an image of 'Crist [...] on the crosse', whereupon Repentance assures him 'Be þe Rode [...] thow romest toward heuene' (C.6.315–30, and see also A.2.133; C.4.131; C.7.69; C.21.323). Sloth, promising reform, declares 'I bihote to þe Rode!', B.5.455, C.7.68, vowing to the Rood of Chester at A.5.233; B.5.460. Reason preaches repentance with a processional cross or crozier, at B.5.11–12; C.5.113. The imagery of Christ as 'conquerour', subjugating the Jewish nation, pictures Jesus 'on cros ycrouned kyng of Iewes', who 'comeþ þus wiþ cros' to guide against temptation to sin (B.19.41–63; C.21.42–64). The motif's culmination is the 'Creeping to the Cross' Good Friday vision where Christ in Piers's arms is 'peynted al blody' (C.21.6, 11). *Peynted*, twice-repeated, recalls a church rood, as does 'bifore þe comune peple', C.21.7, since the rood screen faced the people. Envy's confession includes him coming into the church and theoretically kneeling to the rood, but actually turning round to the congregation with spite-filled gaze (A.5.85, B.5.103), which introduces a directionally conceived portrayal which is poised on that function of a rood in a church as the divider between the people's area and the sanctuary. The narrator's devotions to the cross act as the preface to new visions in C.5.105–08, and C.20.473–21.5.22. An image of turning to the Cross is linked with conversion, and individual reform in several examples above and elsewhere: they include St Augustine turning the whole 'marche' to Christ and 'to Cristendom, and cros to honoure' (B.15.446), and, when Robert the 'ruyflare' looks upon *reddite*, the image evokes a turning towards a depiction of Christ's Crucifixion (A.5.243; B.5.468; C.6.315–24).

Unlike the interior fervour that images of the crucified Christ, as a suffering body and lover, awakened for many mystics, Langland's typical allusion seems frequently more to a cross as an object, carried or in a church (yet, as Davlin showed, in its own spatial religious imagery also completely capable of conveying spiritual meaning, relating God to humanity).[104] The Cross repeatedly commands a central place in Langland's

---

103   Davies, 'The Church', in Ralph Griffiths, *Fourteenth and Fifteenth Centuries*, 87–114, p. 106.
104   Davlin, *The Place of God*.

verbal formulations of the basics of Christian theology. When he contemplates the historical conversion of peoples to the true faith, that change is summarized as 'Criste and […] cristendom, and cros to honoure' (B.15.446). Salvation is granted in a letter, freeing humanity from Lucifer's lordship, whose seal depicts 'Criste and Cristendome and a Croys ther-on to honge' (C.19.7–10, B.17.4–8); Conscience's preaching is 'of Crist and of þe cros' (C.21.200–01); Grace gives Piers the Cross as he starts to build the Church (C.21.323–27); the Cross is the timber on which the Church is built (C.21.323); the origin of Christianity: 'At Caluarie, of Cristis bloed Cristendoem gan sprynge' (C.12.110). The beginning of Christendom is honouring the cross (B.15.531); the essence of the faith is that 'Crist with crois' overcame the Old Dispensation (C.20.112). There is 'no richesse but þe roode' (C.17.198–99, B15.536–37). Langland focuses on a victorious crucifixion, hung high — as on a church rood screen — rather than dwelling on Christ's suffering body: 'conquered he on cros as conquerour noble' (C.21.50), 'vpon Caluarie on cros ycrouned kyng of Iewes' (C.21.41). In Bloomfield's words, 'Not the suffering Christ but the victorious Christ is Langland's theme, and his theology is a theology of glory'.[105]

In this emphasis is familiarity with a regional religious culture an underlying presence? Roods were greatly revered in late medieval Welsh piety, pilgrimage, and poetry. Though there were also major roods in England and Scotland and occasionally hymns to these survive, the numerous intricately-crafted Welsh poems about the rich and renowned roods of particular localities (Chester, Brecon, Welshpool, Llanfaes, Llangynwyd, etc.) constitute a late medieval Welsh literary genre without English counterpart, notable for their number and for some poems the number of extant manuscripts. The relatively good survival of pre-Reformation rood screens in Mid Wales and western English counties, especially Herefordshire and Shropshire, though with only rarely any traces of their Crucifixion scenes, testifies to local fervour: the Reformation destruction commands met strong local opposition.[106] Famed roods, generating large sums in offerings, included the Chester and Brecon roods.[107] Barry Lewis and Kathryn Hurlock identify a special preoccupation with location in Welsh veneration of the rood. This localized spirituality is a feature both of the cults of devotion to the roods of particular holy places and of the religious poetry that celebrates these local objects of veneration. Lewis writes that the Welsh poems to roods 'belong within a wider category of compositions in honour of particular places which attracted pilgrims. Welsh religious poetry of the later Middle Ages is peculiarly devoted to the feeling that God's universal power had a local aspect'.[108] Whereas Langland's references to place-pilgrimage generally are negative, he mentions devotions to roods (including Chester and Bromholm) without such censure.

---

105 Bloomfield, 'Piers Plowman' as a Fourteenth Century Apocalypse, p. 125.

106 Salter, The Old Parish Churches of Mid Wales, p. 8; Davies 'The Church', pp. 112–13. Davlin, The Place of God, pp. 33–35, points to another possible Marcher regional influence on Langland's poem and theological imagery, the prevalence of separate towers, sometimes part of churches, in Herefordshire.

107 Lewis, Welsh Poetry and English Pilgrimage, pp. 26–27; Hurlock, Medieval Welsh Pilgrimage, pp. 113–43.

108 Lewis, Welsh Poetry and English Pilgrimage, p. 26. See <dafyddapgwilym.net>, poem 1 and notes.

Langland introduces 'þe Roode of Chestre' into a passage in passus 5 that is focused on two of his foremost theological preoccupations: restitution (both divine and human) and the special role of the cross in devotion. Passus 5 makes the figure of the thief part of these two themes, and introduces two associated regional references: the unnamed thief's promise to the Rood of Chester in A.5.233, B.5.460, and C's Welsh penitent thief Ieuan replacing him in C.6.308–10. Wordplay on restitution creates an alliterative link between 'Roode' and words signifying restitution, and between C's 'Ȝeuan' and 'ȝelde-aȝeyn', while A and B's Robert the Robber and C's Robert the Rifler 'on *Reddite* loked' (A.5.235; B.5.462; C.6.313), and all announce that they are brothers to Dismas, a figure who combines the identities of robber and convert to redemption on the Cross. Though, of course, they were also found elsewhere, roods of the English–Welsh borders area might have included the figures of the two thieves, though we are now dependent on written records after their destruction: one example is the reference to Dismas in Hywel Dafi's poem on the Brecon Golden Rood.[109] Langland's inclusion of Dismas in this sequence of thieves' names perhaps links to such physical rood screens rather than just general iconography of the Crucifixion. Langland brings Dismas back into the poem at B.12.191; C.14.131–47, and C.20.73–74.

The two thieves figured on rood screens throughout Europe, and, although the frequency of their depiction on medieval British rood screens is now impossible to calculate, was there, in Wales including the Marches, a distinctive cult of personal engagement with the penitent thief as a role model for every Christian, proclaiming the promise of forgiveness and salvation for all sinners from the Redeemer on the Cross? The discovery of triple cross depictions in south-east Wales has been so interpreted by the art historian Madeleine Gray. Three late fourteenth-century (?) stone slabs, inscribed with Christ's cross and the two thieves' crosses, survive: at Margam Abbey, Llangynwyd (whose rood made it a site of pilgrimage), and Laleston, made perhaps for the tombs of individuals, possibly clerics.[110]

The Holy Rood at St John's Church, Chester, was a subject for Welsh poets from the fourteenth to sixteenth centuries, including Guto'r Glyn and Gruffudd ap Maredudd ap Dafydd, and was deeply revered in both Wales and the Marches.[111] Twelve extant Welsh poems celebrate it.[112] Promises made to the Chester Rood were held in such respect that in 1278 Edward I brought ten hostages from among the leading men of

---

109   Parri, 'Crog Aberhonddu' and Jones, *Celtic Britain and the Pilgrim Movement*, pp. 550–58, both contain texts. The thieves appear in the Chester Cycle 'Crucifixion' and the Welsh Passion Play, which from its many manuscripts and variations, may have been widely known and date back 'at least into the fifteenth century'; see Klausner, 'English Economies and Welsh Realities', p. 214.

110   See Diocese of Llandaff, press release: 'Ancient Stone Is Found Hidden under Church Carpet'.

111   Lewis and Thacker, *History of the County of Chester*, v.1, 35, 86; 294–99. Lewis, *Welsh Poetry and English Pilgrimage*. The gilded Holy Rood of Chester in St John's Church was not the same as the stone cross on the Roodee island, mentioned by Bennett, following Skeat, *Piers Plowman*, note to B.5.128, and it is unclear whether it was by some believed to be the cross said to have floated along the River Dee to the city; Jones, *Celtic Britain and the Pilgrim Movement*, pp. 293–312, 550–58.

112   Hurlock, *Medieval Welsh Pilgrimage*, p. 159.

Gwynedd to swear loyalty to his overlordship upon the Holy Rood of Chester.[113] Swearing by the Rood of Chester appears in *Richard the Redeless*, a text which at one point focuses vividly on a northern Marches theme: Richard's II's personal troops of Cheshire archers and Welsh pikemen and their misdemeanours.[114] Denunciations of Richard's Cheshire men were, however, widespread, and the author may be merely echoing Langland. All the same, the absence of 'Rood of Chester' oaths elsewhere might indicate little widespread English familiarity for the object or the phrase.

Reflections

Gerald of Wales described his sense of a double psychological position, between Wales and England, within his own identity: 'Both peoples regard me as a stranger […] one suspects me, the other hates me'. Huw Pryce relates Gerald's attitudes both to class and to typical border-dwellers' mindsets.[115] Complications of class and ethnic divisions, and border dwellers' mindsets, seem at times to be present in some of *Piers Plowman*'s structures of thinking, imagining, and criticizing: something like what Raymond Williams (himself a man of the Marches), famously called a 'structure of feeling', from a life, a time, and a particular world. Lieberman, reading Gerald's quotation of his uncle's analogous declaration that as a Norman lord in Ireland he and his kind were 'English to the Irish and Irish to the English', comments that the inhabitants of the Welsh March might often have felt similarly.[116] Another similarly divided psychological reaction to colonial experience has been explored by Helen Fulton, who shows the 'doubling and split subjectivities' evident as a result of colonial rule in many Welsh poets' work in the fourteenth and fifteenth centuries, hardening further after Owain Glyn Dŵr's rebellion to 'the most bitter and implacably hostile terms' of antagonism towards England.[117] I have argued in this essay that negative images of the Welsh in Langland's poem come out of the experience of the world of the medieval Marches and that an analogous symbiosis appears in the presentation of the speaker, and is related to other structures and constructions of instability and duality in the poem.

It is possible that the emotional and personal identification with the penitent sinner, which both Clopper and Lawton have detected at times in the text, is relevant to a question the Welsh and Marches references prompt: Is it significant that they

---

113 Lewis and Thacker, *History of the County of Chester*, pp. 35, 86, 294–99; McKenna, 'City of Chester'; Morgan, 'Cheshire and Wales', p. 206.
114 *Richard the Redeless*, ed. by Dean, Prol.56; 3.310–70.
115 Huw Pryce, 'A Cross-Border Career', pp. 315–21.
116 Lieberman, 'The English and the Welsh', however, shows how unmonolithic and responsive to context and social class English attitudes to Welsh could be: the local aristocratic context and audience for that Shropshire thirteenth-century romance led to its presentation of Welsh and English (Norman) 'Knights' as equals: the lens of shared class outweighs English claims against Welsh neighbours.
117 Fulton, 'Class and Nation', pp. 201, 202.

appear numerously among the Seven Deadly Sins?[118] It might simply reflect habits of negative images of the Welsh. At a deeper level the psychological relationship between acts of confession and the individual self perhaps drew personal background elements into this section. However, rather than invoking a direct autobiographical input, one might see such a stance instead as akin to the mirroring between the speaker's self-presentation and his presentation of others who are negatively perceived — including the Welsh. Stanley Hussey commented that Langland, in his frequent position as the outsider, is also 'constantly touchy about those who resemble him', drawing lines of demarcation, and condemnation, between himself and the Other and the reprehensible.[119] Such mirroring with the self and also such Othering appear in the poem's images and criticism of individual figures, of wanderers, non-workers, unacceptable minstrels, and so on, and in perceptions of whole groups, which include the Jews and the Welsh, as well as peasants. There are parallels to that symbiosis in another symbiotic relationship, a colonialist relationship, discernible in the signs in the poem of what may be regional English perceptions of the Welsh, as lacking honesty, respectability, and social status, and associated with wildness (just as analogously Ireland is a land of disgraceful priests). Langland's references to the Welsh say more about the English, and the Welsh–English Marches, than they say about Wales.

In considering Langland and Wales, this essay offers answers to questions not usually asked about Langland. But, as raked light helps critics and scholars to reconsider the construction or methods of a painting, so recalibrating the position from which we look at *Piers Plowman* has the potential to reveal new aspects, contexts, and connections for many of its structures, idiosyncrasies, and themes.

Works Cited

Primary Sources

Ancrene Wisse: A Corrected Edition of the Text in Cambridge, Corpus Christi College MS 402, ed. by Bella Millett, EETS o.s. 325, 326, 2 vols (London: Oxford University Press, 2005)

Bede, *Ecclesiastical History of the English People*, ed. and trans. by Bertram Colgrave and R. A. B. Mynors, 2 vols (Oxford: Clarendon, 1969)

Chaucer, Geoffrey, *The Riverside Chaucer*, ed. by Larry D. Benson, 3rd edn (Boston: Houghton Mifflin, 1987)

Chestre, Thomas, *Launfal*, in *The Middle English Breton Lays*, ed. by Anne Laskaya and Eve Salisbury, TEAMS Middle English Texts (Kalamazoo: Medieval Institute Publications, 1995)

Dafydd ap Gwilym, *Cerddi*, ed. by Dafydd Johnston and others (Cardiff: University of Wales Press, 2010)

---

118   Clopper, '*Songes of Rechelesnesse*', p. 309. Lawton, 'The Subject of *Piers Plowman*', pp. 9–10.

119   Hussey, 'The Outsider', p. 13. See also Lawton's observations on parallels between pejorative aspects of Sloth, Envy, and Wrath and the self-presentation of the persona: 'The Subject of *Piers Plowman*', p. 13.

———, <http://www.dafyddapgwilym.net> [accessed 18 October 2020]

The Digby Poems: A New Edition of the Lyrics, ed. by Helen Barr (Exeter: University of Exeter Press, 2009)

Dives and Pauper, ed. by Priscilla Heath Barnum, EETS o.s. 275, 280, 323, 2 vols in 3 fasc. (Oxford: Oxford University Press, 1976–2004)

Geoffrey of Monmouth, *The History of the Kings of Britain*, ed. by Michael D. Reeve, trans. by Neil Wright (Woodbridge: Boydell, 2007)

Gerald of Wales, *Itinerarium Kambriae* and *Descriptio Kambriae*, in *Opera*, ed. by J. S. Brewer, J. F. Dimmock, and G. F. Warner, Rolls Series, 21, 8 vols (London: Longman, Green, Longman and Roberts, 1861–91), VI, 3–152, 155–227

Honorius Augustodunensis, *Gemma animae*, in *Patrologiae cursus completus: series latina*, ed. by Jacques-Paul Migne, 221 vols (Paris: Migne, 1844–64), CLXXII (1854), cols 541–736

Iolo Goch, *Gwaith*, ed. by D. R. Johnston (Cardiff: University of Wales Press, 1988)

The Kalendre of the Newe Legende of Englande, ed. by Manfred Görlach (Heidelberg: Winter, 1994)

Langland, William, *The Vision of William Concerning Piers the Plowman*, ed. by W. W. Skeat, 2 vols (London: Oxford University Press, 1886)

———, *'Piers Plowman': The Prologue and Passus I–VII of the B Text*, ed. by J. A. W. Bennett (Oxford: Clarendon, 1972)

———, *'Piers Plowman': A Parallel-Text Edition of the A, B, C, and Z Versions*, ed. by A. V. C. Schmidt (London: Longman, 1995)

Map, Walter, *De nugis curialium: Courtiers' Trifles*, ed. and trans. by M. R. James, rev. edn by C. N. L. Brooke and R. A. B. Mynors (Oxford: Clarendon, 1983)

The Oldest Anglo-Norman Prose 'Brut' Chronicle, ed. and trans. by Julia Marvin, Medieval Chronicles (Woodbridge: Boydell, 2006)

'Richard the Redeless' and 'Mum and the Sothsegger', ed. by James M. Dean, TEAMS Middle English Texts (Rochester, NY: Medieval Institute, 2000)

Sir Gawain and the Green Knight, ed. by J. R. R. Tolkien and E. V. Gordon, rev. by Norman Davis, 2nd edn (Oxford: Oxford University Press, 1967)

Skelton, John, *The Complete English Poems*, ed. by John Scattergood (Harmondsworth: Penguin, 1983)

Vita Edwardi Secundi: The Life of Edward the Second, ed. by N. Denholm-Young, rev. edn by Wendy R. Childs (Oxford: Clarendon, 2005)

William of Malmesbury, *Gesta regum Anglorum: The History of the English Kings*, ed. and trans. by R. M. Thomson and M. Winterbottom (Oxford: Clarendon, 1998)

Secondary Sources

Adams, Robert, *Langland and the Rokele Family: The Gentry Background to Piers Plowman* (Dublin: Four Courts, 2013)

Baring-Gould, Sabine, *Lives of the Saints*, rev. edn, 16 vols (Edinburgh: John Grant, 1914)

Barratt, Robert W. Jr., *Against All England: Regional Identity and Cheshire Writing, 1195–1656* (Notre Dame: University of Notre Dame Press, 2009)

Barron, Caroline, 'William Langland: A London Poet', in *Chaucer's England*, ed. by Barbara Hanawalt (Minneapolis: University of Minnesota, 1992), pp. 91–109

Barth, Fredrik, *Ethnic Groups and Boundaries: The Social Organisation of Cultural Difference* (Oslo: Waveland, 1969)

Benbrough-Jackson, Mike, *Cardiganshire and the Cardi, c. 1760–c. 2000: Locating a Place and its People*, Cymru: Studies in Welsh History (Cardiff: University of Wales Press, 2012)

Bloomfield, Morton W., *'Piers Plowman' as a Fourteenth-Century Apocalypse* (New Brunswick: Rutgers University Press, 1961)

Bonser, K. J., *The Drovers, Who They Were and How They Went: An Epic of the English Countryside* (Basingstoke: Macmillan, 1970)

Breeze, Andrew, '"Tikes" at *Piers Plowman* B XIX.37: Welsh *Taeog* "Serf, Bondman"', *Notes and Queries*, 40 (1993), 443–45

Brooks, E. St John, 'The *Piers Plowman* Manuscripts in Trinity College Dublin', *The Library*, 5th ser., 6.34 (1951), 41–53

Burgess, Glyn S., '"I kan rymes of Robyn Hood, and Randolf Erl of Chestre"', in *'De sens rassis': Essays in Honor of Rupert T. Pickens*, ed. by Keith Busby, Bernard Guidot, and Logan Whalen (Amsterdam: Rodopi, 2004), pp. 41–73

Clopper, Lawrence M., *'Songes of Rechelesnesse': Langland and the Franciscans* (Ann Arbor: University of Michigan Press, 1997)

Davies, John, *A History of Wales*, rev. edn (London: Penguin, 2007)

Davies, Morgan Thomas, 'Plowman, Patrons and Poets: Iolo Goch's *Cywydd y Llafurwr* and Some Matters of Wales in the Fourteenth Century', *Mediaevalia et humanistica*, n.s., 24 (1997), 51–74

Davies, R. R., *The Age of Conquest: Wales, 1063–1415* (Oxford: Oxford University Press, 1991)

——, 'The English State and the "Celtic" Peoples, 1100–1400', *Journal of Historical Sociology*, 6 (1993), 1–14

——, *The Revolt of Owain Glyn Dŵr* (Oxford: Oxford University Press, 1995)

——, *The First English Empire: Power and Identities in the British Isles, 1093–1343* (Oxford: Oxford University Press, 2000)

Davlin, Mary Clemente, O. P., *The Place of God in 'Piers Plowman' and Medieval Art* (Aldershot: Ashgate, 2001)

Diocese of Llanfaff, press release: 'Ancient Stone Is Found Hidden under Church Carpet' <https://web.archive.org/web/20140306143823/llandaff.churchinwales.org.uk/news/2014/02/ancient-stone-is-found-hidden-under-church-carpet> [accessed 1 July 2020]

Dolmans, Emily, 'Locating the Border: Britain and the Welsh Marches in *Fouke le Fitz Waryn*', *New Medieval Literatures*, 16 (2016), 109–34

Duby, Georges, *France in the Middle Ages, 987–1460*, trans. by Juliet Vale (Oxford: Blackwell, 1991)

Dyer, Christopher, '*Piers Plowman* and Plowmen: An Historical Perspective', *Yearbook of Langland Studies*, 8 (1994), 155–76

Elliott, R. V. W., 'Langland's Country', in *Piers Plowman: Critical Approaches*, ed. by S. S. Hussey (London: Methuen, 1969), pp. 226–44

Faletra, Michael A., 'Narrating the Matter of Britain: Geoffrey of Monmouth and the Norman Conquest of Wales', *Chaucer Review*, 35 (2000), 60–85

Fellowes, Jennifer, and Ivana Djordjević, eds, *Sir Bevis of Hampton in Literary Tradition* (Woodbridge: Boydell and Brewer, 2008)

Fenton, Kirsten, *Gender, Nation and Conquest in the Works of William of Malmesbury* (Woodbridge: Boydell, 2008)

Frome, Robin, 'Kingdoms and Dominions at Peace and War', in *The Short Oxford History of the British Isles: The Fourteenth and Fifteenth Centuries*, ed. by Ralph Griffiths (Oxford: Oxford University Press, 2003), pp. 149–80.

Fulton, Helen, 'Class and Nation: Defining the English in Late-Medieval Welsh Poetry', in *Authority and Subjugation in Writing of Medieval Wales*, ed. by Ruth Kennedy and Simon Meecham-Jones (Basingstoke: Palgrave Macmillan, 2008), pp. 191–212

Galloway, Andrew, *The Penn Commentary on 'Piers Plowman'*, I (Philadelphia: University of Pennsylvania Press, 2006)

Gillingham, John, *The English in the Twelfth Century: Imperialism, National Identity and Political Values* (Oxford: Clarendon, 2003)

Godden, Malcolm, 'Plowmen and Hermits in Langland's *Piers Plowman*', *Review of English Studies*, n.s., 35.138 (1984), 129–63

Goldstein, R. James, '"Why calle ye hym Crist, siþen Iewes calle hym Iesus?": The Disavowal of Jewish Identification in *Piers Plowman* B Text', *Exemplaria*, 13 (2001), 215–51

Gray, Madeleine, 'Saints on the Edge: Reconfiguring Sanctity in the Welsh Marches', in *Rewriting Holiness: Reconfiguring Vitae, Re-signifying Cults*, ed. by Madeleine Gray, Kings College London Medieval Studies, 25 (Woodbridge: Boydell and Brewer, 2017), pp. 89–108

Green, David, 'National Identities and the Hundred Years War', in *Fourteenth Century England*, VI, ed. by Chris Given-Wilson (Woodbridge: Boydell, 2010), pp. 115–29

Griffiths, Ralph, ed., *The Short Oxford History of the British Isles: The Fourteenth and Fifteenth Centuries* (Oxford: Oxford University Press, 2003)

——, 'Crossing the Frontiers of the English Realm in the Fifteenth Century', in *Power and Identity in the Middle Ages*, ed. by Huw Pryce and John Watts (Oxford: Clarendon, 2007), pp. 211–25

——, 'Who Were the Townsfolk of Medieval Wales?', in *Urban Culture in Medieval Wales*, ed. by Helen Fulton (Cardiff: University of Wales Press, 2012), pp. 9–18

Gummer, Benedict, *The Scourging Angel: The Black Death in the British Isles* (London: Vintage Press, 2004)

Hanna, Ralph, *William Langland* (Aldershot: Variorum, 1993)

——, 'MS. Bodley 851 and the Dissemination of *Piers Plowman*', section two of 'Studies in the Manuscripts of *Piers Plowman*', *Yearbook of Langland Studies*, 7 (1993), 1–25 (pp. 14–23) (repr. as chap. 11 of *Pursuing History: Middle English Manuscripts and their Texts* (Stanford: Stanford University Press, 1996), pp. 195–202)

——, 'Robert the Ruyflere and his Companions', in *Literature and Religion in the Later Middle Ages: Philological Studies in Honor of Siegfried Wenzel*, ed. by Richard G. Newhauser and John A. Alford (Binghampton: SUNY Press, 1995), pp. 81–95

———, 'Will's Work', in *Written Work: Langland, Labor and Authorship*, ed. by Steven Justice and Kathryn Kerby-Fulton (Philadelphia: University of Pennsylvania Press, 1997), pp. 23–66

———, *Penn Commentary on Piers Plowman*, II (Philadelphia: University of Pennsylvania Press, 2020)

Harriss, Gerald, *Shaping the Nation: England, 1360–1461* (Oxford: Clarendon, 2005)

'Herefordshire in Wales?' <www.bbc.co.uk/herefordandworcester/content/ articles/2006/11/13/hereford_in_wales_feature.shtml> [accessed 1 July 2020]

Horobin, Simon, 'Langland's Dialect Reconsidered', in *Pursuing Middle English Manuscripts and their Texts: Essays in Honour of Ralph Hanna*, ed. by Simon Horobin and Aditi Nafde, Texts and Transitions, 10 (Turnhout: Brepols, 2017), pp. 63–75

Hurlock, Kathryn, *Medieval Welsh Pilgrimage, c. 1100–1500* (New York: Palgrave Macmillan, 2018)

Husain, B. M. C., *Cheshire under the Norman Earls*, A History of Cheshire, 4 (Chester: Cheshire Community Council, 1973)

Hussey, S. S., 'Langland the Outsider', in *Middle English Poetry: Texts and Traditions; Essays in Honour of Derek Pearsall*, ed. by A. J. Minnis, York Medieval Press (Woodbridge: Boydell and Brewer, 2001), pp. 129–37

Johnson, Eleanor, '*Reddere* and Refrain: A Meditation of Poetic Procedure in *Piers Plowman*', *Yearbook of Langland Studies*, 30 (2016), 3–27

Johnston, Dafydd, 'Iolo Goch and the English: Poetry and Politics in the Fourteenth Century', *Cambridge Medieval Celtic Studies*, 12 (1986), 73–98

Jones, G. Hartwell, *Celtic Britain and the Pilgrim Movement* (London: Honourable Society of Cymmrodorion, 1912)

Jusserand, J. J., '*Piers Plowman': A Contribution to the History of English Mysticism*, trans. by Marion and Elise Roberts (New York: Putnam's, 1894)

Kaske, R. E., '*Piers Plowman* and Local Iconography', *Journal of the Warburg and Courtauld Institutes*, 31 (1968), 159–69

Keats-Rohan, Katharine S. B., 'The Bretons and Normans of England: The Family, the Fief, and the Feudal Monarchy', *Nottingham Mediaeval Studies*, 36 (1992), 48–78

Klausner, David N., 'English Economies and Welsh Realities: Drama in Medieval and Early Modern Wales', in *Authority and Subjugation in Writing of Medieval Wales*, ed. by Ruth Kennedy and Simon Meecham-Jones (Basingstoke: Palgrave Macmillan, 2008), pp. 213–30.

Lampitt, Matthew Siôn, 'Networking the Marches: The Literature of the Welsh Marches, c. 1180–c. 1410' (unpublished doctoral dissertation, King's College London, 2019)

Lawton, David, 'The Subject of *Piers Plowman*', *Yearbook of Langland Studies*, 1 (1987), 1–30

Lewis, Barry, *Welsh Poetry and English Pilgrimage: Gruffudd ap Maredudd and the Rood of Chester* (Aberystwyth: Centre for Celtic and Welsh Advanced Studies, 2005)

Lewis, C. P., and A. T. Thacker, eds, *History of the County of Chester*, 5 vols (Woodbridge: Institute of Historical Research, 2003)

Lieberman, Max, 'The English and the Welsh in *Fouke le Fitz Waryn*', *Thirteenth Century England*, 12 (2007), 1–11

———, *The March of Wales, 1067–1300: A Borderland of Medieval Britain* (Cardiff: University of Wales Press, 2008)

————, *The Medieval March of Wales: Creation of a Frontier* (Cambridge: Cambridge University Press, 2010)

Marsden, Richard A., 'Gerald of Wales and Competing Interpretations of the Welsh Middle Ages, c. 1870–1910', *Welsh History Review / Cylchgrawn Hanes Cymru*, 25 (2011), 314–45

Marx, William, 'Middle English Texts and Welsh Contexts', in *Authority and Subjugation in Writing of Medieval Wales*, ed. by Ruth Kennedy and Simon Meecham-Jones (Basingstoke: Palgrave Macmillan, 2008), pp. 13–26

McKenna, Catherine, 'The City of Chester in Gruffudd ap Maredudd's *Awdl i'r Grog o Gaer*', in *Urban Culture in Medieval Wales*, ed. by Helen Fulton (Cardiff: University of Wales Press, 2012), pp. 205–22

Meecham-Jones, Simon, 'Where Was Wales? The Erasure of Wales in Medieval English Culture', in *Authority and Subjugation in Writing of Medieval Wales*, ed. by Ruth Kennedy and Simon Meecham-Jones (Basingstoke: Palgrave Macmillan, 2008), pp. 27–55

Middleton, Anne, 'The Audience and Public of *Piers Plowman*', in *Middle English Alliterative Poetry and its Literary Background*, ed. by David Lawton (Cambridge: Brewer, 1982), pp. 101–54

————, 'William Langland's "Kynde Name"', in *Literary Practice and Social Change in Britain, 1380–1530*, ed. by Lee Patterson, The New Historicism, 8 (Berkeley: University of California Press, 1990), pp. 15–82

————, 'Acts of Vagrancy: The C Version "Autobiography" and the Statute of 1388', in *Written Work: Langland, Labor and Authorship*, ed. by Steven Justice and Kathryn Kerby-Fulton (Philadelphia: University of Pennsylvania Press, 1997), pp. 208–318

————, 'Playing the Plowman: Legends of Fourteenth-Century Authorship', in *Chaucer, Langland, and Fourteenth-Century Literary History*, ed. by Steven Justice (Farnham: Ashgate Variorum, 2013), pp. 113–42

Moore-Colyer, Richard, *Welsh Cattle Drovers*, Landmark Collector's Library (Midsummer Norton: Richard Moore-Colyer, 2002)

Morgan, Philip, 'Cheshire and Wales', in *Power and Identity in the Middle Ages: Essays in Memory of Rees Davies*, ed. by Huw Pryce and John Watts (Oxford: Oxford University Press, 2007), pp. 195–210

Morgan, T. J., and Prys Morgan, *Welsh Surnames* (Cardiff: University of Wales Press, 1985)

Mulligan, Amy C., 'Moses, Taliesin and the Welsh Chosen People: Elis Gryffydd's Construction of a Biblical British Past for Reformation Wales', *Studies in Philology*, 13 (2016), 765–96

O'Neill, Rosemary, 'Counting Sheep in the C Text of *Piers Plowman*', *Yearbook of Langland Studies*, 29 (2018), 89–116

Opie, Iona, and Peter Opie, *The Oxford Dictionary of Nursery Rhymes*, 2nd edn (London: Oxford University Press, 1997)

Parri, Brynach, 'Crog Aberhonddu', *Brycheiniog*, 35 (2003), 19–36

Pearsall, Derek, 'Strangers in Late-Fourteenth-Century London', in *Strangers in Medieval Society*, ed. by F. R. Akehurst and Stephanie Cain-Van D'Elden (Minneapolis: University of Minnesota Press, 1997), pp. 46–62

Perry, Ryan, 'The Clopton Manuscript and the Beauchamp Affinity', in *Essays in Manuscript Geography: Vernacular Manuscripts of the English West Midlands from the Conquest to the Sixteenth Century*, ed. by Wendy Scase (Turnhout: Brepols, 2007), pp. 131–60

Phillips, Helen, 'Structure and Consolation in the *Book of the Duchess*', *Chaucer Review*, 62 (1993), 1–19

——, 'Reformist Polemics, Reading Publics and Unpopular Robin Hood', in *Robin Hood in Greenwood Stood: Essays on Alterity and Context in English Outlaw Tradition*, ed. by Stephen Knight (Turnhout: Brepols, 2011), pp. 87–111

Price, Adrian, 'Welsh Bandits', in *Bandit Territories*, ed. by Helen Phillips (Cardiff: University of Wales Press, 2008), pp. 58–72

Pryce, Huw, 'A Cross-Border Career: Giraldus Cambrensis between Wales and England', in *Grenzgänger*, ed. by Reinhard Schneider, Veröffentlichungen der Kommission für Saarländische Landesgeschichte und Volksforschung, 33 (Saarbrücken: Saarbrücker Druckerei und Verlag, 1998), pp. 46–48

Richmond, Velma Bourgeois, *The Legend of Guy of Warwick* (London: Routledge, 2020)

Rowley, Trevor, *The Welsh Border: Archaeology, History & Landscape*, rev. edn (Stroud: Tempus, 2001)

Salter, Mike, *The Old Parish Churches of Mid Wales*, 2nd edn (Malvern: Folly, 2003)

Samuels, M. L., 'Dialect and Grammar', in *A Companion to 'Piers Plowman'*, ed. by John A. Alford (Berkeley: University of California Press, 1988), pp. 201–22

Simpson, James, 'The Power of Impropriety: Authorial Naming in *Piers Plowman*', in *William Langland's 'Piers Plowman': A Book of Essays*, ed. by Kathleen M. Hewett-Smith (New York: Routledge, 2001), pp. 145–65

Sobiecki, Sebastian, 'Hares, Rabbits, Pheasants: *Piers Plowman* and William Longewille, a Norfolk Rebel in 1381', *Review of English Studies*, 69 (2018), 1–21

Spence, John, 'A Lost Manuscript of the "Rymes of [...] Randolf Erl of Chestre"', *eBLJ*, 2010, article 6; https://www.bl.uk/eblj/2010articles/pdf/ebljarticle62010.pdf

Stallybrass, Peter, and Allon White, *The Politics and Poetics of Transgression* (London: Methuen, 1986)

Steiner, Emily, *Reading 'Piers Plowman'* (Cambridge: Cambridge University Press, 2013)

Thomas, Hugh M., *The English and the Normans: Ethnic Hostility, Assimilation, and Identity, 1066–c. 1220* (Oxford: Oxford University Press, 2002)

Verheij, Louis J. P., 'New Light on the Author of the Twenty-Four Poems in Oxford Bodleian MS Digby 102', *Neophilologus*, 96 (2012), 641–49

Waldron, Ronald, 'Trevisa's Translation of Higden's *Polychronicon*, Book 1, Chapter 38, *De Wallia*', in *Authority and Subjugation in Writing of Medieval Wales*, ed. by Ruth Kennedy and Simon Meecham-Jones (Basingstoke: Palgrave Macmillan, 2008), pp. 99–136

Weeda, Claire V., 'Ethnic Stereotyping in Twelfth-Century Paris', in *Difference and Identity in France and Medieval Francia*, ed. by Meredith Cohen and Justine Firnhaber-Baker (Aldershot: Ashgate, 2010), pp. 115–35

Williams, Glanmor, 'Some Protestant Views of the Early British Church', *History*, n.s., 38.134 (1953), 219–33

Wright, Joseph, *English Dialect Dictionary*, III: *H–L* (London: Frowde, 1902)

Young, Helen Victoria, *Constructing 'England' in the Fourteenth Century: A Post-Colonial Interpretation of Middle English Romance* (Lewiston: Edwin Mellen, 2010)

JAMIE TAYLOR

Community, Charity, and Penetration

Langland's Queer Ecclesiology

▼ **KEYWORDS** *Piers Plowman*, *Confessio amantis*, ecclesiology, marriage, Lee Edelman, reproduction, Meed, Anima, Barn of Unity

▼ **ABSTRACT** This essay examines the heteronormative expectations — particularly marriage and reproduction — that attach to Langland's depictions of community-formation. Tracking Langland's repeated emphasis on marriage, consanguinity, and kinship as models for understanding spiritual community and its devotional precepts shows that core forms of social and political unity in *Piers Plowman* revolve around heterosexual promise and reproductivity. Yet in tracing the ways Langland tries to assert the poem's 'straightness', this essay argues for the possibility of queer ecclesiology at the end of *Piers*. By paying attention to how *Piers Plowman* strains toward a heteronormative and reproductive path to salvation, we can uncover the queer ways in which that path can work. This essay thus tracks key moments in the poem in which reproductive futurity is depicted as a crucial model of salvation and spiritual righteousness, looking particularly for the cracks where Langland admits the flimsiness of that model.

The apocalyptic end of *Piers Plowman* features a crowd of frightened but hopeful 'fooles' crammed into the Barn of Unity, with Conscience trying to soothe them (B.20.74).[1] The fools are suffering, falling ill physically and spiritually. Conscience calls for a friar to help heal a sick Contrition so everyone can be saved, and when the friar arrives, he promises that he can make salves to help. Acting as the 'porter of Unitee'

---

1   All quotations from the B text are taken from *The Vision of Piers Plowman*, ed. by Schmidt. All quotations from the C text are taken from *'Piers Plowman: An Edition of the C-Text*, ed. by Pearsall.

Jamie Taylor (jktaylor@brynmawr.edu) is Associate Professor of English at Bryn Mawr College.

The Yearbook of Langland Studies, 34 (2020), 93–115   BREPOLS ❦ PUBLISHERS   10.1484/J.YLS.5.121088

(B.20.331), Peace asks him his name. 'Sire *Penetrans-domos*', the friar amiably replies (B.20.341), and Peace reluctantly lets him in, although he voices some concerns:

> 'I knew swich oon ones, noght eighte wynter passed,
> Coom in thus ycoped at a court there I dwelde,
> And was my lords leche — and my ladies bothe.
> And at the laste this lymytour, tho my lord was oute,
> He salvede so oure wommen til some were with childe'. (B.20.344–48)

The image of a lecherous friar is taken from II Timothy 3.6, which warns of hypocritical clerics who creep into houses. More directly, Sir *Penetrans-Domos* comes from the antifraternal satire of William of St Amour and Richard FitzRalph, both of whom focused on the sexual connotations of penetrating mendicants, condemning friars both for lechery and for invading congregants' private spaces alike.[2] Langland's particular deployment of this image invites us to read carefully the ecclesiological claims at the end of *Piers Plowman*. Although Stephen A. Barney calls Sir *Penetrans-Domos* a 'mere sideswipe', this essay argues that Sir *Penetrans-Domos* alerts us to the contours of Langland's ecclesiological experiment: that is, conceptualizing a queer way forward to spiritual truth, albeit without guarantees.[3]

Piers Plowman repeatedly turns to heteronormative models of marriage, consanguinity, and kinship to articulate spiritual community and its devotional precepts.[4] Masha Raskolnikov has argued that *Piers* relies on genealogy to produce 'natural' or affective relationships among diverse people (those occupying the 'fair feeld of ful of folk' (B.Prol.17)) and thus, in turn, to generate a sense of Christian unity. But Raskolnikov further points out that, even as it relies on them, the poem challenges genealogical claims to authority — questioning Meed's parentage, for example, or depicting a testy debate between the Four Daughters of God — so that by the end of the poem, kinship is both an assumed structure of spiritual community and one full of pitfalls.[5] In addition, as Sarah Wilma Watson has shown, Langland relies on a 'poetics of penetration' to 'explore questions of inclusion and exclusion from the heavenly kingdom and the Christian community'.[6] Langland's investment in genealogy and a poetics of penetration are, in fact, mutually supportive, and by the time Sir *Penetrans-Domos* shows up, those heteronormative structures prove to be shaky grounds for ecclesiological unity.

Indeed, such normative models of kinship produce community only among those already able and willing to participate in its narrow demands. Michael Warner and Lauren Berlant point out that although core forms of social and political unity always revolve around heterosexual promise and reproductivity, 'a familial model of society displaces

2 Szittya, *Antifraternal Tradition*, pp. 3–10. See also Scase, *New Anticlericalism*.
3 Barney, *Penn Commentary*, v, 242–43.
4 See Davlin, 'Genealogical Terms'.
5 Raskolnikov, *Body against Soul*, pp. 177–81. See also Raskolnikov, 'Promising the Female, Delivering the Male'.
6 Watson, 'Grace Holds the "Clicket"', p. 208.

the recognition of structural racism and other systemic inequalities'.[7] Likewise, for Lee Edelman, the political imperative of producing and sustaining 'human capital' relies on an idealization of a collective future that rests on parental love for children.[8] Such 'reproductive futurism' maintains 'the absolute privilege of heteronormativity by rendering unthinkable, by casting outside the political domain, the possibility of a queer resistance to this organizing principle of communal relations'.[9] Certainly, the Middle Ages authorized its own codes of heteronormative privilege, for example by focusing intently on sodomy as a crime against nature and the Church as well as by asserting, repeatedly and in multiple venues, the biblical injunction to 'go forth and multiply'.[10] Then as now, the unity fomented and explained via reproductive futurity always marginalizes any non-normative form of social participation, providing for those on the margins 'no future', as Edelman puts it. Although his pessimistic theory has been challenged and qualified by scholars attempting to harness optimism as a feature of political resistance, Edelman's polemic on behalf of 'no future' seems right for *Piers*.[11] The poem itself is an exercise in repeated failure — what D. Vance Smith calls the poem's 'larger movement of negation' and Nicolette Zeeman more gently calls its ongoing 'frustration'.[12]

Still, although the poem perhaps does not offer a (heteronormative) future, ending with the dreamer in despair and the world in chaos, this essay argues that Langland ultimately questions the power of heteronormative genealogies to produce a good and virtuous life.[13] In doing so, he not only reveals that the reliance on reproduction and familial ties is fragile, but also suggests that such fragility might admit different forms of ecclesiological community and provide hope for a salvific future that might be capacious, even inclusive. We might thus conceptualize the Barn of Unity scene as a queer experiment in ecclesiological community.[14] This is not exactly to argue for an optimistic reading of *Piers Plowman*, but rather to trace its ambivalent picture of

---

7   Berlant and Warner, 'Sex in Public', p. 549.

8   Edelman, *No Future*, pp. 111–12.

9   Edelman, *No Future*, p. 2.

10 See Burgwinkle, *Sodomy, Masculinity, and Law*. For a discussion of contemporary political reliance on heteronormative sex and medieval parallels and disjunctions, see Lochrie, 'Presidential Improprieties'.

11 For responses to Edelman, see Muñoz, *Cruising Utopia*; Snediker, *Queer Optimism*; and Ahmed, *Promise of Happiness*.

12 Smith, 'Negative Langland', p. 35; Zeeman, *Discourse of Desire*, p. 34. See also Smith, *Book of the Incipit*, for a discussion of failure as a structural principle throughout *Piers*.

13 We might note here the recent strain of genealogical scholarship in Langland studies, in which renewed attention on the poem's authorship traces the biographical and literary evidence of Langland's relationship to the Essex-based Rokele family. Such genealogical work, as Galloway puts it, focuses on 'how this figure's familial and social circumstances might help us further appreciate one of the most idiosyncratic but widely appropriated poems in late medieval England' ('Parallel Lives', p. 44). See also Adams, *Langland and the Rokele Family*; Adams, 'The Rokeles'; and Johnston, 'William Langland and John Ball'.

14 Lochrie reads *Piers* as an exercise in 'negative utopianism', in which he presses failure into the service of institutional critique and thereby offers a kind of hope, or 'adjunct possibility for alternatives to the present'; *Nowhere in the Middle Ages*, p. 134.

ecclesiological reform, one that both strains toward a new, queer future and worries about the masculinist and heteronormative 'losses' that might accompany it.[15]

In arguing for the possibility of queer ecclesiology at the end of the poem, this essay examines, perhaps counterintuitively, the ways Langland tries to assert the poem's 'straightness'. Although Langland endorses a heteronormative imperative throughout the poem, he also repeatedly suggests a queer short-circuiting of that imperative, often in the very episodes in which heteronormative family life seems most aggressively promulgated. By paying attention to how *Piers Plowman* strains toward a heteronormative and reproductive path to salvation, we can uncover the queer ways in which that path can work. This essay thus tracks key moments in the poem in which reproductive futurity is depicted as a crucial model of salvation and spiritual righteousness, looking particularly for the cracks where Langland admits, perhaps subconsciously, the flimsiness of that model.

Marriage and Scrambled Genealogies in the Visio

In the Visio, Langland establishes the primacy of genealogy for ecclesiological authority, beginning with his depiction of Meed. When Will asks after the richly attired woman he sees, Holy Church sneeringly explains,

> In the Popes paleis she is pryvee as myselve,
> But Soothnese wolde noght so — for she is a bastard,
> For Fals was hire fader that hath a fikel tonge,
> And nevere sooth seide sithen he com to erthe;
> And Mede is manered after hym, right as kynde asketh:
> *Qualis pater, talis filius. Bona arbor bonum fructum facit.* (B.2.23–27a)

As a 'bastard', Meed is automatically suspect because of her untraceable genealogy. Holy Church then tellingly adds,

> I oughte ben hyere than heo — I kam of a bettre
> My fader the grete God is and ground of alle graces,
> Oo God withouten gynnyng, and I his goode doughter. (B.2.28–30)

To Holy Church's frustration, her steadfast obedience to God, articulated here as being a 'good daughter', has not convinced everyone of her superior institutional status. Moreover, Holy Church says that Meed's father is Fals, then tells the dreamer that Meed is preparing to marry 'Fals Fikel-tonge, a fendes biyete' (B.2.41). The idea that Meed might be marrying her father — merely suggested, never followed

---

15   In this ambivalent reading, I generally follow Lochrie's call to conceptualize a medieval past 'that is neither hopelessly utopian nor inveterately heteronormative' (*Heterosyncrasies*, p. 25). For a broader discussion of queerness, the past, and imagined futurities, see the forthcoming collection *Medieval Queer Futurity*.

through — is designed not only to demonstrate that Meed's lineage is unsavoury, but that her kinship practices are as well.

Langland suggests that the only real solution to a trenchant problem like Meed is marriage, which will affix Meed to a 'good' kinship relationship and consequently transform her. The king poses the possibility to Conscience in a rather timid way: 'Woltow wedde this womman', he asks, 'if I wole assente? | For she is fayn of thi felaweshipe, for to be thi make' (B.3.118–19). David Wallace points out that, although it suggests egalitarian bonds within horizontally oriented political communities, 'felaweshipe, a political term, brings a gender politics (more or less visible) to each instance of deployment. It rarely suggests affective neutrality or indifference because it speaks from the condition of being bound up, or closed in, with other people'.[16] That the king uses this word both reveals his institutional, governmental agenda and exposes his normative tactics. Although this marriage is instrumental, the king still maps desire onto Meed ('fayn') to insinuate that it is not and that Meed's desire is driving it.

Edelman points out that such kinship politics is fundamentally conservative, 'insofar as it works to *affirm* a structure, to *authenticate* social order, which it then intends to transmit to the future in the form of its inner Child. That Child remains the perpetual horizon of every acknowledged politics, the fantasmatic beneficiary of every political intervention'.[17] Dynastic systems obviously rely on such a conservative model: genealogy is the very fabric of royal authority, and the Child — that is, the political fantasy of future generations and the figure that generates proper affective response — is the key image that guarantees a better, more humane or more righteous future. A marriage between Meed and Conscience would be such a conservative pairing: not only would it produce children that would authenticate the righteousness of their union, it would preserve Meed's central role in sustaining the realm via gift-giving (or bribes), now and in the future.

Conscience is aghast at the suggestion and, among his many insults and complaints, he says,

> Wyves and widewes wantounnesse she techeth,
> And lereth hem lecherie that loveth hire yiftes.
> Youre fader she felled through false biheste,
> And hath apoisoned popes and apeireth Holy Chirche. (B.3.125–28)

Conscience here clarifies the thorny problem with Meed: she provides dark money to both Church and state institutions, garnering behind-the-scenes influence. That this shadiness might be erased through marriage, and that Conscience rejects the possibility by arguing Meed's suspect genealogy, exposes the tight bond between heterornomative kinship structures and putatively righteous institutional systems. Meed's response is likewise telling, in that she defends her work by promising Conscience that she can support him in the same way she does the King: 'Yet I

---

16 Wallace, *Chaucerian Polity*, p. 73.
17 Edelman, *No Future*, p. 3.

may, as I myghte, menske thee with yiftes | And mayntene thi manhode moore than thow knowest' (B.3.184–85). Kathleen Kennedy has shown that maintenance, as a quasi-political system by which influence could be produced and sustained through personal networks, patronage, and favours, was a practice designed 'to transfer and regulate the power between men'.[18] By making Meed a maintainer, Langland exposes the conceptual overlaps between marriage and maintenance as institutions designed to translate kinship into political alliance and vice-versa.

Conscience pushes back by providing a vision of a future without Meed:

> I, Conscience, knowe this, for Kynde Wit me taughte –
> That Reson shal regne and reaumes governe,
> And right as Agag hadde, happe shul somme:
> Samuel shal sleen hym and Saul shal be blamed,
> And David shal be diademed and daunten hem alle,
> And oon Cristene kyng kepen us echone.
> Shal na moore Mede be maister as she is nouthe,
> Ac love and lowenesse and leautee togideres –
> Thise shul ben maistres on moolde trewe men to save. (B.3.284–92)

Conscience's vision of a future based on 'love and lowenesse and leautee' thinks of Christian community as a collection of 'trewe men', a phrase common in both political and spiritual descriptions of community.[19] The rejection of Meed becomes a rejection of women altogether, a happy future in which love among 'trewe men' provides the only glue necessary for political and spiritual harmony. Men can maintain their own 'manhode', no marriage or women required.

The Meed passūs thus superficially depict a heteronormative model of marriage-as-politics, a conservative form of political and spiritual alliance designed to use affective bonds as supportive material for the realm. But they do so clumsily, as Conscience ultimately provides a men-only vision of political and spiritual community. In some ways, this vision merely affirms patriarchal systems of power, rendering women, even moneyed women like Meed, inconsequential. But we might also read this vision as a turn away from heteronormative politics and toward something less dependent on reproductive futurity.

Such ambivalent depictions of spiritual unity and kinship continue throughout the Visio. For example, when Piers tells Will and a group of demoralized pilgrims how to find Truth's castle, he assembles them into a group via a marital metonym:

> Ye moten go thorugh Mekenesse, bothe men and wyves,
> Til ye come into Conscience, that Crist wite the sothe,
> That ye loven Oure Lord God levest of alle thynges,

---

18 Kennedy, *Meed, Maintenance, and Marriage*, p. 66.

19 *MED*, s.v. 'tre[u]e', 1a, 7a. For a discussion of the shifting relationship between 'truth' and its production of legal, political, and spiritual communities in the later Middle Ages, see Green, *Crisis of Truth*. The phrase 'trewe men' was important to the rebels of 1381 as well as to the lollards; see Justice, *Writing and Rebellion*, esp. pp. 124–25.

And thane youre neghebores next in none wise apeire
Otherwise than thow woldest hii wroughte to thiselve. (B.5.561–65)

Piers's description here pointedly sees heteronormative kinship ties between 'men and wyves' and the wider bonds between Christian neighbours as epistemological pathways. Indeed, Piers says, when one arrives at Truth's gleaming castle, one encounters Grace, the porter, who will allow entrance only if kinship is reiterated as a communal principle:

And if Grace graunte thee to go in this wise
Thow shalt see in thiselve Truthe sitte in thyn herte
In a cheyne of charite, as thow a child were,
To suffren hym and segge noght ayein thi sires wille. (B.5.605–08)

This expansion of Mark 10.15 emphasizes its power structure: here, the child is the central image of submission and truth alike. Like Edelman's Child, this metaphor stabilizes the relationship between political bonds and a sanctified future.

This emphasis is made especially clear when Piers explains how to gain entrance even if one fails to perform submission adequately: 'Ac ther are seven sustren that serven Truthe evere', he explains, 'And arn porters of the posternes that to the place longeth' (B.5.618–19). These siblings, including Abstinence and Chastity, might admit someone who styles himself as kin:

And who is sib to thise sevene, so me God helpe,
He is wonderly welcome and faire underfongen.
And but if ye be sibbe to some of thise sevene,
It is ful hard, by myn heed, any of yow alle
To gete ingong at any gate but grace be the moore! (B.5.625–29)

Raskolnikov points out the elliptical instructions here: one must be(come) kin to these sisters, such that 'to be kind may mean always-already to have had a kinship relationship with these virtues — to be able to trace distant genealogical connections, figuratively speaking, between one's family and theirs, if we are to think this metaphor through'.[20] Still, Piers says, since Mercy is one of the sisters — and Mercy is 'sib to alle synfulle, and hire sone also' (B.5.636) — anyone might claim for themselves a kinship line that extends to their children.

The Visio thus returns, again and again, to cracked or thin models of kinship. We might ask, then, whether those cracks are deliberate challenges to reproductive futurity or merely hairline fractures made larger by interpretive attention. The C-text 'autobiographical passage' suggests the latter, vociferously asserting straight genealogical paths to social and spiritual community. The dreamer awakens next to his wife, Kit, whereupon Conscience and Reason both demand that he account for his intellectual and spiritual labours. He returns to his childhood, saying that his father supported

---

20 Raskolnikov, *Body and Soul*, p. 178.

his schooling and he then followed the correct path set out by his familial station. But such genealogical imperative has gone by the wayside, to society's detriment:

> Bondemen and bastardus and beggares children,
> Thyse bylongeth to labory, and lordes kyn to serue
> God and good men, as here degre asketh,
> Somme to synge masses or sitten and wryten,
> Redon and resceyuen þat resound ouhte to spene.
> Ac sythe bondemen barnes haen be mad bisshopes
> And barnes bastardus haen be erchedekenes
> And soutares and here sones for suluer han be knyhtes
> And lordes sones here laboreres and leyde here rentes to wedde,
> For the ryhte of this reume ryden aȝeyn oure enemyes
> In confort of the comune and the kynges worschipe,
> And monkes and moniales, þat mendenantes sholde fynde,
> Imade here kyn knyhtes and knyhtes-fees ypurchased,
> Popes and patrones pore gentel blood refused
> And taken Symondes sones syntwarie to kepe,
> Lyf-holynesse and loue hath be longe hennes,
> And wol, til hit be wered out, or oþerwyse ychaunged. (C.5.65–81)

Key to the dreamer's complaint is the mismanagement of 'kin', which has scrambled proper social ordering. Indeed, that this impassioned speech begins with him waking up next to his wife suggests that even his own marriage bed operates as the foundation from which he might assert society's political and spiritual woes, animating the ways such domestic relationships undergird conservative communal principles and, at the same time, how those relationships nonetheless might not be able to shore those principles up sufficiently.

Charity and Unity in the Vita

The Visio betrays its own superficially heteronormative principles, struggling and failing to depict marital and kinship relationships as foundational for social order. The promise of reproductive futurity is shaky at best, and that promise continues to splinter as Langland keeps trying to explain its principles in the Vita. For example, when Will seeks Do-Wel, Do-Bet, and Do-Best and Wit instructs him to find Kynde's castle, Wit tells him that Kynde keeps Anima, 'a lemman that he loveth like to hymselve', enclosed in the castle to keep her away from the Devil:

> Ac Kynde knoweth this wel and kepeth hire the bettre
> And hath doon hire with Sire Dowel, duc of thise marches.
> Dobet is hire damyselle, Sire Doweles doughter,
> To serven this lady leelly both late and rathe.
> Dobest is above bothe, a bisshopes peere;
> That he bit moot be do — he biddeth hem alle. (B.9.10–15)

The Castle is guarded by Inwit, who 'hath fyve faire sones by his firste wyve', all of whom protect Anima (B.9.19). Wit goes on to explain that the Castle is metonymic for the body itself:

> Inwit and alle wittes yclosed ben therinne
> For love of the lady *Anima*, that lif is ynempned.
> Over al in mannes body heo walketh and wandreth,
> Ac in the herte is hir hoom and hir mooste reste. (B.9.53–56)

Anima governs the senses, the body, and especially the heart as the 'lady' of the castle.

The domestic relationships within Kynde's castle enact a reproductive paradigm in which each successive generation builds on the virtue of the one before: 'Doing well' gives birth to 'Doing better', and so on. Kynde is designated 'Fader and formour the first of alle thynges' (B.9.27), so that genealogies broaden out to link together the divine and the earthly. In addition, the relationships between actions in the world ('doing well') and the interior mechanisms of morality ('inwit' and 'anima') are understood via deep familial love.[21] The potential threat to this domestic order comes from a 'proud prykour of Fraunce', a villain into whose description Langland packs several insults: the mounted horseman coming in from a 'foreign' space; the venal pride; and, most subtly but importantly, the penetrative phallus the term 'prykour' suggests. This specific fear of the unwanted penetration of Kynde's castle by an outsider anticipates the more obvious Sir *Penetrans-Domos* at the end of the poem.

But Langland also implies there might be another, more embedded threat to the domestic relationships that organize Kynde's castle. Who and where is Inwit's *first* wife? Does he have another?[22] Inwit's second (perhaps third?) marriage suggests the possibility of various lines of kinship, or at least marriage among various actors. 'Fooles that fauten Inwit, I finde that Holy Chirche | Sholde fynden hem that hem fauteth, and faderlese children', Wit says.

> And widewes that han noght wherwith to wynnen hem hir foode,
> Madde men and maydenes that helplese were –
> Alle thise lakken Inwit, and lore bihoveth. (B.9.67–71)

Holy Church can supplement the kinship deficits for fatherless children, widows, and helpless single women; charity is the process by which such fragmented kinship can be caulked under the auspices of Christian unity. However, despite all these insistences, Anima's structural protection against any 'prikours' is threatened as much by an external menace from France as by the domestic relationships within the castle.

Anima next appears in the poem as a 'sotil thyng' (B.15.12) who resembles not so much a maiden in a castle but an open-mouthed enigma. As Elizabeth Robertson

---

21 Harwood and Smith point out that both the *De anima et ejus ad sui et ad Dei cognitionem et ad verum pietatem institutione libri quatuor* and *Ayenbite of Inwyt* use the metaphor of the *paterfamilias* to describe the nature of inwit; 'Inwit and the Castle of "Caro"', p. 651.

22 For a discussion of multiple marriages in the Middle Ages, see McSheffrey, *Marriage, Sex, and Civic Culture*. For a discussion specifically about widowhood and remarriage in church law, see Brundage, *Law, Sex, and Christian Society*, pp. 539–44.

points out, whereas the Anima we meet in B.9 is 'conventionally gendered' in her domestic role in Kynde's castle, the 'sotil thyng' Will encounters in B.15 'evokes gender characteristics just as it denies them'.[23] James J. Paxson has defined Anima as 'transumptive', arguing that they embody the rhetorical trope in which a chain of metaphors 'jumps over' one of its middle terms.[24] Certainly, the most crucial aspect of this Anima is their decentralized multiplicity, an open personification whose body and names alike resist easy categorization. But such a trans(umptive) identity might not be merely rhetorical or grammatical. Indeed, as Alan of Lille famously argues at the beginning of the *Plaint of Nature*, grammar, bodies, and gendered identities are always entangled; Alan worries that 'improper' grammatical pairs are unnatural and, crucially, frighteningly non-productive.[25] If we read this Anima as trans, grammatically and otherwise, then we can trace their transformation from a domesticated female lover to a 'non-productive' personification.[26]

Given Anima's striking appearance, it is notable that the dreamer tries to figure out who this 'sotil thyng' is by asking about their genealogical lines. Anima reassures the dreamer that they are of Christ's kin, going on at length to explain the multiple names that can indicate the multiple directions that kinship lines can go. As they explain, 'I am Cristes creature, and Cristene in many a place | In Cristes court yknowe wel, and of his kyn a party' (B.15.16–17). Kinship and kind — here collapsed in the term 'kyn' — suggest an overlap between 'natural' bodily forms and familial ties, an overlap Anima overtly fragments and scrambles in their own body. Anima here seems understand that kinship and genealogy might not formulate direct paths or immediately legible bodies, and that their multiplicity, nominative and bodily, stretches the assumptions that attach to both kind and kinship to reach 'many a place'.

Yet when the dreamer next asks what charity is, Anima seems to return to a normative, genealogical understanding of spiritual community. Anima follows Matthew 18.3, telling him that it is 'a childissh thyng'. Rebecca Davis argues that

---

23 Robertson, 'Souls that Matter', p. 166.

24 Paxson argues that Anima can be read as 'a rebus of Freud's *vagina dentata* — *sans dentis*', so Anima becomes a 'transumptive vagina' insofar as they 'become' a *vagina dentata* by virtue of the allegorical demands of personification. In other words, rather than articulate the chain of metaphors by which Anima 'becomes' a *vagina dentata*, personification permits Anima to immediately embody it without tracking how they got there. Paxson, 'Queering *Piers Plowman*', pp. 25–26.

25 'The witchcraft of Venus turns him into a hermaphrodite. He is subject and predicate: one and the same term is given a double application. Man here extends too far the laws of grammar. Becoming a barbarian in grammar, he disclaims the manhood given him by nature'; Alan of Lille, *The Plaint of Nature*, trans. by Sheridan, p. 68 n. 12. See Schibanoff's brilliant discussion of Alan's oxymoronic worry: grammatical *vititum* (vice) is actually quite productive, even if what it produces is monstrous or non-normative ('Sodomy's Mark', pp. 30–31). See also Rollo, 'Nature's Pharmaceuticals'; and Guynn, *Allegory and Sexual Ethics*, pp. 93–135.

26 Breen argues that Anima reveals the limits of personification allegory and the limits of linguistic expression. Notably, those limits expose the normative structures of both, as she explains: 'Personification allegory generally makes abstract nouns easier to grasp by assigning them human bodies, along with mothers, fathers, spouses, children, and wardrobes that situate them within a social and conceptual sphere. Anima, in contrast, visibly resists physical description'; 'Langland's Literary Syntax', p. 96.

the 'distinctive liberality' that attaches to children here becomes a salvific promise: 'Like an observant, impressionable child, Charity takes cues for behavior from the people near him and conforms to the affective ambiance of his surroundings'.[27] Such responsiveness is presented as compassionate generosity, the sort that formulates a community based on mutual recognition and love. But there might be a flip side to compassion, as Edelman reminds us:

> What future could one build upon their unforgiving slopes when communal relations, collective identities, the very realm of the social itself all seem to hang on compassion's logic — though that logic, in turn, as Kant insists, may hang on the formal abstraction of compassion's tender touch until it becomes the vise-like rip of duty's iron fist. That fist may then curl back inside compassion's velvet glove, but only the better to pack the punch that, even when stopping us dead in our tracks, always stops us in the name of 'love'.[28]

How is the love that drives charitable compassion defined? What does that love look like? Edelman argues that the heteronormative constraints on political futures renders even compassionate love reliant on a fantasy of childishness that marginalizes non-reproductive relations. Langland's childish Charity seems to suggest affective bonds that are similarly exclusive. In other words, the idealization of charity as childish innocence, without guile or agenda, requires a troubling underside that suggests charity works only in a world in which childhood — and by extension, reproductivity — shapes communal bonds. And yet coming from Anima, such childishness might be extracted from the reproductivity trap. Perhaps childishness could be trans like Anima, a multiplicitous term that signifies differently for different people and in different institutions. Indeed, as we shall see, when Need emerges later in the poem to remind the dreamer of the urgency of compassion and charity, a new, non-reproductive future starts to take shape.

By this point in the B text, Anima has repeatedly explained to the dreamer what charity is and how it works, but the dreamer still presses Anima for further definition. In the next passus, B.16, Anima tries to explain charity using a complex metaphor of a tree. Here, the heteronormative demands embedded in a childish Charity emerge, as the three prongs of the tree (mercy, the trunk; faithful words, the leaves; true speech and kindness, the blossoms) are likened to the Trinity, which in turn is likened to marriage. The metaphor is, as several scholars have noted, difficult and 'thick', perhaps even not fully cooked.[29] However, although the B text certainly offers a more strained metaphor, perhaps we need not dismiss it as merely confusing or unfinished. Rather, we might embrace its confusion as a poetic and theological gesture, one that tries to access the queerness in these normative, 'straight' forms of sanctity and proper devotion. In other words, perhaps the B text's awkwardness reveals something about the limitations of its normative structures or Langland's anxieties about them.

---

27 Davis, 'Childish Things', p. 458.
28 Edelman, *No Future*, pp. 67–68.
29 See, for example, Steiner, *Reading 'Piers Plowman'*, p. 173; and Tavormina, 'Bothe Two Ben Gode'.

Once Anima mentions that Piers tends the tree, the dreamer swoons into an inner dream, in which he sees Piers show the tree Anima had described. In this inner dream, Piers first tells the dreamer about the fruit that hangs from the tree:

Matrimoyne I may nyme, a moist fruyte withalle.
Thanne Continence is neer the crop as kaylewey bastard.
Thanne bereth the crop kynde fruyt and clennest of alle –
Maidenhode, aungeles peeris, and rathest wole be ripe
And swete withouten swellyng — sour worth it nevere. (B.16.68–72)

Given earlier emphases on reproductive models of salvation, it is perhaps a bit surprising that Langland elevates virginity over matrimony here. More surprising is the structural position of a grafted pear ('kayleywey bastard') as a linchpin between the two, interrupting any smooth conceptual line between marriage and virginity.[30]

After Piers shows the dreamer the Tree of Charity and describes how Jesus was betrayed there, the dreamer awakens from his inner dream and, wiping his eyes, looks around for Piers. As he searches, he comes across a grey-haired figure, whom the poem calls Abraham but who introduces himself to the dreamer as Faith. In answer to the dreamer's questions about who he is and what he is doing there, Abraham/Faith tells the dreamer that he is searching for God the Father, the Son, and the Holy Ghost, which then prompts Abraham/Faith to explain the generative processes that formulate these divine relationships. Abraham/Faith tells the dreamer that God sent his son to be an earthly servant until 'issue were spronge', which he clarifies to mean 'children of charite, and Holi Chirche the moder. | Patriarkes and prophetes and apostels were the children' (B.16.196–98). Here, not only is *corpus mysticum* actualized as familial and generational, now the childishness of Charity is embodied in the institutional roles of prophets and apostles. The origins of the Church are to be understood via reproductive futurity, tracking back to God the Father through the apostle-children and Holy Church-mother. Thus 'is mankynde or manhede of matrimoyne yspronge, | And bitokeneth the Trinite and trewe bileve' (B.16.209–10). Moreover, 'Ne matrimoyne withouten muliere is noght muche to preise', Faith says. 'Thus in thre persones is parfitliche pure manhede – | That is, man and his make and mulliere hir children' (B.16.219–21). Although the metaphor of the Trinity-as-marriage would have been familiar from Augustine's *De Trinitate*, Langland's version emphasizes at length a reproductive model of the trinitarian divine.[31] By the end of the explanation, 'matrimony' comes specifically to signal producing children and reproducing that family structure through performing affectively childish acts of charity.

---

30 Discourses around virginity vary widely; it is both a central feature of heteronormative discourse and offers a potentially queer, non-reproductive mode of spiritual futurity. Here, Langland's 'bastard pear' subtly brings to the surface the queer potentiality of virginity — and, by extension, perhaps of marriage, too. See Gaunt, 'Straight Minds, "Queer" Wishes'; and Bly, *Queer Virgins*.

31 Galloway, 'Intellectual Pregnancy', p. 118, argues that Langland's repeated images of reproduction, including this one, 'emphatically place the procreative laity at the center of the poem's social ideals'.

As M. Teresa Tavormina points out, Langland radically revises his explanation of the Trinity in the C text:

> And as thre persones palpable is puyrlich bote o mankynde,
> The which is man and his make and moilere here issue,
> So is god godes sone, in thre persones the trinite.
> In matrimonie aren thre and of o man cam alle thre
> And to godhede goth thre, and o god is all thre. (C.18.234–38)[32]

By simplifying the metaphor in the C text, this passage performs the same work as the C.5 autobiographical passage: to assert, clearly, that the foundational ground for Christian community and its future is marriage and reproduction. In contrast, the meandering explanation in B awkwardly and confusingly tries to think through the relationship between marriage and virginity, somehow including bastardy in that paradigm. But as a twisty, more convoluted passage, the B explanation challenges any simple ideal that might assert normative models of political and spiritual community. The scrambled lineage marked as 'bastardy', here operating along the same continuum as virginity and marriage, offers a curved, wandering, not-always-obvious path toward salvation, one we might call queer.

Need and Impotence in the Final Passus

By the time the poem amps up the speed of action in the final passus, it has collected a number of complications and twists in its genealogical metaphors and images. Those complications erupt forcefully in the final passus, culminating in the attack on the Barn of Unity. At the beginning of passus B.20, the dreamer awakens, hungry and 'hevy-chered' (B.20.2), and he is accosted by Need. Need is the personification of bodily requirements, and as such he makes the dreamer worry about the ethics of poverty, begging, and compassionate, charitable response to others. Need is, at first, depicted as 'straight', insofar as he operates as a direct line between body and its material needs. This is why the dreamer explains that although 'Nede ne hath no lawe', he nonetheless always supports the needy 'anonrighte', a term that is temporal (meaning 'immediately') but also directional, indicating that Need links body and survival without detours into Conscience or cardinal virtues.[33] But, as Louise O. Fradenburg brilliantly maps out, Need is 'impossible to stabilize', in that he also connects bodily needs to more tortuous questions about desire and enjoyment.[34] Fradenburg explains that although 'need' is associated with necessity whereas desire is associated with superfluity, charity muddies such a distinction, in that it works

32 Tavormina, '"Bothe Two Ben Gode"', pp. 320–21. Elsewhere, Tavormina argues that the revisions in the C text demonstrate a reinvigorated commitment to marital and familial (what I have been calling 'reproductive') forms of spiritual community; see *Kindly Similitude*, pp. 140–47.

33 Adams, 'The Nature of Need', pp. 273–301. For a discussion the Church and the cardinal virtues in Langland, see Aers, 'Langland on the Church'.

34 Fradenburg, 'Needful Things', p. 54.

according to the 'good' superfluity, balancing the material excesses of one with the bodily needs of another. In such a system, 'need can slide very easily into excess, precisely because one cannot be thought — or demarcated — without the other'.[35]

By putting charity back on the table for investigation, Need's appearance reasserts the centrality of the child in Langland's exploration of desire, truth, and spiritual community, albeit in a roundabout way. Langland's 'childish' Charity suggests that any blurring between need and desire can be understood in the ways children sometimes view their own desires as needs, demanding toys or entertainment or candy as though they were bodily requirements. And when Need appears at the beginning of passus 20, he chastises the dreamer as though he were a whiny child, suggesting that the dreamer's search for truth has all along been a product of superfluous desire, not material or even spiritual need. Calling him a 'faitour', Need implies that the dreamer's worry over his lack of spiritual knowledge is overblown, particularly in the face of those with real, immediate needs.

When the dreamer falls back asleep, the body and its frailties take on a central role to challenge any residual assumed necessity of reproduction for a salvific future. The dreamer sees Antichrist 'in mannes forme' come to chop away Truth's trees and plant Guile everywhere. Antichrist draws friars, nuns, and kings into his orbit of hypocrisy and lies, so Conscience calls upon the rest — the 'fooles' — to shelter inside Unity, which he now names explicitly as 'Holy Church' (B.20.74–75). Meanwhile, Kynde emerges from the cosmos to dispense

> feveres and fluxes,
> Coughes and cardiacles, crampes and toothaches,
> Rewmes and radegundes and roynouse scalles,
> Biles and bocches and brennynge agues
> Frenesies and foule yveles' throughout the commons. (B.20.81–4a)

This passus thus moves from Need to the Barn of Unity through sickly bodies to express the frightening vulnerability of ecclesiological community but also to promise that healing can happen, in body and in soul.

The specific body upon which this passus centres is Elde, who assaults the dreamer: flying over his head so aggressively that he makes him 'balled before and bare on the croune'; cuffing him on the ear to deafen him; giving him gout; and knocking out his teeth. Worst of all, Elde renders the dreamer impotent, thus affecting both him and his wife:

> And of the wo that I was inne my wif had ruthe,
> And wisshed wel witterly that I were in hevene.
> For the lyme that she loved me fore, and leef was to feele —
> On nyghtes, namely, whan we naked weere,
> I ne myghte in no manere maken it at hir wille,
> So Elde and heo it hadden forbeten. (B.20.193–98)

---

35   Fradenburg, 'Needful Things', p. 50.

As Paxson points out, the last line indicates a bodily depletion, insofar as the dreamer's penis has either been beaten into submission by his wife or enfeebled by age. In either case, the focus is the way Will's will — metonymically encapsulated by his erectile dysfunction — is weakened and unsatisfactory, unable to motivate his uncooperative body to have sex with his wife.[36]

Crucially, earlier in the poem, the verb 'forbeten' signals how Christ will rehabilitate all who suffer death's universal destruction:

> Deth seith he shal fordo and adoun brynge
> Al that lyveth or loketh in londe or in watre.
> Lif seith that he lieth, and leieth his lif to wedde
> That, for al that Deeth kan do, withinne thre daies to walke
> And fecche fro the fende Piers fruyte the Plowman,
> And legge it ther hym liketh, and Lucifer bynde,
> And forbete and adouen brynge bale-deth for evere:
> O Mors, mors tua ero, ero morsus! (B.18.29–35a)[37]

Here, Christ is the triumphant warrior, strong enough to escape death's destruction as well as redeem Piers the Plowman. The verb 'forbete' is part of a series of operations around preventing and punishing Death's unrelenting force (the anaphora 'And' working as a formal signal to indicate that series). Life's promise to 'forbete' Death then moves the passus to its Crucifixion scene, with Christ's body as its soteriological focus.

Not surprisingly, Christ is the ultimate male embodiment of proper devotion and a salvific future.[38] Book refers to him as 'Gigas the geaunt' who has ways 'to breke and to bete adoun that ben ayeins Jesus' (B.18.252–53). Passus 18's repeated focus on beating, particularly voiced through Book, recalls the classroom practices for small boys, for whom *disciplina* signalled both the body of knowledge to be learned (that is, an academic discipline) and punitive, corporeal punishment. Together, the two are meant to develop intellectual and moral fortitude:

> In the language of the Church Fathers, the punitive connotation of *disciplina* is associated with an educative function corporal punishment as deterrent or correction. Here the term *disciplina* becomes linked with *verberare*, 'to flog', and with *vapulare*, 'to get a beating'. The term inevitably acquires civil and legal dimensions: physical punishment by secular authority; the power to inflict punishment; and punitive law itself. Out of its association with flogging and

---

36   Paxson, 'Queering *Piers Plowman*', p. 22.

37   Schmidt reads the verb as *forbiten*, anticipating the *morsus tuus ero* in the next line. But as Burrow and Turville-Petre note in their edition of Bx for the *Piers Plowman Electronic Archive*, 'R's rather odd reading was rejected by other B scribes, who read "forbite" or "for to bete", but it is supported by the P family and three of the X family of C'. Here, I do not want to assert the codicological primacy of either verb, but to point out the hermeneutic possibilities offered by the word *forbete*.

38   Steiner, *Reading 'Piers Plowman'*, pp. 200–01.

beating it also takes on the specialized meaning of flagellation, both in the sense of punishment under law and of self-inflicted scourging.[39]

If we track the term 'forbeten' in passus 18 with an eye toward its redeployment in passus 20, we can see that its associations with schoolboy punishment and learning, as well as with devotional pain and performance, collapse in a way that yokes the 'childishness' of charity with Elde's phallic failure. Notably, the *Elegiae Maximianus*, which formed part of the primer given to young schoolboys, includes memoirs by an old man about his sexual escapades from his younger days.[40] One in particular describes a moment he lost his erection with a Greek woman after she insulted his biceps. Significantly, her anger focuses not on her own lost pleasure but on the social consequences of phallic failure:

> non fleo privatum set generale chaos
> haec genus humanum pecudum volucrumque ferarum
> et quicqid toto spirat in orbe creat
> hac sine diversi nulla est Concordia sexus
> hac sine coniugii gratia summa perit (ll. 110–14)

> > (I mourn a public, not a private, hell,
> > It makes the human race, the herds, the birds, the beasts
> > And everything that breathes throughout the world.
> > Without it there's no union of the different sexes,
> > The highest grace of marriage dies without it.)[41]

Schoolboys learn that erections build worlds and that the 'coming-together' of marriage is crucial to all creation.[42]

At the end of passus 18, the dreamer awakens and calls for his wife and daughter, telling them, 'Ariseth and go reverenceth Goddes resurexioun, | And crepeth to the cros on knees, and kisseth it for a juwel!' (B.18.427–28). Tavormina sees this moment as Langland's return to marital sanctity as a model for spiritual devotion, and Andrew Galloway likewise argues that Will gathers his wife and daughter in recognition of the 'social and epistemological sacralizing of the family and of feminine generativity'.[43] Both miss the erotic dynamics embedded in the scene, however. The command for these women to crawl upon their knees to kiss the Cross offers a key counterpoint for the humiliation suffered by Elde and Will in the final passus. Here, the command is both devotional and sexual, a form of Christological submission that positions these women as performers of heteronormative erotics and power dynamics at the feet of the quintessential male body.

---

39 Copeland, 'The Pardoner's Body', pp. 341–42.
40 Woods and Copeland, 'Classroom and Confession', p. 382.
41 Maximianus, *Elegies*, ed. and trans. by Juster, pp. 70–71.
42 See Hanna, 'School and Scorn', for a discussion of the ways *Piers* links learning with fragile masculinity.
43 Galloway, 'Intellectual Pregnancy', p. 147.

With these contexts in mind, Elde's penile depletion takes on more sedimented meaning, drawing together the figure of the child, Christological erotics, and lost reproductivity. As in the sexual memoirs in the *Elegiae*, Langland's portrait of Elde is designed to instruct readers about the social power and fragility of the phallus as a cornerstone of reproductive futurity. Will's bodily failure is an aggressively heteronormative one: the problem is that Kit, Will's wife, is deprived of pleasure and Will is thus deprived of her love. The family unit is unravelled from the inside out, marital discord stoked not by adultery or temptation but by failure. But, as Jack Halberstam shows us, failure can be rehabilitated as a way to conceptualize paths of desire that skirt the demands of heteronormative kinship. Halberstam understands failure as a way of harnessing and redirecting Edelman's politics of 'no future', in which anti-heteronormativity, understood as non-reproductivity, can find a place in the political imagination. Such harnessing, Halberstam says, can 'offer more creative, more cooperative, more surprising ways of being in the world'.[44] Heteronormative 'failure', in other words, might be reformed into productive queer life, a renewed look at how spiritual community can be accomplished. Thus Daniel F. Pigg reads Langland's Elde as a return to a childish state of potentiality for the dreamer, in which 'Will is learning how to learn in new ways, and we too as readers of the poem are "learning" not to read the ending as a harbinger of imminent destruction, but as the venue for new experiences, the opening of a new discourse'.[45]

The end of *Piers Plowman* anxiously awaits no future, a collapse of the possibility of any good life, as False and Guile run rampant and force Conscience and Contrition to cower. Indeed, the disappearance of Will's daughter — particularly after her mention in passus 18 — highlights the shift from reproductive futurity to something more uncertain. On its surface, Will's anticipated phallic failure registers the precarity of his heteronormative kinship structure — which is to say, the precarity of his status as masculine authority over two women, his wife and daughter. In doing so, it seems to assert the normativity of 'straight' gendered and familial models for social and devotional sanctity: as his masculinity fails, so too does the social fabric of those who just want to 'do well'. But perhaps this 'failure' is a kind of queer opportunity, a rerouting of a salvific path that can become more surprising and more capacious.

We might turn to a more well-studied moment of penile impotence for comparison. Like the end of *Piers*, the end of the *Confessio amantis* turns to the failures of the older male body to express anxiety about phallic futurity, with Amans worrying that despite his best intentions and ardent desires, his wrinkling, aging body will thwart his ability to fulfil his lusty duties.[46] Venus's response is terribly dismissive: 'Er thou make any suche assaies | to love and faile upon the fet', she warns Amans, 'Betre is to make a beau retreat' (8.2414–16). And then she really puts the nail in his coffin. She tells him that it is not really worth the effort, 'Whan that thou art not sufficant | To holde love his covenant' (8.2419–20). In other words, Amans's phallic insufficiency,

---

44 Halberstam, *Queer Art of Failure*, p. 2.
45 Pigg, 'Old Age, Narrative Form, and Epistemology', p. 396.
46 See Carlson, 'Gower's Amans', pp. 67–80; and Rayner, '"How love and I togedre met"', pp. 69–85.

what Venus has already named as his failure, annuls his ability to practice the art of love as a form of political community. Venus thus locates communal love — that is, ennobling love, secular and sacred — in the erect penis, and as such, marginalizes Amans from the institutional communities that draw upon fantasies of love as their affective foundation. Amans's only choice is a 'beau retreat', a return along the same path that is only 'beautiful' or 'excellent' in its assertion of normative, phallic masculinity as structural principle.

But Langland seems to offer a different path. Distraught at having aged out of his marital and social affiliations, he begs Kynde for help, asking the Langlandian question, 'What craft be best to lerne?' (B.20.207). Learn to love, Kynde tells him, and forget everything else. In itself, Kynde's advice is not terribly notable. Throughout *Piers*, Langland advocates for love as a model of divine truth and devotional practice alike; both *kynde* and love are produced and sustained by the actions of those who are dedicated to both.[47] But here, sandwiched between Elde's impotence and the Barn of Unity's destruction, and with Gower's aged Amans in mind, this turn to love invites questions about the ways affect, desire, and communal inclusion encircle one another. For Langland, it is not a straight path from desire to love to unity, but a curved one, in which love can reroute the failure of impotence rather than suffer for it.

Whereas Gower puts male impotence at the centre of his thinking about the affective basis of political community, for Langland it is an ecclesiological question. The dreamer worries specifically that learning to love will not, in fact, support his material needs for food and clothing, but Kynde explains that there is another kind of love, one that exceeds the body and thus counterintuitively cares for the body: 'And thow love lelly, lakke shal the nevere | Weede ne wordly mete, whil thi lif lasteth' (B.20.210–11). Although she sends him on to the Barn of Unity, the dreamer instead roams for a bit before finding his way to the Barn. What the dreamer actually says is that he 'comsed to rowme' (B.20.212), which seems a strange claim for someone who has been roaming about for thousands of lines by now. Obviously, on the most literal level, Will means that he will start moving in this particular dream. But this roaming is different than Amans's 'beau retreat'. This is not a return, but a new beginning — a vagrant, wandering model of Unity rather than a straight path.

Conclusion: Queer Vagrancy in the Barn of Unity

When the dreamer finally comes to the Barn of Unity, he finds a chaotic scene, in which Conscience is trying to protect the Barn. Need is back, advising Conscience to forget the false friars clamouring to enter the Barn. Conscience, surprisingly, 'comsed for to laugh', gallantly inviting them in (B.20.242). Conscience's welcoming of the friars is arguably expected, but his laughter, perhaps, is not. R. James Goldstein has tracked the various moments of laughter in the poem to demonstrate that Langland specifically and repeatedly associates laughter both with complex theological ideas and

---

47   Davis, *'Piers Plowman' and the Books of Nature*, p. 18.

with childlike response.[48] Conscience's laughter here tries to harness the principles of childish charity to shape the friars' entrance into the Barn as an act of communal support and love. Moreover, in using the verb 'comsed' here — just like the dreamer 'comsed' to roam — Langland suggests that Conscience's laughter inaugurates a new beginning, not unlike the dreamer's 'new' wandering, and both suggest possibility, play, even enjoyment.

But that enjoyment does not last long. Envy overhears Conscience and gives friars scholarships to learn philosophy while Coveytise and Unkyndenesse attack Conscience. Conscience retreats into the Barn, putting Peace at the gates. Although those huddling within the Barn are under assault, they remain unified in their faith and their steadfast resistance to those attempting to destroy it. This is a revised picture of Wit's castle from B.9; whereas that building housed and protected domestic relationships in the service of spiritual sanctity, this building collects a diverse group unified by affect (fear) and purpose (safety). As a structure of united purpose and mutual feeling, the Barn of Unity offers with what J. Patrick Hornbeck recognizes as a communitarian ecclesiology, which formulates Church membership as anyone who fulfils the requirements of *redde quod debes*. And judging by the numbers of people stuffed into the Barn, it seems that Langland understands ecclesiological accommodation capaciously. Such a communitarian ethos, Hornbeck insists, is based in optimism.[49]

But as Lauren Berlant reminds us, optimism can be cruel. She explains, 'Where cruel optimism operates, the very vitalizing or animating potency of an object/scene of desire contributes to the attrition of the very thriving that is supposed to be made possible in the work of attachment in the first place'.[50] In other words, we cling to optimistic fantasies as a way to manage anxiety, precarity, the worry of an uncertain future. We find institutions that promise a 'good life' and attach ourselves to those institutions. But those optimistic fantasies do not, in fact, accommodate those who are not already expected by them, and so they promise a universal good life that is not universally available. The institutional object of cruel optimism is thus always both enabling and disabling, a fantasy of political attachments and participations that ostensibly erases the hierarchies and marginalizations by which it continues to function. Conscience's laughter animates the cruel optimism of communal ecclesiology, expressing a kind of future-oriented hope that cannot but remain unfulfilled.

And now we find ourselves back with Sir *Penetrans-Domos*. He emerges as the last, desperate hope for the 'fooles' within the Barn to find a way to return to the fantasy of functional ecclesiology and soteriology, one based in contrition and confession, good intentions and faithful devotion. But Sir Penetrans-Domos penetrates the Barn in a way that Amans and the aging Will never could, and in doing so, he destroys the Barn of Unity, leaving its frightened and sick inhabitants to scatter. However, even though he

---

48 Goldstein, 'Laughter in *Piers Plowman*', esp. pp. 40–51. For a broad overview of medieval laughter, see Classen, ed., *Laughter in the Middle Ages*.
49 Hornbeck, 'Barn of Unity', p. 44.
50 Berlant, *Cruel Optimism*, pp. 24–25.

destroys the structure, he does not necessarily destroy the ecclesiological community gathered within. Rather, he inaugurates the possibility of a queer ecclesiology, one that is based not on architectural structure or institutional recognizability, but in wandering. Thus, when Conscience announces that he will become a pilgrim and 'walken as wyde as the al the wordle lasteth', we can resist reading it as a desperate or angry response to a destroyed world gone mad. Rather, it might be cruelly optimistic, a hopeful turn toward the unknown, the curved, the queer, even as it recognizes the ways failure might subtend those hopes.

Works Cited

Primary Sources

Alan of Lille, *The Plaint of Nature*, trans. by James J. Sheridan (Toronto: Pontifical Institute of Mediaeval Studies, 1980)
Gower, John, *Confessio amantis*, ed. by Russell A. Peck, 2nd edn, 3 vols (Kalamazoo: Medieval Institute, 2006-13)
Langland, William, *Piers Plowman: An Edition of the C Text*, ed. by Derek Pearsall (Exeter: University of Exeter Press, 1994)
——, *The Vision of Piers Plowman: A Critical Edition of the B Text*, ed. by A. V. C. Schmidt, 2nd edn (London: Everyman, 1995)
——, *The Piers Plowman Electronic Archive*, IX: *The B-Version Archetype*, ed. by John Burrow and Thorlac Turville-Petre (Chapel Hill: University of North Carolina Press, 2018), and online at <http://piers.chass.ncsu.edu/texts/Bx> [accessed 1 July 2020]
Maximianus, *The Elegies of Maximianus*, ed. and trans. by A. M. Juster (Philadelphia: University of Pennsylvania Press, 2018)

Secondary Sources

Adams, Robert, 'The Nature of Need in *Piers Plowman* XX', *Traditio*, 34 (1978), 273-301
——, *Langland and the Rokele Family: The Gentry Background to 'Piers Plowman'* (Dublin: Four Courts, 2013)
——, 'The Rokeles: An Index for a "Langland" Family History', in *The Cambridge Companion to 'Piers Plowman'*, ed. by Andrew Galloway and Andrew Cole (Cambridge: Cambridge University Press, 2014), pp. 85–96
Aers, David, 'Langland on the Church and the End of the Cardinal Virtues', *Journal of Medieval and Early Modern Studies*, 42 (2012), 59–81
Ahmed, Sara, *The Promise of Happiness* (Durham, NC: Duke University Press, 2010)
Barney, Stephen A., *The Penn Commentary on 'Piers Plowman': C Passus 2–22; B Passus 18–20*, V (Philadelphia: University of Pennsylvania Press, 2006)
Berlant, Lauren, *Cruel Optimism* (Durham, NC: Duke University Press, 2011)
Berlant, Lauren, and Michael Warner, 'Sex in Public', *Critical Inquiry*, 24 (1998), 547–66
Bly, Mary, *Queer Virgins and Virgin Queans on the Early Modern Stage* (Oxford: Oxford University Press, 2000)

Breen, Katharine, 'Langland's Literary Syntax, Or Anima as an Alternative to Latin Grammar', in *Answerable Style: The Idea of the Literary in Medieval England*, ed. by Frank Grady and Andrew Galloway (Columbus: Ohio State University Press, 2013), pp. 95–120

Brundage, James A., *Love, Sex, and Christian Society in Medieval Europe* (Chicago: University of Chicago Press, 1990)

Burgwinkle, William, *Sodomy, Masculinity, and Law in Medieval Literature: France and England, 1050–1230* (Cambridge: Cambridge University Press, 2004)

Carlson, David Richard, 'Gower's Amans and the Curricular Maximianus', *Studia philologia*, 89 (2017), 67–80

Classen, Albrecht, ed., *Laughter in the Middle Ages and Early Modern Times: Epistemology of a Fundamental Human Behavior, its Meaning, and Consequences* (Berlin: de Gruyter, 2010)

Copeland, Rita, 'The Pardoner's Body and the Disciplining of Rhetoric', in *Critical Insights: The Canterbury Tales*, ed. by Jack Lynch (Pasadena: Salem, 2011), pp. 337–59

Davis, Rebecca, 'Childish Things: Charity and the Liberal Arts', *postmedieval*, 6 (2015), 457–66

——, *'Piers Plowman' and the Books of Nature* (Oxford: Oxford University Press, 2016)

Davlin, Mary Clemente, *The Place of God in 'Piers Plowman' and Medieval Art* (Aldershot: Ashgate, 2001)

——, 'Genealogical Terms in *Piers Plowman*', *Yearbook of Langland Studies*, 26 (2012), 111–32

Edelman, Lee, *No Future: Queer Theory and the Death Drive* (Durham, N.C.: Duke University Press, 2004)

Fradenburg, Louise O., 'Needful Things', in *Medieval Crime and Social Control*, ed. by Barbara Hanawalt and David Wallace (Minneapolis: University of Minnesota Press, 1999), pp. 49–69

Galloway, Andrew, 'Intellectual Pregnancy, Metaphysical Pregnancy, and the Social Doctrine of the Trinity in *Piers Plowman*', *Yearbook of Langland Studies*, 12 (1998), 117–52

——, 'Parallel Lives: William Rokele and the Satirical Literacies of *Piers Plowman*', *Studies in the Age of Chaucer*, 40 (2018), 43–111

Gaunt, Simon, 'Straight Minds and "Queer" Wishes in Old French Hagiography: *La Vie de Sainte Euphrosine*', *GLQ: A Journal of Gay and Lesbian Studies*, 1 (1995), 439–57

Goldstein, R. James, '*Ve Vobis qui Ridetis* (Lk. 6.25): Laughter in *Piers Plowman*', *Yearbook of Langland Studies*, 29 (2015), 25–60

Green, Richard Firth, *A Crisis of Truth: Literature and Law in Ricardian England* (Philadelphia: University of Pennsylvania Press, 1999)

Guynn, Noah D., *Allegory and Sexual Ethics in the High Middle Ages* (New York: Palgrave Macmillan, 2007)

Halberstam, Jack, *The Queer Art of Failure* (Durham, NC: Duke University Press, 2011)

Hanna, Ralph, 'School and Scorn: Gender in *Piers Plowman*', *New Medieval Literatures*, 3 (1999), 213–27

Harwood, Britton J., and Ruth F. Smith, 'Inwit and the Castle of "Caro" in *Piers Plowman*', *Neuphilologische Mitteilungen*, 71 (1970), 648–54

Hornbeck II, J. Patrick, 'Barn of Unity or the Devil's Church? Salvation and Ecclesiology in Langland and the Wycliffites', in *Medieval Poetics and Social Practice: Responding to the Work of Penn R. Szittya*, ed. by Seeta Chaganti (New York: Fordham University Press, 2012), pp. 273–301

Johnston, Michael, 'William Langland and John Ball', *Yearbook of Langland Studies*, 30 (2016), 29–74

Justice, Steven, *Writing and Rebellion: England in 1381* (Berkeley: University of California Press, 1994)

Kennedy, Kathleen, *Meed, Maintenance, and Marriage* (New York: Palgrave, 2009)

Lochrie, Karma, 'Presidential Improprieties and Medieval Categories: The Absurdity of Heterosexuality', in *Queering the Middle Ages*, ed. by Glenn Burger and Steven F. Kruger (Minnesota: University of Minnesota Press, 2001), pp. 87–96

——, *Heterosyncrasies: Female Sexuality When Normal Wasn't* (Minneapolis: University of Minnesota Press, 2005)

——, *Nowhere in the Middle Ages* (Philadelphia: University of Pennsylvania Press, 2016)

McSheffrey, Shannon, *Marriage, Sex, and Civic Culture in Late Medieval London* (Philadelphia: University of Pennsylvania, 2006)

Muñoz, José Esteban, *Cruising Utopia: The Then and There of Queer Futurity* (New York: New York University Press, 2009)

Paxson, James J., 'Gender Personified, Personification Gendered, and the Body Figuralized in *Piers Plowman*', *Yearbook of Langland Studies*, 12 (1998), 65–96

——, 'Queering *Piers Plowman*: The Copula(tion)s of Figures in Medieval Allegory', *Rhetoric Society Quarterly*, 29.3 (1999), 21–29

Pigg, Daniel F., 'Old Age, Narrative Form, and Epistemology in Langland's "*Piers Plowman*": The Possibility of Learning', in *Old Age in the Middle Ages and the Renaissance*, ed. by Albrecht Cassen (Berlin: de Gruyter, 2007), pp. 393–406

Raskolnikov, Masha, 'Promising the Female, Delivering the Male', *Yearbook of Langland Studies*, 19 (2005), 81–105

——, *Body against Soul: Gender and 'Sowlehele' in Middle English Allegory* (Columbus: Ohio State University Press, 2009)

Rayner, Samantha J., '"How love and I togedre met": Gower, Amans, and the Lessons of Venus in the *Confessio amantis*', in *Sexual Culture in the Literature of Medieval Britain*, ed. by Amanda Hopkins, Robert Allen Rouse, and Cory James Rushton (Cambridge: Brewer, 2014), pp. 69–85

Robertson, Elizabeth, 'Souls that Matter: The Gendering of the Soul in *Piers Plowman*', in *Mindful Spirit in Late Medieval Literature: Essays in Honor of Elizabeth D. Kirk*, ed. by Bonnie Wheeler (New York: Palgrave, 2006), pp. 167–86

Rogers, Will, and Christopher Michael Roman, eds, *Medieval Queer Futurity: Essays for the Future of a Queer Medieval Studies* (Kalamazoo: Medieval Institute, 2021)

Rollo, David, 'Nature's Pharmaceuticals: Sanctioned Desires in Alain de Lille's *De planctu naturae*', *Exemplaria*, 25 (2013), 152–72

Scase, Wendy, '*Piers Plowman' and the New Anticlericalism* (Cambridge: Cambridge University Press, 1989)

Schibanoff, Susan, 'Sodomy's Mark: Alan of Lille, Jean de Meun, and the Medieval Theory of Authorship', in *Queering the Middle Ages*, ed. by Glenn Burger and Steven F. Kruger (Minnesota: University of Minnesota Press, 2001), pp. 28–56

Simpson, James, 'Religious Forms and Institutions in *Piers Plowman*', in *The Cambridge Companion to 'Piers Plowman'*, ed. by Andrew Galloway and Andrew Cole (Cambridge: Cambridge University Press, 2014), pp. 97–114

Smith, D. Vance, *The Book of the Incipit: Beginnings in the Fourteenth Century* (Minneapolis: University of Minnesota Press, 2001)

——, 'Negative Langland', *Yearbook of Langland Studies*, 23 (2009), 33–60

Snediker, Michael D., *Queer Optimism: Lyric Personhood and Other Felicitous Persuasions* (Minneapolis: University of Minnesota Press, 2009)

Steiner, Emily, '*Piers Plowman* and Institutional Poetry', *Études anglaises*, 66 (2013), 297–310

——, *Reading 'Piers Plowman'* (Cambridge: Cambridge University Press, 2013)

Szittya, Penn R., *The Antifraternal Tradition in Medieval Literature* (Princeton: Princeton University Press, 1986)

Tavormina, M. Teresa, '"Bothe Two Ben Gode": Marriage and Virginity in *Piers Plowman*', *Journal of English and Germanic Philology*, 81 (1982), 320–30

——, *Kindly Similitude: Marriage and Family in 'Piers Plowman'* (Woodbridge: Boydell and Brewer, 1995)

Wallace, David, *Chaucerian Polity: Absolutist Lineages and Associational Forms in England and Italy* (Stanford: Stanford University Press, 1997)

Watson, Sarah Wilma, 'Grace Holds the "Clicket" to the Heavenly "Wiket": *Piers Plowman*, the *Roman de la Rose*, and the Poetics of Penetration', *Yearbook of Langland Studies*, 30 (2016), 207–26

Woods, Marjorie Curry, and Rita Copeland, 'Classroom and Confession', in *The Cambridge History of Medieval English Literature*, ed. by David Wallace (Cambridge: Cambridge University Press, 1999), 376–406

Zeeman, Nicolette, *'Piers Plowman' and the Medieval Discourse of Desire* (Cambridge: Cambridge University Press, 2006)

WILLIAM RHODES

Personification, Action, and Economic Power in *Piers Plowman*

▼ **KEYWORDS** action, agency, economics, Hawkyn, Hunger, Meed, money, personification, *Piers Plowman*, will

▼ **ABSTRACT** This essay argues that three economically-oriented personifications of *Piers Plowman* — Meed, Hunger, and Hawkyn — form three aspects of an interwoven critique of economic power. These three figures personify respectively the semiotic obscurity of money, the need to eat, and the affective consequences of social hierarchies that invite economic exploitation. Since personification, as a number of recent scholars agree, is a privileged mode for exploring volition and action, *Piers Plowman* exemplifies the ways in which prosopopeia can make visible the determining effects of economic relations on the individual will by, paradoxically, creating fictive agents that enact the constraint or loss of agency in relation to concrete abstractions like money and wages.

As J. M. Bowers notes in an essay on the avoiding of work in *Piers Plowman*, the poem's restless dreamer, Will, 'fails to recognize that the essence of Dowel is *doing*, by working productively and with a sound will, whether that means plowing an English acre or laboring in the Lord's vineyard.'[1] This critique of Will's behaviour, however, depends on the assumption that knowing what one is supposed to do and actually being able to do it are fairly straightforward operations. If, as Bowers contends, sloth is the 'dominant principle of corruption in the Fair Field', then the problem's root lies in 'the free choice of man's will'.[2] But action in *Piers Plowman* is more complicated than that. The poem turns *doing* into a question rather than an imperative, especially when it considers actions in the realm of worldly work, where the differences between 'plowing an English acre' *or* 'laboring in the Lord's vineyard' are not superficial distinctions but fundamental challenges to any individual's agency

---

1 Bowers, '*Piers Plowman*', p. 246.
2 Bowers, '*Piers Plowman*', pp. 239 and 240.

William Rhodes (wrhodes@uiowa.edu) is Assistant Professor of English at the University of Iowa

The Yearbook of Langland Studies, 34 (2020), 117–135   BREPOLS ❧ PUBLISHERS   10.1484/J.YLS.5.121089

to transcend sinful entanglements while working for a living. The fact that most people in late medieval England could not devote themselves to elite religious pursuits, but had to earn a living in occupations that were increasingly defined by wage relations and mercantile networks, meant that the economic context in which anyone sought salvation is of paramount importance in *Piers Plowman*.

In fact, 'economic context' is not strong enough for the poem's treatment of the intimate, compelling forces and relations that determine — or potentially prevent — any action. In this, *Piers Plowman* explores an ever-present tension between doing and making (or *praxis* and *poesis*), which the recent work of Richard Halpern has described as a contradiction between individual and collective forms of agency, where questions of action are inseparably bound up with economic processes of production and exchange.[3] The quest for salvation by means of spiritually beneficial acts frequently finds itself threatened in *Piers Plowman* by economic relations that obscure or block the right path. The most economically-oriented personifications in the B text of the poem — Meed, Hunger, and Hawkyn — give a figural shape to the otherwise dispersed and insensible, but still materially effective, collective processes of production and exchange that constrain people's wills. These figures make visible a form of economic power that works not via an absolutely dominant individual, but through a mixture of affective, economic, ecological, and political compulsions that are activated by the brute fact of inequality. Meed, Hunger, and Hawkyn entangle action with production at a particular late medieval conjuncture and present the poem's readers with a means to grasp the will as both a personal, causal force and a manifestation of the inequities of socioeconomic class. This essay considers how personification's unique approach to the problem of the will allows Langland to enfold the problem of economic agency into *Piers Plowman*'s exploration of the immanent forces that stymie the transcendence of worldly necessities.

Personification, Volition, and 'Real Abstraction'

Understanding the thorny relationships among will, intention, and action is one of the primary affordances of literary personification, as several recent studies have shown vis-à-vis premodern and modern theological, philosophical, and psychological investigations of the nature of the will.[4] According to Andrew Escobedo, personification manifests 'a distinctly premodern intuition about the human will, namely, that the will is both mover and moved, the origin of our actions and the effect of prior determinisms'.[5] This medieval and early modern will was a part of the self, but not fully identified with the self; sometimes it might be governed by an agent's thought

---

3   See Halpern, *Eclipse of Action*.

4   For a survey of premodern ideas of the will in relation to personification in general, see Escobedo, *Volition's Face*, pp. 57–95. See also Zeeman, '*Piers Plowman*'. For an account of the relationship between allegory and modern psychoanalytic theories of agency and compulsion, see Fletcher, *Allegory*, pp. 279–303.

5   Escobedo, *Volition's Face*, p. 4.

and emotions in predictable ways, but at other times it might escape the control of the agent's faculties and execute actions for arbitrary or unpredictable reasons. For Escobedo, prosopopeia is a literary device that captures the intricacy of causation for any action, in which the relationships between self, world, and psychological faculties create ever-changing scenarios for fictional characters to act and be acted upon in turn.

Alongside the concerns of allegorists, the problem of knowing and representing how the will acts in relation to its various affective and environmental determinants was likewise a pressing one for economic ethics in the Middle Ages. Ethical questions about exchange, lending, and wages required consideration of the nature of volition, since an act of exchange or relation of employment had to be free from coercion in order to be just.[6] As the work of Odd Langholm details, these examinations of the nature of volition in economic relations reveal the fundamentally 'mixed' or conditional nature of the individual will when there is uneven access to life-sustaining goods.[7] The will cannot fully be free to choose if the only other alternative might be penury or starvation. Personification, insofar as it is particularly suited for making visible the forces that move the will, can allow us to see the otherwise invisible relations that make up what we now call 'the economy' and that limit the personal will in ways both quotidian and profound. For Langland, personification is a technique that can mediate the individual experience of volitional constraint and the socioeconomic forces that shape the will, an art that illuminates the relationship between self and society. Langlandian personification, according to the introduction to a recent cluster of essays on the topic in this journal, uses names that often join a unique moniker to a general class, like Piers the Plowman or Hawkyn the Active Man, in order to render such a personification 'partly as an individual and partly as a member of a collectivity'.[8] To be partly an individual and partly a member of a collectivity aptly describes the paradoxical status of economic agency, in which an individual might theoretically possess the will to *do* one thing, like renounce worldly commitments, and at the same time be part of a collectivity that demands that individual make a living instead. The collectivity that might make such a demand, however, rarely appears as a visible agent issuing commands, unless we are in the world of *Piers Plowman* and its prosopopoetic concretions of more diffuse or abstract forms of collective power, like money or the conventions of exchange.

Piers Plowman needs personification to give form to things that are materially effective, but do not have a crudely material, sensible appearance. The money economy, for example, is a complex, emergent phenomenon that results from a myriad of processes and relations. It is imperative to make these processes and relations visible in *Piers Plowman* because imagining how individuals relate to the

---

6 For a thorough review of the ethics of the will in medieval economic thought, see Langholm, *Legacy of Scholasticism*. For a summary account of these findings, see Langholm, 'Voluntary Exchange', pp. 44–56.

7 On the roots of the scholastic idea of mixed will in Aristotle's discussions of volition, see Langholm, *Legacy of Scholasticism*, pp. 17–29.

8 Breen, 'Introduction', p. 156.

world in all its complexity might enable readers to know how to do well. This kind of judgement needs figural assistance because the collective nature of economic activity makes individual actions more difficult to analyse ethically. If any action's causes and effects depend upon countless combined actions of other agents in the process of production and exchange, then it is that much harder to know what one ought to do. As Langholm's analysis of economic sins in penitential manuals shows, for example, the criteria for a 'just price' are highly variable depending on the situation, and often rely on some notion of a 'common' or 'ordinary' price for something, determined by an aggregate of transactions.[9] The sphere of political economy, as Halpern reminds us, encompasses the world of aggregates and structures, and it exists in a permanent state of tension with individual action that has troubled writers from Aeschylus to Adam Smith, Karl Marx and Hannah Arendt, who all interrogate in different ways the possibility of meaningful individual action when set against the needs of a collectivity to sustain itself.[10]

Langland's use of personification to confront this inescapable tension bears a telling resemblance to the kind of paradox that the Marxist term 'real abstraction' evokes as it seeks to overcome the simple opposition between the concrete and the abstract. By recognizing that the spheres of production and exchange are materially linked in the process of value creation and its realization as money, the formulation 'real abstraction' hijacks the insensible quality of mere conceptual abstractions in order to apply it to things like labour and value that are simultaneously abstracted and realized within a social process of making, buying, and selling. Concrete labour, for example, is abstracted in its relationship to the value of a commodity, while that value is realized as money in the sphere of circulation.[11] For Marx, this process is simultaneously concrete and abstract, since the concrete act of labour cannot be related to value without the aggregate of so-called abstract or socially necessary labour, and the seeming abstraction of value cannot be thought without the aggregation of concrete productive acts. I've dwelt on this formulation of 'real abstraction' because, in its refusal of the binary opposition between the real and the ideal, it captures how Langland's economic personifications interweave concepts and quantities and moral ideals with feelings and bodies and material infrastructure in order to capture how economic power works on people's wills. In Langland's exploration of economic agency, individual acts of spiritual striving must contend with the real abstractions of an incipient market economy. The episodes of Meed, Hunger, and Hawkyn suggest that the relations that make people do things extend invisibly beyond any concrete, particular act, and each episode's central personifications are attempts to make those relations visible. These personifications are not only a case, as Kathleen Hewett-Smith

9   Langholm, *Merchant in the Confessional*, pp. 245–47.

10 Halpern, *Eclipse of Action*, pp. 11–13.

11 For a definition of Marxian 'real abstraction', see Toscano, 'Open Secret', p. 275: 'these abstractions are not mental categories that ideally precede the concrete totality; they are real abstractions that are truly caught up in the social whole, the social relation'. For overviews of the concept of 'real abstraction' and its elaboration in Marxist theory, see Ngai, 'Visceral Abstractions', pp. 36–45, and La Berge, 'Rules of Abstraction'.

argues of the half-acre scene, of Langland exposing the limits of allegory as a mode of signification that dispenses with historical reality on the way to transcendence, but rather Langland using personification to make visible forces immanent to a late medieval political economy whose combination of corruption, fraud, and force blocks individual flights toward transcendence.[12]

We might say that Langland joins the unending search for an adequate way to represent the impasse of economic agency, with personifications like Meed, Hunger, and Hawkyn prefiguring Marx's axiom: 'Men make their own history, but they do not make it just as they please; they do not make it under circumstances chosen by themselves, but under circumstances directly encountered, given, and transmitted from the past'.[13] These personifications simultaneously consolidate into an imageable form complex and multiplicitous aspects of economic reality 'given and transmitted from the past' while capturing the power these formations have over people's lives as they nevertheless 'make history' in countless daily interactions with the world around them.

A number of recent critics have emphasized different aspects of *Piers Plowman*'s approach to the problem of agency and the demands of economic life. For Mark Miller, the clash between agency and structure defines the poem's repetitive investigation of the mystery of sin, which appears as the inevitable result of the inherent self-division of the Christian subject who is compelled to abide by a seemingly impossible norm.[14] In *Piers Plowman*, as other critics suggest, compulsion is not only a question of inherent sinfulness or deep psychic structures, but of how these human capacities and failures are activated through the machinations of economic power. As Katharine Breen has argued, *Piers Plowman* helps to develop kinds of personifications that serve as 'literary devices and instruments of thought that enable readers to define, manipulate, and evaluate new economic concepts'.[15] As the work of Elizabeth Fowler has shown, the literary construction of social personhood always contends with the fact that any individual's agency is activated and constrained within unequal social, economic, and legal structures.[16] If the will, as Escobedo contends, was understood in premodern sources to be both 'the origin of our actions and the effect of prior determinisms', then *Piers Plowman* always remains attuned to the ways those 'prior determinisms' must include relations of production and exchange that suture the individual experience of sin to the general experience of being at the mercy of economic power.[17] The

---

12 Hewett-Smith, 'Allegory on the Half-Acre', p. 4.
13 Marx, 'Eighteenth Brumaire', p. 329.
14 Miller, 'Sin and Structure', pp. 202, 206, and 219–20.
15 Breen, 'Need for Allegory', p. 187.
16 Fowler, *Literary Character*, p. 132.
17 Escobedo, *Volition's Face*, p. 4. Recent scholarship has shown just how extensively *Piers Plowman* draws from a deep familiarity with the economic, social, and political networks of the London mercantile world, situating the poem in a specific community and its associated technologies of reading, writing, and accounting while also showing *Piers Plowman*'s constant concern with the pressures of communal associations on any individual's economic agency. See Pearsall, 'Langland's London'; Hanna, *London Literature*, pp. 233–304; and Galloway, 'Account Book', pp. 81–92.

characters involved in the episodes of Meed, Hunger, and Hawkyn are, as Nicolette Zeeman says of Will, 'guilty of events that we sense are not fully of [their] own choosing'.[18] These economic personifications deal not just with individual affects and actions, but open toward institutional, 'transindividual' formations that are just as multiplicitous as the psychological forces that make up the self.[19] The following essay takes up in sequence the episodes of Meed, Hunger, and Hawkyn in order to trace how *Piers Plowman* serially examines the tension between individual act and economic power by moving from the epistemological constraints of monetary exchange to the biophysical constraints of the need to eat to the affective constraints of seeking worldly success in rural production and urban exchange.

Meed, Money, and Economic Power

The early episode of Lady Meed seeks to make visible the ways monetary exchange of all kinds can constrain the wills of both giver and recipient, thanks in part to the fundamental ambivalence of money itself as an eraser of concrete particularity that nevertheless has definite material effects in particular contexts of exchange and payment. While J. A. Burrow has cautioned against accepting too easily Meed's identification with money, when a more specific meaning of bribes or improper gifts seems more prevalent,[20] it remains true that she personifies 'the power of money', as John A. Yunck argues.[21] This claim focuses not so much on the physical form of cash, since Meed does not deal in coin alone, but rather the mystery of exchange, in which one thing is made equivalent to another thing through a medium (coins, luxury goods, etc.) that can ideally allow all parties involved to gain, and that therefore exerts a shocking amount of control over how people behave. Lady Meed personifies the process whereby the variegated energies and activities of human beings can be reduced and frozen into the form of moveable wealth, which can then be used in turn to subsume and control the thoughts and wills of even more people. In this sense, seeing Meed as money activates the episode's confrontation with the problem of agency defined as 'an engagement of gears [...] between one person (a principal) and another (the agent)'.[22] Money, as the solvent of particularity, serves as the screen in the Lady Meed episode for anxieties about the impossibility of individual moral agency, because money, in its conventional arbitrariness and ineluctable needfulness, stands for a power, an impersonal force that arises from the momentum of a collectivity, which spurs individuals to do things according to obscure or potentially corrupt causes.

---

18 Zeeman, '*Piers Plowman*', p. 103.
19 The 'transindividual', in Etienne Balibar's reading of Marx, captures the sense in which the human cannot be defined through a static privileging of either the isolated individual or the social whole, but rather in relations among individuals. Balibar, *Philosophy of Marx*, pp. 30–32.
20 Burrow, 'Lady Meed', pp. 113–18.
21 Yunck, *Lineage of Lady Meed*, p. 6.
22 Fowler, *Literary Character*, p. 99.

Whether or not a fully-formed money economy existed or was merely on the rise in Langland's lifetime, the existence of monetary exchange as a widespread practice exerts considerable force over *Piers Plowman*.[23] The poem registers an attempt to create prosopopoetic forms adequate to a materially dynamic and semiotically bewildering world of mercantile exchange. In late medieval London, the growth of a mercantile class spurred thought about the nature of exchange, especially the relationship between the form of money itself and the practices that create its value and the actions that it can make people do in debates about just price, payment for service, wages, and accounting.[24] Meed personifies all of these problems and more. She is an intermediary that means different things to different people, from judges and clerks to friars and food sellers. Meed embodies a logic of exchange that requires the solvent power of the universal equivalent to break down any moral or legal objections to profit making. For example, the narratorial description of Meed's efforts on behalf of brewers, bakers, butchers, and cooks captures the dangerous mingling of the fundamental need for 'lifelode' in the form of food with the motivations of profit that takes the form of money, which in turn becomes investment capital for the acquisition of rents. 'Maires and maceres', we are told, ought 'to kepe the lawes, | To punysshe on pillories and on pynynge stooles | Brewesters and baksters, bochiers and cokes':

> For thise are men on this mold that moost harm wercheth
> To the povere peple that parcelmele buggen.
> For thei poisone the peple pryveliche and ofte,
> Thei richen thorugh regratrie and rentes hem biggen
> With that the povere peple sholde putte in hire wombe.
> For toke thei on trewely, thei timbred nought so heighe,
> Ne boughte none burgages — be ye ful certeyne!
> Ac Mede the mayde the mair heo bisoughte
> Of alle swiche selleris silver to take,
> Or presents withouten pens — as pieces of silver,
> Rynges or oother richesse, the regratiers to mayntene.
> 'For my love', quod that lady, 'love hem echone,
> And suffre hem to selle somdel ayeins reson'. (B.3.76–92)[25]

---

23 Bolton, 'What Is Money?', pp. 1–12, and *Money in the Medieval English Economy*, pp. 18–39, argues that a money economy had emerged in England by the late thirteenth century, although other forms of exchange existed alongside monetary exchange throughout Europe until the early modern period. See also Lavatori, *Language and Money*, pp. 3–13.

24 Smith, '*Piers Plowman*', calls this process of thought about late medieval political economy the 'national noetic' of *Piers Plowman*, in which the poem enacts the process of coming to know economic formations that did not yet have clear discursive manifestations. On wages, see Wood, *Medieval Economic Thought*, pp. 144–47. See also Galloway, 'Account Book', pp. 83–84, on the fundamental epistemological obscurity that inheres in accounting prices for services, and Fowler, *Literary Character*, pp. 122–23, for remarks about the need of 'interpretation and convention' to make exchange work.

25 Quotations of *Piers Plowman* are from *Vision of Piers Plowman*, ed. by Schmidt.

The victuallers sell tainted food at inflated prices in the retail trade, and then buy up properties in town for rent, thereby translating the substance that should fill the bellies of the poor into a source of wealth. This further allows these food producers to enhance their power and prestige by buying the authority of the mayors, which ought to restrain this assault on the basic, physical survival of the population. The amoral acts that allowed these producers to amass such wealth have solidified into the forms of dazzling gleams of silver, rings, and riches that obscure their corrupt origins. The actual labour that goes into making tainted food and the destabilized social relations that result from rent-racking disappear into the form of silver coins, plate, and rings — meed which the mayor can now accept without looking into its origins in corruption and fraud, and which persuades him to 'suffre' these merchants to sell 'ayeins reson'. The verb 'suffre' here captures the passivity that Meed imparts to a figure that should be active in the pursuit of justice, revealing the extent to which she can transfer to others her own ambivalence, which stems from her status as a personification of money, something that is both a tool to be used and a manifestation of a collective social agency that acts upon others.[26]

Within the mercantile world of greedy butchers, bakers, and grocers, Meed's intercessions are clearly corrupt, but amongst the justices at Westminster, she is revealed to be a familiar presence amongst the upper echelons of the state. This signals that the power she represents is less a corruption of the functions of law and government than one of their integral components. Meed embodies the process that makes favourable legal judgements and luxury goods interchangeable when her gifts to the justices at Westminster ensure their continued commitment to Meed's interests:

> Mildely Mede thanne merciede hem alle
> Of hire grete goodnesse, and gaf hem echone
> Coupes of clene gold and coppes of silver,
> Rynges with rubies and richesses manye,
> The leeste man of hire meynee a moton of golde. (B.3.20–24)

Here, Meed does not facilitate corruption and fraud as an intermediary between merchants and political power. Instead, she directly distributes the wealth that maintains the legal apparatus of the state. Meed reveals here her broad significance as the representative of money's ability to traverse the boundary between the economic activities that produce this wealth and the internal wills and dispositions of people who receive money, either from necessity or cupidity. This is the sense in which Meed personifies the power of money. Money renders abstract concepts of value into a concrete form that has real power over individuals who need it, or who want it too much. It translates an invisible thing, 'that social fiction that is value', from the myriad, unequal social relations that produce value into a tangible object.[27] This object can in turn be deployed to further enhance the power of those who have it, albeit in a potentially illusory way, since, as we will see in the conclusion of

26 For an account of patience and agency and their occasionally paradoxical overlaps in Christian thought, see Bugbee, *God's Patients*, pp. ix–xiii, 3–5, and 127–47.

27 Jappe, 'Sohn-Rethel', p. 12.

Conscience's refutation of Meed, both hoarders and recipients of money find their souls endangered. In the figure of Meed, money appears as a reification of past actions motivated by greed, obscuring the processes that created it and confronting those who handle it as a potentially infectious, corrupting agent that robs their agency in turn.

The power of money is a complicated thing, since money is at once a tool to be used and an instrument that uses its user. As Aristotle observes in his discussion of money's unnaturalness, which influenced condemnations of usury and avarice throughout the Middle Ages, money might have been invented in order to allow for the exchange of things not easily transported by substituting a useful and portable thing as a medium of exchange.[28] But once metal money gets stamped into coin, and its function of signifying value supplants its use value in itself as metal, then money as an arbitrary sign system becomes something that can artificially take the place of goods that actually maintain individual and collective life: 'But sometimes, contrariwise, money seems to be empty trash and to exist entirely by convention and not by nature at all, because, when changed by its users, it has no value and is useless for acquiring the necessities, and often someone who is rich in money will be unprovided with the food that is necessary'.[29] Meed captures this contradictory dynamic in which the very qualities that make money useful for exchange — its fungibility, its ease of circulation, its simplifying erasure of the specific qualities of the things for which it stands — are also what makes it dangerous, because it can insinuate itself into any kind of social relationship, even ones that ideally would be outside the realm of monetary exchange, such as the relationship between a human and 'the food that is necessary' to survive.

Money's power in part depends upon the ability to appear as both a natural and benign support for exchange and a conventional, unnatural system that can come between people and a natural good like food. For Aristotle, this creates a problem whereby money can be separated from its realization in the form of a use-value, and its accumulation can become an end in itself, the mere hoarding of exchange-value.[30] The prosopopoetic form of Langland's analysis mirrors the process in which a concrete form stands for an abstract value, but it also inverts it, since the personificational figure presents a face with which humans can interact as a sort of use-value. In each case, however, one face stands for multiple abstract concepts, as a coin or silver plate concretizes an abstract value that has been unmoored from the social relations that produced it. This is why Meed can appear as both culpable and innocent, given that the process she personifies is one in which money simultaneously shields its users from the concrete relationships that give it value and from the concrete effects it has on those to whom it is given as a wage, payment, or gift. This obscuring power is key for Meed's effects, argues Clare Lees, since 'the representation of Meed as both fetishized object of desire ("woman") and pure commodity ("money") conceals and displaces the social relations that produced her'.[31] For Diane Cady, theories of money

28 Hole, *Economic Ethics*, p. 23.
29 Aristotle, *Politics*, trans. by Reeve, 1257b.10–14, p. 14.
30 Aristotle, *Politics*, trans. by Reeve, 1257b.21–40, pp. 14–15.
31 Lees, 'Gender and Exchange', p. 124.

and language in the Middle Ages frequently attempt to resolve their contradictions by projecting onto women the responsibility for the moments when signification and exchange go wrong; that way 'bad practitioners, and not the systems themselves, are assigned responsibilities for their gaps and disruptions'.[32] This gendered dynamic is undoubtedly at work in the Meed episode, but, in Langland's personificational method, the 'bad practitioner' *is* the system. The form of Meed's personification echoes the process whereby the universal equivalent, money, occludes the potentially exploitative relations that give it value and enable its use as a medium of exchange that can overtly or subtly direct people's actions.

Lady Meed, with her strangely active and passive status as a figure who corrupts others while being corrupted in turn by those who seek to use her for advantage, captures an understanding of money that situates the source of its power somewhere in between communal consent, in which money is merely an agreed-upon convention for ease of exchange, and the lure of domination, in which money is a moral danger because it confers 'maistrie' to those who have it over others who need or desire it. In this way, Langland argues that part of money's essence is its mediating status between the individual and the social surround; it is both a feature of the given world that (mis)shapes all human agents, and it is a tool that allows human agents to shape their world. Money, as Lady Meed, is not only a medium of exchange amongst material goods, but a vehicle for some humans to impose their wills on others. Crucially for Langland, this is not just an abuse of wealth in the form of bribes, but also a constitutive feature of all kinds of exchange. As Meed objects in response to Conscience's attacks, in which she is accused of mere bribery, she does more than facilitate corruption; she is there even in seemingly licit and traditional relations of gift, tribute, and wage between different levels of the social hierarchy:

> Emperours and erles and alle manere lordes
> Thorugh yiftes han yomen to yerne and to ryde.
> The Pope and alle prelates presents underfongen
> And medeth men hemselven to mayntene hir lawes,
> Servaunts for hire servyce, we seeth wel the sothe,
> Taken mede of hir maistres, as thei mowe acorde.
> Beggeres for hir biddynge bidden men mede.
> Mynstrales for hir myrthe mede thei aske.
> The Kyng hath mede of his men to make pees in londe.
> Men that kenne clerkes craven of hem mede.
> Preestes that prechen the peple to goode
> Asken mede and massepens and hire mete also.
> Alle kynne crafty men craven mede for hir prentis.
> Marchandise and mede mote nede go togideres:
> No wight, as I wene, withouten Mede may libbe! (B.3.213–27)

---

32 Cady, 'Symbolic Economies', p. 128.

This rhetorically forceful litany of the social relations enabled by Meed puts Conscience on his heels, prompting him to concede Meed's multiplicity before the king: 'Ther are two manere of medes, my lord, by youre leve' (231). There is a good kind, 'mesurable hire' (256), which 'laborers and lowe lewede folk taken of hire maistres' (255), and a bad kind, 'mede mesurelees that maistres desireth' (246). The fact that Langland creates one personification to cover both kinds, rather than, say, staging a prosopopoetic confrontation between Mesurable Hire and Mede Mesurelees, suggests that Langland's project goes beyond a mode of satirical and moralizing personification in which good and bad forms of monetary exchange are sorted and judged. Instead, this episode attends to the relationship between monetary exchange and human action, whether that takes the form of wages or of bribes, not because these are presented as being morally equivalent, but because they both involve a mysterious process whereby people are made to do things out of need or desire for mere stuff that is also more than what it appears to be. Dangerous as it may be, the power of money is an inescapable aspect of the *activa vita*, which includes supposedly licit forms of wages ('mesurable hire') and trade ('permutacion apertly', 258) that Conscience celebrates, as well as the kind of 'mede mesurelees' that allows a kind of mastery that uses the power of money 'to mayntene mysdoers' (247). The ambiguity of personificational fictions, which Meed exemplifies in her multivalent ethical, legal, and political effects, does not exist in some other order of slippery signification than that of monetary exchange, Langland suggests. Rather, they both engage in more or less obscure permutations, subsuming many things under one sign as they mediate between individual and collective existence. For Meed, the fiction of her agency, ambiguously situated between the active distribution of gifts and being passively led to and around Westminster, makes money a partially inscrutable and potentially threatening convention.

As the debate between Conscience and Meed before the King winds down, Conscience gets the last word by chiding Meed's faulty reading of Proverbs and paraphrasing the full verse she had partially cited to the effect that 'thei that yyven yiftes the victorie wynneth' (B.3.334). Conscience provides the conclusion Meed had left off: 'That theigh we wynne worshipe and with mede have victorie, | The soule that the soude taketh by so muche is bounde' (352–53). At the conclusion of this passus, we have a clearer sense of what is at stake in Conscience's fight against Meed's multiple natures. Even though the conclusion of the episode in passus B.4 ends Meed's presence in *Piers Plowman* as the three male figures of King, Conscience, and Reason unite against the corrupt and corrupting Lady Meed, who makes a 'cokewold' (164) of her would-be suitors, this dismissive resolution does not mean that the problems her power raises disappear from the poem. Under the sign of one proper name, in the form of a singular person, Meed represents all manner of payments that bind people's souls. Clearly, this includes bribes, but Meed's two manners undercut Conscience's desire to hold fair wages separate from improper gifts, raising the possibility that even 'mesurable hire' involves a kind of bondage — one that, as Piers the Plowman himself wonders in the next vision, might endanger the soul of the master more than that of the recipient of the wage.

Piers the Plowman's Enforcer

Hunger personifies the meeting point where economic processes that exceed individual control meet the individual experience of bodily suffering — and explores the consequences of attempting to control this contact zone for the purposes of making people work. In a way that complements Meed's exploration of the dangers of both giving and receiving gifts, wages, or bribes, the personification of Hunger raises disturbing questions about 'mesurable hire' as a relation that could imperil the souls of those who exercise mastery over others. The danger is not just for masters that desire 'mede mesurelees', as Conscience maintains, but also threatens a figure as free from the taint of commercial greed as Piers the Plowman, because he finds himself in a role that allows or even requires him to exercise economic power. What does it mean that, for a moment, the poem's ambiguously transcendent figure wields the power of harsh physical necessity that drives people to work for survival? For one thing, it connects Meed's political economic assertion that 'No wight, as I wene, withouten Mede may libbe!' (B.3.227) to the biopolitical deployment of the need for food to live in the organization of the manorial economy.[33] Meed and Piers are brought into surprising alignment when it comes to the problem of work and reward during the course of Piers's experience on the half-acre, since it is survival that ultimately makes people work for wages when they lack the means to sustain their own existence independently.

Langland makes visible the otherwise more generalized and impersonal violence that backs up the exercise of economic power in a space seemingly far removed from, but actually inextricably linked to, the corrupting movement of wealth that Meed represents. After Waster and a Bretoner refuse to work on the half-acre Piers oversees, Piers finally calls upon Hunger to overwhelm their resistance:

> Hunger in haste thoo hente Wastour by the mawe
> And wrong hym so by the wombe that al watrede hise eighen.
> He buffetted the Bretoner aboute the chekes
> That he loked lik a lanterne al his lif after. (B.6.174–77)

Such violence has the effect of making anyone who had previously avoided toil get to work. Frauds and hermits fear Hunger, and so they take up instruments of agrarian toil, abandoning their illicit leisure so that they can legitimately enjoy a humble meal of 'a potful of peses' (186). Even though these people might now be doing what they are supposed to do, Piers nevertheless remains aware that his authority over his workers results from a troubling absence of agency on their part, leaving him perplexed about the ethical way to proceed. As Piers acknowledges to Hunger, 'I am

---

33   On the biopolitics of the Hunger episode, see Rhodes, 'Personification, Power', pp. 95–107.

wel awroke of wastours thorugh thy myghte' (201), but he is clearly uncomfortable with the mastery he now possesses over his 'blody brethren':

> Meschief it maketh thei be so meke nouthe,
> And for defaute of hire foode this folk is at my wille.
> And it are my blody bretheren, for God boughte us alle.
> Truthe taughte me ones to loven hem ech one
> And to helpen hem of alle thyng, ay as hem nedeth.
> Now wolde I wite of thee, what were the beste,
> And how I myghte amaistren hem and make hem to werche. (205–11)

Piers knows that it is only Hunger and the pain he threatens that make his workers pliable, so how can he 'amaistren' them when Hunger leaves, especially since he is called to help his fellow Christians with whatever they need?

Piers is trying to understand how he can exercise economic power over these individuals without sinning. Hunger proffers answers that assure Piers of the biblical warrant for making people work by, for example, only allowing healthy beggars the barest of subsistence, because 'Crist wolde men wroght' (B.6.248). For Hunger, anything that brings those who are able to labour to embrace toil is good, and so Hunger's earlier violence, which allowed Piers to 'amaistren' his workforce, appears as a legitimate component of economic power. But the personificational form of Hunger complicates the words he speaks, as Langland combines the real effects of a legal and economic system that unevenly distributes food with the abstract ideals of *post hoc* defences of the morality of using hunger to enforce obedience. In other words, personification's ability to figurally consolidate multiple aspects of a specific problem allows Langland to simultaneously give voice to the legitimation of economic power and to undermine it. What is shocking about this episode — the individualized, extra-economic violence of Hunger replacing the systemic, economic maldistribution of scarce resources — is that it challenges the anonymity and apparent naturalness of a political economy that unevenly distributes the requirement of labour and the products of labour. The personification of Hunger transforms a crisis of agrarian production and distribution into an action performed by Piers and his grim collaborator, which suggests that things could be done otherwise, even if, paradoxically, the episode underscores the extent to which anyone's ability to do otherwise is constrained by the need to eat and the system of labour organization that attempts to meet that need.

Personification allows a diffuse system of economic power to appear as a dramatic moment of economic action, which exacerbates rather than assuages the possibility that 'synne seweth us ever' (B.14.323), as Hawkyn will lament in the final episode under consideration in this article. The episode of Hunger complements that of Meed by emphasizing the biological compulsion that underlies the wage relation, as the poem moves from a consideration of economic power in the urban marketplace and the halls of Westminster to its manifestation in the agrarian economy. These complementary personifications present an analysis of economic power, which Hawkyn then consolidates as he reveals how the forces that Meed and Hunger represent interact in daily life to overwhelm the intention not to sin.

Hawkyn's 'maistrie'

The way Meed and Hunger personify late medieval England's political economy clarifies what is at stake in Hawkyn's personification of the active life. Hawkyn thrives in a system that rewards amoral deception and fraud, and his activities combine the obscuring power of money exemplified by Meed with the overt relations of mastery and subordination explored in the plowing of the half-acre. Hawkyn tries to answer the question of why he does what he does not just by examining individual affects and faculties, but by taking us outward into humanity's condition as socially embedded creatures. This condition makes Hawkyn the centre of any attempt to grasp what kind of perfection is available to laypeople working for a living in the poem.[34] Hawkyn is domineering, proud, lustful, worldly, and covetous, but his many sins are as much the product of his position in the world as they are a product of his nature — or rather, his prosopopoetic nature is one and the same with his position in the world. At the conclusion of his episode in passus B.14, Hawkyn's anguish about the unavoidability of sin is specifically tied to the moral consequences of his economic role as a landowner:

> 'So hard it is', quod Haukyn, 'to lyve and to do synne.
> Synne seweth us evere', quod he, and sory gan wexe,
> And wepte water with hise eighen and weyled the tyme
> That evere he dide dede that deere God displesed –
> Swouned and sobbed and siked ful ofte
> That evere he hadde lond or lordshipe, lasse other moore,
> Or maistrie over any man mo than of hymselve. (322–28)

Hawkyn, as he makes a living, also sins at the same time, moment by moment, by having land, lordship, and mastery over others to a degree that exceeds his ability to master himself. His regret emphasizes his position within a socioeconomic hierarchy that at once calls forth his active pursuit of a living and renders him vulnerable to the encounters with sin that leave his cloak dirty. Having land, lordship, and mastery in relation to other people overrides whatever intentions Hawkyn might have to keep his cloak clean. He regrets his domination of others insofar as it exacerbates the moral consequences of his lack of self-control, and this lack of self-mastery directly relates to his economic position in which he must behave sinfully in order to inhabit his place in the world. Hawkyn, as Activa Vita, personifies a particular relationship to work, wealth, and commerce that any individual may inhabit and not easily abandon because of responsibilities like Hawkyn's: providing for children and maintaining a household (l. 3). Even though he is trying to make ends meet rather than hoard a large fortune, Hawkyn's lengthy confession to Patience presents a fairly detailed

---

34   The theology of this dilemma is richly described in the account of spiritual perfectionism versus pastoral universalism of Watson, 'Piers Plowman', pp. 83–85. Breen, Imagining an English Reading Public, meanwhile, accounts for the non-elite habitus of Hawkyn in order to illuminate the poem's particular concern with fashioning vernacular readership. Staley, 'Man in Foul Clothes', pp. 27–31, situates Hawkyn within late medieval controversies of sin and judgement in relation to the institutional church.

account of how he practices daily thefts and deceptions to get the goods with which he lives, from the country to the city:

> If I yede to the plowgh, I pynched so narwe
> That a foot lond or a forow fecchen I wolde
> Of my nexte neghebore, nymen of his erthe;
> And if I rope, overreche, or yaf hem reed that ropen
> To seise to me with hir sikel that I ne sew nevere.
> [...]
> And whoso cheped my chaffare, chiden I wolde
> But he profrede to paie a peny or tweyne
> Moore than it was worth, and yet wolde I swere
> That it cost me muche moore — swoor manye othes. (B.13.371–75, 380–83)

Hawkyn's confession offers a moral critique of economic relationships, but it also complicates such moralism by revealing the socioeconomic contacts that elicit certain sinful acts. It is the layout of common fields in strips of land owned by different individuals that enables Hawkyn's overreaching, while the fundamental obscurity, even arbitrariness, of measuring 'worth' in the form of price encourages Hawkyn's false oaths to his customers. In each case, we see Hawkyn admitting to an action, implicitly emphasizing the possibility that he could have done otherwise. But the personificational form of Hawkyn as Activa Vita vitiates the agency that would allow him to freely pursue profit without being domineering or dishonest. This personificational form enables an analysis that combines in a single figure the transindividual nature of economic agency and the individual affective consequences of the lack of moral agency such economic forces entail. By the end of passus 14, Hawkyn desires cleanliness and regrets his sinfulness to the point of tears but seems to lack the ability to be perfect because of his position. All that remains is for Hawkyn to regret that he did not die immediately after his baptism 'for Dowelis sake!' (320–21), an expression of anguish that follows directly from the sense that action — doing well — is impossible. Whatever the theological implications this may carry for the laity, as a form of economic analysis Langland's personification of the active life enables him to bring together the systemic force and the affective motivations that propel the economy — that bewildering creation of a myriad of social relations that nevertheless runs through inhuman mediators like money, and which produces emotional pain and moral angst as a matter of course.

Conclusion

The relationship between master and worker, as the episode of the half-acre in passus B.6 shows, involves a relationship of 'maistrie' that depends upon the diminished agency of the hired person. The labourer must work to survive, and the best way to ensure that the work goes as planned, Piers the Plowman discovers, is to instrumentalize the frailty of the human body. The wasters and healthy beggars that had disrupted the harmonious plowing of the half-acre return to work once Piers calls Hunger to the scene. Piers recognizes that it is 'for defaute of hire foode this folk is at my wille' (206). Langland situates questions of agency in a world where people must work to survive, and in which 'mesurable hire' necessarily involves the kinds of hierarchical relationships that Hawkyn regrets navigating so successfully. Having land, lordship, and mastery over anyone, he suggests, is what led him to his prideful, domineering, and covetous ways. The kinds of exchange that Conscience wants to recover from his condemnation of 'mede mesureless', especially 'marchaundise', are the kinds of things Hawkyn does. According to Conscience, 'In marchaundise is no mede [...] | It is a permutacion apertly' (3.257–58). But when Hawkyn sells, he admits,

> chiden I wolde
> But he profrede to paie a peny or tweyne
> Moore than it was worth, and yet wolde I swere
> That it coste me muche moore. (13.380–82)

For Hawkyn, merchandise is anything but an open and transparent process, but a chance to obfuscate and bully people about prices, because, as Meed's episode shows, value's material manifestation as money in processes of exchange is semiotically obscure, and it is that very obscurity that allows merchants to get *more* than a perfectly equivalent 'permutacion'. Hawkyn's frank admission that he lies about price is not an insight into an idiosyncratically sinful way of doing business; it is, according to this prosopopoetic analysis of the *activa vita*, inherent in commerce, where the confused mechanisms for determining price create a space for deception.[35] The 'permutacion apertly' is Conscience's fantasy, as is the just and sinless wage relation promised by 'mesurable hire', which the episode on the half-acre and the encounter with Hawkyn reveal. The personification of Meed usefully muddles the clean distinctions along moral lines between different kinds of economic activity. Because Lady Meed is one, but meed is many, Langland can deploy the ambiguity inherent in the figural sign to capture the moral ambiguity of economic exchange, whether it be the mastery that defines the wage relation or the slippery 'permutacion' of material goods into various forms that may or may not be truly equivalent. Instead of arriving at a straightforward condemnation of some forms of exchange (bribery) and a celebration of others (wages, open commerce), Langland, as D. Vance Smith suggests, examines a 'phenomenology of exchange [...] in which a close analysis of the marketplace is not subsumed by moralizing conclusions about it'.[36] While personification frequently makes visible unjust social relations in order to serve a polemical purpose in a poem like 'The Simonie', for example, Langland personifies economic relations in a way that does not point his readers to an easy exit from the moral obscurity of the *activa vita*. Transcendence is elusive because, in *Piers Plowman*, working for a living means submitting to a world given and transmitted from the past, with all the necessary constrictions on the individual will that this reality entails.

---

35   Smith, '*Piers Plowman*', p. 242, briefly summarizes the various factors that merchants could use to set a price.

36   Smith, '*Piers Plowman*', p. 251.

Personification is necessary for this kind of analysis, because, as recent studies of the technique argue, it breaks apart and externalizes the affects and psychological faculties of the individual in order to show the multiple determinations that cause the self to act. But at the same time and as part of this disintegrative account of action, personification can also consolidate multiple social processes into singular figures in order to make visible the material relations that force people to do things according to a given economic order.

While not the focus of this essay, the economic networks that bind people together depend upon processes of exchange that at once elicit fears of sinful transgression *and* establish the dynamics by which salvation could be achieved in the translation of sin to grace, the final profit that makes all losses good.[37] But my concern here has been to show that, notwithstanding a long history of critics associating allegory with transcendence and the rejection of immediacy, prosopopeia enables the perception of immanent forces that move people to act.[38] Like the money that Meed in part personifies, a seeming abstraction in the form of a personified concept can appear to erase material specificity and historical particularity even as it emerges from and interacts with a particular historical conjuncture. Langland approaches the dubious possibility of an individual transcending their position within economic networks of production, exchange, and consumption by personifying the limits of agency in economic terms. He does so because so-called economic agency is perhaps our most thoroughly fictional form of agency, in which to win and to waste is the mere exercise of free moral choice, rather than the fulfilment of structural necessities that keep goods and money circulating. Taken together, the episodes of Meed, Hunger, and Hawkyn envision economic personhood as a state in which physical and epistemological limitations (i.e., the need to eat and the inability to transcend the arbitrariness of signs in the process of monetary exchange) make the pursuit of individual perfection impossible without collective transformation.

Works Cited

Primary Sources

Aristotle, *Politics*, trans. by C. D. C. Reeve (Indianapolis: Hackett, 2017)

Langland, William, *The Vision of Piers Plowman: A Critical Edition of the B-Text*, ed. by
     A. V. C. Schmidt (London: Dent, 1995)

Marx, Karl, 'The Eighteenth Brumaire of Louis Bonaparte', in *Karl Marx: Selected Writings*,
     ed. by David McLellan (Oxford: Oxford University Press, 2000), pp. 329–55

---

37 Smith, *Arts of Possession*, pp. 108–53, esp. p. 139.
38 On the history of allegory's longstanding association with the rejection of sensual immediacy and the
     transcendence of the literal, see Hewett-Smith, 'Allegory on the Half-Acre', esp. pp. 2–4, and Brljak,
     'Age of Allegory', esp. pp. 703–05.

Secondary Sources

Balibar, Etienne, *The Philosophy of Marx*, trans. by Chris Turner (New York: Verso, 2014)

Bolton, James, 'What Is Money? What Is a Money Economy? When Did a Money Economy Emerge in Medieval England?', in *Medieval Money Matters*, ed. by Diane Wood (Oxford: Oxbow, 2004), pp. 1–15

——, *Money in the Medieval English Economy, 973–1489* (Manchester: Manchester University Press, 2012)

Bowers, John M., '*Piers Plowman* and the Unwillingness to Work', *Mediaevalia*, 9 (1986 for 1983), 239–49

Breen, Katharine, *Imagining an English Reading Public, 1150–1400* (Cambridge: Cambridge University Press, 2010)

——, 'The Need for Allegory: *Wynnere and Wastoure* as an *Ars Poetica*', *Yearbook of Langland Studies*, 26 (2012), 187–229

——, 'Introduction', *Yearbook of Langland Studies*, 33 (2019), 145–58

Brljak, Vladimir, 'The Age of Allegory', *Studies in Philology*, 114 (2017), 697–719

Bugbee, John, *God's Patients: Chaucer, Agency, and the Nature of Laws* (Notre Dame: University of Notre Dame Press, 2019)

Burrow, J. A., 'Lady Meed and the Power of Money', *Medium Aevum*, 74 (2005), 113–18

Cady, Diane, 'Symbolic Economies', in *Middle English*, ed. by Paul Strohm (Oxford: Oxford University Press, 2007), pp. 124–41

Escobedo, Andrew, *Volition's Face: Personification and the Will in Renaissance Literature* (Notre Dame: University of Notre Dame Press, 2017)

Fletcher, Angus, *Allegory: The Theory of a Symbolic Mode* (Ithaca: Cornell University Press, 1964)

Fowler, Elizabeth, *Literary Character: The Human Figure in Early English Writing* (Ithaca: Cornell University Press, 2003)

Galloway, Andrew, 'The Account Book and the Treasure: Gilbert Maghfeld's Textual Economy and the Poetics of Mercantile Accounting in Ricardian Literature', *Studies in the Age of Chaucer*, 33 (2011), 65–124

Halpern, Richard, *Eclipse of Action: Tragedy and Political Economy* (Chicago: Chicago University Press, 2017)

Hanna, Ralph, *London Literature, 1300–1380* (Cambridge: Cambridge University Press, 2005)

Hewett-Smith, Kathleen M., 'Allegory on the Half-Acre: The Demands of History', *Yearbook of Langland Studies*, 10 (1996), 1–22

Hole, Jennifer, *Economic Ethics in Late Medieval England, 1300–1500* (Cham, Switzerland: Palgrave Macmillan, 2016)

Jappe, Anselm, 'Sohn-Rethel and the Origin of "Real Abstraction": A Critique of Production or a Critique of Circulation?', *Historical Materialism*, 21 (2013), 3–14

La Berge, Leigh Claire, 'The Rules of Abstraction: Methods and Discourses of Finance', in *In the Mind but Not from There: Real Abstraction and Contemporary Art*, ed. by Gean Moreno (New York: Verso, 2019), pp. 43–72

Langholm, Odd, *The Legacy of Scholasticism in Economic Thought* (Cambridge: Cambridge University Press, 1998)

——, *The Merchant in the Confessional: Trade and Price in the Pre-Reformation Penitential Handbooks* (Leiden: Brill, 2003)

——, 'Voluntary Exchange and Coercion in Scholastic Economics', in *The Oxford Handbook of Christianity and Economics*, ed. by Paul Oslington (Oxford: Oxford University Press, 2014), pp. 44–56

Lavatori, Gerard Ponziano, *Language and Money in Rabelais* (New York: Lang, 1996)

Lees, Clare A., 'Gender and Exchange in *Piers Plowman*', in *Class and Gender in Early English Literature: Intersections*, ed. by Britton J. Harwood and Gillian R. Overing (Bloomington: Indiana University Press, 1994), pp. 112–25

Miller, Mark, 'Sin and Structure in *Piers Plowman*: On the Medieval Split Subject', *Modern Language Quarterly*, 76 (2015), 201–24

Ngai, Sianne, 'Visceral Abstractions', *GLQ: A Journal of Gay and Lesbian Studies*, 21 (2015), 33–63

Pearsall, Derek, 'Langland's London', in *Written Work: Langland, Labor, and Authorship*, ed. by Steven Justice and Kathryn Kerby-Fulton (Philadelphia: University of Pennsylvania Press, 1997), pp. 185–207

Rhodes, William, 'Personification, Power, and the Body in Late Medieval and Early Modern English Poetry', in *Personification: Embodying Meaning and Emotion*, ed. by Walter S. Melion and Bart Ramakers (Leiden: Brill, 2016), pp. 95–120

Smith, D. Vance, *Arts of Possession: The Middle English Household Imaginary* (Minneapolis: University of Minnesota Press, 2003)

——, '*Piers Plowman* and the National Noetic of Edward III', in *Imagining a Medieval English Nation*, ed. by Kathy Lavezzo (Minneapolis: University of Minnesota Press, 2004), pp. 234–57

Staley, Lynn, 'The Man in Foul Clothes and a Late Fourteenth Century Conversation about Sin', *Studies in the Age of Chaucer*, 24 (2002), 1–47

Toscano, Alberto, 'The Open Secret of Real Abstraction', *Rethinking Marxism*, 20 (2008), 273–87

Watson, Nicholas, '*Piers Plowman*, Pastoral Theology, and Spiritual Perfectionism: Hawkyn's Cloak and Patience's *Pater Noster*', *Yearbook of Langland Studies*, 21 (2007), 83–118

Wood, Diane, *Medieval Economic Thought* (Cambridge: Cambridge University Press, 2002)

Yunck, John A., *The Lineage of Lady Meed: The Development of Medieval Venality Satire* (Notre Dame: University of Notre Dame Press, 1963)

Zeeman, Nicolette, '*Piers Plowman' and the Medieval Discourse of Desire* (Cambridge: Cambridge University Press, 2006)

LAWRENCE WARNER

Convergent Variation and the Production of *Piers Plowman*

▼ **KEYWORDS** *Piers Plowman*, editing, textual studies, convergent variation, manuscripts, scribes, Michael Madrinkian, George Kane and E. Talbot Donaldson, A. V. C. Schmidt

▼ **ABSTRACT** This essay re-demonstrates the pervasive reality of convergent variation, whereby unrelated manuscripts (here, of *Piers Plowman* A and B) come upon the same unauthorial reading. It does so by testing the data and methodology of Michael Madrinkian's revolutionary proposal about the production of *Piers Plowman* B (*Yearbook of Langland Studies*, 32), which argues that the B-reviser's A manuscript was quite corrupt and that, in a separate set of episodes, many of its readings contaminated the main A-text families. He presents his conclusions as having extraordinary implications that are damning for George Kane and E. Talbot Donaldson's edition of the B text. Yet Madrinkian mischaracterizes or misunderstands both the nature of the (A)B agreements and the workings of convergent variation, especially coincident substitution. Nothing that he presents as evidence leads easily to his conclusions, and substantial evidence points away from them.

Michael Madrinkian's essay 'Authorship and Error' (*Yearbook of Langland Studies*, 32) is one of the most exciting contributions to Langland textual studies of recent years. Adapting and expanding Charlotte Brewer's list of **A**-version variants that appear as well in **B** manuscripts, which form a group of 357 readings he calls (**A**)**B** agreements, he asks the 'simple' question: 'how and why did this correspondence between the **B** archetype and the minority **A** manuscripts occur?'[1] His answer: 'the scribally corrupt readings in Bx that are attested in some **A** manuscripts would be remnants of the corrupt **A**-text exemplar that Langland used to revise the **B** text', an argument that,

---

1 Madrinkian, 'Authorship and Error', p. 184.

Lawrence Warner (lawrence.warner@kcl.ac.uk) is Professor of Medieval English at King's College London. He was co-editor of the *Yearbook of Langland Studies* from 2004–12 and Director of the International *Piers Plowman* Society from 2013–17.

The Yearbook of Langland Studies, 34 (2020), 137–173   BREPOLS ❧ PUBLISHERS   10.1484/J.YLS.5.121090

he claims, 'would have extraordinary implications for our understanding of the **B** version of *Piers Plowman* and would alter the long-held theory of Bx's corruption'[2] and would be 'damning [...] for the Athlone editorial method', i.e., that of the great edition overseen by George Kane, who edited **A**, co-edited **B** with E. Talbot Donaldson, and co-edited **C** with George Russell, 'and indeed, for any attempt to discover a lost "authorial **B** text", since this copy may never have actually existed'.[3] His argument produces a 'blurring of the boundaries between authorial and scribal revision', so that 'we must redefine the way we understand scribal error in the **A** and **B** texts, as error underpins the textual tradition at every stage, even permeating the author's own compositions'.[4]

This is a bold set of claims, which demand testing. Having worked carefully through Madrinkian's data and methodologies, I conclude that nothing he presents as evidence leads easily to his conclusions, and substantial evidence points in the opposite direction. My broader point is that it is time to take seriously the Athlone editors' claims for the pervasiveness of convergent variation, the attestation of variants in common via modes other than descent from a common ancestor. To Madrinkian's credit, 'Authorship and Error' pushes to the limit, explicitly and forcefully, a conviction probably more widely held than it is committed to print: that Kane and his colleagues were somehow playing us. Those editors said convergent variation was everywhere — but *really*? Few have been willing to build an essay on the premise of such scepticism, but Madrinkian has finally done so, a very important and belated step in the history of *Piers Plowman* scholarship.[5] We can now see what the alternative looks like, and need no longer wonder: the editors were right, and it is thanks to his boldness (as well as Kane's original demonstration) that this lurking suspicion can be laid to rest.

Madrinkian's argument rests on this series of claims: first, Kane and Donaldson's (implicit) attribution of these **(A)B** agreements to convergent variation cannot account for the high number, 357, or the 202 of these that appear in four or more **A** manuscripts. Second, the uneven distribution of these **B**-type readings among the **A** manuscripts, with members of A. V. C. Schmidt's **m** family averaging many more than those of his **r** family (or its presumed constituent r^1 and r^2 families), is not what one would expect were convergent variation the cause.[6] Finally, a good forty readings are too 'lengthy and complex' to be explained as coincidental, which, as we shall see, is what he takes 'convergent' to mean.[7]

---

2 Madrinkian, 'Authorship and Error', pp. 194–95.

3 Madrinkian, 'Authorship and Error', p. 217.

4 Madrinkian, 'Authorship and Error', p. 217.

5 Others who have been willing to reject the logic of convergent variation, though certainly not as a principle or argument, are Hanna, 'George Kane', and Wood, 'Nonauthorial *Piers*'. See Warner, 'Ilchester Prologue'.

6 See *Piers Plowman: A Parallel-Text Edition*, ed. by Schmidt, II, 92–93, for these families: **m** = EAMH³W (E through 7.213; A lacks Prol.1–1.141, 2.18–145, 3.114–229, 7.33–85, 8.32–80; H³ from 5.106, W from passus 10); r^1 = TH²ChDRU; r^2 = VHJLKWN (W through passus 9). But see below for important qualifications.

7 Madrinkian, 'Authorship and Error', p. 186.

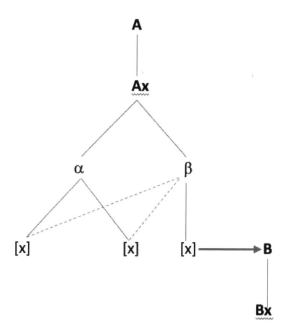

Figure 11. Theoretical **A**> **B** Revision (Madrinkian's diagram).

Madrinkian's alternative history of the transmission of *Piers Plowman* **A** and **B** is in part represented by the diagram above (fig. 11), though in my judgement it accords only very loosely with its explanation. He says, in short, that 'β represents a more corrupt version' of the **A** version, 'no longer extant, that was used for the composition of **B**' — the '[x]' below the β must therefore represent either what he elsewhere calls 'ur-**B**' or, if his '**B**' is that entity, a scribal **A** copy made from β to which he never refers. Whatever the case, β's 357 errors also 'made their way into the other subgroups of **A**', as indicated by the dashed lines, though, again, the diagram has unexplained '[x]'s where those subgroups, **r** (or its constituent members r^1 and r^2) and **m**, would be expected.[8] Madrinkian also uses the symbol 'α' for what is conventionally known as 'Ax' in Langlandian textual studies, i.e., the archetype behind all extant copies of the **A** version, while his own '**Ax**' is what Schmidt calls '(A-θ)', a scribal copy from which the archetype was copied.[9]

Madrinkian does not specify the means by which the readings 'made their way' from β to the **A** copies. His decision not to represent **r** (or r^1 and r^2), **m**, and ur-**B**, and his remarks along the lines that β 'contained at least 357 errors not found in the other strands',[10] and that, for example, 'TH²HNZ have replaced the Ax

---

8   Madrinkian, 'Authorship and Error', pp. 195–96.
9   See Schmidt, *Parallel-Text*, II, 91.
10 Madrinkian, 'Authorship and Error', p. 195.

reading *conseyuede* with *comsede*' at **A**.7.35,[11] make sense only if the readings entered into the **A** manuscripts (e.g., TH², H, N, and Z) directly, i.e., via consultation by individual scribes rather than via descent from the ancestors of the **m** and **r** (or r^1 and r^2) groups. If they had 'made their way' into those ancestors, after all, the readings *were* 'found in the other strands' and it was not TH²HNZ who replaced the archetypal reading. Conversely, however, his emphasis on the 'genetic' character of the agreements, reference to their 'process of their descent' through the **A** tradition, and arguments concerning the relative numbers of errors found in each family make sense only if he is proposing something quite different from, and incompatible with, that idea: that it was indeed the scribes of **m** and **r** (or r^1 and r^2) who consulted β and between them (and quite often together) substituted these 357 lections for the archetypal readings, with **m** taking on substantially more than **r** or than r^1 and r^2.[12]

Which of these two irreconcilable options is the more likely to be what Madrinkian intends? My hunch favours the second, in large part because the first, i.e., the idea that each manuscript consulted this postulated 'β', is wholly undermined by its reliance on thousands of episodes of the most difficult form of convergent variation, which ill suits an argument targeting 'Kane and Donaldson's assumption of convergent variation' (in its simplest form).[13] Indeed I find it impossible to believe this option could ever occur, no matter how compelling the supposed evidence for it. The other reason for rejecting it is the simplicity with which one can treat the '[x]'s and comments at issue as shorthand ways of referring to the second option. The symbols would thus indicate the diagram's provisional status,[14] and comments like 'TH²HNZ have replaced the Ax reading' would indicate the replacement of the reading by those manuscripts' ancestors, **m** and **r** (or **m**, r^1, and r^2), rather than by the scribes of TH², H, N, and Z.[15] Endorsement of the second option permits

---

11   Madrinkian, 'Authorship and Error', p. 199.

12   See below, n. 16, and Madrinkian, 'Authorship and Error', pp. 192 ('textual subgroups display different levels of **B**-type readings, indicating that the agreements are most likely connected in some way to the genetics of the textual tradition') and 196 ('these scribal readings inconsistently corrupted all of the extant **A** manuscripts and further evolved in the process of their descent, leaving an inconsistent and scattered number of agreements throughout all of the extant **A** texts'). The diagram and an impulse for simplicity support the case that Madrinkian intends **r** alone; the treatment of the two **r** subgroups as distinct at Madrinkian, p. 186 n. 21, supports the case that he means r^1 and r^2 differently. The latter fits his interpretation of the data better but is hampered by its need for one more scribe to have consulted β, which is not only all the more unlikely on its face but also undermines Madrinkian's argument in that it adds 50 percent more convergent variation to his narrative, which is supposedly the *alternative* to convergent variation (see below on his confusion regarding this matter).

13   Madrinkian, 'Authorship and Error', p. 186.

14   I.e., as representations of the comment of Madrinkian, 'Authorship and Error', p. 195: 'this should not be taken as a definitive stemma, but rather as a general representation of how the early revisionary transmission might have occurred'. If so, it might have been helpful for Madrinkian to have informed his readers and to have indicated the status (definitive?) of those items that *are* represented on the diagram.

15   Madrinkian, 'Authorship and Error', p. 199.

what Madrinkian presents as 'one of the best arguments against' that 'assumption of convergent variation' to remain: the one that 'suggests a genetic factor to their distribution', whereby **m** and **r** (or **m**, r^1, and r^2) took on the errors, which 'descended' to TH^2, H, N, Z, and the rest.[16]

Before turning to the supposed problem this is intended to solve, let us look at this proposal's own implications. What would prompt these two or three scribes to take on 357 readings 'indeed attributable to scribal error' and 'which display, for the most part, a distinctly scribal character' from another copy, so as to substitute *wel* for *ful*, *for* for *be*, *shal* for *shuld*, *Ac* for *And*, zero for metrically necessary *as wolues*, *the* for zero?[17] '[T]here seems to be no logical explanation why scribes would trouble themselves to deliberately replace one insignificant reading with another equally insignificant reading', as Madrinkian remarks when he is casting doubt on the notion that **A** scribes would do so from **B** manuscripts.[18] The **A** version has about 2450 lines, averaging about 9.5 words per line, resulting in about 23,275 lections. Every copy has these sorts of variants, which are found in nearly every line. There is no way to measure the odds, but I find it difficult either to understand why two scribes would separately decide to seek out 300-odd meaningless variants from the same copy or to believe that both lighted upon more than a small handful in common, not to mention 216 (if the scribes were **r** and **m**).[19] The believability diminishes on the addition of a third scribe (if it was r^1, r^2, and **m**) likewise seeking to replace insignificant readings in his copy with ones in this same hypothetical β: if that is what Madrinkian means, they home in on eighty-seven in common from the thousands of options.

How did the 'correct' reading enter the **A** tradition for those 216 or eighty-seven readings, which, after all, could no longer descend to the extant copies from **m** and **r** (or r^1 and r^2)? Madrinkian acknowledges that his proposal in general 'would again require some level of scribal conflation' to explain why the errors taken on from β are so randomly dispersed in the **A** tradition; for the readings under discussion at least one manuscript must have been 'corrected' against Ax or a still earlier copy, with the others corrected against that copy, or the archetypal/pre-archetypal copy, or each other in turn, although it is not clear that he realizes as much.[20] Kane and

---

16   Madrinkian, 'Authorship and Error', p. 186.
17   Madrinkian, 'Authorship and Error', pp. 186 and 190. The examples are taken from p. 229: **B**.10.214, 338, 392, 143, 212, and 150.
18   Madrinkian, 'Authorship and Error', p. 191, critiquing the account of interversional micro-contamination offered by Adams, 'Editing *Piers Plowman B*'.
19   See above, n. 6, for the **A** families used by Madrinkian. A reading attested by, say, H^{2}LMZ(VH) (see **B**.Prol.44 in Madrinkian, 'Authorship and Error', p. 219) would have been taken on by all three scribes, r^1's instance descending to H^2 (only), r^2's to LVH, and **m**'s to MZ; a reading just in EM descended from **m** only; and so forth. I went through and tallied the results: 216 readings appear in at least one **r** and one **m** manuscript, of which eighty-seven appear in both **r** groups. In the latter scenario, r^2 and **m** shared 114 readings, r^1 and **m** fifteen, and r^1 and r^2 thirty-six.
20   Madrinkian, 'Authorship and Error', p. 196.

Donaldson posit such correction of a **B** manuscript against an early 'good' copy as the explanation for its unique correct readings, but their reward from Madrinkian is an accusation of bad faith.[21]

A simpler such approach, if still in my judgement not very plausible, would place these errors in Ax itself, so that **r** (or *r¹* and *r²*) and **m** simply copied them, and Langland as **B**-reviser used it rather than the invented β.[22] It would be no more difficult to attribute the 216 **rm**, or eighty-seven *r¹r²***m**, errors to the Ax scribe — indeed they are in effect archetypal readings — than to the β scribe, and not only because the Ax scribe is not merely hypothetical. It is inconceivable that the source of those errors did not also provide other readings, erroneous or not, and no reason to exclude the possibility that it was the source of lines, passages, passus, the **A** version itself. This would still require extensive correction by many scribes against a pre-archetypal copy, though. Simpler still would be to go along with Schmidt in accepting the great majority of the Bx readings in question as authorial: he deems only twenty-one erroneous.[23] Jill Mann, who like Madrinkian 'address[es] the problem posed by these **BC** readings in **A** manuscripts, namely, how did they get there?' (her answer is that

---

21 *Piers Plowman: The B Version*, ed. by Kane and Donaldson, pp. 165–73, interpret F's correct readings where the other manuscripts of **B** err, often in agreement with **A**, as evidence that F accessed pre-archetypal materials. And yet Madrinkian, 'Authorship and Error', pp. 181, 182, offering no support for the claim, writes that these editors 'were well aware' of the 'fact' that F 'is known to have been heavily contaminated by **A** at some point in its textual history', and that they 'choose to use F for their **B** reading against all other extant manuscripts simply because it supported Kane's original choice in **A**'. The facts, by contrast, are these: Kane and Donaldson, p. 221, identify a single **A** line in F, after Prol.94. What Madrinkian cites as a 'fact' is, rather, Schmidt's interpretation of a portion of the readings in question. See Schmidt, *Parallel-Text*, II, 143–44 (Madrinkian, p. 181 n. 15, wrongly cites Schmidt, II, 275). Any accusation of bad faith on Kane and Donaldson's part ought at least to acknowledge the force of this sentence (p. 172): 'Correction of F was, finally, from a manuscript of the **B** version and not severally from manuscripts of **A** and **C**: this is indicated by the superiority of a number of F's readings to those of the archetypal **C** tradition and confirmed by F's possession of intrinsically more authoritative readings in that part of the poem, also, where **B**'s text is unique', and, better yet, the readings to which it refers, analysis of twenty-three of which the editors offer as 'an appropriate end' to their illustration of the phenomenon. Madrinkian, p. 181, n. 15, in passing cites Adams's attempt to downplay this material ('Editing *Piers Plowman* B', p. 53), but Kane and Donaldson's approach cannot be explained away as an after-the-fact attempt to justify Kane's choices of **A** readings.

22 It can even, though need not, have included the **r**-only and **m**-only errors, which would have disappeared from the one tradition via the correction of the other tradition's inaugural copy against the pre-archetypal copy that so many other subsequent scribes would later access.

23 Schmidt, *Parallel-Text*, rejects the Bx reading for the following relevant items on Madrinkian's list: **B**.Prol.76, Prol.78, Prol.231, 1.43, 1.88, 1.191, 2.8, 5.467, 6.291, 6.323, 7.97, 7.106 (x2), 7.173, 8.74, 8.110, 9.26, 9.34, 10.55, 10.56, 10.72. There are a good number of items on Madrinkian's list that do not belong, e.g., where the **B** error is not Bx's (see below), where the question of Schmidt's endorsement or otherwise is moot. Madrinkian, 'Authorship and Error', cites Schmidt with regard to many local textual issues: pp. 181 (F); 186 (stemma); 188, 190 n. 27, and 213 n. 73 (**Z**); 189 n. 25, 191 n. 31, and 196 (**A** scribes' consultation of other copies); 194 n. 42 (the **B** reviser's corrupt **A** manuscript); and pp. 198 and n. 47, 199 n. 53, 210 and nn. 67–68, and 211 and n. 70 (individual lections). But nothing on his acceptance of these readings.

'**A** derives from **B** rather than the reverse'), has also argued for the authorial status of a handful of these 'errors'.[24]

Schmidt also proposes that a number of these minority **A** readings converged with (correct, in his estimation) **B** via their scribes' consultation of members of that version.[25] Madrinkian at least mentions this idea (as opposed to Schmidt's endorsement of Bx at the large majority of readings in question (see above, n. 23)), rejecting it on the grounds that 'there is no evidence in any of the extant **A** manuscripts of such comprehensive scribal conflation of **A** and **B** before the sixteenth century'.[26] But the stakes are high, and some readers might wonder at the demand of evidence for the phenomenon in general as some sort of prerequisite, instead taking this body of data on its own to constitute that evidence. This logic, that a phenomenon must already be identified elsewhere before it can be identified anywhere, prevents it from ever being identified at all; even the sole exception Madrinkian acknowledges, London, British Library, MS Harley 3954 (sigil H of **A** and H[3] of **B**), could not be an **A-B** combination by such logic.[27] It also does away with his β, given the absence of evidence in any manuscript of such comprehensive scribal conflation from a hypothetical copy that left no trace other than as a source of error everywhere else. One might also wonder whether medieval readers were so attuned to the differences between **B** and **C** as is Madrinkian, which differences enable exclusion from consideration of the many manuscripts conflating **A** and **C**. His exclusion of the **A-B-C** conjoint manuscript San Marino, Huntington Library, MS Hm 114 (Ht) and of Oxford, Corpus Christi College, MS 201 (sigil F of **B**) on the grounds that they are 'eccentric' and 'highly divergent' is inexplicable.[28] He overlooks the group of manuscripts attesting **C**.Prol.–2.131 (sigils OLB), **A**.2.1–3.29, and **B**.3.30–end (sigils BmBoCot [=collective

---

24 Mann, 'Was the C-Reviser's Manuscript Really So Corrupt?', pp. 453 (see Madrinkian's quotation attached to n. 1 above) and 464. Mann, pp. 454–58 and 462–63, endorses Bx at 2.6, 3.158, 5.213, and 8.22 and observes, p. 466 n. 15, that 'Schmidt's edited text of **B** agrees with the Bx readings in all the examples I cite' with one exception on which she agrees with him. To be fair, I should note that Mann presents this answer 'in passing', remarking that 'this assumption is not a necessary foundation for skepticism about Kane and Donaldson's case for the **C**-reviser's "corrupt" **B** manuscript' (p. 464), but it is the only answer to the question as stated that I can find in her essay.

25 Schmidt, *Parallel-Text*, II, 92 ('The hypothetical family original **m** [...] was copied [...] after the **B**-Text had been composed, as is indicated [...] by its occasional inclusion from **B** of Bx readings that seem inauthentic'); 97 ('W reveals extensive recourse to [...] **B**'); 98 ('K's value 'is reduced by its extensive conflation from **C** (and in one instance **B**)'); and 117–18 ('Possible **B** Contamination in the **A** Version').

26 Madrinkian, 'Authorship and Error', p. 192.

27 Madrinkian, 'Authorship and Error', p. 193.

28 Madrinkian, 'Authorship and Error', p. 192, where he claims that '[r]ather than a scribe conflating minute line-by-line variations between the versions', Ht 'is a wholesale revision of the poem', which, even if it were accurate, is irrelevant to the point at issue. It is true that most of the conflations are on the level of passage, but not that its scribe did not conflate minute line-by-line revisions. Russell and Nathan, 'A *Piers Plowman* Manuscript', p. 120, say that the version created by this scribe is one 'in which the individual **B** line is often modified by a reading imported from one or other of the texts'. See above, n. 21, on Madrinkian's treatment of MS F.

B]), for whose absence from his **A** edition Kane later apologized,[29] and the **A-C** splice Aberystwyth, National Library of Wales, MS 733B, which has '**B**' material throughout.[30] Finally, this rejection of the viability of **B**> **A** contamination conflicts with his absolute reliance on the 'abundant evidence', likewise Schmidt's, 'of [**A**] scribes correcting their exemplars with other copies of the *same* version', which is of absolutely identical character.[31]

Madrinkian's Langland, too, is a figure opposite the one who grows from analysis of the whole spectrum of readings rather than 357 interpreted in a particular way. His poet 'chose not to emend minor variations from his own *usus scribendi* in this scribal copy [i.e., one contaminated by β] before transmitting them to his **B** text composition'; 'Unlike Chaucer, who prays of his book in *Troilus and Criseyde* "that non miswrite the"', he 'seems generally unconcerned, in this first revision, with the transformative effects of textual transmission and is willing to accept possibly erroneous scribal readings as a legitimate basis for his extended version'; his 'literary persona' is 'more concerned with improving the theological force of the poem than improving its artistic merit at the level of the line'.[32] The question is whether Madrinkian's case is so strong that these statements, which clash with those put forth by previous students of the issue, must be accepted.

Madrinkian's invocation of Chaucer might be profitably compared with Schmidt's remark that *Piers Plowman*'s excoriation of those foolish scribes who miswrite charters by skipping over sections and mistreating copy (**B**.11.303–06/**C**.13.118–20) 'strongly suggests that Langland cared as much for accuracy in a copyist as did Chaucer'.[33] And the notion that he accepts errors as a 'legitimate basis' for **B** revision seems quite far from Kane's, 'that Langland once or even twice either missed or did nothing about' only ten or twelve scribal mistakes in his **A** copy that issued in unmetrical lines in **B**,[34] and especially Russell and Kane's: 'A turn of language which he sensed to be not his

---

29 *Piers Plowman: The A Version*, ed. by Kane, p. 459. He has the **A** material concluding at the end of passus 2, but its continuation for twenty-nine more lines is convincingly argued by Davis, 'Rationale for a Copy of a Text'.

30 I actually do not think this is **B** material at all, so in that sense Madrinkian implicitly endorses my argument. See Warner, *Lost History*. Yet my explanation, that it is early **C** matter that contaminated Bx, might transgress his supposed rule, and is the opposite of the belief of Madrinkian, 'Authorship and Error', p. 218, that Bx 'may bring us [...] far closer' to the ur-**B** text, 'indeed, than Kane and Donaldson's laborious reconstruction'. My point here is that somehow Madrinkian needs to account for NLW 733B if he is to adopt this approach.

31 Madrinkian, 'Authorship and Error', p. 196 (emphasis in original), citing Schmidt, *Parallel-Text*, II, 100–01, to support the point. This relies in part on Madrinkian's earlier rejection (p. 189 n. 25) of Schmidt's analysis of **B**> **A** contamination: 'Schmidt seems to neglect the fact that **B**-type readings appear in *all* subgroups of **A**' (emphasis in original), another way of saying that he does not propose any contamination of r¹ by **B**. It would be just as fair to accuse Madrinkian of 'seem[ing] to neglect the fact that' these are not '**B**-type readings' but instances of coincident variation. Either remark would beg the question.

32 Madrinkian, 'Authorship and Error', pp. 214, 215, and 216.

33 *Vision of Piers Plowman*, ed. by Schmidt, p. lx.

34 Kane, *The A Version*, p. 463. See also Kane and Donaldson, *The B Version*, p. 211 n. 172, and Russell, 'Evolution of a Poem', p. 42. All are mentioned by Madrinkian, 'Authorship and Error', pp. 193–94.

own, or imperfect alliteration, or nonsense error that caught his eye would sharpen the critical attitude already implicit in the intent to revise, giving local application to general dissatisfaction. Quite often his reaction was to repair by rewriting, even to the extent of incorporating the scribal reading in the revised line or passage.'[35] In 'most instances' where the **C** reviser's **B** manuscript was corrupt 'the scribal corruption has disappeared or appears adapted or corrected'.[36] Madrinkian evinces some awareness of the difference between his **B** reviser and Russell and Kane's **C** reviser: 'The later recognition during the **C** revision of the corruption inherent in the **B** tradition and the large-scale emendation that took place also suggests that there was something recognizably alien about the *usus scribendi* of these readings.'[37] But wouldn't the poet correct these alien readings on his first encounter with them? Madrinkian does not explain.

---

35 *Piers Plowman: The C Version*, ed. by Russell and Kane, p. 67. See Kane and Donaldson, *The B Version*, pp. 98–127, and, for other 'instances of Langland's incorporation of an unoriginal reading in his **B** copy into a revision', Russell and Kane, p. 90 n. 2. This theory has not been universally accepted. See especially Mann, 'Was the C-Reviser's Manuscript Really So Corrupt?', and below, n. 37, for Madrinkian's own very brief engagement with the topic. Like Madrinkian (see above, n. 21), Mann, p. 453, takes the premise that 'Kane's procedure in editing **B** was heavily influenced by his need to defend his **A** text', so that her conclusions are predetermined, and her reader is left in no doubt that indeed she 'could work through the rest of Kane and Donaldson's examples in the same way' as she does a small proportion of them in the essay (p. 464). As for the examples Mann does discuss, her suggestion re **A**.5.128 is attractive (see below, n. 130), but not so much her analysis of **B**.3.158 *þe lawe*. Kane and Donaldson, p. 102, adduce this as 'manifestly inferior in sense' to **A**.3.148 *lawe*: 'The definite article destroys the personification.' Mann, p. 455, citing as well VEKWN's agreement with Bx, writes that '*in that very line* in **B**' that established the personification, '"him" follows "þe lawe", not "lawe" […] If the definite article is not felt to destroy the personification there, why should it do so in line 158?' (emphasis in original). But this is what Mann, p. 459, herself describes as 'a classic example of Langland's use of what might be called intermittent personification: the vacillation between "þe lawe" (abstract noun) and "Lawe" (a fully fledged personification, who is "so lordlich …") continues throughout': 'And liþ ayein þe lawe [*abstract*] & lettiþ *hym* [*personification*] þe gate' (**B**.3.156, my emphasis), the a-verse indicating that Meed 'opposes "the law"' — an abstract entity — 'with lies'. See Kane, *Piers Plowman: Glossary*, 'lye(n), leiȝe', citing this line; likewise *MED*, 'lien' (v.(2)), 1a.

36 Russell and Kane, *The C Version*, p. 72.

37 Madrinkian, 'Authorship and Error', p. 213. Madrinkian, p. 204, writes that 'of the readings used to justify **BC**'s opposition to **A**' in Kane and Donaldson's account of the **C** reviser's **B** manuscript, 'almost 50 percent are in fact attested in some extant **A** manuscripts', remarking that the editors 'again write them off as convergent variation. Yet, if we accept the possibility that these readings were, in fact, corrupt **A** readings present in the ur-**B**, then Kane and Donaldson's postulated relationship between the three versions becomes much more problematic.' See also Madrinkian, p. 205 and n. 62, for his very brief engagement with Kane and Donaldson's evidence. He offers no support for the claims either that Kane and Donaldson 'used' readings in order 'to justify' the conclusion, or that they 'wrote off' inconvenient evidence to the contrary. And the only counter-evidence to that postulate that I find in his essay is the possibility that his own conclusion is right. Such circularity invites a turning of the tables: if one accepts the possibility that Kane and Donaldson were acting in good faith, then Madrinkian's postulated (and unexplained) belief that the existence of meaningless variants somewhere in **A** shows that the **B** reviser's **A** manuscript was corrupt becomes much more problematic. In any case, the attribution of these agreements to convergent variation is simple (I would say necessary as well) while Madrinkian's alternative is extraordinarily difficult. Hence this essay.

Convergent Variation and its Vicissitudes

What, then, is the problem that this proposal intends to solve? Madrinkian's target is the Athlone reliance on 'what is known as "convergent variation", wherein two or more readings agree in error through pure coincidence by scribes making the same mistakes independently of one another', a principle that gave the editors 'a convenient way of explaining the numerous seemingly inexplicable agreements between various unrelated manuscripts of *Piers Plowman*'.[38] This is the means by which, in the face of such agreements as those between minority **A** and Bx, editors 'write them off', he says twice, and attempt to 'explain away' their import.[39] His phrase 'through pure coincidence' indicates that Madrinkian here has in mind 'coincident substitution', which, as further indicated by the adjective 'pure' and his ironic tone ('convenient', 'seemingly inexplicable'), he takes to instance *Oxford English Dictionary*, 'coincidence (n.)', 4, 'a notable concurrence of events or circumstances having no apparent causal connection'. If that were accurate, then his depiction of the phenomenon as something of a refuge for scoundrels might be justified; but in textual studies the term 'coincidence' is used in its neutral sense, *OED*, 'coincidence (n.)', 1(a), 'The fact or condition of being coincident; the occupation of the same place or part of space.' For the point of the phenomenon is precisely that there *is* a causal connection between the readings: 'Coincident substitution', write Russell and Kane, 'occurred because every piece of text in its context contained inducements to certain classes of substitution, from its content or language or metrical form.'[40] For instance: critics of Middle English alliterative poetry frequently mistake the adjective 'Other' in the essay title 'Feminine Knots and the Other *Sir Gawain and the Green Knight*' as a noun, an entity found 'in' the poem, whose title is not modified by 'Other' but is rather the object of the added preposition.[41] The popular 1990s genre of the critical essay including 'the Other in [X]' in its title was a strong inducement to the error.[42]

The previous paragraph was about 'coincident substitution', but Madrinkian claims he is discussing 'convergent variation'. These terms are not synonymous: the former is a subset of the latter. Readers will need to weigh up the extent to which they consider

---

38 Madrinkian, 'Authorship and Error', p. 180.

39 Madrinkian, 'Authorship and Error', pp. 183 and 204 (both: 'write them off') and 186 ('explain away').

40 Russell and Kane, *The C Version*, p. 59.

41 The adjectival status of 'Other' is clear in the text itself: Heng, 'Feminine Knots', p. 501, argues for 'a feminine text in *Sir Gawain*'. Until recently I assumed the title included the *in*; when I realized my error I because curious as to its extent. A search of 'feminine knots and the other in sir' (within quotation marks) on Google Books, 22 June 2019, and on jstor.org, 23 December 2019, produced about a dozen hits. If they are indeed genetically related, then the likely source is a 1995 publication which, however, I find cited by only one other later example and whose topic is rather far from the others as well. Another influential essay of 1998, too, is cited by one later publication that has the error. But citations are of little help in diagnosing causes; I knew the 1998 essay well, but it is doubtful that I attended to its bibliography so closely that it interfered with my reading of Heng's title. Another recent citation places a colon after Heng's 'Other', which supports my general sense: it is obviously separate from all this, while also arising from the cause I identify at work.

42 E.g., Vine, 'The Wuther of the Other'; Ferriss, 'The Other'; and Makarushka, 'Tracing the Other'.

Madrinkian's conflation of the two to affect his argument. For while the Athlone editors' reliance on convergent variation is, rhetorically at least, his target, his own reliance is just as extensive, perhaps more so. Russell and Kane identify a second mode of convergent variation, 'memorial contamination', close enough to 'coincident substitution' that it need not detain us;[43] but the third, 'consultation of another copy', is at the heart of Madrinkian's own argument. Russell and Kane explain that 'in textual criticism the term "correction" has three meanings. One implies the "good intention" of the copyist, a second the quality of the alternative exemplar available to him and the third the circumstance that (except in the special situation of authorial direction) his judgement of that quality would be based on the same criteria that directed his conscious or subconscious substitutions'.[44] When Madrinkian says that the **(A)B** agreements 'further evolved in the process of their descent' from a common exemplar, a postulate that would 'require some level of scribal conflation',[45] he is putting into different words a narrower version of Kane's conclusion 'that convergent variation (whether correction or coincident error) has so obscured the evidence by which common descent might be ascertained that no clear or unquestioned genealogical picture takes shape'.[46]

Kane's parenthetical aside shows that he has no particular investment in *how* the evidence for genetic relationships got cloudy. His point is *that* it did, and these, coincidence and conflation, are the two options. Now, Kane certainly considers coincidence to have occurred far more frequently than conflation: on the one side is 'the principle that the possibility of explaining a variation easily implies a likelihood of its recurrence'; on the other, that conflation 'is unlikely to extend to such variants' as what W. W. Greg called the 'herd of dull commonplace readings' that are so abundant in lists of shared errors.[47] For that matter, Madrinkian, despite excoriating Kane for

---

43 Russell and Kane, *The C Version*, p. 59: 'The scribe would "pick up", that is, visually memorize a piece of text, and then turn his eyes to the page, writing from memory and consciously attending to the formation of the letters and the look of the page. Any part of the text he had so far copied, or any part of the whole text if he was copying it for a second time, could intrude in the system of messages from eye to brain to hand and substitute another reading.' Madrinkian, 'Authorship and Error', p. 191, refers in passing to '**A** scribes consciously or unconsciously contaminating the **A** text with **B** readings perfectly or imperfectly recalled from memory'. He remarks, 'many modern close readers of the poem, upon reading a less familiar version, may easily find themselves recalling memorable portions of text from the other versions. Yet the idea of *memorability* is key here; recalling significant words or phrases from the other versions is plausible, while recalling minute lexical variations is not' (p. 192). This reference to the 'memorability' of a phrase seems based on the assumption that it is akin to the way we might get earworm from hearing a catchy hook in a pop song, but it is, rather, a neurological and physical phenomenon pertaining to the specific material circumstances of scribal practice. See also Kane, *The A Version*, p. 144. In any case, for our purposes 'coincident substitution' and 'consultation of another copy' are the two that matter.

44 Russell and Kane, *The C Version*, p. 59.

45 Madrinkian, 'Authorship and Error', p. 196.

46 Kane, *The A Version*, p. 55.

47 Kane, *The A Version*, p. 59, citing Greg, *Calculus of Variants*, p. 57; also, Kane and Donaldson, *The B Version*, p. 168. See also Russell and Kane, *The C Version*, p. 59: 'Generally speaking, random groups in the *Piers Plowman* situation seem most likely to have been formed by coincident variation and memorial contamination.'

his supposed blind, or wilful, support of coincidence, agrees with him: on the one side, he characterizes the 357 **(A)B** agreements as 'attributable to scribal error', and presents no reasons for rejecting the principle 'that the possibility of explaining a variation easily implies a likelihood of its recurrence', in fact acknowledging its effects on occasion; and on the other, he observes there 'to be no logical explanation why scribes would trouble themselves to deliberately replace one insignificant reading with another equally insignificant reading'.[48]

Madrinkian's agreement with the Athlone editors on all the fundamental issues at stake makes it difficult for me to understand the heated language ('damning') and accusations of bad faith (see above, nn. 21 and 37) that characterize his response to their work. His only substantive complaint is the narrow one that Kane and Donaldson harbour an 'assumption' that the **(A)B** agreements are attributable 'entirely to convergent variation'.[49] Since **A** and **B** did not receive the errors via descent from a common ancestor, as Madrinkian acknowledges — hence the dashed lines on his diagram — it turns out, again, the editors were correct. This is not an 'assumption', but a 'conclusion' that is 'beyond doubt', one that by definition applies in situations like this one.[50] He homes in on their supposed failure to recognize that the data pointed to his own conclusion, that Langland was happy to allow hundreds of errors to stand in his **B**-revision copy and that consultation among **A** copies, even pre-archetypal ones, occurred everywhere and all the time. Here is the heart of his logic:

> What this assumption [that convergent variation explains **(A)B** agreements] does not account for, however, is the persistence and regularity of the agreement across numerous manuscripts of **A**; in the body of data, there are 202 agreements that are attested in four or more manuscripts of **A**, which must certainly constitute a significant persistence. Statistically, the more manuscripts of **A** attesting any given

---

48   Madrinkian, 'Authorship and Error', pp. 186, 191. He allows the 'distinct possibility […] that not all **(A)B** agreements reflect transmission from an **A**-text exemplar to the ur-**B**' and that 'some may, indeed, be attributable to convergent variation or conflation' (p. 196) and grants that 'the inversion of' one phrase 'may have happened coincidentally in all three traditions' (p. 211). But Madrinkian clearly does not really believe this occurred: he 'does not categorically deny the existence of convergent variation or interversional contamination' (p. 196), the qualification revealing the strength of his rejection of the concept; his point is to deny that all 357 agreements could have arisen thus, and his allowance of the phenomenon is confined to twenty-five **A** readings that agree only with the beta family of **B**. See Madrinkian, p. 197: 'the fact that only twenty-five **(A)B** agreements can be proven to be post-archetypal is telling in itself', showing that the vast majority of **B** readings attested in minority **A** manuscripts were also present in the **B** archetype'. Conversely, he categorically claims that 'the [**A**] manuscript used in the **B** revision […] contained *at least 357 errors* not found in the other strands' (p. 195; my emphasis) and says that the evidence that the **B** reviser's **A** manuscript was corrupt 'may give some cause to suspect' (p. 211) that the inversion of the phrase in question is in fact not coincidental at all. But such resistance is not on theoretical grounds; Madrinkian could hardly reject the logical force of Kane and Donaldson's remark on its own terms.

49   Madrinkian, 'Authorship and Error', p. 185. Madrinkian often refers to the 'assumptions' of Kane and Donaldson, where 'conclusions' or 'arguments' might be more accurate: pp. 181 n. 13, 186, 188, 205 n. 61, and 212. But this does not seem part of his assault on their integrity; he also uses it thus for his own argument (pp. 194–95, 199).

50   Kane, *The A Version*, p. 55.

variant the less likely it is that this can be attributed to coincidence. When, for instance, a minority **A** reading is shared by numerous **A** manuscripts in agreement with Bx, it becomes increasingly improbable (though not technically impossible) that they could be coincidental and independently reproduced error. Where the improbability of coincidental agreement becomes overwhelming, the possibility of a genetic relationship must be considered.[51]

Madrinkian is here in effect saying — though I am not certain he realizes this — that for a large proportion of his data set we need to reverse the genetic group (no longer the correct one) and the convergent group (no longer the erroneous one). Otherwise his argument, so far as it is inferable, that the erroneous readings made their way from β into **r** (or r^1 and r^2) and/or **m** and thence descended into the **A** manuscripts would make no sense.

At **A.1.47** 'And **he** askide of hem of whom spak þe lettre', for instance, 'the possibility of a genetic relationship must be considered' for incorrect RH² (r^1)-JLKW (r^2)-E (**m**) *god* — for it is very improbable that seven manuscripts could have independently produced this error — so that it is now correct TChD (r^1)-VH (r^2)-M (**m**) *he* that must be the result of convergent variation: not coincidence, which Madrinkian seems to believe almost never occurred (see above, n. 48), but 'some level of scribal conflation', despite the absence of any logical explanation why scribes would trouble themselves to do this, and which, as discussed above, necessitates consultation by at least one scribe of Ax or a still earlier copy.[52] This same set of difficulties attends every 'erroneous' reading on his list that appears in both **r** and **m** copies, or possibly just the r^1, r^2, and **m** copies (as here). Where one family does not attest the error, consultation of it by other members, again despite the absence of a reason for doing so, could in theory explain their 'correct' readings. What prompts Madrinkian's promotion of this very difficult scenario, we remember, are the 202 agreements that are attested in four or more manuscripts of **A**, which for reasons that seem to him self-evident 'must certainly constitute a significant persistence'; he later cites 'the overwhelming persistence of (**A**)**B** agreement'.[53] He does not specify whether that persistence inheres in the number of agreements (357/202), the number of manuscripts attesting the latter group of agreements (four or more), or some combination. It does not matter much, but I will consider the two main options in turn.

Madrinkian's list contains 351 (not 357) items, of which 195 (not 202) are agreements attested by four or more manuscripts. In addition, readers need to know that some 120, over a third, including fifty-five of those 195 in four or more manuscripts (28 percent) and seventeen of the forty 'lengthy and complex' readings (42.5 percent), do not belong (see the appendix). One or two such oversights are inevitable — no doubt some of my own remain in this essay — but this constitutes a substantial and serious discrepancy between a data set and its presentation by an essay analysing it. Over a third of these 120 are readings where Bx is in fact correct and which thus,

51   Madrinkian, 'Authorship and Error', p. 185.
52   Madrinkian, 'Authorship and Error', p. 196.
53   Madrinkian, 'Authorship and Error', pp. 185 and 201.

obviously, do not belong on a list of Bx errors. Madrinkian's main source was a list of **A**-manuscript agreements with **B** manuscripts, not necessarily Bx, in Charlotte Brewer's Oxford D.Phil. thesis, but he missed her explanation that the items in her catalogue 'are not all necessarily [...] readings which agree in error; some [...] *are* [...] "right" readings' — this is a very important point for her — and he did not, it seems, check against the Athlone edition.[54] Some of those in this category are his own additions, however. Another third of the 120 comprise instances in which the agreement does not exist, sometimes where Madrinkian has misunderstood what is going on but usually where 'disagreements' between Bx and correct **AB** (e.g., sg. for pl., *wel* for *ful*, *thou* for *ye*) are treated as 'agreements' when occurring between Bx and erroneous **A**, or within the **A** tradition.[55] About 20 percent of these 120 are items where Madrinkian selects as the 'Bx' error a reading unlikely in fact to be Bx; this is usually where editors consider either F or R of alpha correct on account of **AC** support.[56] A handful of the 120 are items the Athlone editors exclude from consideration as unlikely to have genetic significance; and a small number fit more than one of these categories.

That brings Madrinkian's figures down to 231 **(A)B** agreements, of which 140 appear in four or more **A** copies. So far as I am aware, the Athlone edition both includes these remaining readings and classifies them as Bx errors, but a few other categories not listed in the appendix could have joined the above. Brewer excludes from her collection of **AB** agreements such variants as 'addition or omission of *and* within or at the beginning of a line, or of *that* before an object clause',[57] leading Madrinkian to call into question her willingness to allow her judgement about Kane's work to grow

---

54 Brewer, 'Some Implications', p. 10 (her emphasis); her catalogue is on pp. 93–168. See Madrinkian, 'Authorship and Error', pp. 183, 189 n. 24, and 219 n. 88, for his use of this material. A quick if not fool-proof way to tell whether any given agreement in Brewer's list is erroneous in **B** is to see whether 'KD' appears in the margin next to the entry: Brewer, p. 11, specifies that that symbol indicates that Kane and Donaldson 'adopt Kane's reading as an emendation of the reading of the **B** manuscripts', meaning that the absence of 'KD' indicates that they do not emend. I checked the seventeen that I list as readings where Bx is correct and four or more **A** manuscripts share the reading, of which fifteen lacked 'KD' (the two which erroneously are thus marked are Prol.16 *diches* and 5.586 *maner*).

55 Many of these are what Madrinkian, 'Authorship and Error', pp. 197, 201–02, calls 'imperfect agreements' which, '[i]f the direction of error' he suggests for them 'is accurate, [...] would represent readings in transition, erroneous readings in **A** directly causing new erroneous readings in **B** and **C**, and would thus further support the theory that Langland revised from a scribal **A** manuscript', wording that makes clear the circularity involved in including such items in the list providing the evidence that Langland revised from a scribal **A** manuscript.

56 For one important exception see above, n. 21. I tend to be conservative, not including readings like **B**.Prol.63, where Kane and Donaldson's reading *hire* (2) is attested by WHmCr (as well as much of **A** and **C**), or **B**.6.128, which Madrinkian, 'Authorship and Error', p. 226, presents as 'not: A.7.120† noþer] not TDCh' ('†' = his addition to the list of Brewer, 'Some Implications'), where Kane and Donaldson's reading *not* is both the reading of BmBoCr and accepted as authorial by Schmidt. The former is accepted by neither Schmidt nor *Piers Plowman Electronic Archive: The Bx Archetype*, ed. by Burrow and Turville-Petre, while the latter is accepted as authorial but not archetypal by Schmidt, *Parallel-Text*, II, 365, who takes BmBoCr to instance correction against **C**.

57 Brewer, 'Some Implications', p. 10, citing Kane, *The A Version*, pp. 122 and 131.

from, rather than determine, the data set: 'Given Brewer's later rejection of Kane's editorial criteria, this seems an ironic choice to incorporate into her methodology, and one which limits the sample still more. By not including agreements in minor mechanical errors and substitutions, this method limits our perspective on the largely scribal character of the (**A**)**B** agreements.'[58] There are at least twenty-three of these (eleven in four or more manuscripts) not already excluded.[59] Also, *wel/ful* variants might 'easily have been unconscious, even habitual', say Russell and Kane, in which case they would be meaningless for the classification of manuscripts (eleven; eight in four or more manuscripts),[60] while 'singular/plural alternations should be treated as non-indicative of genetic origin since they are largely unconscious', in Schmidt's judgement (twenty; seventeen in four or more manuscripts).[61] No classification of manuscript groups as genetic would stand or fall on the basis of such agreements, but that is not necessarily true for Madrinkian's argument. Exclusion of all of these agreements would further reduce the relevant figures to 177, of which 104 are in four or more **A** copies. Madrinkian claims that his theory 'challenges [...] the notion that all 357 agreements can be attributed to later scribal activity': would he still have pursued the point had he followed this application of his criteria and concluded that the relevant figure is instead at most 231, possibly as few as 177? Should we pursue it ourselves? If so, the situation is still not straightforward: in the absence of any precedent for this method of counting a given manuscript's readings (Bx's) across another set of seventeen manuscripts (**A**), readers are left in the dark as to whether 177, 231, or even the original 357 shared readings present the difficulties Madrinkian claims.

To turn to the other belief subtending Madrinkian's reference to 'significant persistence', i.e., 'Statistically, the more manuscripts of **A** attesting any given variant the less likely it is that this can be attributed to coincidence' (hence his categories of two-to-three and four-plus **A** manuscripts with the erroneous **B** reading): Madrinkian calls this 'a basic editorial principle, and one with which Kane and Donaldson certainly agreed in theory'.[62] Madrinkian's attempt to substantiate this remarkable claim only underscores the non-existence of this supposed editorial principle. This is his citation not of Kane and Donaldson, but instead R. W. Chambers and J. H. G. Grattan: 'variants

---

58 Madrinkian, 'Authorship and Error', p. 189 n. 24.

59 Here and below, readings shared by four or more manuscripts are asterisked. All of these are Madrinkian's additions to the list of Brewer, 'Some Implications' save the second at 3.140 according to his own list: **B**.Prol.22, 1.78, *1.80, 1.89, 1.99, *2.164, *2.202, 3.123, 3.137, 3.140 (x2, *both), 4.22, *4.57, 4.184, *5.211, *6.157, *6.291, *7.127, 7.173, *8.45, 8.86, 8.125, and 10.55. There are a number of other additions to Madrinkian's list with initial 'For' and the like that are probably also products of such exclusion by Brewer, 'Some Implications', not included here.

60 Russell and Kane, *The C Version*, p. 99. See Adams, 'Editing *Piers Plowman B*', p. 45 n. 21, for a critique of the treatment of this trivial variant by Kane and Donaldson. These are: *B.Prol.26, 2.74, *3.37, *3.124, 4.183, *5.21, *5.98, *5.263, *5.268, 6.44, and *7.58.

61 See Schmidt, *Parallel-Text*, II, 108. Those on Madrinkian's list are: *Prol.2, *Prol.73, *Prol.224, *1.187, 1.195, *2.137, *2.224, *3.220, *4.31, *5.47, 5.72, *5.214, †*5.445, *5.596, *5.604, *5.612, *6.76, †*6.122, 7.10, and †*7.105.

62 Madrinkian, 'Authorship and Error', pp. 185–86.

consisting merely in the *substitution of similars* can prove relationship only when they occur constantly and repeatedly. It is not the occurrence of such variants, but their occurrence *in overwhelming proportion*, that provides the argument for common origin.'[63] But this has nothing to do with Madrinkian's assertion. What Chambers and Grattan are discussing is indeed a basic editorial principle: that the number of *errors* in which given manuscripts agree, not the number of *manuscripts* attesting those errors, can indicate genetic relationships. Hence Kane: 'the persistence of the groups RU, VH and WN probably establishes their genetic character', and Kane and Donaldson: the 'impressive body of evidence' comprising over five hundred agreements in error between R and F 'must powerfully suggest genetic relation.'[64] Such large bodies of error in common do establish manuscripts as genetic groups; by contrast, though, the attestation of, say, *And* by TDChH²JLM (**A**.Prol.87), *dedes* H²VHJEMZ (**A**.Prol.102), or *wi3t* ChKWHRVJ(E)M (**A**.1.61), to take random examples from early in Madrinkian's list, does not render those agreements genetic by virtue of the large number of witnesses to the error in question. Any such 'basic editorial principle' as that cited by Madrinkian, if it existed, would be instantiated by actual genetic groups featuring many manuscripts. Kane identifies 1000 variational groups of four or more manuscripts in the **A** tradition, of which four are persistent and likely to be genetic (TDChH²; TRUDChH²; AWMH³; EAMH³), another three perhaps 'explicable as agreements of a larger group [TRUDChH²] when one or another of its members is absent.'[65] But to cite TRUDChH² or AWMH³ as support for H²VHJEMZ's genetic character would be no more valid than to cite VH, RU, or WN, all certainly genetic couples, to support the case that, say, HL and ChA are genetic.

As it happens, fifteen of the 231 items whose presence on Madrinkian's list is probably legitimate by his criteria (6.5 percent) are attested entirely and only by ten of the genetic groups identified by Kane, i.e., by the three pairs just cited, or TChH², or the various permutations of EA(W)MH³.[66] In addition I spot two items attested by more than four manuscripts and that point to genetic relationships for those readings, which are quite clearly archetypal readings where a single manuscript 'acquired an original reading by felicitous correction', with the erroneous reading being 'a scribal substitution which occurred in the first phase of transmission' of the

---

63 Chambers and Grattan, 'The Text of *Piers Plowman*', pp. 17–18 (emphasis in original), cited by Madrinkian, pp. 185–86 n. 20.

64 Kane, *The A Version*, p. 85, and Kane and Donaldson, *The B Version*, p. 28.

65 See Kane, *The A Version*, pp. 91–97 (quotation at p. 96).

66 Cited by **A** line number: TChH² (10.212), RU (6.62, 8.121, and 11.236), VH (3.71, 3.197, 3.220, and 4.66), EM (1.46), EAM (alone: 3.112 and 4.65; with Z: 3.5 and 4.31 *agayns*), AWMH³ (8.101 and 11.226). Kane's groupings do not include Z, which Kane, '"Z Version"', considers a scribal redaction of **A**. Though Madrinkian, 'Authorship and Error', p. 190, agrees with Kane that 'Z is no more than a heavily revised **A** text', he nevertheless includes those readings in his list, having his cake and eating it, on the grounds that Z 'contains a relatively high quantity of **B**-type readings' the 'persistence and substance of' which 'suggests they cannot be explained away as coincidental'. The issue does not affect anything here: for Kane Z's readings here are no more relevant than **B**'s, while for Madrinkian they are simply part of the **m** genetic group and thus still belong here.

A and **B** traditions, as the Athlone editors believed regarding some instances.[67] By definition each of these readings was the product of a single scribe, their agreements with Bx thus being the products of two scribes. These agreements are no different from those on Madrinkian's list attested by a genetic group with one additional witness, such as VHL (A.1.76), RUE (1.101), RUK (11.90), RUW (Prol.109), WNA (3.2), WNH (3.169), WNM (3.126, 6.54), and HEAM (5.103), or two genetic groups, such as VHAMH³ (8.87).[68]

The ease with which agreements like these attested by (in effect) only two witnesses can be attributed to convergent variation is what prompts Madrinkian to play up **(A)B** agreements attested by multiple **A** manuscripts, which supposedly manifest the 'basic editorial principle' that the more manuscripts sharing a given reading the more likely they are to be genetically related. But the problem is that the rest of those agreements with multiple manuscripts, i.e., those other than the fifteen items mentioned in the opening sentences of the previous paragraph, are *not* genetic and therefore must be random. Genetic groups by definition manifest single witnesses, their agreements with Bx thus relatively easy to explain as convergent; multiplicity, in his mind, points away from convergence and thus towards genetic explanations further back in the poem's transmission (e.g., in **r** rather than RU), but in reality do not, the opposite instead being the case. What Madrinkian takes to be 'a *prima facie* likelihood that manuscripts will agree in variation more often through common descent than through convergent variation', as Kane and Donaldson call such a belief,

> is manifestly not absolutely determinable; moreover it depends on two assumptions which are far from easy. The first is that the frequency of convergent variation is somehow limited. But for such limitation there is no evidence; indeed on the showing of our analysis it must have occurred with extreme frequency. The second assumption is that all transmission is uniformly corrupt, that genetic relation will always be indicated by relatively abundant agreement in error. If this assumption is put in another form, that all the human agents of manuscript transmission were equally inefficient, its difficulty appears.[69]

The substantial amount of data that generated these comments provides the relevant context for Madrinkian's discussion. He does not engage with this material, or with any of the Athlone editors' extensive demonstrations of the extreme frequency with which convergent variation must have occurred.

Readers might have noticed that Kane's identification of genetic groups, summarized above, does not mention the **r** group, the putative existence of which generates (Madrinkian's words) 'in fact one of the best arguments against Kane and Donaldson's

---

67 Russell and Kane, *The C Version*, p. 93, describing Kane and Donaldson's approach to authorial readings attested in **B** by 'a single manuscript or a very few', where the majority erroneous reading was shared by the archetypal text of **C**. See the first two items in the section on 'lengthy' agreements below. See also Kane and Donaldson, *The B Version*, p. 120 n. 43.

68 Kane, *The A Version*, p. 83: 'Of course, once a group is treated as genetic, its sigils, appearing within a larger group, must reflect that genetic relation.'

69 Kane and Donaldson, *The B Version*, pp. 19–20.

assumption of convergent variation', the notion that the **m** scribe took on more β errors than did the **r** scribe, or those of r^1 and r^2.[70] This is because the putative '**r**' family is Schmidt's creation, the evidence for which he cites as '108 agreements in error (some 50 major) of r^1 and r^2', nearly all of which, however, Madrinkian, who is quite consistent on such matters, either accepts as *correct* or would clearly do so if they qualified for his list.[71] Of the eleven 'major' agreements where Madrinkian would endorse Schmidt's judgements, only six, at three sites in the poem, appear exclusively in all candidates of the putative family.[72] The 'minor' agreements provide no further support.[73] The problem is with r^2, which sigil Schmidt uses 'mainly for convenience in differentiating the seven manuscripts' readings from those of r^1 on the one hand and **m** on the other (despite frequent agreement with **m** where r^1 errs)'.[74] If Madrinkian's claim is that **m** took on from β substantially more errors than did **r**, it

---

70 Madrinkian, 'Authorship and Error', p. 186.

71 Schmidt, *Parallel-Text*, II, 99. Of **r**'s fifty-four 'major' agreements in error there cited, Madrinkian takes forty-three to be correct, citing the **m** reading instead as the error in his list, pp. 219–29 (listed in the order given by Schmidt, II, 100): +**Z** 7.270 and 8.54; +**ZB** 1.106, 1.112, and 2.87; +**ZBC** 2.124, 2.146, 2.154, 3.146, 6.13, 6.71, 7.5, 7.60, 7.86, and 7.233; comparable with **ZBC**: +**Z** 8.101, 8.111 (x2), 10.32, and +**BC** 5.116, and 10.22. The other 'major' supposed agreements in error that Kane, and thus presumably Madrinkian, if they qualified for his list, instead take to be authorial are: +**Z** 1.110, 2.94, and 8.61; +**ZB** 7.15 and 7.60; +**ZBC** 5.256 [=Kane 5.254], 6.9, 6.82–84, and 7.230; comparable with **ZBC** 7.59 and 7.294; +**B** 8.54*a*; +**Z** 8.100; and +**BC** 5.126, 5.163 [= after Kane 5.162], 5.167 [= after Kane 5.165], 7.61, 7.68, and 8.136. Those with no other parallel are 5.79, 11.154, and 11.182.

72 Kane, *The A Version*, p. 98: 'One is prepared for the agreements supporting larger groups to be fewer than those supporting, say, genetic pairs. The remoteness of the act of copying their exclusive common ancestor establishes a probability that further variation will have obscured many of its errors, or correction have removed them. But an indispensable requirement of evidence for grouping manuscripts is actual agreement, and particularly, agreement in the same unoriginal variant or in unoriginal variants demonstrably stemming from a common variation.' Again, from Schmidt, *Parallel-Text*, II, 100, the six that appear entirely and exclusively in **r** are: 5.243 [=Kane 5.241] *reddere* **m**] red non / no red / no reed TH²ChDRUVHWNJLK; four readings at 11.194–96 (*line div.*; Dredles] God wot; wot þe soþe] *om*.; ben in office] benefices); and 11.245 shewiþ […] aftir] *om*. The remaining five cited as support for '**r**' despite the existence of contradictory evidence are: 7.128 (x2), where for both readings at least one **r** member agrees with correct **m**; 5.249 [=Kane 5.247], where the error (*gilt* for *coupe*) is shared with half of the **m** family (MH³); 5.87, where W, which Schmidt deems part of **r** here, agrees with **m** in attesting the line missing from the rest of **r**; and 8.105, where MS A agrees with **r** in reading *liflode* for MH³ *belyue*.

73 Again, from Schmidt, *Parallel-Text*, II, 100, I find the following 'minor' agreements in error among **r** manuscripts appearing as correct in Madrinkian's list: +**ZBC** 1.161, 2.75, 3.5, 3.129, and 4.106; +**ZB** 1.46, 4.31, and 4.33; +**B** 6.47; and +**BC** 6.110, 6.112, 6.116 [these three =Kane, 6.107, 6.109, 6.113], 8.87, and 11.5. Of the remainder I find none that Kane takes to be authorial (on a few occasions I was unclear as to what precisely was the error Schmidt was identifying in **r**).

74 Schmidt, *Parallel-Text*, II, 96. Other than the r^2 agreements in error with r^1 discussed above, the only two errors unique to r^2 that feature in all extant manuscripts are: 10.214 *schrewe* VJK (rest *same*), which I imagine was probably induced by both *shuln* in that line and the arrival, in the first line of passus 11 five lines later, of Dame Study (K probably influenced by C.11.24 *schrewes* likewise at line end; see note 100 below), and the trivial 11.217 *þo* JK (rest *þis, þe, þes, þese*). See Schmidt, II, 96, for a list of supposed r^2 agreements in error, for every other one of which, however, either at least one supposed r^2 witness does not agree, frequently aligning with **m** or r^1, or at least one non-r^2 witness joins the group, as can be seen by checking against Kane. Schmidt still does occasionally treat r^2 as if it existed even

collapses with his own endorsement of Kane's approach to the readings. If his claim is rather that **m** took on more than r^1 and r^2 in turn, it might be salvaged by replacing r^2 with VH, J, L, K, and WN, which would, however, in effect mean endorsing the first of his proposals, the one I rejected above as both self-defeating and impossible to believe.[75] Again, he presents this as his strongest evidence.

Length, Complexity, and Coincidence

My points so far have been that Madrinkian does not exhibit as complete control over the concept of 'convergent variation', or over his body of data, as might be expected in a data-driven essay on that topic, especially one whose claims are so dramatic. We turn now to the qualitative aspect of his argument, its final plank: his claim that 'the more lengthy and complex the error the less likely it is that multiple scribes all independently reproduced the same erroneous reading' and that forty (twenty-three, by my count) such 'substantive (**A**)**B** agreements are difficult to explain away as convergent variation' by the **A** scribes on the one hand and an early **B** scribe on the other.[76] The large number and 'substance' of these agreements, so he argues, means they 'must be explained' as lateral transmission from β to the **A** families, and vertical from β to ur-**B** and from **r** (or r^1 and r^2) and **m** to **A** copies.[77] In my judgement this sense that these agreements cannot evidence convergent variation, if accurate, would at best suggest the need to follow Schmidt in accepting the readings as authorial. I do not see that as necessary, though, and present the following in large part to make the point that the seeming difficulty of these readings is a function of the viewer's experience and desires rather than anything substantive.[78]

Madrinkian just presents the raw data — lemma and variant — rather than any support for his dramatic claims regarding how these agreements 'must be explained' in this manner. In their contexts, however, all but two of these twenty-three, which is also to say all but two of all the items on which Madrinkian's argument is based, are

---

while confirming its chimerical status, e.g., 11, 93: 'r^2's individual members exhibit the capriciousness characteristic of all extant **A** copies. Thus their combined attestation of the sub-family ancestor's readings remains uncertain as well as imperfect.'

75 One might also query the reliance of Madrinkian, 'Authorship and Error', p. 186 n. 21, on the 'average' number of β errors in each of r^1, r^2, and **m**, as it seems to me that the relevant figures instead would be the total number attested by **r** (or r^1, r^2) and **m**. For what it's worth — and remembering that the inclusion or not of any given item, e.g., *And* at line-beginning or *wel/ful*, has a substantial impact, nearly always only on r^2 and **m** — of the items legitimately on Madrinkian's list, I find that 191 appear in r^2 (whether alone or with r^1 and/or **m**), 183 in **m** (whether alone or with r^1 and/or r^2), and 101 in r^1 (whether alone or with r^2 and/or **m**). Or if only **r** and **m** are counted, the figures are 209 in **r** (of which fifty-four **r** alone) and 183 in **m** (of which twenty-eight in **m** alone), figures that would lead to a conclusion opposite the one Madrinkian draws.

76 Madrinkian, 'Authorship and Error', p. 186.

77 Madrinkian, 'Authorship and Error', pp. 187–88 (list) and 188 (quotations).

78 Kane, *The A Version*, p. 62 n. 1: 'The attitude of textual critics to this phenomenon [i.e., coincident substitution] seems to depend more on their experience than on theoretical considerations.'

most easily explained as coincidental. The non-difficulty of their substance in turn negates whatever power their number might have carried. There is neither support for Madrinkian's argument nor any given reason to endorse or to reject Schmidt's alternative here. The latter is a separate issue. In a few cases, the supposed 'minority' **A** reading is clearly that of Ax, which either calls its appearance on Madrinkian's list into question or, assuming it is accepted into the list, necessitates consultation by at least one **A** scribe of a pre-archetypal copy, which is intolerable to Madrinkian (see above, n. 21). The following list is keyed to the line numbering of the **B** version; '†' marks Madrinkian's additions to Brewer's list:

1. 2.183/**C**.2.196 rennen: **A**.2.144 iotten] rennen RUDVJKLHWNMZ; ganges E. Ax *rennen* is clear, *iotten* being attested accurately by only T and confusingly by its congeners H² (*Iotton*) and Ch (*trotten*). The term cannot have descended to their common ancestor, Schmidt's **t**, via Ax.[79]

2. †10.172 þynges: **A**.11.124 wyttes] þinges RUVJKAWMH³. In Madrinkian's paradigm authorial *wyttes* TH²ChD, which Kane takes to mean not 'the mind, human reason' as elsewhere in the episode, but 'departments of knowledge',[80] could have appeared in Schmidt's **d** only via correction against a pre-archetypal **A** copy.[81]

Next come three agreements that are not lengthy and complex but short and simple:

3. 2.160 bad hem alle: **A**.2.124 alle] bad hem alle MZ. E's *þaim alle* shows that M's *hem alle* comes from their exclusive ancestor, **m**. M added *bad*, like the other scribes who supplied **b**-terms for what seemed a deficient a-verse: *þat vche beorne* L; *Til/ To her bodes* WN. Initial *And bad* line 109 (again 171) and the seeming need for a vb. here parallel to 123's *And let* (for which H substituted *And bad*) were inducements.

4. †6.186 potful: **A**.7.174 potel] potful VJLKWN. This is straightforward 'visual error induced by the context'.[82] A *potel* is a vessel, a pot (*MED*, s.v.), so the terms are nearly identical.

5. 7.129 vs: **A**.8.111 vs anoþer] *om.* W; vs NAMH³. Donaldson deemed the sort of putative contamination here proposed, from something to nothing, 'utterly impossible to accept'.[83] Note that the omission occurs not in five but rather two **A** witnesses, the common ancestors of WN (Schmidt's 'w') and of AMH³ (**m**).[84]

---

79 See Kane, *The A Version*, p. 436, who suggests that *iotten* 'is probably a past tense of the verb "to go"', and *MED*, 'jotten', which assumes it to be onomatopoeic but deems Kane's idea possible. Schmidt, *Parallel-Text*, II, 322, says that scribal activity is most likely. See Schmidt, II, 95–96, on the t group, identified as well by Kane, pp. 85–86 and 89.

80 Kane, *The A Version*, p. 455; also Kane and Donaldson, *The B Version*, p. 86. This is *OED*, 'wit', III, 11a. Schmidt, *Parallel-Text*, II, 389, endorses þinges: *wyttes* is 'the more explicit reading and could have been induced by preceding *wyt* 123'.

81 See Kane, *The A Version*, pp. 91–93, and Schmidt, *Parallel-Text*, II, 94–95, on TH²ChD, the latter of whom identifies 'd' as its mutual ancestor.

82 Kane and Donaldson, *The B Version*, p. 99. See Schmidt, *Parallel-Text*, II, 366, for his endorsement of *potful*.

83 Donaldson, 'MSS R and F', p. 209.

84 See Schmidt, *Parallel-Text*, II, 97 and 100–01, on 'w' and AMH³ as the 'core-group' of **m**, and Kane, *The A Version*, pp. 77–78, 82–85, 87, and 89 on these groups.

Others barely differ from the postulated original and/or are ones in which the manuscript record proves the agreement to be coincidental:

6. 3.38/**C**.3.40 boþe: **A**.3.37 ichone] boþe HNM. The senses of *both* and *each one* are interchangeable.[85] M of **C** substitutes *echon* for *bothe*; at **B**.14.81, F does the reverse. Inducement to error by attraction to the previous phrase, 'be þe', is also likely; at **B**.14.257, C substitutes *beþe* for terminal *boþe*.[86]

7. 3.71 dele: **A**.3.62 giue] dele JA; delyn M. Kane finds here mere 'dialectal variation',[87] for the terms are synonymous; *MED*, 'delen', 3(a) ('to give'), cites a line from *Mandeville's Travels*, translating French *homme* […] *donne*, which appears as *He* […] *delez* in London, British Library, MS Egerton 1982 and *men ȝeuen* in London, British Library, Cotton MS Titus C.xvi. Schmidt suggests that this might instance 'scribal substitution of a familiar collocation [*dele dolis*], in part alliteratively induced', where 'agreement of (the genetically unrelated) J with **m** points to the likelihood that *dele* is of scribal origin, and possibly influenced by awareness of the **Bx** tradition here'.[88]

8. 4.44 ayeins: **A**.4.31 in to] agayns EAM. Schmidt, who accepts the **Z**-**m**-Bx 'error' *agayns* as authorial, says '*in(to)* **r** looks like a scribal attempt to remove a perceived ambiguity in the preposition that commonly signifies opposition'.[89] *MED*, 'in-to' (prep.), 19 ('against, in opposition to'), cites the Wycliffite Bible (early version), 1 Corinthians 6.18, 'He that doth fornycacioun, synneth *in to* his body', where the later version reads *aȝens*.[90] The **A** tradition also records: to V; vnto LK; on to Ch; toward N; *om.* I IJ.

9. 5.200 wayte: **A**.5.116 loke] wayte AMH³. Both terms mean 'watch, look' (*OED*, 'wait', 4a ('look'), quots. 1–3).[91] Cf. **A**.8.127/**B**.7.145/**C**.9.294 waitide] lokede VW, G, P², where the substitution disrupts that line's alliteration on *w*. In L the Dreamer went wide in this world 'wondres to wayte', i.e., 'to seek' (**A**.Prol.4; *MED*, 'waiten', 1a, d).[92]

10. 5.208 liser: **A**.5.124 list] lyser JU (overlooked by Madrinkian), leser RNWH³. 'The variants *lyser* and *list* are identical in sense (see *MED* s.vv. *liser* n. and *liste* n(2))',

85 Kane and Donaldson, *The B Version*, p. 100, call *boþe* a 'contextually easier reading'.
86 Kane, *The A Version*, pp. 117 (repetition of same word within a line) and 119–20 (confusion of *e* and *o*).
87 Kane, *The A Version*, p. 140 n. 4.
88 Schmidt, *Parallel-Text*, II, 326.
89 Schmidt, *Parallel-Text*, II, 335.
90 Kane and Donaldson, *The B Version*, p. 150, remark upon 'the practical impossibility of editorial decision in many cases of trivial differences between the **B** and **C** versions where no motive for revision or unambiguous indication of direction of variation by scribes suggests itself', such as *out of* / *fro*. Kane and Donaldson, p. 86, cite Bx's reading as 'more explicit' than A's here.
91 Kane and Donaldson, *The B Version*, p. 99, cite Bx's *wayte* as a 'lexically easier reading' than A's *loke*.
92 See the apparatus in Kane, *The A Version*, ad loc. The reading is confirmed by transcription at the wonderful 'International *Piers Plowman* Manuscripts Archive', ed. by Matsushita, source for all presentations of **A** readings beyond simple lemmas.

that is, the border or selvage of a cloth, and 'were in free variation', Schmidt says (all three versions attest both terms in this line).[93]

11. 6.94 his masse: **A**.7.86 mynde] his masse AMH[3](Z). The church is beholden to have Piers in mind by holding Masses for him; Cr reads 'to *mind* me in his *masse*'.

12. †7.119 atweyne: **A**.8.101 assondir] on tweyne AH[3]; atwynen M; a two W. Kane and Donaldson take Bx to be 'more explicit' than **A**; *OED*, 'a-twain', 2 ('asunder'), directs readers to *OED*, 'atwin', citing a text from 1400.[94]

13. †9.167 welþe: **A**.10.188 wele] welþe VChJAW. See also **C**.15.304 wele] *all MSS save W*, welth W; **B**.19.285 wele] WR, welþe HmCrLMF; **B**.20.38 wele] WHmCrYOCBLM, welthe C²GRF. This very common substitution arose from the term's derivation from *wele*, the *-th* suffix probably by analogy with *health* (see *MED*, 'welthe').

14. †10.376 **A**.11.257 make] lette AWM. The term *lette* is a 'more explicit' word for *make*, both of which mean 'to prevent'.[95] Cf. **B**.5.450 *lette* vs. **AC** *make*.[96]

Many of the readings, if not instancing substitution of synonyms, are nevertheless mundane scribalisms, as confirmed by the presence of the same error elsewhere in the *Piers* textual tradition:

15. 3.118 quod þe kyng if: **A**.3.107 ȝif] quod þe kyng ȝif VJM. Such medial 'quod [x]' additions, 'designed to express the sense of the text more fully', may 'record a probably unconscious protest against the necessity for unremitting, intelligent attention to meaning'.[97] See the Athlone apparatuses at **A**.2.16/**B**.2.20/**C**.2.19; **A**.3.5, **C**.3.155, **A**.7.36/**B**.6.34, and **A**.8.120/**B**.7.138 (this erroneously appears in Madrinkian's list; see the appendix).

16. 3.210 mede to men: **A**.3.197 hise men mede] meede to men VH. A simple case of transposition; also **C**.3.290 men mede] mede to men PE.[98]

---

93   Schmidt, *Parallel-Text*, II, 348. Kane and Donaldson, *The B Version*, p. 153, cite this as their first example of the editorial imperative to choose between variants found in all three versions: the choice here 'is between partially synonymous *list* and *liser* attested in manuscripts of all versions'. Kane and Donaldson, p. 154, determine that 'at V 208 substitution of *liser* can have been induced by attraction to the following *lenger*, while the local text has no features to suggest the reverse; therefore *list* is presumed original'; Schmidt, however, p. 348, objects that *lyser* 'seems to be the rarer word, and the distribution of manuscript support points to its having been archetypal in the later versions and probably also in the earliest'.

94   Kane and Donaldson, *The B Version*, p. 86.

95   *MED*, 'maken', 21(h), and 'letten', 5, and Kane and Donaldson, *The B Version*, p. 86. Schmidt, *Parallel-Text*, II, 393, says the minority **A** reading here 'could be original in **A** or reveal contamination here from **B**; but no serious issue of meaning is involved'.

96   Both Kane and Donaldson and Schmidt emend: Bx is 'more emphatic and explicit' (Schmidt, *Parallel-Text*, II, 356) and 'lexically [...] easier' (Kane and Donaldson, *The B Version*, p. 79).

97   Kane, *The A Version*, p. 131, including **A**.3.5 as an example. Schmidt, II, 327, considers the phrase 'possibly a Bx intrusion, omitted in G (presumably following an **A** source); but it could have been added in **B** and deleted again in **C** as one of various (small) revisions in' this and the following line.

98   Kane and Donaldson, *The B Version*, p. 79: 'A particular manifestation of the scribal tendency to produce an easier text is variation which makes the expression of the sense more explicit', such as this Bx error.

17. 5.126 þe beste: **A.**5.103 goode] þe best HEAM. Cf. **A.**1.133, betere] best E, which Kane includes among those errors that demonstrate how scribes 'consciously or unconsciously, if sometimes without intelligence or taste, strained to participate in the experience that [the poem] recorded, as well as to contribute to its purpose'.[99]

18. †10.5 quod she to wit: **A.**11.5 wyt quaþ she] quod sche to witt KMH[3] and Cx (11.5); it is likely that K here attests **C.**[100] Kane and Donaldson characterize this as substitution of a more explicit reading; it recurs at **C.**11.78 wit quod she] quaþ hue to wit PERMVAQSZFKGN.[101]

Some difficult or rare words, meanings, or constructions led scribes to substitute easier terms:

19. Prol.42/**C.**Prol.43 Faiteden: **A.**Prol.42 Flite þanne] Fayteden HM(JZW). The sentence concerns bidders and beggars who either beg under false pretences (*MED*, 'faiten', 1(b)) or argue noisily (*MED*, 'fliten', 1(a)). But a glance at the Athlone apparatus shows that scribes of all traditions went wild here. Kane and Donaldson deem *Faiteden* 'lexically and contextually easier' than *Flite þanne*.[102]

20. †9.178 togideres: **A.**10.199 ysamme] togeder ChH[2]KAWMH[3]. The terms are synonymous (*MED*, 'isame' (adv.), 1a ('in a group, together')). Kane and Donaldson plausibly remark that '**B**'s *togideres* is a gloss of the difficult word *ysamme*; in the next line *þe same* is a conscience-salving homœograph of the word just supplanted.'[103]

Reasons for many of these errors reveal themselves upon examination of their context, not apparent when one isolates the lemma and variants as in Madrinkian's list, as exemplified by this instance:

21. †10.339 heris: **A.**11.227 ʒeris] heris MH[3]; heres K; heers W. A one-letter difference. Kane: 'one heris ende means simply "the very least amount"; the phrase adopted, a legal formula […] here has the meanings "in due course, as a sure consequence, at the day of judgement". heris was introduced either because this was not perceived, or because the alliteration *Hélpiþ héueneward óne* was missed.'[104]

---

99 Kane, *The A Version*, pp. 138–39. Schmidt, *Parallel-Text*, II, 346, considers this possibly **B**> **m** contamination, but equally possibly original to both **A** and **B**, the other **A** family 'attempting to tone down the optimism'.

100 K = the **A** portion of Oxford, Bodleian Library, MS Digby 145, copied by Sir John Fortescue; its **C** portion is sigil D². Some of its **C** readings are collated in Kane, *The A Version*; e.g., its **C.**Prol.17a *And sawe a depe dale* appears as a variant of **A.**Prol.15a *A dep dale benethe* (the b-verse is certainly **A**); its **C.**7.158a *But ther ne was wight none so wise* is collated at **A.**6.1 *Ac þere were fewe men so wys*.

101 Kane and Donaldson, *The B Version*, p. 152.

102 Kane and Donaldson, *The B Version*, p. 100. Cf. Brewer, 'Some Implications', pp. 177–87, and Schmidt, *Parallel-Text*, II, 307.

103 Kane and Donaldson, *The B Version*, p. 110. See also Kane, *The A Version*, p. 454. Schmidt, *Parallel-Text*, II, 385, deems *togyderes* original: 'the superficially harder synonym *ysamme* may have been induced by *same*' in the following line.

104 Kane, *The A Version*, p. 456.

I agree with Madrinkian that two of these agreements are not easily attributable to coincident variation:

22. 5.190 eiȝen as a blynd hagge: **A.**5.109 eiȝen] eyn as a blynd hagge AM; ene like a blynd asse E; eyne blynd as an hagge H³. Schmidt speculates that 'the poet's **A**-MS could itself have been of **m** type; but more probably **m** here shows contamination from the Bx tradition, similar signs of desire to expand the Sins' descriptions appearing after **A** 110'.[105] Or a reader of a manuscript in Bx's line of transmission might have remembered having seen the phrase in an **A** manuscript and inscribed a marginal gloss that was subsequently taken into the main text.

23. 5.303 Hastow ouȝt in þi purs: **A.**5.153 Hast þou] hast þou ouȝt in þy pors VHN(ULJA). ULJA are here for attesting *ouȝt* alone, but as Schmidt observes, 'The shortness of the line may have prompted the needless scribal filler *ought* in several **A** mss' — as may have the seeming need for an object for *hastow*: cf. '"**Knowist þou ouȝt** a corseint", quaþ þei, "þat men callen treuþe? | **Canst þou** [**ouȝt** WJE; WHmLMR] wisse vs þe wey where þat wy dwelliþ?"' (**A.**6.20–21/**B.**5.532–33).[106] As for *in þi purs*, Schmidt suspects **B** contamination, yet even here a few scribes could have wanted Glutton's query of Betoun the Brewster to identify the location of his desired quarry: 'Do you have anything' — where? — 'in your purse? For instance, any hot spices?'[107] Metathesis (*spice> purs*) would also have played a role.

Save perhaps the last two items, nothing in these materials 'must be explained in some way other than Kane and Donaldson's assumption of coincidental reproduction of error'.[108]

In sum, Madrinkian's revolutionary argument relies on a series of misunderstandings of the data and of the phenomenon of convergent variation. His own argument relies, perhaps more extensively, on a much more difficult form of convergent variation than does the Athlone argument. He seems under the impression that Kane and Donaldson had a vested interest in promoting 'coincident substitution' so as to 'explain away' agreements, when they were merely arguing that the agreements in question could not be used to edit by recension — an argument that Madrinkian endorses. His figures are substantially higher than warranted, and even if they were still considered particularly high, it would be much easier to follow Schmidt's simple approach than Madrinkian's difficult one. Madrinkian's beliefs that the more manuscripts attest an erroneous reading the less likely it is convergent, and that this is a basic editorial tenet, are without foundation. And the 'lengthy and complex' (**A**)**B** agreements in error, which supposedly cannot instance coincidence, in fact epitomize that phenomenon.

Michael Madrinkian is quite right to insist that a critical comparison of variants across the postulated authorial versions of *Piers Plowman* must be at the heart of Langland

---

105   Schmidt, *Parallel-Text*, II, 347. Kane and Donaldson, *The B Version*, p. 80, cite the Bx reading as 'more emphatic' than **A**, deeming it 'explicable as the result of scribal participation in the sense and feeling of the poem', but they do not mention its existence in the **m** family of **A**.

106   Schmidt, *Parallel-Text*, II, 352.

107   Schmidt, *Parallel-Text*, II, 352. Schmidt attributes 'the fuller and more explicit *ought in þy pors*' in VHN to 'contamination from a **B** source, as elsewhere in Passus V'.

108   Madrinkian, 'Authorship and Error', p. 188.

textual study, and it is to his credit that he put that conviction to such sustained use, even if the variants in question did not support the conclusion he drew. He is also quite right that we should not accept as a given the account of the development of *Piers Plowman* proposed by the editors of the twentieth century. That account calls for continual testing, and the fact that the results of my own testing of his claims do not support his argument has little bearing on this much more important larger point. The very definition of '*Piers Plowman*' is at stake, and it would behove all critics of that great poem to follow Madrinkian's lead in working through the mass of data at the bottom of the Athlone editions. But it will be difficult to come upon any new knowledge if convergent variation is assumed from the outset to be a cheap escape hatch for editors, or coincident substitution to be all but impossible. It is everywhere.

Appendix: Readings Erroneously Included among Madrinkian's 357 (A)B Agreements in Error[109]

Excluded from classification by Athlone as 'unlikely to have genetic significance' (seven in total; those with four or more **A** manuscripts agreeing identified parenthetically).[110] The variants *and* or *but* for *ac*, excluded 'because linguistic change made coincidence in these variations almost inevitable': †Prol.214 (attested by seven **A** manuscripts), †8.22 (eight), †8.119 (seven), and †10.143.[111] Plus/minus inflexion of romance words ending in *-ce: iustice/iustices* 2.137 (four).[112] Excluded 'because independent substitution seems particularly likely': *†7.130: *we sholde no3t be / þat are not* (thirteen); [* with prev.] 7.130 *besy / to besy* (seven).[113]

Both same as prev. and correct **B** where Bx is not in question: 4.59 *mayde* presented by Madrinkian as an error for *maiden*, a variant (here only in **A**; seven manuscripts) excluded by Athlone.[114]

Both excluded from classification as 'unlikely to have genetic significance' and choice of Bx reading is dubious, where editors' identification of another reading in the **B** tradition as correct relies on its archetypal status: †3.11 *And* beta-F; Kane and

---

109 In this appendix '*' marks readings included in Madrinkian's list of forty 'lengthy and complex' instances; '†' marks his additions to Brewer's original list; and '$' marks 'imperfect agreements', in which Madrinkian, 'Authorship and Error', p. 197, claims it to be 'possible [...] to conjecture as to the direction of the error'. Unless otherwise indicated, line numbers refer to the **B** version.

110 Kane and Donaldson, *The B Version*, p. 18 n. 13. What Kane, *The A Version*, p. 122, calls '[t]he most numerous and difficult of' variants that 'bring us to the border between mechanical error and deliberate alteration of copy', 'the small ones', are for the most part still included in the tally by Kane and Donaldson, and thus not here.

111 Kane and Donaldson, *The B Version*, p. 18 n. 13. The exclusion was first noted by Kane, *The A Version*, p. 68.

112 Exclusion noted by Russell and Kane, *The C Version*, p. 20.

113 Kane, *The A Version*, p. 68. Madrinkian, 'Authorship and Error', divides this into two, but all of the readings in question fall under Kane's exclusion of 'VIII 112 þat ... not]'.

114 See Russell and Kane, *The C Version*, p. 20.

Donaldson, Schmidt, and John Burrow and Thorlac Turville-Petre (in their edition of Bx) endorse BmR *Ac*.[115]

Correct **B** readings where Bx is not in question: I present these sometimes slightly differently from how they appear in Madrinkian's list, by **B** line number and spelling. Those attested by four or more **A** manuscripts (seventeen in total): Prol.16 *diches*, 1.192 *and to alle*, 2.223 *cloutes*, 3.73 *half*, 3.146 *sixe*, 3.220 *myrþe*, 3.251 *bittre*, 4.31 *harmes*, †5.305 *A ferþyngworþ*, 5.452 (*recte*, for Brewer's and Madrinkian's 5.453) *matyns and masse*, *5.584 *In-no-manere-ellis-noȝt*, 5.586 *Manoir aboute*, 5.604 *keye*, 5.614 *wiþouten*, *6.5 *acre and sowen it after*, 6.76 *tiþe*, and 6.249 *Contemplatif lif or Actif lif*.

Same, those attested by two or three **A** manuscripts (twenty-five in total): Prol.219 *Brewesteres and Bochiers*; 1.114 *þat felawshipe*; 2.123 *For Dignus est operarius his hire to haue*; 2.123 *hire*; 2.193 *I cache myȝte*; *3.22 *coppes*; 3.156 *hym þe gate*; *3.198 *his men murye* (Kane and Donaldson accept *his* and *murye*); 3.198 *lette*; 4.107 *hewen*; 4.115 *haten alle harlotrie to heren*; *4.160 *Mekenesse* (sole **AB** term in common); *5.28 *Tomme Stowue*; *5.227 *vse*; †5.308 *warner*; 5.467 *Robbere*; 5.545 *Ido* (**B**: *I do*); 5.552 *hewe*; 5.559 *lasse*; †5.587 *oute*; 6.6 *wiþ yow and þe wey teche*; 6.66 *haue leue*; 6.105 *Perkyn*; 7.52 *þe Sauter bereþ witnesse*; and †10.21 *is cleped* (Kane and Donaldson read [*are*] *cleped*).

Madrinkian's choice of erroneous Bx reading is dubious, where editors' identification of other readings in the **B** tradition as correct relies on the archetypal status of Bx, those that appear in four or more **A** manuscripts (nine in total; this does not include those items where Madrinkian misidentifies the secure Bx reading, either as above, or below where the error does not exist):

1. 1.191 *no men* WHmCrOC²LM, *no man* YC, *non men* H. Both Kane and Donaldson and Schmidt endorse GF *non* given its support from **AC** (and **Z** for Schmidt); as Burrow and Turville-Petre remark, F's *non* 'may represent **Bx**'. Readers will want to remember that RF (alpha) together constitute a family of equal authority to WHmHm²CrGYOC²CBLMH (beta). F is frequently wild, but when it agrees with **A** and/or **C**, especially where R is absent, as here, it can reasonably be taken to record alpha.[116]
2. 3.6 *moolde* WHmHm²CrGYOC²CLMH. All three editions endorse BRF-**AC(Z)** *world*.
3. 3.63 *seye* WHmHm²CrGYOC²CLMH (B *siegge*). All three editions endorse RF *see*, supported by **A** and the X family of **C** (P family *sey* DGN; *see* and *seye* rest).

---

115   Burrow and Turville-Petre, *The B-Version Archetype*, note both that *Ac* 'is supported in the less obvious reading by the X family of **C**. The P family omits the conjunction', and that Kane, *Glossary*, 'ac', glosses *the term* as 'moreover' here. See the initial list and n. 111 above. Unless otherwise noted all quotations from this edition come from the notes to the line in question, which I usually consulted in the online version by clicking the 'note' symbol. Madrinkian, 'Authorship and Error', p. 183 n. 18, says that he has cross-referenced the readings with the lections presented in Burrow and Turville-Petre.

116   See Kane and Donaldson, *The B Version*, pp. 25–28 (RF) and 54–59 (WHmHm²CrGYOC²CBLM). These were first called alpha and beta in Schmidt, *Vision*, p. lxi.

4. †3.130 *in* WHmCrGYOC²CBLM. All three editions endorse RH *and*, supported by most **A** manuscripts and the X family of **C** (P family *alle*). Burrow and Turville-Petre: 'The apparent illogicality of the expression (what lies between heaven, hell and earth?) perhaps prompted beta to revise to *in* and F to revise to *þey men al erthe sowhte*.'

5. †3.162 *she* WHmCrGYOC²CBLMH. Both Kane and Donaldson and Schmidt endorse R *he* (F: *it*), supported by **A** and the X family of **C** (P family *she*): 'given the habitual association of justices and barristers with the legal process, the masculine form is preferable'.[117]

6. 5.214 *Spynnesteres* WHmCrGYOC²CBLM, **C**. Kane and Donaldson deem RF's singular reading, shared by TChH²RK of **A**, archetypal and correct. A coin toss.

7. †5.533 *he* GYOC²CB. All three editions endorse WHmCr²LMF *wye* (Cr¹³R *wight*), supported by **A(Z)** (**C** *treuth*).

8. 5.596 *men* WHmCrGYOC²CB. All three editions endorse *man* LMRF-**AC(Z)**.

9. †7.186 *Is noȝt* WHmCrGYCBLM (OC² absent). All three editions endorse RF *It is noȝt*. Burrow and Turville-Petre: 'Alpha's resumed subject is perhaps more likely to have been lost than added. **A** and **C** also vary, though *It* is supported by the X family of **C**.'

Same, two or three **A** manuscripts (sixteen in total):

1. 1.40 *folwen þe* CrYOC²CLMRF. Burrow and Turville-Petre think Bx might have picked up erroneous *þe* from the previous line, but WHmGH's reading, *folwen*, is accepted as archetypal and authorial (together with **AC(Z)**) by both Kane and Donaldson and Schmidt. Attribution of *þe* to a few post-archetypal scribes is easy.

2. 1.73 *asked* WHmCrGYOC²CLMH. Taking this to be Bx's error relies on two stages of interpretation that are plausible but not certain: F's provision of the correct reading, *halsede,* via consultation of **A**, and R's spelling *hasked* as a reflex of Bx (thus Schmidt, Burrow and Turville-Petre)[118] rather than being a form that 'shows that it does not reproduce an archetypal **B** error but reflects a reading *halsede* of its group ancestor (RF)' (Kane and Donaldson).[119] Of thirty-seven other appearances of the vb. *asken*, R spells only one with initial *h-* (10.160), and *halsede* is the reading of **A** and JOBUDMF of **C**.1.70 (LN *askide*).[120] The reading *asked* can be treated as a Bx error only by begging the question.

117 Schmidt, *Parallel-Text,* ii, 329.

118 Schmidt, *Parallel-Text,* ii, 313. See above, n. 21.

119 Kane and Donaldson, *The B Version,* p. 168. They see *asked* as an easier reading substituted for archetypal *halsede* (p. 154).

120 I found the spellings of *asken* via a search of a text-only file of R which was published with the early CD-ROM edition of *Piers Plowman Electronic Archive: London, British Library, MS Lansdowne 398 and Oxford, Bodleian Library, MS Rawlinson Poetry 38,* ed. by Adams, and included in the online version in earlier iterations but is no longer there. I thank Jim Knowles, Managing Editor of the project, for providing it. See Adams, 'Introduction', III.2.2.2, on loss of initial aspirate /h/ in this text.

3. 2.113 *I assele* YOLMRF (*I ensele* WCrG). Burrow and Turville-Petre: *I assele* 'must be **Bx**, though HmC *ys aseled* is the **AC** reading', where the need for 'must' undoes its force. Both Kane and Donaldson and Schmidt adopt HmC, the latter's comment that '**Bx** *seems* to have had *I assele*' (my emphasis) likewise recording the reasons for doubt.[121] This is just the other side of the line and thus should not be included in any list that presents itself as constituting the evidence of **A** agreement with Bx in error.

4. †3.63 *euery* WHmHm²CrGYOC²CBLMH. This is the reading of both Schmidt's and Burrow and Turville-Petre's editions, with support from **C**, while Kane and Donaldson opt for *ech a* RF, with support from **A**. An even split.

5. †3.78 *and* WHmCrGYOC²CBLMR. Kane and Donaldson and Schmidt endorse, and Burrow and Turville-Petre equivocate regarding, *and on* FH-**AC**.

6. 3.182 *gold* WHmCrYOC²CLMRH. Kane and Donaldson and Schmidt endorse BGF-**AC** *gold and*. It is not difficult to imagine R dropping the ampersand.

7. †3.229 *wel worþi* WHmCrGYOC²CBLMH. All three editions endorse RF-**AC** *worthy*.

8. *5.215 *weyed* HmYOC²CBM. All three editions endorse WCrGLRF-**AC** *peisid*.

9. 5.217 *barly malt* WHmCrGYOC²CBLMF. All three editions endorse *barly* R-**AC**, *malt* being an 'easy addition […] made by beta and F' (Burrow and Turville-Petre).[122]

10. 6.76 *take* WHmCrGYOC²CBLMF. All three editions endorse *aske* R-**AC**. The F-beta reading 'is an easy error, typical of F in increasing the alliteration, especially in a line where the pattern puzzles some scribes, and indeed it is found as a minor variant in both **A** and **C** mss' (Burrow and Turville-Petre).[123]

11. *7.129–30 divided after *by foweles* WHmCrGYOC²CBLM. It is not the line division but the reading that is in question. Burrow and Turville-Petre's text reads this because they are following copy-text; they grant that Schmidt might be right to endorse *be foles* RF.

12. †8.24 *alwey* WHmCrGYOC²CBLMR. Kane and Donaldson cite *alwey*><*amonges* attraction as the explanation for beta-R's error, endorsing F *alwey at hoom* as Bx, supported by **AC**.[124] It is difficult to maintain absolute consistency in one's treatment of situations of F-**AC** agreement: cf. item 15 in this section, and Schmidt's endorsement of *at hoom* as authorial but not Bx ('F presumably has it from **A**').[125]

13. *†8.50 *þi soule* WHmCrYOC²CBLMF (*þe soule* G). Kane and Donaldson and Schmidt endorse *þi selue* R-**A**. F uniquely attests the previous line, **A**.9.45 (= Kane

121 Schmidt, *Parallel-Text*, II, 320.

122 Kane and Donaldson, *The B Version*, p. 168 n. 89, place this among 'the commonest sorts of variation' in which F and beta converge: here, of a 'more explicit' reading.

123 Kane and Donaldson, *The B Version*, 168 n. 89, cite this as a careless beta-F substitution 'of an alliterating near-equivalent'.

124 Kane and Donaldson, *The B Version*, p. 169.

125 Schmidt, *Vision*, p. 377. Kane and Donaldson, *The B Version*, pp. 168–69, discuss readings where, despite the fact that F 'is hardly so innocent' as R, 'actual evidence of R varying coincidentally with the larger group survives' (p. 168).

and Donaldson **B**.8.49), one of the main pieces of evidence for what Madrinkian takes to be **A**> F contamination (above, n. 21), so he cannot take it as support for beta.[126]

14. †8.119 *were war* WHmCrYC²BoCotM; *weryn war* F; (*were(n) ywar* GOCBmL; Bm notes correct order). Kane and Donaldson and Schmidt both opt for *war were* R-**A** and the X family of **C**, which Burrow and Turville-Petre acknowledge 'may be right'.[127]

15. †8.128 *dowel* WHmCrGYOC²CLMR. Kane and Donaldson and Schmidt endorse *dowel and* BF-**AC**. See item 12 in this section.

16. †9.179 *Wydwes and wideweres* WGYOC²CBLM. All three editions endorse *Wydeweres and wydewes* RF-**A** (F reads *with* for *and*) and P of **C**; HmCr join alpha for *wydewes* (the spelling *wydwes* for the first term is Hm's).

Same and the agreement does not exist, four or more **A** manuscripts (two in total):

1. Madrinkian presents: '3.39 þei3] And Falsnesse (**C**.3.41 And Falshede): **A**.3.38 And þei3 falshed] þei3 *om.* NM; falshed] falsness RUHJ'. Lots of problems: a) initial *& þey* is attested only by MS F, which Burrow and Turville-Petre proclaim to be 'from **A**', undermining Madrinkian's acceptance of this as Bx (see above, n. 21); b) neither is *And Falsnesse* WCrGYOC²CLMH archetypal, all three editions endorsing instead *falsede* R, which 'presumably represents alpha (with F reading *Fals*) and is supported by **AC**' (Burrow and Turville-Petre); c) neither **A** group cited agrees with either possible Bx reading; and d), J reads *falnesse*, not *falsness* as here recorded.

2. 5.34 (*corrected*) chasten: **A**.5.32 chastice] chasten RHVKZ. First, Bx is in doubt: chasten CrGCL(R), Schmidt, Burrow and Turville-Petre; chasti3en WYOC²BM(HmFH), Kane and Donaldson. Second, it is questionable whether Langland or the poem's scribes treated this a substantive variant. Both terms mean 'chastise' < OF *chastier* (*OED* 'chaste' (v.), 'chastise' (v.)). Wherever either appears, its alternate almost invariably does as well: e.g., **A**.4.103 chastised] chasted URDNV; **A**.7.46, 299 chaste] chastise H³JCh, TChH³A; **B**.6.51, 11.425 chaste] chastise OC²BF, HmC²F; **B**.17.323, 334 chastised] chasted LYCCotR, CrYCLMR; **C**.5.136 chasten] chastysen RUD; **C**.19.303, 314 chasted] chastised JD²DH²ChW, JD²DChW. Genetic groups split between the alternatives; scribes go back and forth. The terms appear separately in Kane's *Glossary* as in the dictionaries, but the Athlone editors generally accept the given version's copy-text even where it conflicts with other versions and provide ample support for emendation (e.g., **B**17 chastised vs. **C**19 chasted; **A**.7.46 is a rare site where copy-text is rejected).

---

126 Another instance in which Kane and Donaldson, *The B Version*, p. 168 n. 89, place the F-beta agreement among 'the commonest sorts of variation', here, a misreading 'induced by the context'.

127 Yet another entry into Kane and Donaldson, *The B Version*, p. 168 n. 89: careless substitution 'of prose order' by F and beta.

The agreement does not exist, four or more A manuscripts (twenty-two in total):

1. Prol.84, presented as: 'parisshes (paryschenes HmF): **A**.Prol.81 parissh] paryschenes (H²)URHK'. This conflates two separate terms: parishes WCrGYOC²LM, H² is *MED*, 'parish(e' (n.), 1 ('parish, an ecclesiastical division'), which cites R of **A**'s attestation of two lines just prior: 'þe *parissh* prest & þe pardoner parte þe siluer | Þat þe pore peple of þe *parissh* shulde haue' (78–79); paryschenes HmF, URHK is 'parishioner', member of a parish, *MED*, 'parishen' (n.(1)), 1, citing V's version of the two lines just quoted: the priest and pardoner part the silver that 'haue schulde þe pore *parisschens*'.

2. 1.187 þe dedes: **A**.1.161 þe dede] þe dedes E(AMZ). Of these only E attests the reading: A *þine dedes* (cf. on his list 2.3 þe] þat, 5.575 þin] ȝour); M *gode dedes*; Z *dedus* (1.101; cf. 3.99 (*recte*, for Madrinkian's 3.127), 3.158). Readers willing to overlook these contextual variations could salvage an agreement of number alone, though see n. 61 on Schmidt's exclusion of sg./pl. variants.

3. 2.20 quod she haþ: **A**.2.16 haþ] quad he hath Z; quoþ heo þat haþ HV; quod sche þat […] hat M. Cf. on his list 8.77 Where] where þat, contradicting this Bx-HVM 'agreement'. One of the most common scribalisms.

4. Madrinkian cites, '2.163 And Fauel fette forþ þanne: **A**.2.127 fette fauel] Fauuel fette forþ VHLE(UM)'. None of these **A** witnesses agrees with each other or with Bx: Bot Fauuel fette forþ VH [a single witness; above, note 64]; And fauel fet forth L; And fauuell fochis forth E; Þanne fette fauel forþ U; And þan fauel fette M. See also **A**.2.108 for similar variation: Þanne fette fauel forþ TH²ChDRHK; and þanne fecchide fauel forþ U; Þan fet forth fauel JL; Þan fauuel fochyd furth E; Than fet favel WNM.

5. $†2.190 priked his palfrey: **A**.2.151 prikede forþ on his palfray] prikede on his palfray VHJWNM. On the one side, Bx lacks *on*; on the other, WN is in present tense, *prikeþ* (see, on his list, 5.101 hatide] hate; 7.175 passiþ] passed). Madrinkian speculates that Bx's lack 'inadvertently caused a further corruption' by Langland, who (he writes 'in **B**, which'), now taking *prikede* to mean 'urged' rather than original *prikede forþ on* 'galloped forth on', dropped superfluous *on*.[128]

6. †3.99 (cited as 3.127 [= **C**] but appearing in the right location), which Madrinkian cites as 'houses and the homes: **A**.3.88 hous and home] houses and homes VHJLAKNM (hous and homes TRUDChH²E)'. No **A** MS attests any of this, all attesting the definite article Madrinkian finds in Bx only, and grouping thus: sg. / pl. TRUDChH²; pl. / pl. VJLAKNM; pl. / sg. E; sg. / sg W. Madrinkian could have cited: 'houses: **A**.3.88 hous] houses VJLAKNME', though that might not have provided a fair picture of what is going on here.

7. $4.46 wel wisely a gret while: **A**.4.33 a gret while wel wisly] ful wysly a gret while EAMZ (*wittely* A). See above, n. 60, on *wel/ful* variation.

8. Madrinkian presents: '†4.90/**C**.4.86 And amende: **A**.4.77 Amende] & amende VHJEW'. But Bx reads *And so amende*, with which no **A** MSS agree.

---

128 Madrinkian, 'Authorship and Error', p. 201.

9. Madrinkian presents: '$4.98 Pitously Pees þanne: **A.**4.85 Pees þanne pitousliche] Pytously þan pes EAM(Z)'. The need for multiple agreements led Madrinkain to put present the sole actual agreement, Z, as if it merely provided indirect support of **m**'s non-agreement, which is perhaps closer to Ax than to Bx in being a straightforward transposition of the two alliterative terms.

10. Madrinkian presents: '†4.190 ride: **A.**4.153 raike] ryde RULEAKJWNM; wende TDH²'. Yet 'correct' *raike* is attested only by Ch, and Bx's 'error' comprises *ride fro me*, unattested in **A**, for the putative original *raike henne*. Kane takes *raike* to be an original reading 'uniquely preserved, the variants of the other manuscripts being groups of coincident substitutions that give a false appearance of unanimity against Ch', which hardly seems conducive to an argument against convergent variation.[129] The phrase *fro me* must be a post-authorial error in Bx, which, once granted, renders it much easier to attribute *ride* to Bx as well. This sort of dilemma crops up all over the place once one begins to examine the actual variants on which Madrinkian's argument is based.

11. Presented as: '5.190 *Divided after* baberlipped: **A.**5.109 *Divided after* baberlypped RDEAMH³'. But Bx is divided after *also*, which no **A** MSS attest.

12. $*5.213 webbe: **A.**5.129 wynstere] webstere MAWH³J. Madrinkian speculates: '**A** *wynstere*> (A) *webstere*> **BC** *webbe*. If the erroneous **B** reading is causally related to the existing error in **A**, moreover, it must have been first introduced into the ur-**B**.'[130] I assume that '(A)' means what is elsewhere called 'β'.

13. Presented as: '5.513 wiȝt noon: **A.**6.1 were fewe men] was non EAMH³(Z)'. Since Bx's only error here is *wiȝt* (*noon* is authentic), the supposed **(A)B** agreement here is of terms that are correct in Bx. So too is Z's *was weye* an agreement with correct Bx (it lacks *non*, though). See above, note 100 for the only near-agreement to be found in Kane's apparatus.

14. Presented as: '5.515/**C.**7.160 late was: **A.**6.3† late] late was N(VHKW)'. Only N agrees: V was late; HKW hit was late. Elsewhere transpositions are treated as errors (items 7, 18, 20 in this section; also, Prol.231, 2.193, 9.3). HKW agree not with Bx but with F only.

15. Presented as: '5.555 þe wey: **A.**6.42† riȝt] þe way DH²(TChUV)'; but the parenthetical readings are: þe riȝt way TCh; þe wey right U; þe wey hom V. The Bx error is in fact *witterly þe wey*, with which no **A** MS agrees. The same questions regarding *fro me* (item 10 in this section) apply here.

---

129 Kane, *The A Version*, p. 161. See Kane's endorsement of that proposal (among four options) at p. 162, and cf. Schmidt, II, 339.

130 Madrinkian, 'Authorship and Error', p. 198. For discussion of this notorious crux see Kane and Donaldson, *The B Version*, p. 102 and nn. 4 and 5; Schmidt, *Parallel-Text*, II, 348; and Mann, 'Was the C-Reviser's Manuscript Really So Corrupt?', p. 456, who intriguingly proposes that 'the nonce-word "wynstere" arose by anticipation of copy under the influence of "spynstere" in the following line — a kind of scribal error that Kane elsewhere shows to be common'. Cf. Madrinkian, p. 198 n. 48, noting his inability to 'discern any logical or mechanical evidence of how a corruption from *webstere* to *wynstere* would have taken place'.

16. 6.24 ye profre yow so faire: Madrinkian cites omission of *for* LW and *fayre* for *lowe* A at **A**.7.26 for þou profrist þe so lowe. Such a presentation obscures the absence of agreement by any of these: **þou** profrest **þe** so **lowe** W; **þou** proferest **me wel lowe** L; **for þu** proferist [*om.*] so fayre A. Cf. on Madrinkian's list 7.189 þou] ȝe; 7.199 þe] ȝou.

17. $6.33 þanne comsed: **A**.7.35 conseyuede] comsede TH²HNZ. The **A** reading cited is not in TZ, which are in present tense (see item 5 above). As for the absence of H²HN agreement with Bx, Madrinkian wonders 'whether the **BC** reading corrupted **A** or vice versa'.[131]

18. Madrinkian presents: '6.286 cole plauntes: **A**.7.270 cole plantis] plante colis AMH³Z'. A disagreement, obviously, cannot be taken as an agreement. The Bx 'error' is in fact attested in **A** by TChRUDVHLJKWN, which Kane considered correct in 1960 but no longer in 1988, when he endorsed **m**Z, Athlone **B** having since emended in that direction.[132] Madrinkian could thus have presented 'cole plauntes: **A**.7.270 plante colis] cole plantis TChRUDVHLJKWN'. It seems clear, though, that **m** strayed from Ax.

19. $7.106 here on: **A**.8.88 vpon] here vpon HLAW; is her vppon V; here in þis M. In fact all three editions take R(F) *upon* to be archetypal, so the addition of *here* is the only relevant issue. It seems to owe its existence to being the obvious solution to the need for a long dip in the deficient b-verse *upon/on þis erþe*.

20. $†9.192 ilke derne dede: **A**.10.205 dede derne] *trp.* RUDJKW. 'Although the inversion of this phrase may have happened coincidentally in all three traditions' (P of **C** *dede derne*), writes Madrinkian, 'the evidence for **B** revision from a scribal **A** manuscript that we have seen thus far may give some cause to suspect that the occurrence of the error in numerous manuscripts of **A**, **B**, and **C** is due to the reading having been passed through the ur-**B**': a clear articulation of the circularity of including these 'imperfect agreements' in any list that claims, in large part because of the large number of items it contains, to instantiate 'the evidence for **B** revision from a scribal **A** manuscript'.[133]

21. †10.150 þe while (**C**.11.88 þe while): **A**.11.102 while] the while KM. Madrinkian wrongly includes, in parentheses, TH² þer whiles. K might be following **C** (see nn. 100 and 138), leaving only M.

22. †10.231 frendloker: **A**.11.174 frendliere] frendloker DChH²VJW. Both are comparative forms of the adv. *frendli*. Kane and Donaldson print *frendlier* because it is the reading of their copy-text, W (it appears as well in Cr), while *frendloker* appears in the apparatus as the result of their policy to 'record formal variants about which we can be reasonably certain that they alter the syllabic value of the alliterative line'.[134]

131   Madrinkian, 'Authorship and Error', p. 199.
132   See Kane, *The A Version*, p. 461. Brewer, 'Some Implications', pp. 197–98, discusses this reading as well.
133   Madrinkian, 'Authorship and Error', p. 211.
134   Kane and Donaldson, *The B Version*, p. 218.

Same, two or three **A** manuscripts (twenty-one in total):

1. Madrinkian presents 'Prol.37 þei schulde / wolde: **A**.Prol.37 hem list] þei wolde HL'. But his list includes 3.5 wol] schal; 10.392 shal] schuld. Kane finds the scribal desire 'to embellish the metrical form of the text by increasing alliteration' to be 'most strikingly illustrated in the variants of L', including this example.[135]

2. Presented as: 'Prol.228 vntil hem: **A**.Prol.106† to hem] on tyll hym EM', but E's actual reading *vnto þaim* disagrees with Bx-M in both preposition and pronoun (sg./pl.). Cf. L *to heom*; D *til hem*. Compare, on Madrinkian's list, substitutions of preposition: 1.44 on] of; 3.2 to] befor; 3.84 of] wyth; 3.293 to] aȝeyne; 4.44 in to] agayns; and of pronoun: †5.108 hym] hem.

3. Presented as '2.198 wol loke: **A**.2.159 lokis] wole loke H(A)'; the parentheses indicate non-agreement, MS A omitting alliterating *loke* and thus agreeing only with F of **B** (*will*).

4. 2.227 '**That he scholde** (F: **wolde**) wonye with hem watres to loke': **A**.2.186 For to] Þat he schuld H; Þat he wolde L. See discussion at item 1 in this section. Here L seems to be attempting to supply a needed alliterative term.

5. 3.232 graunteþ: **A**.3.219 gyueþ] grantyt M(H). As H's actual reading, *haþ grauntid*, makes clear, the tense is not identical (see prev. section, item 5).

6. *4.15, presented as 'And seide [hym] as þe kyng bad/sayde: **A**.4.15 Seide] & seide as þe king bade HW'. F only reads '& tolde hym as þe kyng sayde'; beta-R lack *hym* and read *bad*. Authorial **A** actually reads 'Seide hym as þe kyng sente', and W's initial *&* is shared with N (see also above, n. 59), so the only relevant variant might be: sente] bade HW. Schmidt, preferring *sayde* over *bad* as authorial **B**, writes that Bx 'presumably substituted *bad* through stylistic objection to repetition of the verb',[136] while Kane and Donaldson have it that *bad*, 'as more explicit and incidentally unmetrical, glosses original *sente*', which applies to HW as well (H's partner V reads *sende*; W's partner N, *sente*).[137]

7. $*5.526 oure lordes Sepulcre: **A**.6.14 þe sepulcre] þe sepulchre of oure lord KAH³Z. Madrinkian explains this non-agreement in his account of 'progressive revision within the **C** tradition'.[138]

8. $†5.609, presented as: 'þat is a: **A**.6.95 þat] for he is a VA', already a non-agreement, but this is very misleading. It is VA's omission of the following term, **AB** *wykkide*, that explains these MSS' independent additions.

---

135 Kane, *The A Version*, p. 141.

136 Schmidt, *Parallel-Text*, II, 335.

137 Kane and Donaldson, *The B Version*, p. 107.

138 Madrinkian, 'Authorship and Error', pp. 207 (quotation) and 210–11 (discussion). Regarding KAH³Z *sepulcre of oure lord*, Schmidt, *Parallel-Text*, II, 358, suggests that perhaps K is contaminated by an X-family **C** copy, AH³ by **B**, and Z by **C**, to which Madrinkian, p. 211 n. 68, objects: 'Considering that KAH³Z all use exactly the same reading, however, there is no indication of how or why the editor distinguishes different sources of contamination.' But K's text here, at least, is part of a twenty-three-line **A** passage sandwiched between **C** matter that influenced other sites in this **A** portion as well. See Kane, *The A Version*, p. 37 and n. 1. See also above, n. 100. Madrinkian's objection might be valid, save K's role, were his own argument already established, but otherwise there is no warrant for any treatment of KAH³Z as genetically related.

9. $*†6.155 forpynede: **A.**7.142 pilide] pyned MH³; foule pyne A. The latter is particularly far from Bx. If *forpynede* is to be treated as a synonym for *pyned*, so too ought *wiþheld* be treated as a synonym for *helden* (see *MED*, 'holden' (v.(1)), 11b ('withhold')), but cf. 2.231 on Madrinkian's list. That aside, this is not a 'lengthy and complex' disagreement, but one of a single letter, all three resulting terms fitting context perfectly well: *pilide* is a term of abuse derived from a ppl. meaning 'shorn of hair, tonsured' (*MED*, 'pilen', 6b, citing this instance), while *pyned* and *forpyned* mean 'tortured' (*MED*, 'pinen' and 'forpinen').

10. $†6.292 'Al þe pouere **peple þo** pescoddes fetten': **A.**7.276 peple] peple þan WN. Bx *þo* 'those' modifies *pescoddes*; [WN] and G of **B** *þan* 'then' modifies *fetten*.

11. $7.26, presented as: 'myseise folk/**C.**9.30 mysese men: **A.**8.28 myseyse to] myseise men to LAZ', but MS A in fact reads *myssede* for *myseise*. Madrinkian proposes that Bx altered β *men to helpe* to *folk helpe*.[139]

12. $†7.138 'Abstynence þe Abbesse **quod Piers myn** a b c me tauȝte': **A.**8.120 myn] quoþ he myne HW. The proposed *he-Piers* agreement is incompatible with Madrinkian's *perkyn-peris* disagreement (6.105). See item 15 in the discussion of 'lengthy and complex' agreements above.

13. †7.151/**C.**9.300 Piers þe Plowman: **A.**8.132 peris loue þe plouȝman] peris þe plouȝman KM. K is probably following **C** (see above, nn. 100 and 138), so only M can be identified as agreeing with Bx in this most obvious instance of coincident variation, among those 'induced by more common collocations'.[140]

14. †$8.74 presented as: 'what þow art: **A.**9.65 art þou] þou art DM'. But the **A** equivalent is **who art þou**, DM retaining *who*, with only MS A agreeing: who art þou] what þu art.

15. †8.77/**C.**10.75 Where þat: **A.**9.68 Where] wher þat VK. See item 13 in this section on K's disqualification from such instances.

16. †8.89, presented as: 'and: **A.**9.80 or] and RU'. But in context Bx's reading is *heeld and*, RU retaining **A** *hadde*. It would be fair to ask, if the argument in whose service this and all these instances are cited is accurate, what would prompt a scribe to home in on that meaningless variant while ignoring substantive *hadde/heeld*. RU is a genetic group (see above, n. 64), so this is among the many sites in which it is not an issue of multiple **A** witnesses that point away from coincident substitution.

17. †8.110, presented as: 'noon ooþer: **A.**9.100 oþere] non oþere WM'. This is very misleading; an accurate presentation would be: 'noon ooþer wise: **A.**9.100 oþer wise & ellis nouȝt] non oþer wise / Ne elles not W (ll. 99–100); noun oþere wyse ne ellis M. In this case, W's and M's addition of *non* is clearly connected to their substitution of *ne* for *&*, confirming that the reading must be taken as a whole: 'Unconscious promotion of the notion appearing more important' in Bx, its resulting xa/ay alliteration 'inferior with respect to verse technique'.[141]

---

139   Madrinkian, 'Authorship and Error', p. 200.
140   Kane and Donaldson, *The B Version*, p. 99.
141   Kane and Donaldson, *The B Version*, pp. 82, 81.

18. *†9.34, presented as: 'likkest: **A**.10.35 ymage] like AM.' Again, very misleading, an accurate presentation being: And made man likkest to hymself one: **A**.10.35 Saue man þat he made ymage to himselue] Saue man þat he made like to himselue AM. The single, trivial variant Madrinkian isolates is not an agreement, at least if the inclusion of 5.126 *goode* vs. *þe beste* on his list is legitimate. 'Substitution of an easier and more emphatic statement' in Bx (see **A**.10.6/**B**.9.6 *lik to hymselue*) resulted in botched metre (aa/xy vs. **A** aa/ax).[142] K *Image like* suggests that scribes found the noun *ymage*, in apposition to *man*, difficult and thus changed it to the adv. *like* or *likkest*: 'and made man like(st) himself', or as K (redundantly) has it: 'man, that he made a likeness like to himself'.

19. †9.161, presented as: 'mariages: **A**.10.184 weddyng] maryages ChH³'. This is incorrect; Ch has sg. *mariage*, which, if not an oversight, suggests that Madrinkian, too, considers the twenty sg./pl. disagreements on his list 'non-indicative of genetic origin' (Schmidt; see above, n. 61).

20. †10.56, presented as: 'forþ a: **A**.11.42 forþ] forþ a A(KW)'. KW omit *forþ*; in any case K is probably following **C**.11.37 here (see above, nn. 100 and 138).

21. $†10.202 For he: **A**.11.151 And] He MH³. See above, n. 59, on Brewer's probable omission of such items (when they actually occur) from her list. That the error arose coincidentally in M and H³ is clear from correct *And* in their respective congeners A and W.

Works Cited

Manuscripts and Archival Resources

Aberystwyth, National Library of Wales, MS 733B
London, British Library, Cotton MS Titus C.xvi
———, MS Egerton 1982
———, MS Harley 3954
Oxford, Bodleian Library, MS Digby 145
Oxford, Corpus Christi College, MS 201
San Marino, Huntington Library, MS Hm 114

Primary Sources

International *Piers Plowman* Manuscripts Archive, ed. by Tomonori Matsushita <http://piersplowmanmss.sakura.ne.jp> [accessed 1 July 2020]
Langland, William, *Piers Plowman: The A Version*, ed. by George Kane, rev. edn (London: Athlone, 1988)
———, *Piers Plowman: The B Version*, ed. by George Kane and E. Talbot Donaldson, rev. edn (London: Athlone, 1988)

---

142 Kane and Donaldson, *The B Version*, p. 89.

——, *The Vision of Piers Plowman: A Critical Edition of the B-Text*, ed. by A. V. C. Schmidt, 2nd edn (London: Dent, 1995)

——, *Piers Plowman: The C Version*, ed. by George Russell and George Kane (London: Athlone, 1997)

——, *Piers Plowman: A Parallel-Text Edition of the A, B, C and Z Versions*, ed. by A. V. C. Schmidt, 2 vols (Kalamazoo: Medieval Institute, 2011)

——, *The Piers Plowman Electronic Archive*, VII: *London, British Library, MS Lansdowne 398 and Oxford, Bodleian Library, MS Rawlinson Poetry 38*, ed. by Robert Adams <http://piers.chass.ncsu.edu/texts/R> [accessed 1 July 2020]

——, *The Piers Plowman Electronic Archive*, IX: *The B-Version Archetype*, ed. by John Burrow and Thorlac Turville-Petre (Chapel Hill: University of North Carolina Press, 2018), also available online <http://piers.chass.ncsu.edu/texts/Bx> [accessed 1 July 2020]

Middle English Dictionary <http://quod.lib.umich.edu/m/middle-english-dictionary/> [accessed 1 July 2020]

Oxford English Dictionary <http://www.oed.com> [accessed 1 July 2020]

Secondary Sources

Adams, Robert, 'Editing *Piers Plowman* B: The Imperative of an Intermittently Critical Edition', *Studies in Bibliography*, 45 (1992), 31–68

Brewer, Charlotte, 'Some Implications of the Z-Text for the Textual Tradition of *Piers Plowman*' (unpublished D.Phil. thesis, University of Oxford, 1986)

Chambers, R. W., and J. H. G. Grattan, 'The Text of *Piers Plowman* I. The A-Text', *Modern Language Review*, 4 (1909), 357–89

Davis, Bryan P., 'The Rationale for a Copy of a Text: Constructing the Exemplar for British Library Additional MS. 10574', *Yearbook of Langland Studies*, 11 (1997), 141–55

Donaldson, E. Talbot, 'MSS R and F in the B-Tradition of *Piers Plowman*', *Transactions of the Connecticut Academy of Arts and Sciences*, 39 (1955), 179–212

Ferriss, Suzanne, 'The Other in Woody Allen's *Another Woman*', *Literature/Film Quarterly*, 24 (1996), 432–38

Greg, W. W., *The Calculus of Variants: An Essay on Textual Criticism* (Oxford: Clarendon, 1927)

Hanna, Ralph, 'George Kane and the Invention of Textual Thought: Retrospect and Prospect', *Yearbook of Langland Studies*, 24 (2010), 1–20

Heng, Geraldine, 'Feminine Knots and the Other *Sir Gawain and the Green Knight*', *PMLA*, 106 (1991), 500–14

Kane, George, 'The "Z Version" of *Piers Plowman*', *Speculum*, 60 (1985), 910–30

——, *Piers Plowman: Glossary* (London: Continuum, 2005)

Madrinkian, Michael, 'Authorship and Error: Reconsidering the B Revision of *Piers Plowman*', *Yearbook of Langland Studies*, 32 (2018), 177–233

Makarushka, Irena, 'Tracing the Other in *Household Saints*', *Literature and Theology*, 12 (1998), 82–92

Mann, Jill, 'Was the C-Reviser's Manuscript Really So Corrupt?', in *New Directions in Medieval Manuscript Studies and Reading Practices: Essays in Honor of Derek Pearsall*, ed. by Kathryn Kerby-Fulton, John J. Thompson, and Sarah Baechle (Notre Dame: University of Notre Dame Press, 2014), pp. 452–66

Russell, George, 'The Evolution of a Poem: Some Reflections on the Textual Tradition of *Piers Plowman*', *Arts*, 2 (1962), 33–46

Russell, George, and Venetia Nathan, 'A *Piers Plowman* Manuscript in the Huntington Library', *Huntington Library Quarterly*, 26 (1963), 119–30

Vine, Stephen, 'The Wuther of the Other in *Wuthering Heights*', *Nineteenth-Century Literature*, 49 (1994), 339–59

Warner, Lawrence, *The Lost History of 'Piers Plowman': The Earliest Transmission of Langland's Work* (Philadelphia: University of Pennsylvania Press, 2011)

——, 'The Ilchester Prologue, the Penultimate Passus of Corpus 201 (F), and a New School of *Piers Plowman* Textual Studies', *Journal of English and Germanic Philology*, 118 (2019), 486–516

Wood, Sarah, 'Nonauthorial *Piers*: C-Text Interpolations in the Second Vision of *Piers Plowman* in Huntington Library, MS HM 114', *Journal of English and Germanic Philology*, 114 (2015), 482–503

Teaching Reflection

SARAH TOLMIE

Langland, Milton, and the Weird Trees

Teaching and Learning through Piers Plowman *and*
Paradise Lost

▼ **KEYWORDS** Milton, teaching, experiential learning, theological
poetry, counterintuitiveness, enigma, work, reading

▼ **ABSTRACT** This essay about teaching and learning
compares *Piers Plowman* and *Paradise Lost* as enigmatic teaching
texts that offer students, especially undergraduates, irreplaceable
experiences both in class and in private reading. Both poems
are deliberately counterintuitive and lead readers and teachers
constantly into challenges that they cannot win. While these
techniques were devised to create the conditions for Christian
humility, they still have a lot to offer to the post-secular world.

> *A learning experience is one of those things that says,*
> *'You know that thing you just did? Don't do that'.*
>
> Douglas Adams, *The Salmon of Doubt*

I will never teach *Piers Plowman* again. So I'm having to make do with *Paradise Lost*. There are worse problems. It is not absolutely necessary to teach on the topics of our own research. Nonetheless, the opportunity of teaching Langland to undergraduates fifteen years ago led me to publish on the poem in ways I would never have achieved otherwise. At that time, I could get away with offering a semester-long course on Langland in the one Non-Chaucerian Middle English undergraduate slot we had available. No one has taught that course in years. Students have, I am told condescendingly in department meetings, 'voted with their feet' against pre-1800 literature. If they wish to study literature at all, they prefer contemporary literature. Much more popular are our various rhetorical options, especially anything to do with digital media or gaming, and a growing list of courses in writing pedagogy.

Sarah Tolmie (stolmie@uwaterloo.ca) is an Associate Professor of English at the
University of Waterloo.

The Yearbook of Langland Studies, 34 (2020), 177–199   BREPOLS ❧ PUBLISHERS   10.1484/J.YLS.5.121091

The fact that all these options jostle under one departmental roof is the product of a perhaps uniquely Canadian compromise. Where in the American institutional landscape these things tend to divide explicitly into departments of Literature and Language versus Rhetoric and/or Communications, the brief of my institution — a polytechnic foundation of the 1960s — has always been to combine them under various guises. Literary study was intended to look applied from the outset. Thus conflicts sometimes spread over several humanities fields have unfolded at very close quarters. Today rhetoricians and writing studies scholars outnumber literature faculty by two to one, a transition aided by a university-level commitment to communications courses for STEM students. I make this complaint only to clarify why I am offering an essay about teaching Milton to an audience of Langlandians.[1] My brief here is to explain how and why having read and taught Langland makes me a better teacher and reader of Milton. In the midst of this Pyrrhic endeavour, I am going to make a case for some fundamental approaches to difficult poetics that I believe the two writers share despite their differences, and suggest that the rebarbative operations of the will required to make sense of either *Piers Plowman* or *Paradise Lost* mean that both poems rely on the process of experiential learning.[2] If literature, especially old literature, can offer anything to the twenty-first-century pedagogical community, it is this: both 'work' and 'experience' once had broader existential remits than the almost exclusively corporate-professional understanding of these terms that prevails today. My experience of teaching these enormous and complicated poems successively is what drives the following pages. Engagement with the scholarly tradition of either Milton or Langland studies is light, consisting mostly of those few selected sources I would typically acknowledge in an undergraduate lecture class.

Langland is a medieval poet, a Catholic reformer; Milton is an early modern radical Protestant determined to do away with Catholic institutions. These are real differences and we can't get around them. Nonetheless, my experience of reading these poems — and particularly, of teaching them to mystified undergraduates who

---

1   Readers looking for essays specifically about teaching Langland should see the recent volume *Approaches to Teaching Langland's 'Piers Plowman'*, edited by Thomas A. Goodmann. For a completely different take on the value of experiential learning and its relation to teaching about poverty in *Piers*, see Kate Crassons's 'Going Forth in the World: *Piers Plowman* and Service Learning' in this collection. In the same volume, C. David Benson's essay '"Lewed" Langland and the Delights of Difficulty' shares some ground with my main point about teaching either Langland or Milton. William E. Rogers, one of my favourite readers of *Piers Plowman*, contributes an essay on 'Repeating our Agonies: An Approach to Teaching Langland' (notably one that emerges out of teaching the poem specifically to undergraduates) that also focuses on what the poem does to readers and as such bears comparison to what I say here about teaching both these poets. Nicholas Watson's '*Piers Plowman* as Theology: Pedagogy, Politics, Pastness' offers a characteristically clear statement about the value of teaching theological poetry to secular students; this value applies equally well to teaching Langland or Milton, in my view.

2   There are many ways of approaching this term. I do so very broadly. One influential theorist of experiential learning, for example, is David A. Kolb. His approach stresses the need for improvisation, for moving knowledge from one domain to another, for trial and error, and for personal reflection. All of these are required to read or teach *Piers Plowman* or *Paradise Lost*. His initial influential work was 1984's *Experiential Learning: Experience as the Source of Learning and Development*.

know little European history or theology — has brought them together in my mind in two interrelated ways. Firstly, Milton and Langland are both profoundly theological poets. This status has certain entailments that makes them different from most poets students have previously encountered. Secondly, they share a Christian epistemology totally committed to experience, and perhaps even more importantly, to a poetics that places experience at the heart of reading.

Langland and Milton are theologians who write in poetic form, and poets who write theology. The tasks are inseparable and mutually dependent. The kind of theology that they write can only exist in poetry and neither one of them would have written his major poetic work for anything other than theological purposes. Theology is their art. This poetic art anticipates, and is even in many ways coextensive with, the concerns and techniques of secular poetry as it seeks to represent reality and experience, but the world that they represent is entirely conceived in theological terms. At the same time, vernacular poetry alone has the affordances to do the theological work that these writers perform.[3] It cannot be done by biblical commentary, preaching, liturgy, catechism, law, prayer, contemplation, pilgrimage, participation in sacraments, discussion, translation or anything else, not even by the sacred texts themselves. It has its own authority: the fallible authority of fiction. That is why we have *Piers Plowman* and *Paradise Lost* and why they take the disconcerting forms they do. Langland and Milton share a mission despite their wide separation in time, supervening even the drastic differences in the landscape of religious authority in their two cultures. Their impetus for writing is to 'justify' (Milton's term at 1.26) the ways of God to man, while necessarily having to accept that divinity is the ultimately foreign object, uncontainable in either human language or consciousness. Committed to the claims of heaven, they must discuss them in the terms of earth. Both are, therefore, necessarily, poets of failure. It is critical to understand this about both of them, as it divides them utterly from the suasive inheritance of classical oratory and the didactic aims of classical pedagogy. Rhetoricians do not set out to fail. Poets often do, and theological poets must.

My main evidence for this is the notable extent to which both poems get in their own way. Both *Piers Plowman* and *Paradise Lost* are thoroughly bass-ackward, I have told students repeatedly, and it isn't because Langland or Milton was incompetent. In the case of *Piers Plowman*, readers spend their time following the errant Will on a quest with an ever-diminishing likelihood of completion, chiefly because its parameters keep changing according to whomever he is talking to at the time. In the case of *Paradise Lost*, we are faced with foregone conclusions from the first line — which conclusions are parodically reinforced and hyperbolically inflated with insistent iterations for twelve encyclopaedic books. In neither case is there

---

3 There is a large body of scholarship on vernacular theology in the medieval period, following on from Nicholas Watson's 'Censorship and Cultural Change in Late Medieval England' and related works. James Simpson has written books carrying aspects of this tradition across the medieval/early modern divide, among them *Reform and Cultural Revolution, 1350–1547* and *Cultural Reformations*, co-edited with Brian Cummings. The present essay does the same, though less masterfully.

any possibility of suspense. Not even Milton's epic machinery, which he may have borrowed specifically because it existed in order to animate familiar myths, succeeds in creating any. In Langland's case, Holy Church gives the game away to Will before he's even out of passus 1 and there are nineteen more to go. If suspense is not what keeps us reading, neither can it be the educational strides made by the protagonists, all of whom appear to learn nothing. Adam and Eve fall despite every kind of warning. Will has not ceased his restless and unsatisfied journeying even at the end of his book. Students expecting (albeit anachronistically) a *Bildungsroman* in either case are grimly disappointed. Conventional narrative satisfactions are hard to come by in both these poems. Langland and Milton are astonishingly ready to prejudice and defy easy understanding of, or smooth progress through, their works at almost every level from basic grammar upward. Frustration is a key tool for both of them. They are, I think, at their most alike in being Christian poets in a love/hate relationship with secular poetry — if not with language itself, or even representation — and in using the tensions produced by this to theological effect.

Both of these great, weird, long poems grapple with one big two-part question: Why did we fall, and what can we do about it? Milton concentrates more on the first part of the question, Langland on the second: they are, nonetheless, inextricably linked as the 'overwhelming question'[4] continuously posed by Christian writers, the answer to which is the human condition. Milton deals with the question proleptically and Langland *in medias res*, which explains the huge difference in atmosphere between the two poems. However, living through the plague years, as Langland did, or the civil wars, as Milton did, certainly casts the question that necessarily precedes this one into similarly high relief: namely, why is living in the world as horrible as it is? From an epistemological point of view, in particular, how is it that knowledge — the gift and burden of the Fall — can so consistently fail to guide us? I will spend the remainder of this essay looking at a few among the many scenes of unpropitious teaching and learning that occur in both *Piers Plowman* and *Paradise Lost*. If what we expect of pedagogy is clear transmission of information from authoritative teacher to receptive and obedient student (the classical model), these scenes are failures. If what we expect of pedagogy is playful and interactive delivery of age-and-culture-appropriate material from facilitators to learners (the progressive, learner-centred model), they are still failures.[5] Nor can we say with certainty that we, as readers, are supposed to take them all as negative *exempla*. I do not think that either Langland or Milton wishes us to profit, simply and smugly, from the misery of their literary characters. That hardly takes much willpower and both writers are obsessively interested in the human will.

---

4   Eliot, 'The Love Song of J. Alfred Prufrock', l. 10. To my mind, this poem is another stop on the road of English vernacular theology and a lineal descendant of both *Piers Plowman* and *Paradise Lost*, particularly the former.

5   By this I mean the tradition that traces back to early and mid-twentieth-century education scholars like Jean Piaget and John Dewey and that is broadly normative in public education throughout the English-speaking world. Progressive education, at minimum, consists of a network of theories and practices that are child- or learner-centred. An attempt to come to grips with what the umbrella term means in the Canadian context is Davies, 'The Paradox of Progressive Education'.

Let us begin with the scene from Milton that gives me my title. This is the hilarious and pathetic moment in book ten in which Satan, expecting the applause of his demonic host after his successful mission to earth to tempt Eve and Adam, and doubtless planning to follow it up with an exordium of self-praise, is unexpectedly turned into a snake (10.504–45). Slithering in mute terror and embarrassment out of the great hall of Pandaemonium, he finds his army likewise transmogrified and busy iteratively chomping on the fruits of a grove of trees which has suddenly appeared there:

> There stood
> A grove hard by, sprung up with this their change,
> His will who reigns above, to aggravate
> Their penance, laden with fair fruit, like that
> Which grew in Paradise, the bait of Eve
> Used by the Tempter: on that prospect strange
> Their earnest eyes they fixed, imagining
> From one forbidden tree a multitude
> Now ris'n, to work them further woe or shame;
> Yet parched with scalding thirst and hunger fierce,
> Though to delude them sent, could not abstain,
> But on they rolled in heaps, and up the trees
> Climbing, sat thicker than the snaky locks
> That curled Megaera; greedily they plucked
> The fruitage fair to sight, like that which grew
> Near that bituminous lake where Sodom flamed;
> This more delusive, not the touch, but taste
> Deceived; they fondly thinking to allay
> Their appetite with gust, instead of fruit
> Chewed bitter ashes (10.548–66)[6]

This scene immediately recalled to me two memorable scenes from *Piers Plowman*, one being that of the fruitless and recursive confessions of the Seven Deadly Sins in passus 5, capped as it is by the repulsive image of dogs returning to their own vomit in Gluttony's section (B.5.355–56), and the other being the bizarre Tree of Charity with its squelching and writhing fruit in the inner dream of passus 16 (19–167). Langland's latter passage is too diffuse to quote in its entirety but here are some salient lines:

> I prayed Piers to pulle down an apple, and he wolde
> And suffre me to assaye what savoure it hadde.
> And Piers caste to the croppe, and thanne comsed it to crye;
> And wagged Wydwehode, and it wepte after;
> And whan [he] meved Matrimoigné it made a foule noyse. (B.16.73–77)

---

6   Citations are from the edition from which I teach Milton, namely the *Norton Anthology of English Literature*, ed. by Greenblatt and others. Likewise, Langland citations are from *Piers Plowman: A Norton Critical Edition*, ed. by Robertson and Shepherd. This edition contains the Donaldson translation, indispensable to my students.

This unpromising start is followed by the violent striking-out of Piers in 'pure tene' after the fruit-stealing devil, 'happe how it myghte' (B.16.86–87). Then the text goes on to provide a brief overview of Christ's birth, ministry, and Passion in which Piers is implicated (presumably as *humana natura*). It remains unclear exactly how Will receives this information — whether as a visionary witness or as the recipient of narration from Piers, or both. Finally, as we recall, Will

> awaked therewith and wyped [his] eyghen
> And after Piers Plowman pryed and stared
> Estwarde and westwarde. (B.16.167–69)

Here are two spectacular instances of Doing The Wrong Thing With The Tree, parodies that we might expect in works broadly having to do with the Fall. In the case of Milton, snakes do not eat tree fruits, and would have a comically hard time plucking them. Nor do they have the teeth to chew them or the intestinal tract to digest them.[7] This is an exercise in futile animal foraging that is meant to map on to the theological impossibility of the fallen angels ever acquiring knowledge by a means designed for humans. After all, when Eve and Adam ate the fruit from their tree, it did not turn into ashes in their mouths, did it? No, rather, it turned *them* to ashes — to consumable material beings, capable of changes of state. Milton's angels are not capable of such transformations. They can only change their shape, a process much less metaphysically consequential. In this they resemble Langland's Sins in passus 5, hopelessly unchanged even after their dramatic confessions.

Milton goes on to state brusquely that this parodic incident in book ten shows the angels 'like in punishment | As in their crime' (10.544–45). This certainly makes it sound cut and dried. Yet it entirely fails to tally with the Gormenghast weirdness of the scene. We realize that it is doubly pointless for the angels to re-enact the Fall. They have already fallen, and they didn't fall that way. Perhaps, indeed, it is triply pointless, as the Fall that they imagine to be their great triumph is, in fact, a nullity — recuperated and exceeded by the Son's sacrifice. Ontologically, what we have in this scene are non-snakes climbing non-trees to eat non-fruit due to an induced illusory hunger. Really, why write the scene at all? Or, perhaps more pointedly, why write the scene and then gloss it so reductively?

Firstly, Milton cannot help himself. He is a poet and poets write this way, in artful combinations of word and image. He wants wordplay and dramatic sound and a visual emblem that sticks in readers' minds. At the same time, he cannot resist both pointing out his own genius (see what I did there?) and pedantically nailing down at least one primary meaning by providing the gloss — not to mention modelling, in so doing, one powerful, if reductive, way to interpret his poetry. He coaches the reader through the act of reading. Every time he does this (which is quite often) he betrays himself as a control freak. This is the Milton who has always annoyed me. Until quite recently I thought he was the only Milton. Then I began to recall how much

---

7   Presumably they might once have done in their prelapsarian state. But, as Milton is at pains to point out, we are postlapsarian readers and bring our native assumptions to bear.

these kinds of thing — proleptic explanations, otiose glosses, ridiculously drawn-out allegorical names — always annoyed me in Langland's work. They still annoy me, but I now understand what they are doing. I accept that I am supposed to be annoyed.

Here I'm going to invoke a recent book I liked a lot, and one that helped me to uncover another Milton, a secret — or at least enigmatic — Milton, who I believe is also operative in this scene, and ones like it. This is Curtis Gruenler's *'Piers Plowman' and the Poetics of Enigma: Riddles, Rhetoric and Theology*.[8] I doubt that Gruenler would be too sanguine about Milton's chances at enigma, given what he says about the decline of the theology of participation in the early modern period.[9] In his book he describes two poles of theological-poetic discourse, the didactic and the esoteric, of which enigma is the middle point: my guess is that Milton would fall at the didactic end in his accounting. Yet I think there is considerable room for enigma in *Paradise Lost*. This passage shows traces of it. Gruenler points out, in passing, how important the idea of change of state is to the corpus of riddles, the most ubiquitous form of enigma in English. They often concern water and ice, seed and tree, chicken and egg — the mysteries of the material world. Here is Milton doing the same with wood and ash.[10] I suggest that this places his poem in the enigmatic part of the spectrum. In these lines he shows the fallen angels' blindness to changes of state, as timeless beings. A tree might as well be ash to an angel. If we read these lines as having a riddling quality, we gain an additional insight into angelic ontology and perception. This detail reinforces the limitations of angelic understanding. Creatures so easily induced to confuse wood and ash would never be able to understand the change from life to death (and back to life again) that overtakes humans after the Fall. We can shoehorn these enigmatic meanings into Milton's summative statement about the angels being 'like in punishment | As in their crime' without much pressure — that is, the fallen angels remain themselves, blind and limited, before and after the Fall — yet they tend to exceed it. The dyad punishment/crime is based on one element answering another reciprocally. The fallen angels, seeking to harm, are harmed. Or, seeking to poison humanity with fruit, they are poisoned with fruit. However, the third element, the transition from wood or tree to ash, messes up this neat tit-for-tat. It suggests a problem unique to angels, that has no parallel in humanity. An angel's problem is eternity. A person's is mortality.

All this is to say: we need both the poetic episode and its gloss to eke out the fullest range of meanings from Milton's lines. Moreover, we need a reader, preferably a wilful one. The episode, as described, would stand on its own: any reader used to allegory would get it. The gloss, in offering up its aphoristic reduction, introduces a new problem: the know-it-all narrator. In a poem about the perils and responsibilities of knowledge this is likely to set our teeth on edge. It is our resistance to the pat conclusion of the glossing

8 I would like to thank Curtis Gruenler for reading an early, and very different, draft of this essay, upon which he offered valuable comments. The same thanks are due to the anonymous *YLS* readers.

9 Gruenler, *Poetics of Enigma*, p. 383.

10 Really, it is the tree fruit that the fallen angels eat, not the trees. But I think we might take the fruit as synecdoche for the whole tree. It is the remarkableness of the grove of trees, and its sudden appearance, that the passage dwells on.

poet, Milton, that does the final work of this passage. Without it, it cannot happen. The enigma made possible by the little conundrum of wood-to-ash encourages the reader to resist, or at least to amplify, what the poet has so securely concluded himself.

Milton's poetic voice is so stentorian that it can be hard to disagree with him. Yet if you can do so, even transiently — set your will against his, insist, or even speculate, that you are right and he is wrong — another order of meaning opens up in the poem: the experiential order. Immediately, poetic knowledge becomes a matter of contest. Adversarial, acquisitive, name-calling possibilities arise. Chiefly, the idea of indirection becomes thinkable: that knowledge might be propagated obversely, readers sent down paths because of barriers erected before them — and that even the poet's own authoritative persona might be such a barrier. Readers of Chaucer, witty master of the unreliable narrator, or of Langland, in whose work this authorial posture achieves its quintessence, may feel a curious familiarity at such points. It is just that it is, overall, more challenging to identify the narrator of *Paradise Lost* as unreliable than Chaucer's moribund poet figure in *The Book of the Duchess*, or the hopelessly wonky Will. The idea that the magnificent voice in charge of *Paradise Lost* could be, as it were, staging his own failure in order to further our learning opportunities is not immediately obvious. I have liked Milton a lot more since I realized that this was the case.

There are other counterintuitive elements in Milton's hellish orchard scene in book ten, but for the moment let us turn our attention to Langland's equally bizarre passage about the Tree of Charity. It is also about failure. Will spectacularly does the wrong thing in asking Piers to pluck fruit from the tree for him. To be fair, it is difficult to determine what the right thing would be. On the one hand, surely any questing Christian should beware of apple-plucking scenarios. Yet most of us, as bipedal creatures with opposable thumbs who are perfectly capable of eating tree fruits, if confronted by a laden tree in a garden — even a dream garden, and notwithstanding what we might know about the Fall — might very well reach for a fruit, especially if our equally human-shaped better self, apparently its custodian, is standing next to it, intent on displaying its wonders. Will might even be commended for charting the middle course and asking Piers to pick the fruit. Refusing all interest in the fruit looks like inertia; grabbing one himself looks like greed. Asking the authority figure to intervene seems like wisdom. Of course, it turns out to be a mistake. Langland's allegory, in this instance, leaves room for Will to use his human affordances in the wrong way. Indeed, even more remarkably, he allows the man-shape of Christ, as it is manifested to Will in the form of Piers for the sake of comprehensibility, to be similarly misused. As it happens, this allows for a uniquely brilliant mistake. Langland, to his credit, does not gloss it. He allows it to hang there, enigmatically, the unpicked fruit. Of course it is Piers, human nature, the humanity of Christ, who touches the fruit. He is the one in whom the unending desire for knowledge resides.[11] This does

---

11   Nicolette Zeeman, in *'Piers Plowman' and the Medieval Discourse of Desire*, explores the deep relationship between volition and desire in Langland, and this observation owes much to her thinking. The importance of failure in the project of Christian learning that her book suggests overall has also informed this essay.

not prevent this action from being a mistake. If Christ is going to be a man, he is going to be fallible: it goes with the territory. It may also be that, in him, the desire for knowledge — crucially, the knowledge of death, something to which he would normally not be subject as an immortal divine being — may mysteriously coincide with the desire for sacrifice. (In most people, most of the time, as both Langland and Milton demonstrate, the desire for knowledge is tantamount to the desire for control.) Perhaps it is this that Piers signals to Will as he glances at the tree 'egrely' — saying to his human counterpart, in effect, 'you and me, eh?' (16.64).

However that may be, at minimum we can say that putting humans in a garden setting is completely different from putting snakes there, in terms of allegorical affordances. People make and use gardens. Having said that, it is worth looking quickly at the fabulous appearance of Satan-as-snake in Milton's book nine:

> enclosed
> In serpent, inmate bad! and toward Eve
> Addressed his way: not with indented wave,
> Prone on the ground, as since; but on his rear,
> Circular base of rising folds, that towered
> Fold above fold, a surging maze! his head
> Crested aloft, and carbuncle his eyes;
> With burnished neck of verdant gold, erect
> Amidst his circling spires, that on the grass
> Floated redundant: pleasing was his shape. (9.494–503)

And as he makes his final approach:

> So varied he, and of his tortuous train
> Curled many a wanton wreath in sight of Eve,
> To lure her eye (9.516–18)

This is scarcely less ludicrous than the parody in book ten. Satan is in snake drag, teetering along like a performer in ten-inch heels. It is history's first burlesque. Rarely do we think of Milton as funny, but the sheer awkwardness of this attempt of a long, skinny, armless snake to imitate a human moving erect has its comical aspects. He has fictionally expanded the few lines about the snake in Genesis in precisely this way in order to highlight the foolishness of the whole endeavour. Thus when we read the book ten passage about the army of snakes swarming the forest of trees, we are reading a burlesque of a burlesque.

The baffling events that occur to Satan's army and to Will in their encounters with their respective weird trees ultimately have different meanings. Satan and the other fallen angels are forced to devour the empty and non-nourishing fruits of the mock trees, gaining nothing, but also expending nothing, and needing nothing (as their 'empyreal substance' is not in need of food or diminished by activity) (1.117). It all adds up to zero. My Foucault-saturated students are usually keen to see this parodic episode as appropriate punishment for the angels, taking the poet's 'like in punishment | As in their crime' to apply to the plot. As I see it, Milton's angels are incapable of acting meaningfully in a plot.[12] Plots — narrative schemas that unfold in space and time, with cause and effect — are human devices. Angels are no more capable of performing in them at any length than Langland's personifications can sustain a narrative, and for the same reason. They are functions, not human characters. It took me some time to perceive this fully in *Paradise Lost*, as they are so prolix; they can sustain speech, if not action, for much longer than any single personification in Langland can. As Raphael, Michael — and even Satan — gassed on for books at a time I found myself haunted by a sense that this was all very familiar. Finally I realized that they share the robotic quality of many of Langland's personifications: Reason, or Conscience, or Theology. If Abdiel, say, were simply called Servant of God this would all be a lot clearer. However, in the end their ambits are similarly restricted and local, and their interactions with humans similarly oblique, as I hope to demonstrate below.

Why would God punish the fallen angels by making them eat ashy fruit? Punishment is a teaching tool, at least in the hands of a beneficent God who does not inflict it for pleasure. Yet no one in this scenario can be taught: not Satan, not his followers, and not us. The fallen angels cannot be corrected. To use the word 'penance' in connection with them, as Milton does at l. 10.551, can be nothing less than irony — the same contrary indication that the trees-and-ashes riddle provides, showing the distance between angels and men. Angels do not participate in sacraments. The very idea is ridiculous. (An idea that follows hard upon this, of course, is that sacraments are ridiculous. And as angels are impossible penitents, making a joke of that sacrament, so their pointless and iterative chewing on a substance that will not change them makes a brief and scathing comment on the Eucharist also.) Humans can learn nothing from the fate of angels; our conditions are too different. Indeed, it's pretty clear throughout *Paradise Lost* that humans have very little to learn from angels at all. About as little, it would seem, as Will is able to learn from the numerous hectoring personifications with whom he interacts. If the narrator's statement does not properly apply to the plot — if it is so easily misread — why, then, is it there? I would say: precisely because it is so easily misread. It is, frankly, tempting. It invites novice readers to make the same kind of misrecognition of angels as people as Satan does, the misrecognition that allows him to pretend to be the hero in an epic plot. This is the same kind of observation that Stanley Fish made long ago, and I agree

---

12   Angel-to-angel plot interactions are completely ineffective. Abdiel fails to persuade Satan's rebel army to turn back and this is known before he even returns to base with his message (6.20). The angel army fails to defeat Satan in heaven and has to be saved by the Son (6.807). The fallen angel parliament is divided and follows the path of least resistance in book two. Satan easily fools Uriel (4.681). Satan and Gabriel have an inconclusive and preening standoff that doesn't even lead to a fight (4.968–96). Angel watchdogs fail to keep Satan out of Eden, twice. Angels are incompetent. All of this serves to highlight the ineffectiveness of angel-to-human transactions: Satan's temptation and Raphael's and Michael's instruction. Angels are better at being than doing, the inverse of humans. For an overview of Milton's angels, see Joad Raymond, *Milton's Angels*. Raymond, however, attributes more efficacy and freedom to them than I do.

with him; it's only that I arrived at it via reading Langland.[13] The same may well be said of Fish, of course.

The human Will, on the other hand, is genuinely punished for disturbing the fruit on his tree (even by proxy), first by its farting outcry, which shocks him, and then by being summarily dismissed from his heightened level of dream insight and losing track once more of the elusive Piers. Once again in his frustrating experience the buzzer beeps, the proffered treat retracts into its panel in the wall, and Will is forced to scurry on again in his maze. This is not a gratifying spectacle, but it is one from which Will learns through both positive and negative reinforcement, whether it be by encountering various dead ends, bouncing off various walls, charging heedlessly through various delicate barriers, or earning small tasty morsels from Holy Church, Piers, Conscience, or whomever. Those of us who persevere with Will through to his inconclusive end — in which he simply escapes into a larger maze — appreciate that he is not so much taught as *tamed*, but Milton's fallen angels are not granted even this privilege. It's also worth noting that we have no sense that Piers learns anything in the Tree of Charity scene. Piers, in his various guises, never does. Apparently he does not need to. He changes but his function remains the same; he is Will's objective correlative. Dynamic as he seems, he too is a just a personification: the personification of divine personhood, which changes according to Will's perception of that role.

Moving past these specific scenes with the weird trees — scenes in which we learn as much or more through failures as we do through successes, whether they be made by author, character or reader — I want to consider, briefly and broadly, the pedagogical landscapes of both poems. It is hard to see them as anything other than negative. A tremendous volume of information is taught, to Eve and Adam by angels, and to Will by a series of personifications, to horrifically little effect. Books six through eight, and then eleven and twelve, of *Paradise Lost* consist mostly of Adam being lectured at by the archangels Raphael and Michael. Will, as we know, spends the majority of his poem careering from one master to another, alternately pugnacious and hangdog, never seeming to take in what they say. He is the kind of student most professors would fail. Readers, therefore, find themselves passing their eyeballs over tracts and tracts of learned material that the in-text learners almost magnificently fail to process. I once had a student memorably say that *Piers Plowman* was 'the worst poem in the English language' for this reason. Teaching appears to occur almost entirely at cross-purposes.

In *Paradise Lost*, for example, Adam asks impertinent questions of Raphael during his long lecture on cosmology in book eight and gets imperiously smacked down (8.168–69). Eve does not even wait to hear the lecture but abandons the taught-astrophysics curriculum in favour of the hands-on biology lab that is Eden (8.44–56). If she has to deal with abstractions she prefers to get them in digest form from Adam later, a teacher and a format she likes better. She is the student who relies on a note taker or reads the lecture notes on the website; she arranges her own accommodations, and she is free to do so. Raphael does not miss her. He considers

---

13   In *Surprised by Sin*, first published in 1967.

her disabled, and disabling. From an accessibility point of view, there is no question that the Fall of Man might have been avoided had Eve been better accommodated. Milton understands this perfectly. She is his ideal student for experiential learning. He did not consider women capable of university-type learning (and had been contemptuous of his own university experience). Moreover, he knew well that the main engine of experiential learning is error. (Living through the disastrous failure of the Commonwealth would tend to point this out.) This is what distinguishes it from learning by precept. Hence he makes sure that Eve is in a position to learn her most important lessons extracurricularly — and she does, taking us all with her.

The experiential learning process ought to be obviated, or at least supplemented, by intellectual learning or systematic pedagogy. Teaching by precept is, in principle, more efficient — the unwieldy experience of trial and error conducted by generations of instructors is distilled into a set of positive principles, facts, techniques or heuristics that can be learned without wasting time. This is the main evolutionary advantage of culture. Yet in *Paradise Lost* everything that Adam, a seemingly receptive student not disabled by femininity, learns from Raphael, and later Michael, seems gruesomely trivial in comparison to Eve's learning experience. Who can even remember all the speculative detail about the organization of the universe that Raphael spouts off in book eight (it always makes me think of Sherlock Holmes's brusque rejection of Copernican theory as a waste of mental space, leading to Watson's agonized rejoinder, 'But the solar system!')?[14] Or the pedantry of Michael's biblical history in books eleven and twelve? New science and old theology both fall flat. In this respect Adam resembles Will being endlessly instructed in the long middle of *Piers Plowman*. Eve's exclusion from the male world of institutional learning gets her out of these backwaters and makes her learning curve dangerously more dramatic. Adam, meanwhile, plods on in conversation with his angelic tutors. He is, like Will, variously corrected. He gets into various human tunnel-vision problems that the angels find contemptuously amusing.[15] He learns that angels do not share his material desires — for Eve, for example. They do, however, demonstrate the desire to instruct, and occasionally to listen. Raphael is interested to hear Adam's narrative about his own creation; Michael is keen to gain an acknowledgement from Adam that he has finally understood the salvific role of Christ (8.225–78; 12.466). As (apparently) male beings, they have some intellectual passions in common.

This sometimes-adversarial, sometimes-chummy interaction transforms Eden into a classroom (one into which Eve is rarely admitted) and suspends Adam's gardening work. Plants run wild as Adam chats on about abstractions, and who knows what is going on in Eve's head? Is this whole pedagogical enterprise therefore a dangerous waste of time? Should we likewise skip over the entire third vision of *Piers*

---

14 This occurs in the introductory story, *A Study in Scarlet*, first published in *Beeton's Magazine* in 1887; it was later included in the collection *The Adventures of Sherlock Holmes*, p. 14.

15 At 8.78–86 Raphael is mocking and dismissive of human attempts to understand the solar system, and identifies Adam as the first one to do so, following on from his query about the inefficiency of the geocentric model of the universe at 8.15–35.

Plowman in which Will has his fruitless discussions with the university disciplines? I fear that most of the proponents of experiential learning that I have encountered in the academy recently would say yes. There is a depressingly common consensus that whatever goes on in a classroom does not count as experience. More insidious and damning is the effortless assumption — so effortless that it is often not even uttered, merely assumed — that reading cannot be an experience. It is configured, de facto, as its polar opposite.[16] Now we have to admit that among allegorical writers, among whom we must include Langland and Milton — or, let's say, C. S. Lewis and Jo Rowling — there is a tendency to move in this dismissive direction and to make a running joke of formal instruction. We are looking at it here in *Piers Plowman* and *Paradise Lost*. It gives us the picture of the already-dead Professor Binns droning on in History of Magic in the Harry Potter series, or the instructor Miss Prizzle in Narnia, whose lecturing is so dry that running off to become a Maenad appears to be a good idea.[17] All of these books suggest instead the alternate pathway of imaginative story as the primary means of learning.

Unlike Lewis or Rowling — or their powerful precursor in writing about education, Dickens, in whose work almost all school scenes are appalling and punitive — both Langland and Milton include, verbatim, much of the curriculum that is offered to their in-text learners. You will look in vain for this in *David Copperfield*. There the only solution is to get out of the classroom. Piaget and Dewey must have felt something similar as they pioneered the methods of progressive education. However, it means something quite different if the author — as pedagogue — leaves all the learned material in his text, no matter how well or badly his in-text learners cope with it. Langland and Milton allow the unpropitious learning scenarios they describe to be enabling, not to say ennobling. Adam and Will undergo pedagogical processes, variously embarrassing; we, as readers, witness them doing so. Some percentage of the learned material rehearsed by the angels (in Milton) or personifications (in Langland) both we, and they, take in; more passes by us (and them) without full comprehension or sympathy. If we are lucky, we may arrive at these later, by reflection or re-reading, or at a future moment at which the information is called into practical use. The point is that all of us, inside and outside the text, are the same kind of interpreter: selective and wilful. The intellectual content is trotted out regardless. It exists and is there to read. We are thus able, crucially, to make our own mistakes with the available curriculum, bringing us into a community of experience that we share with the texts' protagonists. Perversely, the undigested chunks of pedagogical material that stick out in both *Piers Plowman* and *Paradise Lost* enable increased readerly choice and a kind of informed identification with the in-text experients. At the same time, the fact that all this ineffective teaching is performed by angels and/or personifications is also instructive. Humans are needed in order to teach humans — and one of the most crucial criteria of humanity is fallibility. If nothing else, it adds interest. The

---

16 For example, consider the wording at my institution: 'Experiential Learning'. In practice, nothing is designated experiential unless it involves an industry partner.

17 The classroom scene occurs on p. 214 of *Prince Caspian*, first published in 1951.

dull asymmetrical power relations that obtain between teachers and students in *Piers Plowman* and *Paradise Lost* are completely unhelpful, and the main thing that they are there to demonstrate is the frustrating and exhausting interface between the individual and all forms of authority. (Philip Pullman, one of the most productive recent readers of Milton, makes this very clear throughout *His Dark Materials* by calling his illusory antagonist The Authority.)

Langland and Milton, as writers of long, hard poems (and as sufferers-through of oppressive educational regimes, whatever exactly these might have been) expect our readerly attention to phase in and out; they expect oscillating emotions that will enhance or distract from our learning experience; they expect us to gloss over some passages and linger over others. Both Adam and Will model such reactions. Through them, the poets anticipate our misunderstanding. Reading *Piers Plowman* or *Paradise Lost* offers the same opportunity for error as any other worldly experience does — more than many, in fact, due to their complexity. At no time do their authors assume that knowledge can be seamlessly transferred from one consciousness to another simply by uttering it, requiring nothing from the auditor or reader but passive absorption. All the angelsplaining that goes on in *Paradise Lost* is meant to be boring; it is meant to show us that we are not angels. This is the beginning of the poem's morality. It's no struggle to be an angel. Satan's struggle comes about because he thinks he's a person. Likewise, no individual speaker is actually Theology or Study or Holy Church or Clergy; they are institutions. Will's ongoing dilemma in *Piers Plowman* lies in his being a person surrounded by personifications, which inevitably leads to some interpretative gaps. It is what he does in these gaps — the fuming and backtracking and wandering and persevering — that marks him out as a human learner. *Piers Plowman* accomplishes, in the single character of Will, in fact, what Milton has split off into the two gendered characters of Adam and Eve. There is no doubt that Will has his Eve side. Eve is won over by Satan's specious rhetoric in book nine because she feels disempowered and he appeals to her desire for equality and inclusion. Will, angry and fearful of being left out, seems to bring out these qualities in his interlocutors; time after time, as soon as he gets into their proximity, they begin to rant defensively about the truths native to their domain and to call out any that impinge on them. Spatially, Adam stays still while Eve wanders in *Paradise Lost*; Will does both.

During the long section of the poem in which Will seeks learned help with the Do-Wel, Do-Bet, Do-Best triad, it is Patience and Conscience who come to the fore as his chief aides, not Dutiful Listening or Fanboy or even Intelligence. Will is catapulted into the third (pedagogical) vision by Wit and received out the end of it by Imaginatif. His mental faculties are equally present before and after. As he encounters the arts and the theological curricula, Patience helps him to put up with blinkered professional opinion; Conscience helps him to sift through (and frequently to reject) it. His guides are not intellectual but moral and affective. What is being modelled in this section of the poem is the act of difficult reading (or being taught) itself: the encounter of a wilful mind with hard material. What's more, this material is domain-specific and its purveyors feel proprietary about it. To get hold of it you either have to wrest it from them and carry it away, out of context, or convince them that you belong to the in-group to whom it belongs. Will sometimes manages to do one of these things. If he does, he has learned something. When he is handed off to Imaginatif, the presiding spirit of vernacular poetry, he is not necessarily in possession of clearer information, as the academic opinion he received was contradictory. He has, however, retained his imagination through, or perhaps uncovered it by, this learning process. In one of the operations in which this poem excels, he has not gotten what he wants but has been left with what he needs.

Imaginatif, as he appears here, looks forward to the strange hybrid figure of Urania whom Milton equivocally invokes at the beginning of book seven, just over the halfway point of the whole poem, and again — though not by name — at the beginning of book nine, the book in which he finally and very fictively re-tells the core myth of the Fall (7.1–20; 9.21–22). At both points he dwells briefly on his uneasy status as poet: blind, aged, under political threat, and parochial as an English writer (7.23–32; 9.41–47). Urania is supposed to be the muse of astronomy, a discipline Milton dismisses as short-sighted in book eight (through the pedagogical voice of Raphael lecturing on cosmology). Yet she is a muse of looking upward to explain things, and while she once guided poets wrongheadedly to celebrate epic wars and to soar over Olympus — a place that cold and damp England is wrongly placed to catch sight of, as Milton remarks in a tellingly Langlandian aside — Urania nonetheless becomes the more or less workaround muse of English theological poetry at its most ambitious, the power Milton needs to get through the upcoming sections (9.25–42; 8.3; 9.44–47).[18] Imaginatif, I think, is a similar repurposing, in this case of a figure from faculty psychology, into a highly specific emblem of English poetry writing of a kind that Langland saw nowhere before him and consequently had to make up. It is here that he discusses his distracting career of 'medlyng with makyngs' and how it has failed to endow him with authority, while at the same time using it to begin to understand how such messy 'medlyng' can serve as evidence of authentic experience, authority's necessary and powerful human counterpart (B.12.16).

Langland's vision of experience, like Milton's, has everything to do with making mistakes. So obsessed are both poets with the human will and its erroneous power of teaching us through experience — experience bitter and iterative, but useful and above all, desirable — that in reading and then teaching them one after the other I was finally able to bring into focus a paradox that has always troubled me about Christian doctrine, namely the value of sacrifice. I have been able to reconsider it as a pedagogical technique, a deliberate embrace of error. For what it's worth, this must be chalked up specifically to the kind of medieval-to-early-modern English poetic theology that Langland and Milton create. Theology was intrinsically part of everything in their world, and they are virtuosic in it. Yet, as poets writing in their own language, they are able to tell stories with a complexity and verve that

---

18 According to the Norton editors, Urania had already been rebranded as a muse of Christian poetry by Guillaume de Salluste Du Bartas in his 'L'Uranie' (1584). Yet Milton feels compelled to do this work again for his English poem.

the Bible cannot achieve, nor any academic theologian. Augustine's conversion narrative never succeeded in making the value of sacrifice clear to me, and neither has any later religious writer, not even one as powerful as Tolstoy. I think this has to do with the religious moment of Langland and Milton, one in which Christianity had been hegemonic in Europe for centuries — even the massive disruptions of the Reformation only proved its sheer centrality. Augustine is fighting rhetorical battles with Rome, and Tolstoy with Russia, colossal empires that had other fish to fry than Christian doctrine in their respective moments. However that may be, while neither Langland nor Milton has succeeded in converting me into a Christian, the ways in which people behave in their books, and also while reading or teaching them, has clarified two things: one, that ignorance can be precious, and two, that error and sacrifice — which, if they are not exactly the same are at least on a spectrum — are powerfully implicated in learning.

Readily-admitted ignorance is necessary to reading either *Piers Plowman* or *Paradise Lost*. Both poems beat us over the head with proliferating domains of knowledge about which we don't know enough and demand that we look them up or seek expert help. At the same time, both involve us in the opposite problem: the more learning we have, the more reluctant we are to admit to ignorance. We are very familiar with this problem as academics. It is embarrassing to be caught out in ignorance, and consequently some of us generalize out our domains of knowledge so that they seemingly apply to everything. Yet the humility that follows from admitting that you don't know something is the precondition for genuine inquiry. It is the first step in experiential learning. It is the foundation of the scientific method. Do we ask meaningful questions to which we already know the answers? No. We are stuck with those vile instrumental things, rhetorical questions. Fiction, however, that great experiment, affords us the opportunity to create new learners, which is what Milton and Langland do in their epistemological poems, via their characters of Eve, Adam, and Will. Through them, both poets undertake the deeply unexpected work of trying to make the too-familiar question 'why did we fall?' resolutely unrhetorical. Instead they try to translate them into experience. *Paradise Lost* and *Piers Plowman*, therefore, if taken together, are probably the most significant allegorical thought experiment about the foundations of knowledge in the English language.

Will, or Adam and Eve — or even Satan, though he is self-consciously forcing the issue — make choices the outcomes of which they alone cannot foresee. From their perspectives, they behave contingently — freely, or ignorantly — and so, to us, convincingly. Adam and Eve did not know in advance that they would fall in *Paradise Lost*. Will does not know, even at the end of his poem, that he is his own worst enemy. Their ignorance enables their own learning, and also ours. The feat that both Milton and Langland perform transcends simple dramatic irony (itself an incredibly powerful effect) in an act of highly specific imaginative induction: knowing the answer (i.e., that humans fell, the effects of which are palpable to them in all aspects of disorderly experience) they have tried to work back to the question (why?). They seek to recover a lost question in all of its urgency: Would it ever have been possible not to fall? Or, in Langlandian terms, for the will not to be wilful — humans not human? Can the will be tamed, or erased? In the epistemological sphere, this is like imagining a world without gravity. It is pure science fiction, if by *science* we mean knowledge. This operation explains the chronic ass-backwardness of both poems, as I have been telling my students lately. Why else would Milton emphasize, at every possible opportunity, that Eve and Adam, despite the story we are reading, have already fallen, and consistently offer precursor parodies of every significant event or speech? And how can Will, whose heart is in the right place, possibly be so stupid?

Milton (like Langland) is trying to recover the power of primal ignorance — the state of not knowing that must precede knowing and that enables the act of learning. Not-knowing is, as it were, the root position or the first position of learning.[19] In their insistence on this, Milton and Langland alike begin from precisely the opposite position than do the progressive or learner-centred educators of today (though they do converge with them later in recommending experience as a learning tool). The progressive idea is that students cannot learn, and will not learn, until they have reached the appropriate mental stage, however that be construed, for whatever the material in question is. Education consists in sympathetically figuring out student needs, and offering information in stages so that students can take it in. (To some extent we can see Will conforming to this paradigm, though with the Langlandian proviso that Will is never let in on the secret that this is going on, which explains his combative attitude.) On the other hand, *Piers Plowman* and *Paradise Lost* confront their learners with facts and states that nobody can take in at once (or arguably, at all). There is no conceivable stage of human life in which they can be processed — certainly no single one. If they can be glimpsed, it can be only over an unfolding lifetime of experience. They are faced with choices that no one can be ready for, and they must make them anyway. That is what learning fundamentally is in these books. It is the wilful proceeding through trial and error. Both success and failure are equally necessary and learning results from both of them. This is to say that there is no way for Eve and Adam to understand the prohibition against eating fruit from one tree when all other tree fruits are edible and the punishment for doing so is death, which is meaningless to them. It is an impasse and the only way through it is to act and try it: the result is knowledge. In Will's case, when Holy Church tells him early on in the poem that truth is the best treasure, he cannot be expected to take it in. Holy Church is in possession of that truth because she represents a complex institution that has been around for 1400 years. Perhaps it is obvious to her, but from Will's perspective it might make a nice T-shirt.

Eve and Adam, in Milton's poem, are paradoxical children: newborns in adult bodies. Milton goes out of his way to emphasize this. Will, although an adult male, has childish tantrums. It's not that either Milton or Langland is oblivious of life's stages. It is rather that, as Christian poets, they consider the problems that their protagonists are facing to be universal: the facts of death and inequality. In front of these facts, we

---

19 Another word that could be used here is the fraught one, innocence. I think we should distinguish this childlike ignorance from any neutral blank state such as Locke's *tabula rasa*. Implied within it by both poets is aggression and wilfulness. Blake's later poetic vision of innocence is similar.

are all children. Children are wilful. Adam and Eve, crucially, make their decisions to fall with their uncorrupted wills. They act wilfully in Eden before the Fall. The will is the basis of human action. In *Piers Plowman*, Will is culpable of the wilful sins of anger, jealousy, greed, and even despair but he has no option but to persevere using willpower, a force which is also adaptive and transformative. I should interject here that it was only through appreciating Eve and Adam's Edenic wilfulness, combined with the liberatory potential of Satan's (for everyone but him), that I reached a new sense of the Promethean power of Langland's Will. I had always identified Will too strictly as a Kafkaesque victim of circumstance.

Both these monstrous poems are trying to allow readers — and teachers — to recover 'the beginner's mind'.[20] This is a state of deliberate unpreparedness. They are each confronting the problem that their fellow Christians in their respective periods just know too much about the Fall and its consequences. They are alike in trying to get them to unlearn it so that it can be refreshed, and so that people can as-if-newly understand their implication in it. The flailing around of Will — so extreme that we are constantly driven to ask 'OMG, *now* what's his problem?' — is specifically designed to make us (wilfully, sinfully) lose patience, so that eventually we realize that we are doing to him what he does to everybody else: what humans do. Milton's notorious poetic difficulty is performing a similar task. In his grammatical inversions, multiplication of allusions, genre play, and so on — that is, in the isometric, self-cancelling effort that is Christian epic — we see a poet who is furiously throwing spanners into the work accomplished in Genesis. He wants us to forget it. He overwrites it. He indulges himself in showing off his classical chops and his knowledge of natural philosophy. Only then, after all the parsing and looking things up, after our interpreting wills are exhausted, do we realize that we have tottered over the same finish line as Adam and Eve: we have sought knowledge despite serious barricades being thrown up against it. In fact, if we have managed to make sense of certain highly-staged cruces in the poem that emphasize their 'mysterious terms' (such as the apportioning of blame between Satan and the serpent in book 10.164–74 from which this phrase is drawn), I would go so far as to say that we have insisted on knowledge in the face of prohibition. Knowledge is something that we universally make happen, as humans. Then, of course — as *Piers Plowman*, in particular, makes very clear — we are prone to hoard it, fostering inequality.

My point about error and sacrifice and their role in human learning is more difficult to explain and more tendentious. It revolves around the fact that in both *Piers Plowman* and *Paradise Lost* erroneous decisions are made much more often than correct ones. There's a lot about this that simply feels like life. You'd think that, statistically, given human intelligence, this would not be the case. Yet, pessimistically, many of us feel that it is; various kinds of psychological bias affirm it, and so on.[21] Indeed, I have to assume that it is this pervasive feeling that led to the elaboration of the theory of the Fall (as opposed to the other way around, as Langland and Milton, as Christian

---

20   This translates the Zen term *shoshin*.
21   For example, so-called negativity bias: 'Negativity Bias'.

believers, must have it). Christianity is a pessimistic religion; it exists in order to account for all the things that go wrong (and then to excuse and transcend them). Very broadly speaking, classical culture, even its pantheistic religion, is optimistic; it exists to extol and explain human power and success, and to keep inimical forces (i.e., the gods) at bay as much as possible. So, I think, René Girard would say in his theory of religion.[22] To him, certainly, the idea of sacrifice (accepting it in person rather than ritualistically performing it upon animals as propitiatory destruction of wealth) is the watershed of Christianity: the game-changing element that made the cult successful. While I admire his argument, it has never satisfactorily brought home the human and local reasons why people in everyday life might wish to imitate, or participate in, Christ's sacrifice. Indeed, because of his divinity, it is, de facto, inimitable. Only Christ was capable of accepting death, experiencing it, and then rising from it in that unique way. Why anyone would wish to imitate the impossible (and necessarily fail) remained opaque to me.

Yet, in both *Piers Plowman* and *Paradise Lost* people are asked to do the impossible. They are required to act in situations in which they cannot predict the outcomes at all. The outcomes are overwhelmingly likely to be failures given the limitations of their resources. They act anyway. They take the risk. On the face of it, it is irrational. (It is not news to anybody, I suppose, that Christianity is an irrational religion. Yet it feels like news in these poems.) The result of these decisions — often terrifying, often negative — is knowledge. Experiential knowledge. As it happens, such knowledge may kill you, as it does Eve and Adam, eventually. Experimenting with their tree is like experimenting with radium. Yet even if it does kill you, whatever you learn in so doing may become the property of your culture. You will have arrived at knowledge that cannot be gained by any other means. To make a sacrifice means to embrace risk for the sake of knowledge. We do this all the time, every time we move forward in a decision that we know might be wrong. If and when it proves to be wrong, we learn on the basis of the error. In miniature, this process underlies the scientific method, dialectic, and much human reasoning. We have to be willing to make the mistake. Bizarrely enough, this is what Christ did. Not only did he undertake a task that ought to have been needless, that was itself the result of mistakes (the erroneous Fall, the violent Crucifixion) but he did so in a mistaken, or experimental — risky — way: Incarnation, with its necessary concomitant, death. Why would an eternal Hebrew deity attempt death? Can we even say he satisfactorily achieved it? He, too, was asked to perform the impossible.

What Langland, and then Milton, supreme voluntarists, finally got into my head is the fact that the Christian understanding of the will twins man and God specifically in the ability to make sacrifices — right across the gap between humanity and divinity. This is Kierkegaard's leap of faith, and I never got it from reading Kierkegaard. They allowed me to understand sacrifice as a gambit of thought, an epistemological move

---

22   These works are Girard's *Violence and the Sacred, Things Hidden since the Foundation of the World*, and *I See Satan Fall Like Lightning.*

both practical and prudential, one that has meaning even for secularists.[23] Will's continuous willingness to get things wrong in *Piers Plowman*, Eve's choice to disobey and discover an unknown state in *Paradise Lost*, Adam's decision follow Eve into this unknown state because he loves her, Christ's decision to undertake Incarnation and Passion: these now appear to me to be continuous — as attempts to gain knowledge that is not otherwise accessible. (Logically, what knowledge might an undying omniscient deity lack except an experiential knowledge of death?)

This commitment to the value of learning things the hard way is the polar opposite of the classical inheritance that rationally weighs options, calculates in positives, and seeks to avoid error as damaging. Without finding this inheritance as entirely self-serving and repugnant as Augustine did — it is his enemy in *City of God* — I can see one major deficiency in it more clearly now: as a way of being in the world, seeking only to do or be right (that is, correct, not erroneous) cannot account for value produced by doing or being wrong (erroneous, incorrect).[24] There is a lot of the latter, not least all the information produced by experiment or trial and error. Moreover, wrongness outweighs rightness in most people's experience of the world: it is more salient because of its association with risk, which we are by nature primed to avoid. It is culture that teaches us the value of incorporating it. The kink of Christianity — its embrace of sin, Fall, and sacrifice, these negative capabilities or ways of accommodating error — must therefore be reckoned its cultural triumph. Girard would be happy with this conclusion, though I am only reluctantly so. Consider, however, the futility of Will's search for Do Well, Better, and Best. He never finds them, only endless competing (positive, often correct) definitions of them. What he finds instead, ubiquitously, is Fucking Up. He observes this in others who are hoarding or peddling their knowledge and he enacts it as he goes in his interactions with them (negatively). What learning he accomplishes is fundamentally the result of the latter. He does not learn intellectually or systematically about doing well, better, or best but perversely, by doggedly continuing in his Christian experience, may end up performing well, and even better and best, even as he feels himself to be failing ever more drastically. It may be that his final correctness is in losing sight of these categories altogether. It may be that Will wins some complex game of loser-takes-all by running off the final page of his book, gaping. The poem is an enigma, so I cannot say.

One thing, however, of which I am absolutely certain is that in teaching these poems to students the very last thing that we are doing is passively spoon-feeding them unimpeachable information, thereby precluding their experience or our own. *Piers Plowman* and *Paradise Lost* are about people making disastrous mistakes, and the necessity of mistake is encoded into them. They are, in fact, about — rather

---

23   Thomas Prendergast has more to say about the value of a 'Postsecular Piers' in his essay in Goodmann's volume.

24   Adam exclaims at 12.470 over the fact 'That all this good of evil shall produce'. This phrase applies to Christ's sacrificial redemption but also to the knowledge gained in the welter of violent and erroneous human history that Adam has just witnessed — and from which he himself has painfully learned.

grudgingly — welcoming all comers into the community of mistake. We may contend with these texts and come to some degree of (possibly mistaken) comprehension of them; we may make the mistake of abandoning them and thereby learning that we are not capable of getting anything out of them at the present time; or we may make the worst mistake of all and believe ourselves to have mastered them. The last is a particularly Satanic delusion, in Miltonic terms. It is impossible to get through either poem without constantly disentangling your interpreting will from both the blandishments of authority and the illusions of rebellion. I cannot think of a better use of class time.

Piers Plowman and *Paradise Lost* are critically useful in the classroom. Having lost one I will cling to the other. If complex, monumental, and alien works such as these are dropped out of the curriculum they cannot be replaced. More accessible later works cannot perform the work they do. They are predicated on difficulty and they problematize the acts of teaching and learning in unique ways. Their far-awayness in time, in fact, is one of their chief strengths in our contemporary setting; they present a level playing field of genuine ignorance. Students from Christian backgrounds today are as clueless about the topics Langland and Milton discuss as anybody else. Yet the texts provide high moral-existential stakes to which students are receptive. (The same is less true of many postmodern texts with a comparable level of formal difficulty.) Moreover, the inevitable dog's breakfast that even the best prepared professor has to make out of teaching them — the stopping and starting, the frank admissions that you don't really know exactly what is going on here, the frequently failed attempts to answer or anticipate students' questions — not to mention the gruelling task of reading the poems outside of class, privately, underline exactly what the poems exist to prove: that the experience of learning is messy and frustrating. It is work. Being in class is a work experience. Reading is a work experience. An event does not have to have a corporate moniker on it in order to constitute an experience from which you must learn by doing, while attending to other people's arbitrary whims.

Works Cited

Primary Sources

Conan Doyle, Arthur, *A Study in Scarlet*, in *The Adventures of Sherlock Holmes* (Ware: Wordsworth Editions, 1992)

Eliot, T. S., 'The Love Song of J. Alfred Prufrock' <https://www.poetryfoundation.org/poetrymagazine/poems/44212/the-love-song-of-j-alfred-prufrock> [accessed 3 January 2020]

Langland, William, *Piers Plowman: A Norton Critical Edition*, ed. by Elizabeth Robertson and Stephen H. Shepherd (New York: Norton, 2006)

Lewis, C. S., *Prince Caspian* (New York: Harper Trophy, 1994)

Milton, John, *Paradise Lost*, in *The Norton Anthology of English Literature*, I.B, ed. by Stephen Greenblatt and others, 10th edn (New York: Norton, 2018), pp. 1493–1727

Secondary Sources

Benson, C. David, '"Lewed" Langland and the Delights of Difficulty', in *Approaches to Teaching Langland's 'Piers Plowman'*, ed. by Thomas A. Goodman (New York: Modern Language Association Publications, 2018), pp. 54–59

Crassons, Kate, 'Going Forth in the World: *Piers Plowman* and Service Learning', in *Approaches to Teaching Langland's 'Piers Plowman'*, ed. by Thomas A. Goodman (New York: Modern Language Association Publications, 2018), pp. 197–208

Davies, Scott, 'The Paradox of Progressive Education: A Frame Analysis', *Sociology of Education*, 75 (2002), 269–86

'Experiential Learning', University of Waterloo, Centre for Teaching Excellence <https://uwaterloo.ca/centre-for-teaching-excellence/support/integrative-learning/experiential-learning> [accessed 3 January 2020]

Fish, Stanley, *Surprised by Sin: The Reader in Paradise Lost*, 2nd edn (Boston: Harvard University Press, 1998)

Girard, René, *Violence and the Sacred* (Baltimore: Johns Hopkins University Press, 1979)

——, *Things Hidden since the Foundation of the World* (Stanford: Stanford University Press, 1987)

——, *I See Satan Fall Like Lightning* (New York: Orbis, 2001)

Goodmann, Thomas A., ed., *Approaches to Teaching Langland's 'Piers Plowman'* (New York: Modern Language Association Publications, 2018)

Gruenler, Curtis, *'Piers Plowman' and the Poetics of Enigma: Riddles, Rhetoric and Theology* (Notre Dame: Notre Dame University Press, 2017)

Hickman, Larry, and Thomas Alexander, eds, *The Essential Dewey*, 2 vols (Bloomington: Indiana University Press, 1998)

Kolb, David A., *Experiential Learning: Experience as the Source of Learning and Development*, 2nd edn (New York: Pearson, 2015)

Müller, Ü., J. Carpendale, and L. Smith, eds, *The Cambridge Companion to Piaget* (Cambridge: Cambridge University Press, 2013)

Prendergast, Thomas, 'Postsecular Piers', in *Approaches to Teaching Langland's 'Piers Plowman'*, ed. by Thomas A. Goodman (New York: Modern Language Association Publications, 2018), pp. 73–78

'Negativity Bias' <https://en.wikipedia.org/wiki/Negativity_bias> [accessed 3 January 2020]

Raymond, Joad, *Milton's Angels: The Early Modern Imagination* (Oxford: Oxford University Press, 2010)

Rogers, William E., 'Repeating our Agonies: An Approach to Teaching Langland', in *Approaches to Teaching Langland's 'Piers Plowman'*, ed. by Thomas A. Goodman (New York: Modern Language Association Publications, 2018), pp. 67–72

Simpson, James, *Reform and Cultural Revolution, 1350–1547*, Oxford English Literary History, 2 (Oxford: Oxford University Press, 2002)

Simpson, James, and Brian Cummings, eds, *Cultural Reformations: Medieval and Renaissance in Literary History* (Oxford: Oxford University Press, 2010)

Watson, Nicholas, 'Censorship and Cultural Change in Late Medieval England: Vernacular Theology, the Oxford Translation Debate and Arundel's Constitutions of 1409', *Speculum*, 70 (1995), 822–64

———, '*Piers Plowman* as Theology: Pedagogy, Politics, Pastness', in *Approaches to Teaching Langland's 'Piers Plowman'*, ed. by Thomas A. Goodman (New York: Modern Language Association Publications, 2018), pp. 67–72

Zeeman, Nicolette, *'Piers Plowman' and the Medieval Discourse of Desire* (Cambridge: Cambridge University Press, 2006)

Notes

JENNIFER SISK

'Grace is a gras'

Theological Uses of Metaphor in Piers Plowman[1]

▼ **KEYWORDS** metaphor, theology, grace, volition, Imaginatif, Samaritan, Mary Clemente Davlin

▼ **ABSTRACT** Langland's most potent explorations of the mystery of grace occur via richly developed and shifting metaphors that play with the question of how and whether God's gift is impacted by human effort. This essay closely analyses the contributions of Imaginatif and the Samaritan to Will's education in grace and to *Piers Plowman*'s poetic approach to this theological problem.

in memory of Sr. Mary Clemente Davlin, OP

Will encounters many interlocutors in *Piers Plowman* who pass on distinctly theological messages in response to his questions. These teachers display an impressive arsenal of pedagogical strategies in their engagement with Langland's dreamer, whose initial posture as a deferential listener sometimes gives way to that of a recalcitrant or even rebellious student. But his interlocutors tend to be as stubborn as he is, and like good teachers of *Piers Plowman* today they will not let their student rest easily. Instead they privilege pedagogies that highlight the complexity of issues under debate, provoking questions more readily than delivering tidy answers.[2] Difficult theological topics in *Piers Plowman* become occasions for extended meditation rather than doctrine and for

---

1   This essay began as an offering to a session honouring the late Sr. Clemente at the 2019 International *Piers Plowman* Society meeting in Miami, Florida. I would like to thank the session organizers, Thomas Goodmann and Elizabeth Robertson, and all in attendance for their engagement with ideas I present here, as well as the anonymous readers for *YLS*.
2   A common theme across the contributions to *Approaches to Teaching Langland's 'Piers Plowman'*, edited by Thomas Goodmann, is the value of discussion-oriented pedagogies that foster emerging questions.

Jennifer Sisk (jsisk@uvm.edu) is Associate Professor of English at the University of Vermont

The Yearbook of Langland Studies, 34 (2020), 203–210   BREPOLS ॐ PUBLISHERS   10.1484/J.YLS.5.121092

the associative work of metaphors, analogies, and figurative expressions that illuminate rather than explain.[3] This essay offers a case study of Langland's theological poetics at work in two related instances that richly treat the topic of grace: Imaginatif's use of a striking botanical metaphor and the Samaritan's transformation of a Trinitarian analogy in which he develops ideas latent in Imaginatif's words to locate grace in the cooperative interplay of divine and human agency, a theological position I take to be the very heart of *Piers Plowman*. These two instances exemplify the centrality of metaphor to Will's education in the theology of grace.

The first of these teachers, Imaginatif, appears at one of the dreamer's low points, after Scripture has delivered an unpleasant message that launches him into a fit of predestinarian thinking, according to which human effort of all kinds is pointless. Imaginatif's instruction redeems the effort of learning for Will, as it re-establishes the value of 'clergy' (revealed knowledge) and teaches Will, as Michelle Karnes has argued, to reconcile it with 'kynde wit' (natural knowledge derived from the senses and intellect) so that he is able to see the spiritual in the natural.[4] Seeing one thing and by means of it 'seeing' something else is work akin to encountering a metaphor in a poem: it requires thinking figuratively, and Imaginatif's words to Will encourage such work as a means toward spiritual knowing. Cristina Maria Cervone has pointed out that the word *figurative* itself 'encodes the expectation that the sought thing cannot be comprehended fully at once in its own nature but must be understood by means of something-it-isn't, expressed in language-it-isn't — perhaps in and through time as a series of something-it-isn'ts'.[5] Cervone's discussion draws attention to the necessity of figurative language to any attempt to comprehend the divine: the one-off nature of God is something the fallible mortal mind can only approach through precisely such it-isn'ts, so it is no surprise that Imaginatif tries to explain grace to Will by means of a metaphor.

'Grace is a gras' (B.12.58/C.14.23), Imaginatif declares, playing on homophones and pointedly depicting grace as something-it-isn't: a living plant that Will himself can see in the natural world, and through which (Imaginatif seems to hope) he can approach 'seeing' the full truth of grace. This 'gras' is a medicinal herb, Imaginatif says, that remedies various metaphorical sicknesses or sins (in the B text, private individual maladies of miserliness and being puffed up with knowledge; in C, public hypocrisies such as unworthy lordship, teaching by the unlearned, and misdirected charity on the part of the Church). Though he speaks of grace using botanical imagery, he avoids scientific explanation of its source of life, moving directly to the

---

3   While this observation is by no means new, I hope that the localized close readings offered here will provide food for thought for scholars and students of Langland's poetics. Serious consideration of the theological work of Langland's poetics has flowered in literary criticism attentive to vernacular theology following seminal work by Bernard McGinn (1994) and Nicholas Watson (1995, 1997) and also in more recent literary criticism influenced by New Formalism. Jim Rhodes deserves special credit for avoiding jargon and naming the phenomenon with no-frills clarity in the title of his 2001 book, *Poetry Does Theology*.

4   Karnes, 'Will's Imagination', pp. 27–28.

5   Cervone, *Poetics of the Incarnation*, p. 26.

larger question of why it exists in the first place, which can't be addressed without recourse to theology. It is, he insists — in a wonder-inducing declaration that opens still more questions — nothing less than 'a gifte of God' (B.12.68/C.14.33). Like any other plant, it needs a place and the means to grow: in the B text its nurturing fields are 'Pacience and pouerte' (12.61), 'lele lyvynge men' (12.62), and 'lif holy' (12.62), and in the C text it thrives when 'gode-wil' (14.24) brings rain. God in the person of the Holy Spirit gives this gift, but the metaphor in both B and C suggests that proper human intention and action are what enable it to survive and flourish. This metaphor is in fact a touchstone of what Robert Adams and others have taken as Langland's 'semi-Pelagianism', a theological position manifested as the poem's dominant treatment of the relationship between divine and human will, according to which the operation of grace depends on what people do, how they think and feel and live.[6]

Scholarship emphasizing Langland's insistence on this understanding of grace has of course never denied the agency of God in the theology of *Piers Plowman*, but its special focus on the importance of human agency has tended to reduce the work of the divine to an originary force that fades from attention in the face of Langland's engagement with the ongoing work of human volition. Such discussions focus readerly attention on what the poem says human will and effort can do (and it says a great deal) and draw less attention to Langland's claims about divine interaction with human agency as that plays out over time (a topic no less theologically interesting and no less relevant to a consideration of grace). Curtis Gruenler notes that the term 'semi-Pelagianism' itself suggests a compromise or middle way, which may not do justice to the complexities of an orthodoxy capable of 'embracing seemingly incompatible truths as mystery' and maintaining 'the paradoxes of grace and works and of divine and human agency as productive tensions rather than mere dichotomies'.[7] Langland's figurative descriptions of grace express in highly nuanced ways just such mystery and paradox, revealing a theology centred on divine and human cooperation, not a middle way but a complexly realized both/and.[8]

Piers Plowman is in fact not narrowly focused on human agency, even though it establishes a theology that insists on the importance of human effort and good will. Imaginatif makes clear the necessary human part played in the cultivation of grace, but in the C text he also emphasizes God's sending of the 'Seynt Espirit' to make love

---

6 Adams, 'Piers's Pardon and Langland's Semi-Pelagianism', p. 393; Lawler, *Penn Commentary*, p. 413. While 'semi-Pelagianism' is a prominent theological term in the significant chapter of *Piers Plowman* scholarship inaugurated by Adams's 1983 essay, in more recent years it has fallen into less frequent use both in broader theological discourse and in *Piers Plowman* scholarship, where its utility as a descriptor of Langland's theology has been called into question by Aers, *Salvation and Sin*, pp. 83–131, esp. pp. 84–85.

7 Gruenler, *Poetics of Enigma*, pp. 296, 38.

8 Gruenler uses the term 'participation' to describe this relationship of human and divine, situating it in relation to Christian Platonism such that a creature 'participates' in the Creator in a way analogous to a particular 'participating' in a universal or Platonic form, according to Platonic and Neoplatonic philosophy. Gruenler offers a fascinating history of the specifically theological use of this term, which he traces in the English tradition back to Chaucer's translation of Boethius (see *Poetics of Enigma*, pp. 13–21, 31–80).

'sprynge' up as its fostering condition (C.14.27). The verb suggests spring growth, analogous but prior to that of 'gras', prompted by the energetic work of the Holy Spirit instead of the good will of people. In the parallel passage in B, moreover, Imaginatif continues his speech in a way that draws special attention to the presence of divine mystery, thereby problematizing the effort to locate catalysing agency with any specificity. As he proceeds to teach Will the distinction between 'clergy' and 'kynde wit' and the value of both for Christian knowing, he says about grace that 'of greet love' it 'spryngeþ', and it is perhaps telling that he neglects to indicate whether this love is human or divine or both, for he concludes, 'Knew neuere clerk how it comeþ forþ, ne kynde wit þe weyes' (B.12.68–69). Here grace is considerably less knowable than the grass of the metaphor, much more *other* than *like*, a mystery analogous to the blowing of the Spirit that floats through Imaginatif's speech in Latin lines from John's gospel: '*Spiritus vbi vult spirat* [...] *Nescit aliquis vnde venit aut quo vadit*' (The Spirit blows where it will [...] No one knows where it comes from or where it goes)' (John 3.8; B.12.63a, 69a). If 'grace is a gras' was initially intended to reveal the importance of human agency to the workings of grace, it is as if here Imaginatif retracts the metaphor's explanatory power to illuminate instead inscrutable divine mystery. In this figuration the operation of grace is finally not given to Will to know, even with his interlocutor's most potent theologizing. What Imaginatif says about it is a figure of speech and, as he himself admits, *just* that, a brilliant illumination of something unknowable, something that even the most learned men never knew.

The mysterious workings of grace described by Imaginatif receive further and lengthier illumination by the Samaritan who becomes Will's teacher in a later vision. Here Langland turns from relatively compact comparison to more thickly descriptive analogy, reinforcing the sense that the truth of grace can be expressed better through a metaphor's conjuring of something-it-isn't than through more head-on consideration. Yet the Samaritan's pedagogical strategy differs from Imaginatif's in a significant way. Unlike the B-text's Imaginatif, he doesn't evacuate his metaphor's explanatory potential to showcase unknowableness but instead uses it to illuminate a theologically rich paradox. He works with his extended metaphor, bending it and allowing it to transform until it breaks into even richer theological meaning. Robert Frost once said, 'All metaphor breaks down somewhere. That is the beauty of it'.[9] In Will's interaction with the Samaritan Langland seems to have been of the same mind, and half a millennium earlier.

Instead of providing a direct metaphor for grace (as Imaginatif does with 'gras'), the Samaritan instead obliquely engages the question of grace in the second of his extended analogies for the Trinity, the long passage likening the Trinity to a torch or a taper that follows its comparison to a hand.[10] The Samaritan explains that Christianity's triune God is like a torch: the Father is the wax; the Son is the wick; the Holy Spirit is the fire — but those identities are not what he dwells on, and in fact for part of the

---

9   Frost, 'Education by Poetry', p. 723.

10   The Samaritan's lengthy torch analogy is essentially the same in the B and C texts; citations hereafter follow B, with any differences in C beyond alternative spelling noted.

passage the burning torch is replaced by a glowing coal (or gleed) whose fieriness can be either quickened or quenched. Grace, in this metaphor, is closely associated with the living quality of the fire figured as the Holy Spirit — it is the light and heat that can be extinguished or brought to brighter blazing. The Samaritan explains that divine grace is quenched by unkindness (which in *Piers Plowman* is the Sin against the Holy Ghost), and that, conversely,

> þe Holy Goost gloweþ but as a glede
> Til þat lele loue ligge on hym and blowe.
> And þanne flawmeþ he as fir on Fader and on *Filius*
> And melteþ hire myȝt into mercy. (B.17.224–27/C.19.190–93)

Human 'lele loue' is what makes the Spirit flame forth, causing the might of the first two persons of the Trinity to soften and to become merciful through heat that is intensified by a loving human disposition. The considerable emphasis on human volition here makes this passage, like 'grace is a gras', another go-to for accounts that emphasize Langland's insistence on human effort in the workings of grace. But like 'grace is a gras' this passage's figurative language actually points to a rich interplay of divine and human agency. While the entire passage repays close analysis, I will focus on three moments in which the Samaritan's complex metaphor does some sort of extra work that illuminates divine and human effort working together.

The first moment occurs in the passage quoted above, when the Samaritan explains how latent fire (the Holy Spirit as a glowing gleed) is quickened by the blowing of 'lele love' (B.17.225).[11] In a beautiful exposition of this passage, Davlin observes, 'When Jesus gave his disciples the Holy Spirit in the gospels, he breathed on them. Here, the loyal, loving human blows on the Spirit in a remarkable reversal, with amazing results'.[12] Davlin's comparison reveals her sensitivity to the rich work of the verb here. By metaphorically rendering the relevant human action as *blowing* in a passage focused on the Holy Spirit, Langland prompts readers familiar with the New Testament to draw several associations: to Jesus's account of the unpredictable blowing of the Spirit (alluded to in Latin in Imaginatif's earlier description of grace), to the resurrected Christ's purposeful giving of the Spirit by breathing on his disciples (to which Davlin refers), and perhaps even to the fire-producing wind of Pentecost.[13] Langland's use of a verb with these particular biblical associations invites readers to dwell on divine love in biblical scenes featuring wind/breath/Spirit, even as the Samaritan's speech focuses instead on the work of human love, 'blowing' on metaphorical fire to quicken its flames. Davlin acknowledges that the spiritual efficacy of human effort — 'lele loue' — is what takes centre stage here, but she emphasizes the role of divine agency as well, pointing out that the Samaritan teaches that 'loyal love is itself the gift of the Trinity'.[14] Indeed, at the very beginning of his analogy the Samaritan establishes

---

11   The parallel passage in the C text has 'loue and bileue' in place of B's 'lele loue' (C.19.191).
12   Davlin, 'The Kindness of God', p. 278.
13   John 3.8; John 20.22; Acts 2.2.
14   Davlin, 'Kindness of God', p. 278.

that what the Trinity-torch does is nothing less than foster 'amonges folk love and bileve' (B.17.210/C.19.176). In other words, human love — the agent that quickens the flame — is itself fostered by the flame it quickens. There's a circularity here, or a reciprocity — a relationship more complex than originary stimulus and response. Mary Raschko hits exactly the right note when she says that the Samaritan's speech characterizes the relationship between human love and God's love as 'symbiotic'.[15]

The torch metaphor is complicated again a little further into the passage, when the Samaritan provides three examples that serve to illustrate the need of fire for fuel. At this point the influence of love (and its opposite, unkindness) on the working of the metaphor has conditioned readers to understand that the full flaming forth of grace is a response to human effort. The Samaritan teaches in the first example that just as wax and a warm coal will burn and blaze, so the Father will forgive mild-hearted men who 'ruefully repenten and restitucion make' (B.17.236/C.19.202). The second example works similarly: as a wick and fire will burn and blaze, so Christ will forgive and forget, interceding with the Father provided that 'men crye hym mercy' (B.17.242/C.19.208). The third example switches gears to point out that when fuel is lacking, fire will not flame forth, a powerful image of 'grace wiþouten mercy | To alle vnkynde creatures' (B.17.249–50/C.19.215–16). It's clear that human agency (love, or active kindness) would provide what's missing in the third example, and attention here to human agency on account of its devastating absence retrospectively affects the impression given by the first two examples so that mild-heartedness, repentance, and restitution (in the first example) and the contrite cry to God for mercy (in the second) seem to be acts of human agency analogous to kindness. The logic of this reading suggests that, like kindness, these dispositions and behaviours should function as kindling similar to the 'tache', 'tonder', or 'broches' without which four hundred winters of striking fire from flint is lost labour (B.17.245/C.19.212). But that is not what the larger metaphor says. The literal fuels in the first two examples are in fact *wax* and *wick*, which the full passage has already identified metaphorically as divine persons, the Father and Son of the Trinity (the wax and wick of the Samaritan's original torch). With this sequence of three examples Langland alters the terms of the original metaphor with the athleticism of a later metaphysical poet like Donne. The result is that the Samaritan's words deliver a double sense of what fuels grace: human *and* divine agency, working together as one. The cumulative effect of this passage is to deliver a message that adds theological flesh to Imaginatif's bare-bones statement in the C text that 'grace withouten grace of God, and also gode werkes, | May nat be' (14.28–29).

Langland figures human and divine cooperation in the workings of grace one more time in the Samaritan's speech, in a final moment of metaphorical play in which the Samaritan takes the vehicle that has worked so hard for him to illuminate something about God and puts it to work on a different tenor: not God this time,

---

15   Raschko, 'Love of God and Neighbor', p. 68. Davis describes what she sees as 'a circularity in the condition of grace' in a discussion of a different part of the poem (*Piers Plowman and the Books of Nature*, p. 190).

but the human person. In the original metaphor, Father, Son, and Holy Spirit were wax, wick, and fire. The Samaritan's representation of the effects of unkindness on the operation of grace, however, established the image of a dysfunctional torch in which human effort was missing. That image of a non-flaming fire is picked up again when the Samaritan likens any rich yet unkind person to a 'blynd bekene'. 'Ye brenne but ye blaseth noughte', the Samaritan says, chiding the imagined sinner (B.17.264/C.19.230). He then reverses the image, pointing out by way of contrast that 'euery manere good man may be likned to a torche | Or ellis to a tapur, to reuerence the Trinitee' (B.17.278–79/C.19.260–61). It's at this point that the initial comparison gives way to something new, as every good person is described in exactly the same way in which the Samaritan's lengthy discourse has trained Will to understand God. Yet herein lies a paradox. With the notable exception of Christ, a human person simply is *not God*, and much of what creatures in Langland's tradition say and believe about their Creator is grounded in God's *other*ness. But even so, Christian tradition also teaches that humans are made in God's image, so there is a metaphorical aptness to the Samaritan's non-equation — a likeness that encompasses otherness — and it's precisely the complication of the original comparison that gives it its theological depth. The contributions of divine agency and human agency to the workings of grace now seem to be poetically — and also theologically — intertwined.

The explorations of grace in Will's schooling by Imaginatif and the Samaritan provide us with a window into the poem's theology through the richly developed metaphors voiced by these interlocutors. Very little can be claimed with certainty about the author of *Piers Plowman* known as William Langland, but beyond any shadow of a doubt he was a poet, and someone who cared passionately about Christian theology. And for him, theology seems to have been inseparable from the work of poetry, for his deepest theological thinking is aided by poetic devices, often figurative language that enables the associative power of words — and, through them, minds and hearts — to approach that which exceeds the knowledge of things seen. The metaphor of the divine torch teaches something about the triune nature of the Christian God, but more than that, it illuminates a rich theology of grace, Imaginatif's living 'gras'.[16] Interestingly, although grace in both of these metaphors is most closely associated with the Holy Spirit, the Trinity's third person, it is in some ways parallel to the *second* person, for it emerges as the spiritual locus of human and divine cooperation, intermingling, even union — not the hypostatic union, of course, but a coming together of divinity and humanity in the arena of ethical effort. It is Langland's poetic manifestation not of God's being but of what it means to live a Christian life of spiritual integrity. It's clear that for Langland divine grace involves the work of God-given human nature, the kindness enacted through love of neighbour that in *Piers Plowman* is one and the same as the work of the God-torch in the world.

---

16 Lawler makes a similar point about the Samaritan's torch analogy but describes it differently: 'the torch/taper (candle) simile […] is not really a companion piece to the hand simile, though it seems at first to be that; rather, it focuses nearly from the start not on the Trinity but on love of neighbor and the part it plays in salvation' (*Penn Commentary*, p. 413).

Works Cited

Primary Sources

Frost, Robert, 'Education by Poetry', in *Collected Poems, Prose, and Plays* (New York: Library of America, 1995)
Langland, William, *Piers Plowman: A Parallel-Text Edition of the A, B, C, and Z Versions*, I, ed. by A. V. C. Schmidt, 2nd edn (Kalamazoo: Medieval Institute Publications, 2011)
The Vulgate Bible, VI, ed. by Angela M. Kinney (Cambridge, MA: Harvard University Press, 2013)

Secondary Sources

Adams, Robert, 'Piers's Pardon and Langland's Semi-Pelagianism', *Traditio*, 39 (1983), 367–418
Aers, David, *Salvation and Sin: Augustine, Langland, and Fourteenth-Century Theology* (Notre Dame: University of Notre Dame Press, 2009)
Cervone, Cristina Maria, *Poetics of the Incarnation: Middle English Writing and the Leap of Love* (Philadelphia: University of Pennsylvania Press, 2012)
Davis, Rebecca, *'Piers Plowman' and the Books of Nature* (Oxford: Oxford University Press, 2016)
Davlin, Mary Clemente, 'The Kindness of God: The Holy Spirit in *Piers Plowman*', *Spirituality*, 10 (2004), 275–79
Goodmann, Thomas A., ed., *Approaches to Teaching Langland's 'Piers Plowman'* (New York: Modern Language Association of America, 2018)
Gruenler, Curtis A., *'Piers Plowman' and the Poetics of Enigma: Riddles, Rhetoric, and Theology* (Notre Dame: University of Notre Dame Press, 2017)
Karnes, Michelle, 'Will's Imagination in *Piers Plowman*', *Journal of English and Germanic Philology*, 108 (2009), 27–58
Lawler, Traugott, *The Penn Commentary on 'Piers Plowman'*, IV (Philadelphia: University of Pennsylvania Press, 2018)
McGinn, Bernard, 'Meister Eckhart and the Beguines in the Context of Vernacular Theology', in *Meister Eckhart and the Beguine Mystics: Hadewijch of Brabant, Mechthild of Magdeburg, and Marguerite Porete*, ed. by Bernard McGinn (New York: Continuum, 1994), pp. 1–14
Raschko, Mary, 'Love of God and Neighbor: The Communal Ethics of Langland's Samaritan Parable', *Yearbook of Langland Studies*, 26 (2012), 49–75
Rhodes, Jim, *Poetry Does Theology: Chaucer, Grosseteste, and the Pearl-Poet* (Notre Dame: University of Notre Dame Press, 2001)
Watson, Nicholas, 'Censorship and Cultural Change in Late-Medieval England: Vernacular Theology, the Oxford Translation Debate, and Arundel's Constitutions of 1409', *Speculum*, 70 (1995), 822–64
——, 'Visions of Inclusion: Universal Salvation and Vernacular Theology in Pre-Reformation England', *Journal of Medieval and Early Modern Studies*, 27 (1997), 145–87

THOMAS KITTEL

Contact between *Piers Plowman* and *The Prick of Conscience* in Rawlinson Poetry 139

▾ **KEYWORDS** *Piers Plowman*, *The Prick of Conscience*, Rawlinson poetry 139

▾ **ABSTRACT** This note identifies a group of inserted passages in a manuscript of *The Prick of Conscience* which contain Latin quotations borrowed from *Piers Plowman*. These short passages, in Oxford, Bodleian Library, MS Rawlinson poetry 139, modify *The Prick*'s discussion of pardons and draw on the Latin of *Piers* in making their new claims. The note identifies these passages and shows that their most likely source is in a now-lost B-text manuscript of *Piers*, examining alternatives including pastoral and penitential texts in Middle English and Latin. Alongside this new evidence for the transmission of the B text to the north-west Midlands, where Rawlinson is localized on the basis of its dialect, the note explores what the passages indicate about the reviser's response to both *Piers* and *The Prick*. It argues that the reviser read *Piers* mostly for its Latin, paying relatively little attention to its English verse, in contrast to the approach taken by most modern readers. It ends with the suggestion that accounts of medieval reading should engage more thoroughly with trends in the medieval reception of Middle English texts which are misaligned with our own interest in these writings.

A manuscript of *The Prick of Conscience* seems to contain a strange error. Oxford, Bodleian Library, MS Rawlinson poetry 139 organizes the poem according to an unusual system of rubrics, which in the early parts do not correspond to the prologue and book divisions seen in other copies. The rubric for book 3 is particularly surprising: this book is given the heading 'Passus tertius' (fol. 23^r), the same term used for the structural divisions in *Piers Plowman*. No other manuscript of *The Prick* and indeed very few other Middle English texts, none of them widely circulated, use the term *passus*. Andrew Galloway notes that although a number of other alliterative texts

Thomas Kittel (thomas.kittel@protonmail.com) has recently completed a DPhil in English at the University of Oxford.

The Yearbook of Langland Studies, 34 (2020), 211–221   BREPOLS ❧ PUBLISHERS   10.1484/J.YLS.5.121093

use the cognate Middle English term *pas*, only *The Wars of Alexander* (surviving in two manuscripts) and a single copy of *The Siege of Jerusalem* use *passus* to describe textual divisions.[1] Given their restricted dissemination, it seems unlikely that either is the source of Rawlinson's use of the term, so the apparent slip indicates familiarity with Langland's poem.

Rawlinson contains further evidence suggesting a relationship with *Piers*. Its text of *The Prick* also contains a group of unique interpolated passages, short insertions of fifteen to twenty lines, clustered in book 4. They challenge statements made in the poem about the process of salvation, and were produced by a reviser who wanted to reshape *The Prick of Conscience* from a more restrictive theological position. Several of these insertions contain embedded Latin quotations, in imitation of the style of the poem, and some of these quotations were taken from a copy of *Piers*. This note identifies these interpolated passages for the first time, exploring what they suggest about the reviser's response to *Piers*, and drawing some broader conclusions about the relationship between *Piers* and *The Prick of Conscience* at the beginning of the fifteenth century.

The Prick was written in Yorkshire around the second quarter of the fourteenth century. In part a translation of an Anglo-French text, *Les Peines de Purgatorie*, it also brings together a wide range of mostly Latin material into a manual for salvation.[2] The poem is divided into a prologue and seven books, which deal with the wretchedness of man, the world, death, purgatory, Judgement Day, the pains of hell, and finally the joys of heaven. Modern readers of Middle English might be forgiven for not having picked up a copy, but whatever one thinks of the quality of this lengthy specimen of northern religious verse it was evidently extremely popular with medieval readers. Over 120 witnesses survive from all over England, more than any other work of Middle English verse and substantially more than *Piers*, and it was rewritten into several new versions and translated into Latin.[3]

The Prick had a significant relationship with *Piers*, of which the text in Rawlinson represents a small part. Six scribes are known to have copied both, three in single manuscripts and three in separate books, so the addition of Rawlinson brings the total number of medieval copyists with access to both poems up to seven.[4] A larger but now mostly invisible community of readers or listeners presumably surrounded these books in their original contexts, broadening the reach of the two poems as

---

1 Galloway, *Penn Commentary*, I, 19–21.

2 This and other sources are discussed in *Richard Morris's 'Prick of Conscience'*, ed. by Hanna and Wood, pp. lii–lxi.

3 The most up-to-date list of manuscripts is available in *Richard Morris's 'Prick of Conscience'*, ed. by Hanna and Wood, pp. 378–83. On its relative popularity, see Sargent, 'What Do the Numbers Mean?'. The poem's dissemination, including adaptations and translations, is discussed in Lewis and McIntosh, *A Descriptive Guide to the Manuscripts*, pp. 1–15.

4 These manuscripts are London, Society of Antiquaries, MS 687; Oxford, Bodleian Library, MS Eng. poet. a.1 (the Vernon); San Marino, Huntington Library, MS Hm 128; London, British Library, Additional MS 34779/Manchester, John Rylands Library, MS English 90; Oxford, Bodleian Library, MS Rawlinson poetry 137/Oxford, University College, MS 142; and Durham, Ushaw College, MS 50/ Oxford, Corpus Christi College, MS 201. The identification of a shared hand in Rawlinson poetry

a pair. Despite growing interest in *The Prick* in recent years, the lack of research into almost all areas of its dissemination has meant that Langlandians have largely overlooked this relationship.[5]

In some ways *The Prick* is very unlike *Piers*, yet the two have some significant subject matter in common. Both are concerned with self-knowledge as a step on the road to salvation. Both depict scenes of the apocalypse, and both discuss the nature of pardons — an aspect discussed in more detail below. It should not be entirely surprising, therefore, to see the two together in the hands of medieval readers, but still their conjunction produces interesting reflections on both. Rawlinson suggests how such readers may have engaged with the two poems principally as Latin texts, with only minimal interest in their English.[6]

Rawlinson is a single-text parchment manuscript, written by one scribe in textualis throughout. Its copy of *The Prick* belongs to the 'Vernon-Simeon group', a family of eight texts named after its two best-known members.[7] This group was apparently disseminated from the Lichfield area, according to a recent argument placing the production of Vernon in that city.[8] The Vernon-Simeon group is related to another group of seven copies also associated with Lichfield, known as the Lichfield group.[9]

Rawlinson is something of an outlier among this constellation of manuscripts, which is otherwise marked by evidence of close and overlapping production. Vernon's Scribe A was responsible for part of two other manuscripts in this group,[10] while the hand of the scribe known as the Lichfield Master, possibly identifiable as one John Scriveyn, is found in three.[11] One further hand appears in two copies,[12] while

---

137 and University College 142 was made by Horobin, 'The Scribe of Rawlinson Poetry 137', and the identification of the same scribe in Corpus Christi College 201 and Ushaw College 50 was made by Doyle, 'Ushaw College, Durham, MS 50'.

5 For recent interest in manuscripts of *The Prick*, see Sawyer, *Reading English Verse in Manuscript*; Marshall, 'Literary Codicologies'; Johnston, *The Reading Nation*; and Killian, 'Menacing Books'. For recent literary-critical studies of the poem, see Rentz, *Imagining the Parish*, pp. 122–48; Galloway, 'Gower's *Confessio amantis*, the *Prick of Conscience*, and the History of the Latin Gloss'; and Chickering, 'Rhetorical *Stimulus* in the *Prick of Conscience*'.

6 On *Piers*'s reception as a Latin text, see Warner, *The Myth of Piers Plowman*, pp. 53–71.

7 The Vernon-Simeon group is described in Lewis and McIntosh, *A Descriptive Guide to the Manuscripts*, pp. 7–8.

8 Horobin, 'The Scribes of the Vernon Manuscript'.

9 Lewis and McIntosh, *A Descriptive Guide to the Manuscripts*, p. 8. More detail on this group, including a stemmatic analysis, is given in Dareau and McIntosh, 'A Dialect Word'.

10 Oxford, Trinity College, MS 16A and Wells (Norfolk), Holkham Hall, Earl of Leicester's Library, MS 668. See *The Vernon Manuscript*, ed. by Doyle, p. 13; Lewis and McIntosh, *A Descriptive Guide to the Manuscripts*, pp. 54 and 121; and Horobin, 'The Scribes of the Vernon Manuscript', p. 45.

11 London, British Library, MS Harley 1205, London, College of Arms, MS Arundel 57, and Manchester, John Rylands Library, MS English 50. See Horobin, 'The Scribes of the Vernon Manuscript', p. 28, repeating earlier partial identifications in McIntosh, 'A New Approach to Middle English Dialectology', p. 7, and separately *The Vernon Manuscript*, ed. by Doyle, pp. 13–14.

12 Hand B of Oxford, Trinity College, MS 16A has been identified as the scribe of Oxford, Bodleian Library, MS Douce 156; Horobin, 'The Scribes of the Vernon Manuscript', p. 46.

the artist of the initials in Vernon has been identified in another.[13] Meanwhile, the *Linguistic Atlas of Late Mediaeval English* places the dialect of Rawlinson poetry 139 in south-east Shropshire, close to the border with Staffordshire.[14] This isolated position might reflect the transmission of a Vernon-Simeon group exemplar some distance away from Lichfield, though scribal dialect does not, of course, always reflect provenance: the dialect of Vernon's Scribe A, for example, is localized to Worcestershire, some way south of Lichfield.[15] Nonetheless, the marked difference in layout between the tall and narrow format of Rawlinson and other Vernon-Simeon and Lichfield manuscripts might indicate separateness from these more consistent productions. The others share layout features including bracketing for rhyme, but all are produced in more standard shapes. Rawlinson's proportions are that of the 'holster book', a format historically associated with public reading, though this theory has since been disputed.[16]

This geographical isolation reflects the unique state of its text. As mentioned above, Rawlinson contains insertions of material not found in the Main Version of *The Prick* or in any other copy of the poem, added to the discussion of purgatory in book 4. The reviser who composed them appears to have taken issue with some of the poem's theological views: although they mimic the form of the Main Version, in rhymed octosyllabic couplets, they challenge its statements about the help available to souls in purgatory and insist that only the individual Christian can save their own soul.

Three of the insertions contain Latin quotations which also appear in *Piers*. On fol. 49[v], between ll. 3833–34 in book 4, a nineteen-line passage is inserted containing verse 41 of the Athanasian Creed: 'Qui bona egerunt ibunt in uitam eternam qui uero mala in ignem eternam'.[17] This quotation is familiar, of course, from all three versions of *Piers*, in which it constitutes the pardon sent by Truth to Piers.[18]

Later in the text of Rawlinson, ll. 3924–25 are omitted and replaced with six lines of new material incorporating two pieces of Latin. The first is a quotation from Psalm 50.19: 'Cor contritum et humiliatum deus non despicies' (fol. 50[r]), found also in the B text at 13.58a and 15.194, and in cognate C-text passages at 15.62 and 16.336a. The second resembles closely a line found only in the B text: 'sola contricio delet peccatum' (11.81a), a unique phrase with parallels, though not an exact source, in other writings.[19] In

---

13   Oxford, Bodleian Library, MS Ashmole 41; see *The Vernon Manuscript*, ed. by Doyle, pp. 7–8. Horobin, 'The Scribes of the Vernon Manuscript', p. 39, further suggests that the scribe of Ashmole may be the same as the copyist of part of the episcopal register of Bishop Stretton of Lichfield.

14   McIntosh, Samuels, and Benskin, *Linguistic Atlas*, III, 426.

15   McIntosh, Samuels, and Benskin, *Linguistic Atlas*, III, 553.

16   Taylor, 'The Myth of the Minstrel Manuscript'.

17   Line numbers refer to *Richard Morris's 'Prick of Conscience'*, ed. by Hanna and Wood. All references to the text of the poem are to this edition. Italics in manuscript transcriptions represent expanded abbreviations.

18   *Piers Plowman: The A Version*, ed. by Kane, 8.95–96; *Piers Plowman: The B Version*, ed. by Kane and Donaldson, 7.113–14; *Piers Plowman: The C Version*, ed. by Russell and Kane, 9.287–88. Further references to the text of *Piers* will be to these editions.

19   Gray, 'Langland's Quotations from the Penitential Tradition', p. 56.

Rawlinson, it appears as 'Sola contr*icio* deleþ om*ne* peccatu*m*' (fol. 50^r), giving the Latin 'delet' an English ending.[20]

A third interpolated passage follows on fol. 50^v, where five new lines are inserted between ll. 3929–30, incorporating a quotation from Matthew 3.2 and 4.17 which appears in slightly different form in other biblical books: 'Penite*nci*am agite q*uia* ap*ropinqua*bit regnu*m* celoru*m*'.[21] This finds a less exact parallel in *Piers*, but might also be derived from the poem. At B.13.49, part of this line is embedded in the English verse, in the form found in Job (21.2) and Ezekiel (18.30): 'He sette a sour loof toforn vs and seide "*Agite penitenciam*"'. The likelihood of a Langlandian source for this very common piece of Latin is strengthened both by its proximity in the manuscript to the preceding insertion and by its proximity in *Piers* to the quotation from Psalm 50, '*cor contritum ...*', a few lines later in passus 13.

These quotations were widely dispersed in late medieval England, and the Rawlinson reviser could conceivably have accessed them independently of *Piers*. The creedal verse and the quotation from Psalm 50 were both used liturgically, as John Alford notes, while all have a clear relevance to discussions of penance and are found in several penitential works.[22] '*Agite penitenciam*' appears in the Latin manual *Fasciculus morum*, as does '*Cor contritum*'.[23] Although '*Sola contricio delet peccatum*' appears to be a unique Langlandian formulation, parallels appear in other texts: one of these is the *Summa* of Robert Courson, which also contains '*Penitenciam agite*' (quoted from Matthew).[24] A later text, the Middle English sermon cycle *Jacob's Well*, contains '*Sola contricio*' in the same form found in *Piers*, suggesting that *Piers* may have been a source; this text, like Courson's, also contains '*Penitenciam agite*', and shows how these quotations were relevant to a range of writers concerned with pastoral care.[25]

There are three further insertions in book 4 (two on fol. 47^r and one other on fol. 50^v) which contain five quotations in total, all biblical, not found in *Piers*, indicating that the reviser had access to other sources. However, Rawlinson's close reproduction of Langland's '*Sola contricio*' suggests that *Piers* is its most likely source, and although the four quotations overlapping with *Piers* were available separately, their presence together in Rawlinson seems most easily explained as the result of the reviser's reading passūs 7–13 of the B text. I have identified no Latin or vernacular source which contains all four quotations, and they may have been less common in instructional writing than the above occurrences suggest: none appear, for example,

---

20 The englishing of Latin verbs has been noted in other contexts, for example in a sixteenth-century ownership inscription discussed by Wakelin, '"Thys ys my boke"', p. 26.

21 Alford, *Guide to the Quotations*, p. 82.

22 Alford, *Guide to the Quotations*, pp. 56–57, 83, 82.

23 *Fasciculus morum*, ed. by Wenzel, p. 480, l. 229 ('*Agite penitenciam*', quoted from Ezekiel). Two similar quotations also appear on pp. 484, l. 57 (from Matthew) and 486, l. 96 (from 1 Peter). '*Cor contritum*' appears at p. 438, l. 96; this phrase alone is also used earlier in the text without reference to its source, at p. 282, l. 135.

24 Identified in Gray, 'Langland's Quotations from the Penitential Tradition', p. 56; see Kennedy, 'Robert Courson on Penance', p. 294.

25 *Jacob's Well*, ed. by Brandeis, pp. 172, 174, 167. See Gray, 'Langland's Quotations from the Penitential Tradition', p. 56 n. 21.

in the Parson's Tale, Chaucer's imitation of penitential literature, or *The Lay Folks' Catechism*, the English form of the syllabus issued by Archbishop of York John Thoresby in 1357.[26]

Other evidence supports the relationship between the insertions and *Piers*. In addition to the manuscript's *passus* rubric, the new context into which the Latin material is placed in Rawlinson also suggests that it was borrowed from the poem. The first of the three insertions outlined above, containing the creedal verse found in the pardon-tearing scene, is used to make a point about pardons. The second and third insertions contain quotations found also in the 'Feast of Conscience' scene (B.13), which stages a dramatization of the sacrament of penance in which Patience and the dreamer eat foods representing 'shrifte' (13.55). These quotations are used also to support the reviser's view on pardons, incorporated into insertions which insist that only penance, and not indulgences, can save the soul. The other quotation in the second insertion, taken from the first inner dream in B.11, occurs during the dreamer's rebuke of the friars for neglecting their duty of baptism, in favour of the more lucrative sacrament of confession. Associated thereby with opposition to clerical corruption, it bolsters the reviser's stance against indulgences. These parallels make clear that the context of the Latin in *Piers* is related to its new setting in Rawlinson.

Looking at the first of the three insertions containing Langlandian Latin in closer detail shows how the reviser was guided by the context of the material in *Piers*, while at the same time redeploying it in a different style. The first insertion occurs during the discussion of pardons in book 4. The *Prick* poet describes pardons as follows:

> Pardon helpes þam, als clerkes says,
> Þat it has purchased in þair lif-days,
> For pardon of papes and bisschopes,
> Þat es granted here als men hopes,
> May availe þair saules in purgatory
> Þat has purchaced it here worthyly,
> If þai of þair syn had contricion
> And war shrifen byfor þat pardon. (ll. 3802–09)

This position was apparently too generous for the Rawlinson reviser, for the manuscript contains an added passage challenging this some lines later:

> Of al þis þat I haue said bifore
> Is gederid holy chirche tresore (ll. 3832–33)
>
>   [Interpolated material begins here]
> Þat is grauntid to hem þat haue uerrey contricion
> And after her power makeþ satisfaccioun
> Of alle wrongwise takyng in her lyue
> And of alle her synnes clene hem schryue
> In his bulle to oþer grauntid þe pope neuer pardon

---

26   On the *Catechism*, see Swanson, 'The Origins of *The Lay Folks' Catechism*'.

Ffor if he hade aȝeyn oure crede hade he don
Þat in quicunque wlt [*sic*] saiþ þus
And al holy writ þerto bereþ witnes
Qui bona egerunt ibunt in uitam eternam qui uero
mala in ignem eternam
Þat is to say þat goode werkes don in charite
In euerlastynge lif her wonyng schal be
And þei þat yuel wirche *and* so ende
Into fuir for euer schul þei wende
Þer is no pardon þat schal hem saue
Þanne it is to drede leste fewe it haue
In þis forme to peter þis tresour crist dide ȝiue
Among his disciplis whil he dide lyue
Goode to louse *and* yuel to bynde
And þis power haden þe apostles alle we fynde (fol. 49ʳ)

The inserted material makes explicit a more restrictive view than the Main Version. From the reviser's perspective, papal pardons are a misunderstanding of church doctrine, as they contradict the Athanasian Creed. The passage suggests instead that Christ is the source of the power to pardon, deputized to the Apostles. Like the priest in the pardon-tearing scene, the reviser sees 'no pardon' in the Creed. This insertion suggests that the reviser found *The Prick* dangerously ambiguous in its treatment of the subject of pardons, and drew on the Latin in *Piers* to compose an insertion clarifying a more correct position.

Although the insertion borrows material from the poem, the views it expresses are not straightforwardly derived from *Piers*. In the B text, the words of the Creed borrowed by the reviser are destroyed in the pardon-tearing scene. Following the tearing, Piers declares that,

Of preiers and of penaunce my plouȝ shal ben herafter,
And wepen whan I sholde werche þouȝ whete breed me failleþ
The prophete his payn eet in penaunce and in sorwe
By þat þe Sauter vs seith, and so dide othere manye. (B.7.124–27)

These lines are part of a speech in which Piers seems to lament the injustice of the Creed. He asks, 'The foweles in þe firmament, who fynt hem at wynter? […] Haue þei no gerner to go to but god fynt hem alle' (B.7.133, 135). The position taken here is complicated: Piers laments the suffering of the poor and the weak, yet seems also to assert faith that God will protect them. The emphasis on penance and on a return to the sacraments as the source of redemption is tonally ambiguous, resigned yet also acknowledging the security offered by the 'Sauter'. The position in the inserted passage is not entirely dissimilar. It emphasizes the responsibility of individuals to atone for their own sins, but maintains that forgiveness is possible through penance. Nonetheless, this insertion flattens the scene in *Piers*, discarding its ambiguity and emotional conflict and translating its underlying point into the discursive style of *The Prick*.

This loss of ambiguity is reflected also in the treatment of Latin in the new insertions. The Rawlinson text emphasizes the clarity of the guidance offered by Scripture and other authoritative Latin materials; unlike *Piers*, it admits no sense of confusion or difficulty of interpretation. This is unsurprising, given the reviser's evident concern with possible errors in *The Prick* and his attempts to control its interpretation by the intended readers of the new version, but it also represents another kind of assimilation. In almost every case, *The Prick* offers only one interpretation of the Latin material it quotes, minimizing any sense of disagreement or instability. This is the style adopted by the Rawlinson reviser.

Also significant is the reviser's exclusive interest in Latin. While the creedal quotation inserted between ll. 3833–34 contains a gloss on the Latin like that of Langland's priest, the revision makes no direct borrowing of English material from the poem. Instead, *Piers* was mined for the Latin it contains, and it was in the Latin that the reviser found authoritative support for his views on pardons and other contentious subjects. The Rawlinson revision put *The Prick* in contact with *Piers* through this most visible of their shared formal features, and suggests that the reviser treated Langland's text as a repository of Latin scaffolded with English.

In addition to evidence for the reviser's response to *Piers*, Rawlinson also suggests some conclusions about the relative status of *Piers* and *The Prick*. The Rawlinson revisions indicate a desire to maintain the wholeness of the Main Version: even while directly challenging material in the poem, the reviser chose not to omit those statements he clearly found troubling. This fidelity might imply that *The Prick* had an authoritative status of its own. It was certainly important within the local textual culture which produced it, and among the nearby group of scribes around Lichfield who generated one of the largest surviving local clusters of a single text. This culture appears to have favoured works of northern Middle English verse: copies of *Speculum vitae* and *Cursor mundi* are copied in the hand of the Lichfield Master.[27]

In contrast, while Rawlinson offers the first evidence that the B text was present in the north-west Midlands in this period, the poem still appears to have been very sparsely copied in the area. Rawlinson and Vernon's A text are a lonely pair of witnesses to Langland's poem compared to the abundance of *Prick* manuscripts surrounding them. The material evidence for the substantially greater popularity of *The Prick* compared to *Piers* among medieval readers is a challenging prospect for our field, accustomed as it is to viewing the two in almost oppositional terms. Where *Piers* is regularly lauded, not undeservedly, for its ambition, complexity, and interpretative openness, *The Prick* has mostly experienced neglect.[28] We must take seriously the interest of medieval readers in the latter text, to understand better the textual culture inhabited by early readers of Langland.

---

27 Doyle, 'Codicology, Palaeography, and Provenance', p. 15; Horobin, 'The Scribes of the Vernon Manuscript', p. 30; Dareau and McIntosh, 'A Dialect Word', p. 22.

28 See, for example, Galloway's praise of the poem in 'Madame Meed', esp. p. 229: 'the most ambitious and scandalous invitation *to* topicality that any poet in English of his century carried out', and in 'Non-Literary Commentary and its Literary Profits', esp. pp. 22–23.

The Rawlinson revision presents another challenge. There has been a tendency in scholarship to look for creativity and originality in medieval reading practices, but these qualities are not apparent in the work of the reviser.[29] The insertions instead suggest concern over ambiguity and a conservative approach to form, seemingly disengaged from the attributes of the poem celebrated today. So, how can we address medieval reception when it is opposed to the ways we ourselves want to see medieval texts? Without returning to the George Kane school of thought, which unhelpfully chastised the supposed incompetence of scribes,[30] it may be productive to consider ways in which medieval reading could sometimes be simplifying, dogmatic, and reductive. A balanced view of the medieval past must embrace the 'bad' readers, as well as the good.

Works Cited

Manuscripts and Archival Resources

Durham, Ushaw College, MS 50
London, British Library, MS Additional 34779
——, MS Harley 1205
London, College of Arms, MS Arundel 57
London, Society of Antiquaries, MS 687
Manchester, John Rylands Library, MS English 50
——, MS English 90
Oxford, Bodleian Library, MS Ashmole 41
——, MS Douce 156
——, MS Eng. poet. a.1
——, MS Rawlinson poetry 137
——, MS Rawlinson poetry 139
Oxford, Corpus Christi College, MS 201
Oxford, Trinity College, MS 16A
Oxford, University College, MS 142
San Marino, Huntington Library, MS Hm 128
Wells (Norfolk), Holkham Hall, Earl of Leicester's Library, MS 668

Reference Works

McIntosh, A. I., M. L. Samuels, and Michael Benskin, *A Linguistic Atlas of Late Mediaeval English*, 4 vols (Aberdeen: Aberdeen University Press, 1986)

---

29 See the influential view of the value of scribal variation as a form of literary criticism in Windeatt, 'The Scribes as Chaucer's Early Critics'.

30 Articulated, for example, in '"Good" and "Bad" Manuscripts', esp. p. 208.

Primary Sources

Fasciculus morum: A Fourteenth-Century Preacher's Handbook, ed. by Siegfried Wenzel (University Park: Pennsylvania State University Press, 1989)

Jacob's Well: An English Treatise on the Cleansing of Man's Conscience, ed. by Arthur Brandeis, EETS o.s. 115 (London: Kegan Paul, Trench, Trübner, 1900)

Langland, William, *Piers Plowman: The A Version*, ed. by George Kane (London: Athlone, 1960)

——, *Piers Plowman: The B Version*, ed. by George Kane and E. Talbot Donaldson (London: Athlone, 1988)

——, *Piers Plowman: The C Version*, ed. by George Russell and George Kane (London: Athlone, 1997)

Richard Morris's 'Prick of Conscience': A Corrected and Amplified Reading Text, ed. by Ralph Hanna and Sarah Wood, EETS o.s. 342 (Oxford: Oxford University Press, 2013)

The Vernon Manuscript: A Facsimile of Bodleian Library, Oxford, MS. Eng. poet. a.1, ed. by A. I. Doyle (Cambridge: Brewer, 1987)

Secondary Sources

Alford, John A., *Piers Plowman: A Guide to the Quotations*, Medieval and Renaissance Texts and Studies, 77 (Binghamton: Center for Medieval and Renaissance Studies, 1992)

Chickering, Howell, 'Rhetorical *Stimulus* in the *Prick of Conscience*', in *Medieval Paradigms: Essays in Honour of Jeremy Duquesnay Adams*, ed. by Stephanie Hayes-Healy, 2 vols (New York: Palgrave Macmillan, 2005), pp. 191–230

Dareau, Margaret Grace, and Angus McIntosh, 'A Dialect Word in Some West Midland Manuscripts of the *Prick of Conscience*', in *Edinburgh Studies in English and Scots*, ed. by A. J. Aitken, Angus McIntosh, and Hermann Pálsson (London: Longman, 1971), pp. 20–26

Doyle, A. I., 'Ushaw College, Durham, MS 50: Fragments of the *Prick of Conscience*, by the Same Scribe as Oxford, Corpus Christi College, MS 201, of the B Text of *Piers Plowman*', in *The English Medieval Book: Studies in Memory of Jeremy Griffiths*, ed. by A. S. G. Edwards, Vincent Gillespie, and Ralph Hanna (London: The British Library, 2000), pp. 43–49

——, 'Codicology, Palaeography, and Provenance', in *The Making of the Vernon Manuscript: The Production and Contexts of Oxford, Bodleian Library, MS Eng. poet. a.1*, ed. by Wendy Scase (Turnhout: Brepols, 2013), pp. 3–25

Galloway, Andrew, *The Penn Commentary on 'Piers Plowman'*, I (Philadelphia: University of Pennsylvania Press, 2006)

——, 'Gower's *Confessio amantis*, the *Prick of Conscience*, and the History of the Latin Gloss in Early English Literature', in *John Gower: Manuscripts, Readers, Contexts*, ed. by Malte Urban, Disputatio, 13 (Turnhout: Brepols, 2009), pp. 39–70

——, 'Non-Literary Commentary and its Literary Profits: The Road to Accounting-ville', *Yearbook of Langland Studies*, 25 (2011), 9–23

——, 'Madame Meed: *Fauvel*, Isabella, and the French Circumstances of *Piers Plowman*', *Yearbook of Langland Studies*, 30 (2016), 227–52

Gray, Nick, 'Langland's Quotations from the Penitential Tradition', *Modern Philology*, 84 (1986), 53–60

Horobin, Simon, 'The Scribe of Rawlinson Poetry 137 and the Copying and Circulation of *Piers Plowman*', *The Yearbook of Langland Studies*, 19 (2005), 3–26

——, 'The Scribes of the Vernon Manuscript', in *The Making of the Vernon Manuscript: The Production and Contexts of Oxford, Bodleian Library, MS Eng. poet. a. 1*, ed. by Wendy Scase (Turnhout: Brepols, 2013), pp. 27–48

Johnston, Michael, *The Reading Nation in the Age of Chaucer: Copying and Reading Middle English Books, 1350–1500* (forthcoming)

Kane, George, '"Good" and "Bad" Manuscripts: Texts and Critics', in *Chaucer and Langland: Historical and Textual Approaches* (London: Athlone, 1989), pp. 206–13

Killian, Ann, 'Menacing Books: *The Prick of Conscience* and the Rhetoric of Reproof', *The Yearbook of Langland Studies*, 31 (2017), 5–41

Lewis, Robert E., and Angus McIntosh, *A Descriptive Guide to the Manuscripts of 'The Prick of Conscience'* (Oxford: Society for the Study of Mediaeval Languages and Literature, 1982)

Marshall, Helen, 'Literary Codicologies: The Conditions of Middle English Literary Production, c. 1280–1415' (unpublished doctoral thesis, University of Toronto, 2014)

McIntosh, Angus, 'A New Approach to Middle English Dialectology', *English Studies*, 44 (1963), 1–11

Rentz, Ellen K., *Imagining the Parish in Late Medieval England* (Columbus: Ohio State University Press, 2015)

Sargent, Michael G., 'What Do the Numbers Mean? A Textual Critic's Observations on Some Patterns of Middle English Manuscript Transmission', in *Design and Distribution of Late Medieval Manuscripts in England*, ed. by Margaret Connolly and Linne R. Mooney (York: York Medieval Press, 2008), pp. 205–44

Sawyer, Daniel, *Reading English Verse in Manuscript c.1350–c.1500* (Oxford: Oxford University Press, 2020)

Swanson, R. N., 'The Origins of *The Lay Folks' Catechism*', *Medium Ævum*, 60 (1991), 92–100

Taylor, Andrew, 'The Myth of the Minstrel Manuscript', *Speculum*, 66 (1991), 43–73

Wakelin, Daniel, '"Thys ys my boke": Imagining the Owner in the Book', in *Spaces for Reading in Later Medieval England*, ed. by Mary C. Flannery and Carrie Griffin (New York: Palgrave Macmillan, 2016), pp. 13–33

Warner, Lawrence, *The Myth of Piers Plowman: Constructing a Medieval Literary Archive* (Cambridge: Cambridge University Press, 2014)

Windeatt, B. A., 'The Scribes as Chaucer's Early Critics', *Studies in the Age of Chaucer*, 1 (1979), 119–41

Reviews

Stephen H. Rigby, ed., with Siân Echard. *Historians on John Gower*. Cambridge: D. S. Brewer, 2019. Pp. xxiv + 555.

It is not an exaggeration to say that this will immediately be a requisite volume for anyone working on Gower. *Historians on John Gower* represents work from a range of perspectives, bringing historical contexts to Gower's writing to an extent we have not yet seen. There are essays here that unquestionably break new ground, essays that offer insights into possible re-readings of familiar works, and essays that outline the inevitable gaps in the historical record we cannot ignore. But perhaps what is most notable and useful is the way in which the disciplinary perspective of these essays displays previously unexamined qualities of Gower's work (and by extension, work on Gower). Gower's relationship to history is deep, and seeing his corpus through a decidedly historical lens not only illuminates areas of his writing in new ways, it also offers an opportunity for literary scholars to interrogate their own assumptions about the perspectives and aims they bring to their reading practice. This is fundamentally a useful and valuable thing.

Perhaps the most elementary effect of looking at Gower from an historical perspective lies in which texts these essays seem to favour. In most collections or monographs, we tend to find the majority of critical attention paid to Gower's English works, and to the *Confessio amantis* in particular. In this volume, however, there is a startling and refreshing turn to Gower's non-English writing: the *Mirour de l'omme* and the *Vox clamantis* play starring roles in nearly all of the arguments in the collection. A tendency to read these poems in an encyclopedic manner, treating them like a repository of perspectives on various elements of the medieval world, is longstanding in the critical tradition; if one wants a representative stance on a particular estate or historical phenomenon, Gower's Latin and Anglo-Norman works offer readers a catalogue of commentaries to choose from. And many of these essays do just that, looking at these texts as indicative of Gower's approach to monasticism, the perils of the chivalric ideal, the events of 1381, and more. But within this framework, the approaches the essays bring to the material are useful in their break with many of the inherited assumptions literary scholars might bring with them. Thus, even when Gower comes across as often deeply conservative in his approach to the state of the world, the essays themselves can move our thinking about Gower in new directions.

The Yearbook of Langland Studies, 34 (2020), 223–226 BREPOLS ❧ PUBLISHERS   10.1484/J.YLS.5.121094

The chapters in the collection are divided into clusters focusing first on Gower's life and works, and then move on to discussing Gower through his approach to lay society, the church, gender, politics, and cosmography. The relationship drawn between Gower's texts and these historical contexts addressed by each essay fall, however, into three main categories.

First, there are essays that present documentation and new archival discoveries, or essays that are fundamentally interested in the figure of Gower the poet. This category is dominated by Martha Carlin's masterful account of Gower's life records, drawn from an impressive range of documents. She offers readers a host of invaluable resources for placing Gower within the legal networks of fourteenth-century England and gives perhaps the most complete picture of the poet we have coming from documentary evidence. Provided material includes useful chronological tables, including likely places of residence; a listing of known associates and their relationship to the poet; relevant maps; and document transcriptions. The level of detail she offers and the information her work makes available to readers is quite simply extraordinary. Of particular interest is her analysis of Gower's marriage and relationship to Agnes Groundolf, for whom Carlin offers an alternative picture from other Gower scholars: neither an opportunistic climber nor an exploited convenience, Agnes emerges as an educated and perhaps propertied women who commits to a marriage that brings affection and tenderness with it. Also in this category, Stephen Rigby details a likely chronology of Gower's writing, with a focus on establishing a timeline for the various parts of his literary career. The essay gives a useful overview of the dating problems with the *Confessio Amantis* in particular, along with an argument about Gower's process of repeated revision. Both of these pieces together offer readers a picture of Gower that is remarkably vivid. For Carlin, Gower can be both unscrupulous in his dealings and lofty in his ambitions, but nevertheless poignantly lonely in his lack of close and abiding ties with others. Whereas in Rigby's depiction, we see the difficulty in teasing out a compositional timeline for Gower's works emerge from his tendency to rework his past pieces in response to political and personal developments. Gower becomes a poet for whom past work is never entirely left behind.

The advantage to this perspective is that we get to know Gower the man before we turn to Gower's works proper. With a corpus as large as that Gower offers us, it is perhaps understandable that we understand him primarily through his literary output. But in these essays, even when we move to Gower's literary production, we are still looking at a depiction of a person rather than just a poet. It might seem a facile observation that beginning a volume with a portrait of the artist is a worthwhile approach. But in this particular case we can also see these opening chapters as making space for a more present, living Gower — who in turn becomes more essentially part of his works — than we might encounter elsewhere.

Second, there are essays that contextualize Gower's poetry within various historical frameworks — the bulk of the collection. To take one representative example, Anthony Musson writes about Gower's probable connection with the law courts, arguing that while we certainly see a great deal of legal language in Gower's writing, this does not necessarily indicate any particular legal training or practice in Gower's professional life. This is a direct contrast to the dominant opinion since John Fisher's influential biography of the poet. In doing so, Musson presents a useful overview of how varied the legal profession was at this time, as well as how we might begin to locate Gower's criticisms of legal practice throughout his three major poems. And even if Musson is circumspect about making any definite claims as to how knowledgeable in the practice of law Gower might have been, he clearly demonstrates that attention to legal contexts in the language Gower uses (found not just in circumstances ostensibly addressing the law, but in puns and moments of wordplay as well) should be something that careful readers have in mind as they move through the poems.

This second type of essay is primarily interested in defining the historical contexts within which to locate Gower and his work. Most include a discussion of the estate or cultural structure the author will address, drawing strongly (as one might expect) from source evidence. James Davis, for example, discusses in detail the way in which mercantile production in London is regulated by the civic government, giving an admirable level of detail. But this information is used to then demonstrate how closely Gower's concerns over trade in the *Mirour* follow the current debates and statutes of his immediate surroundings. We see a similar method in how David Lepine locates Gower's complaints against the papacy and secular clergy within systems of clerical critique; or in Mark Bailey's account of how Gower's castigation of the peasants in the *Visio Anglie* reads when placed against other, contemporary concerns about social order; or in Jens Röhrkasten's argument about Gower's lack of clear connection to fraternal (or extra-fraternal) critiques of the mendicant orders. These are the essays that will be oft-cited for their succinct and valuable descriptions of the social, cultural, and political structures that occupied much of Gower's experience and thought.

Third and finally, there are essays that present new arguments about how we should see Gower's texts within his historical moment. These are arguments that focus principally on the poems. To this end, Michael Bennett's extensive investigation into Gower's approach to Richard II and Henry IV feels like the culmination of many ongoing conversations about how the poet might have politically aligned himself in the later years of his life. Of obvious interest here are the multiple versions that have survived of the *Confessio Amantis*, but the essay also spends much of its time arguing for a compositional strategy for Gower's much less discussed *Cronica tripertita*. Bennett postulates that each of the three sections of Gower's verse chronicle was written shortly after the events discussed took place, rather than in a single consolidated effort after 1400. This would not seem to be the most obvious place through which to establish Gower's political calibration, but Bennett uses it to demonstrate how Gower's position evolves over the course of the late 1380s and into the 1390s. The result is an argument that considers both Gower's biography and his historical surroundings, but the ultimate effect is to recast how this particular poem functions as a document in its own right. We might think also of Rigby's second contribution to the collection, his essay on Gower and political theory. Also treating the *Cronica*, the argument seeks to intervene in how we see Gower's approach to monarchic indiscretions and draws deeply on literary and historical sources to do so. The conclusion, however, is not about documentation or even Gower's position on Richard in particular, but rather in the distinction between political language and political ideals: while the latter may well be firmly held for Gower, the former may be (and often is) remarkably adaptable.

Each of these three approaches demonstrates how useful seeing familiar material from a new disciplinary perspective can be. This is not to say that there are not moments for which readers might draw counterarguments. The discussions of gender, for example, might feel overly perfunctory to literary scholars who do not necessarily expect Gower to exhibit a unified theory of masculinity, or who would like to look beyond presentations of powerful women in the political sphere. It is difficult to think of asking for additional essays on gender in a volume that is already marked by its notable heft, but the possibility for more work is certainly there. But this is also perhaps the most productive aspect of this volume as well: it provides such rich ground to explore. It strikes one that this is a book that cries out to be worked with and built upon. To return to the way in which Gower's texts are deployed across the essays, we can think of the turn to his non-English works as an example of this. On the one hand, the *Vox*, the *Mirour*, and the *Cronica* are used in familiar ways: as representative of a medieval understanding of the social order. But the collection also demonstrates that within this representation is a wealth of opportunity for new investigation. Perhaps because of the disciplinary difference, these texts are not seen as handmaidens to the *Confessio*, but central to our understanding of this poet. And it is to be hoped that scholars of all disciplines who turn to Gower will take this impulse and expand upon it.

This brings us to the other interesting effect of seeing Gower without some of the traditional assumptions that usually accompany him. The perhaps inevitable comparison between this collection and its sister-volume, *Historians on Chaucer*, ed. Rigby and Alastair Minnis (Oxford: Oxford University Press, 2015), is instructive in the structural differences between the two. Whereas Chaucer's pilgrims take centre stage, grounding the descriptions of medieval estates and stations in characters from the General Prologue, the presentation of Gower is contextualized quite differently: more abstract and diffuse on the one hand, but also more focused on the poet himself. But for all that Chaucer is deployed in the essays here, another contemporary also comes surprisingly (and in a most welcome manner) to the light: William Langland. Critical opinion has long seen Langland and Gower as firmly located in two opposing camps. In part, this is due to the emphasis scholars have placed on English (rather than Anglo-Latin or Anglo-French) Gower, and in part this is due to book 1 of the *Vox clamantis*. However, once assumptions about which of Gower's texts 'count', and which literary contexts (and communities) we place the poet within, are removed, new and productive lines of analysis and commentary begin to emerge — the initiation of which is, of course, the highest praise one can offer any piece of scholarly production. I have a feeling that Gowerians have much to look forward to coming out of this volume and keenly anticipate the development of the new avenues of thought and investigation that are certain to emerge from it.

STEPHANIE L. BATKIE
The University of the South
slbatkie@sewanee.edu

Andrew Albin. *Richard Rolle's 'Melody of Love': A Study and Translation with Manuscript and Musical Contexts*. Toronto: Pontifical Institute of Mediaeval Studies, 2018. Pp. xx + 468.

The *Melos amoris* has long been one of Richard Rolle's most enigmatic and inaccessible works. Among Rolle's longer texts, it probably represents the most sustained alliterative prose ever accomplished in Latin. Both in form and content, it addresses a major theme of Rolle's mysticism: the idea that the highest stage of contemplation is an experience of heavenly song. However, its dense alliterative style produces long and confusing sentences, which even pioneering Rolle scholar Hope Emily Allen found difficult to understand. Accordingly, many earlier scholars gave scathing and dismissive accounts of its style (which now seem unfair), and even deemed it 'untranslatable'. Despite being one of the most unusual and elaborate texts in the broader category of fourteenth-century mysticism, it has received surprisingly few devoted readers, and its intrinsic interest along with its importance for understanding Rolle's corpus remain largely untapped.

Andrew Albin's new English translation and commentary provides an indispensable guide to this neglected text, going far beyond the usual remit of a translation. Alongside the translation itself, it comprises an introduction with 'Ten Ways In' to the *Melos amoris*. After an initial discussion of the content, form, and audience of the *Melos*, each section of the introduction contextualizes and discusses the text from a range of perspectives: stylistic traditions, putative sources, manuscript reception, Rolle's biography, the human being, angelology, medieval music theory, and its interplay with Scripture (and the tenth 'way in' introduces the translation). The introduction is thus designed to make this lengthy and disordered text accessible to students through a variety of critical approaches and by highlighting its thematic threads.

Appendices at the end provide a wealth of further supplements. The first three appendices edit, translate, and discuss additional manuscript content. Appendix 1 presents a compilation of alliterative extracts from Rolle's *Incendium amoris* which appear as an extra chapter in several manuscripts and once independently. Appendix 2 contains extensive marginalia to the *Melos* found in Lincoln College MS Latin 89, and appendix 3 transcribes and discusses musical gatherings found in the same manuscript. Appendix 4 gives again the text of this music with selected extracts from the *Melos*, corresponding to a series of performances and readings available online. Lastly, appendix 5 gives a glossary of unusual Latin terms in the *Melos*. The companion website offers further material, including a full transcription of the *Melos* and its marginalia from MS Latin 89, links to images of the musical manuscripts, and extracts of Albin's translation without commentary (reportedly to be available in full for free at some point in the future, according to the website).

Albin's translation is the first into English, and it is notable for Albin's decision to translate Rolle's Latin alliteratively. The decision to privilege what could be seen as a stylistic gimmick over faithfulness to the Latin was a risky one, but from the

The Yearbook of Langland Studies, 34 (2020), 227–230 BREPOLS ❧ PUBLISHERS 10.1484/J.YLS.5.121095

perspective of this reader it has paid off. Reading Albin's translation is an extraordinary experience, and his text represents an object of aesthetic interest in its own right. His translation foregrounds the work's alliterative style, which pushes and pulls against its semantic sense, making it impossible to ignore, and thus replicates the experience of reading Rolle's Latin. Additionally, by rendering this complex text into intelligible prose, Albin's translation contributes to an ongoing reappraisal of Rolle's work, drawing attention to the *Melos* as an unusually crafted work which is as interesting for its content as for its form.

Some cautions should be exercised in using the translation. Firstly, as Albin acknowledges, the translation is based on E. J. F. Arnould's faulty edition (recently criticized by Ralph Hanna in 'The Oldest Manuscript of Richard Rolle's Writings', *Scriptorium*, 70 (2016), 111). In an ideal world, a new edition would have preceded this translation, though perhaps it will turn out to be Albin's translation that ultimately precipitates the academic interest leading to a new critical edition. Additionally, Albin does occasionally correct Arnould's edition when it makes obvious mistakes and incorporates further identifications of Bible passages (drawing on François Vandenbroucke's French translation as far as I can tell).

Secondly, readers should be aware that Albin's decision to translate alliteratively means that his departures from the Latin are more substantive than in a typical translation. Rolle's alliterative style does lead him to reach for a wide and unusual range of vocabulary; however, this effect is greatly amplified in Albin's translation, as for instance when he translates *puerulo* ('little boy') as 'pint-sized pup' (p. 189), or *amati* ('the beloved's') as the 'Sugarplum's' (p. 268). Albin often usefully provides the Latin in footnotes when he deviates significantly, as he does in the latter example just cited. The words *dives* ('rich man'), *divitia* ('riches'), and *donum* ('gift') often appear with other 'd' words and prove particularly difficult to render into English equivalents; accordingly, ducat-rich dukes with dowries and dividends necessarily abound across Albin's work (condemnation of the wealthy being one of Rolle's major themes). The translation often adds words to sustain the alliteration or convey the sense of the original which are not found in the Latin. Albin explains and justifies his decisions in his introduction, giving an unusually detailed account of his translation process. Overall, despite the constraints of translating alliteratively, Albin has produced a translation which is in many places more faithful to the Latin than the only previously available (French) translation by Vandenbroucke, which is non-alliterative, but cuts Rolle's long sentences into more manageable proportions and at times tends towards paraphrase. Thus, Albin's translation offers an invaluable guide to a difficult Latin text, though its readings should not be relied upon without reference to the Latin (a point Albin himself stresses). Albin's translation also comes with light notes which comment on Rolle's claims, point the reader towards contextual information, and highlight parallels elsewhere in the text, and which thus helpfully make the work more approachable.

The materials in Albin's introduction offer the best current introduction not only to the *Melos amoris* but to Rolle's work as a whole. One hopes that students of Rolle's Middle English will not neglect it for appearing in a volume concerned with Rolle's Latin. While Albin's previous research on Rolle approached his work from the niche perspective of 'sound studies', here Albin reaches far and wide across different approaches to literary criticism and produces a rich and detailed panorama of major critical issues pertaining to Rolle's work and this text. Many of Albin's sections usefully summarize and examine previous scholarly discussion of the *Melos*, or bring together what we know about his life and sources. Others offer a more interventionist approach. For example, the section on manuscripts questions the claim that the *Melos* was not widely read — though its ten extant full copies are dwarfed by the surviving copies of Rolle's other works, this textual footprint easily ranks amongst other mystical works which have received far greater attention, and Albin shows that scribal responses to Rolle demonstrate a number of readers engaging closely with the text. (Albin's manuscript list should be compared with A. I. Doyle and Hanna's recent updated *Hope Allen's Writings Ascribed to Richard Rolle*: Albin omits two excerpts listed by them, but also eliminates another, and includes a compilation which Doyle and Hanna discuss elsewhere on p. 51.) Albin's sections on angels and medieval music bring in concepts which are not usually discussed in relation to Rolle. In particular, his section on music contains interesting insights into how Rolle uses and puns on technical terms from medieval musical theory. My only quibbles were with Albin's ninth 'way in' on Scripture, which, by asking questions that are only implicit in Rolle's writing, sometimes tends towards wresting fine distinctions from Rolle's text which he is not necessarily making. This aside, Albin's accounts are generally rich with detail, carefully nuanced, usefully summative of previous work, contain much discriminating analysis, and offer refreshing perspectives.

The appendices offer further important contributions to enable future scholarship on Rolle's work and its reception. The spurious chapter in appendix 1 is edited and translated here for the first time. This text is an important response not only to the *Melos* but to Rolle's *Incendium amoris*, so it is a welcome addition to this volume. Appendix 2 offers perhaps the most important supplement: the extensive glosses in MS Latin 89. To my knowledge these have never been discussed at length, but contain what appear to be important responses to Rolle's work, including quotations from the *Life* of Saint Guthlac and from the *Incendium amoris* and an early scribe discussing Rolle's mysticism. Albin selects only the 'substantial narrative glosses' for transcription but makes full use of the companion website by providing a transcription of the entire copy online — both text and all glosses — allowing readers to check for themselves the whole set of annotations and how they compare to this manuscript's version of the text. In appendix 3, Albin's introduction is rightly cautious about inferring a close connection between Rolle's text and the music found in MS Latin 89. Albin points out that any putative connection would contradict Rolle's account of the internal nature of heavenly song elsewhere (a point which previous scholars have not always made strongly enough). Appendix 5, a glossary of unusual terms, usefully highlights Rolle's wide vocabulary (though a few choices, such as *acies*, *incola*, and *tela*, seem fairly common words to me). After a bibliography, an index of motifs and themes in the *Melos* follows, again offering readers more ways to make sense of the text.

Overall, this book offers an indispensable guide to a difficult and neglected text, providing a wealth of material to make the text more accessible and to animate future scholarship. Well-timed amidst the current resurgence of interest in Rolle, it makes a compelling case for a major rehabilitation of this important work.

(One final minor erratum is a reference to a copy of the *Melos* bequeathed to King's Lynn Dominican Friary in 1382 by Thomas Lexham, listed with other medieval records of the text on p. 60. It appears in a volume containing several of Rolle's works, and, if accurate, would be amongst the earliest records of Rolle in circulation. However, I am informed that this was an error on the Medieval Libraries of Great Britain (MLGB3) website; it should appear as reported by Leland at the Carmelite Friary in London almost two centuries later, and as also listed by Albin. Since it will disappear from the website at some point, its presence in Albin's book may confuse future readers, so it is noted here.)

Timothy L. Glover
University of Oxford
timothy.glover@exeter.ox.ac.uk

**Ralph Hanna. *The Penn Commentary on 'Piers Plowman':
Volume 2: C Passūs 5–9; B Passūs 5–7; A Passūs 5–8*.
Philadelphia: University of Pennsylvania Press, 2017.
Pp. xxvi + 416.**

Ralph Hanna's volume 2 of the ambitious *Penn Commentary* series is a searchingly conceptualized book, partly, of course, a well-researched gloss on the assigned passūs, but more unexpectedly also a full conceptual reading of the poem's deep structure. As such it is a 'twofer', and something of a departure from prior volumes in the series. Therein lies its main point of tension with its predecessors, which Hanna's unusually detailed preface aims to resolve (his volume was preceded by two of the five in the series, Andrew Galloway's in 2006, and Steven Barney's of the same date, but before Traugott Lawler's volume in 2019; the late Anne Middleton's volume is now being completed by Steven Justice). Prior volumes in this series had already set the bar high, not only because of the now somewhat notorious difficulty of *Piers Plowman* studies, with its multifoliate layers of textual, editorial, poetic, and intellectual challenges, but also because the original team aimed to replace W. W. Skeat's indispensable commentary (p. vii), which had nurtured generations of Langland scholars since 1886. Everything therefore about the *Penn Commentary* was designed to be monumental, representing the aspirations of a distinguished generation of Langlandians, a monumentality wryly hinted at in the self-satirizing nickname they chose, 'The Gang of Five'. Throughout his preface Hanna refers affectionately to The Gang of Five, underlining, perhaps unconsciously, the marathon history of this mega-project. Ironically, the nickname itself now requires glossing for many

The Yearbook of Langland Studies, 34 (2020), 230–235   BREPOLS ❦ PUBLISHERS   10.1484/J.YLS.5.121096

younger Langlandian scholars: 'The Gang of Five' rose to enormous power during China's Cultural Revolution (1966–1976) under Chairman Mao, eventually coming to infamy. In common Western parlance the nickname signalled uncompromising power and notoriety by the 1970s. Though adopted by the *Penn Commentary* team satirically, even self-deprecatingly, it is no accident that their project cast a powerful shadow, perhaps second only to the Athlone Press editions' themselves.

Hanna's preface, then, does a service to all Langlandians in tracing this history. Begun when most were University of California employees, Hanna details with candour their early animated debates over the proper interpretive extent of the annotator's reach. For him, the annotator is to have sweeping powers of critical interpretation, and his preface offers an *apologia* for the series itself, and his own departure from the more conventional tendencies of the earlier volumes (by Galloway and Barney):

> The substantial volumes already published present themselves in a rather 'stand alone' mien. Like most published writings [...] they strive to obscure, as irrelevant to the product, an underlying discussion and changes of course. As a result, exactly how the authors' work [...] and subsequently published collaborations [...] [are] to be construed remains slightly opaque (and has provoked some querulousness among reviewers). (vii)

What follows, then, is a kind of defensive driving, both a retrospective defence of the project, and 'a personal statement'. And no matter which side the reader prefers to take, Hanna's preface will remain a lasting account.

The preface also reviews how the team treated all three versions as one developing poem, dismissing the reigning ideology that B was 'the only imaginatively complete version' (p. viii). Even though for Hanna 'the poem's central and abiding enigma' is B's Tearing of the Pardon episode, he realized that in the passūs he covers Langland 'substantially retools the standing B text', most notably via two extensive new initiatives in C.5 and C.9 which 'in certain respects compensated for' its loss. This is very heartening for scholars of C, who have shared this view at least since Pearsall's 1978 edition. I hope Hanna's careful account may help stem remaining prejudices about B as the sole *Piers Plowman*, especially as he notes, 'it should go without saying that [Langland's] reformulation amounts to an implicit authorial rejection of the frequently read B version'. And since the *Commentary* itself is keyed to C as testimony to Langland's 'last words' (p. xviii), it has a natural prominence throughout. Most interesting critically, however, is his early realization that, 'given our sense of the poem's *unity of intention*, if not of execution, much of my work would need to account for the substantial changes' Langland had made (my emphasis).

Hanna here follows with admirable integrity the essentially New Critical philosophy of 'unity'. This had been a very sensitive issue for mid-twentieth-century Langlandians because of C. S. Lewis's 'sneering reference' (in Hanna's words) to *Piers Plowman* as 'fragments but not a poem'. So, of course the 'Gang' initially wrestled with the long shadow of Lewis's contempt by striving to 'address the (now perhaps old-fashioned) concern that a poem forms "an organic unity"' (p. ix). I would add that this sense of organic unity also animated the Athlone Press editions, and continues, as Hanna tells us here, to animate the *Penn Commentary* volumes — though not uncritically, of course. As the late Lee Patterson wrote at a parallel juncture: 'While this may seem a distressingly unstable basis for historical knowledge, I would ask the reader to reflect on the possibilities of any other' (*Negotiating the Past: The Historical Understanding of Medieval Literature* (Madison: Wisconsin University Press, 1987), p. 48).

A related challenge for the team was isolating the 'units' of text, especially those longer than the poem's 'verse paragraphs', that must be demarcated for explication, which Hanna lucidly calls 'units of sense by which the poet prosecutes his argument' (pp. ix–x). Of course, to demarcate these units in *Piers* is often to make interpretive judgement calls. Hanna's readers will naturally find themselves having to ask whether they always agree. Similarly, the perennial issue of voice in *Piers Plowman* requires frequent judgement calls — here again the reader will need to be attentive to Hanna's attributions of voice in a given passage. Especially tricky are the *Commentary* passages that seesaw between calling the I-speaker 'Will' or 'L' (Langland) at a moment's notice. This problem is not unique to Hanna, of course — we've all been there. As he stresses, *Piers* is distinctive in proceeding not so much via 'a plot' as 'conflicting voiced opinions' (p. x). But the commentary genre itself assumes a kind of authoritativeness that ordinary critical studies do not, so while Hanna's attributions of voice are arrived at thoughtfully, they do represent only one opinion. Hanna, however, has much to say against what he calls the 'normative' scholarship on assigning voice in the poem (intriguingly, 'normative' throughout is not a complimentary adjective). For him *Piers* is

> predicated on differing discourses, available elsewhere (yet always […] within a claim of internal discursive completeness). Yet here these separate voices are unified within the same text. Normative study, which has constructed the poem's enigmatic status, has been predicated upon a refusal to recognize that quality of 'voice', to refuse to contextualize statements. Rather the tendency has been to take all statements, unless glaringly partial, as equally fervent statements of authorial opinion. (xvi)

There is much to unpack here. First, while Langland certainly uses various external authoritative sources, I think we want to be careful about assuming that they all make claims to 'internal discursive completeness'. Scholastic sources, for instance, were by nature dialogic, nor would many of the French texts such as Grosseteste's *Château d'Amour*, the major satires, and more fit this description easily. Nor, based on recent brilliant work by Arvind Thomas on Langland's use of and *contribution to* evolving canon law, does this work even for canon law. Moreover, we should note that all critics ('normative' or otherwise!) — and, by the way, all editors — face the problem that there is no real equivalent of modern quotation marks in medieval manuscripts (at least none employed by *Piers* scribes, beyond their demarcation of the Latin). So modern readers depend heavily on editorial choices for insertion of quotation marks, and while Hanna is right that some critics do jump to conclusions in assigning 'authorial' speech, it is also fair to say that many have tried to distinguish voicing carefully, and that good editor's notes (e.g., Derek Pearsall's to C) offer much precision on voicing — and even, in spots, frank admission of defeat. Hanna, too, has tried valiantly to think through the question of voice, but Hanna's is also, finally, an interpretation. Whether we'll ever know in certain passages how to sift, say, Will's voice from the author's ('L' in the *Commentary*) is an open question, and Hanna does often use both attributions interchangeably (see, among many examples, his gloss to C.5.5's 'made' ('composed') on authorship issues in this line). In short, we are all in the same boat on this one — and that boat may always have holes, even though our best editors and interpreters have tried to mend them. Even medieval annotators of the poem, a group I know well, were equally divided on the issue of who was speaking, so this boat has had holes for a long time.

On textual issues, Hanna and the Penn team are fiercely, and I'd say refreshingly, passionate in their belief that the problems modern readers encounter in understanding the poem are ours, not the author's: 'Langland was engaged in trying to write a coherent and "smooth" narrative (even if addressing a subject that resisted coherence)'. Therefore, Hanna notes, 'we [...] would reject such an argument as that of [D.]V[ance] Smith 2009, that the poem's inexplicitness about its own procedures keeps the text open to continual interpretation' (p. xi). While fully acknowledging theoretical fashions of the late twentieth and early twenty-first centuries, Hanna and the team are also refreshingly unapologetic in championing as needed a traditional (i.e., *pre*-postmodern) deference to the poet and his text. He notes, for instance, the team 'assumes the capacity of the author to generate multiform meanings, that he is more intelligently capacious than we, more widely read [...] and considerably more verbally adept' (p. xiii). In 2020 this is a bracing, indeed courageous statement — and I believe it may ultimately be a welcome one in these bewilderingly politicized and anxious days. It is good to be reminded of *why* we read our best poets, and why we keep returning to them. Hanna's preface above all advocates compellingly for taking a great poet seriously, much as George Kane did when defending his Athlone press work. Though everyone will not agree all of the time, and some may disagree a lot, the Kanean 'take-no-prisoners' school of *Piers* criticism lives on vibrantly in Hanna's new volume. And we should be grateful for its powerful advocacy for our poet.

Though Hanna is often gracious in his treatment of prior scholarship, and more often entirely and deliberately silent on great swathes of it, he does not mince words on certain points, taking issue for instance with both Wendy Scase's and Lawrence Warner's attempts to isolate independent textual traditions outside of the A-B-C models (p. xix, and elsewhere). Hanna also evinces impatience with the advocates of Z — on this as on so much else, his textual positions are Kanean. On the massive achievements of A. V. C. Schmidt's learned parallel texts edition, Hanna nonetheless questions Schmidt's very approach to annotation. While conveying appreciation for his treatment of Langland 'as a poetic craftsman', he says of Schmidt's notes, 'while filled with brilliancies concerning grammatical relations and local poetic detail, [...] [they] fall largely within what we call "grammatical annotation". One gains very little sense from Schmidt of poetic argument (as opposed to local poetic craft)' (p. xxii). This will raise eyebrows among those who think that an annotator's job is perhaps more appropriately 'local', and the critique stems from Hanna's adamant insistence that annotators must take account of — and also make definitive decisions about — the deep structure of the poem. Anything less, for Hanna, is a kind of failure.

Thus, the biggest thrust of the preface is Hanna's thesis on why an annotator must make major interpretive choices *before* beginning to annotate. 'Not all the "Gang of

Five"' in fact, he notes, would accept his position on this: 'unlike a grammarian, I strive to enunciate a view of the whole' (p. xiii). He provides some instances, particularly at some well-known cruxes, of how he had to first arrive at a reading of an entire episode within the poem. One such example at C.9.305 turns on his very fine interpretation of Will's hope about his dream ('if hit so be myhte'), which Hanna intuitively relates back to key passages in C.5 and elsewhere as a matter of deep structure. In fact, Hanna is so intent on making the case that his commentary demanded such deep analysis that he is willing to downplay his own role in the more 'objective' matters (e.g., explaining discrete lemmata, grammatical obscurities, or historical facts), even referring the reader back to prior annotators sometimes. In the instance above he wants us to know that we are reading not just annotations, but a *fully developed thesis* of C.5–9 (and the AB equivalents).

Hanna's assignment in this volume gives him the enviable but daunting task of explicating the famous C.5 *apologia pro vita sua*. This is challenging terrain through which critics have charted multiple paths, including E. T. Donaldson's classic contribution on what it reveals about Langland's ordination status; or John Burrow's timely warnings about not underestimating the historicity of medieval autobiography; or Anne Middleton's brilliant connections with the Statute of Labourers of 1388; or the abrupt reversals of C. David Benson's anti-historicist 'Langland myth', recently reversed again in the hyper-archival speculativism about the historical William de Rokayle (e.g., in work by Robert Adams or Andrew Galloway). Hanna's commentary on the *apologia*, however, negotiates all these vicissitudes via decisive cherry-picking and conscious silence on everything else (especially on the post-Middleton trends). Still, in glossing the *apologia* he offers prolific, back-breaking detail on even a single line or phrase. He does this largely by hewing closely to Anne Middleton's reading of the passage as an interrogation of Will under the labour statute of 1388, and while I delight (as a co-editor of the volume in which her article first appeared) in seeing her fine work so carefully used, I must add a real caveat here. Langland employed or took for granted many other kinds of knowledge and allusion in the *apologia*. Some of these are not much evident in Hanna's commentary (e.g., issues of *probatio*, ordination, clerical employment, and other types of non-Statute examination echoed in Reason's and Conscience's questions). Given Hanna's own lovely assertion (above) of belief in 'the capacity of the author to generate multiform meanings', I would suggest that it is especially true of the *apologia*. Having said that, Hanna does strive in his annotations to the passage to cover several key allusions, e.g., to biblical allegory, and to possible twelfth-century goliardic associations (following Jill Mann). Looking forward, he even asserts the passage's influence on Hoccleve, which I was delighted to see (having argued for it myself in 2012).

My one general caveat about Hanna's volume is that it tends to fish too often in the same critical pools — and, though perhaps understandably, these are most often the pools of his fellow annotators. Citation of younger Langlandians is more rare. Of course, we all tend to over-represent our own cohort in our work, so this problem is not unique to Hanna, and Hanna is very self-aware about his choices. He is explicitly comfortable with the fact that his volume will likely be treated less as an 'objective' commentary, and more as a specific set of interpretive choices. Speaking for myself,

I find many of these choices superb. Other choices, however, will remain controversial for many. Perhaps we expect too much of our commentaries if we believe that they can be all things to all people. At least in this volume, Hanna has been utterly frank, even front-loading his belief that the honest annotator must make large, indeed formidably large, interpretive choices.

KATHRYN KERBY-FULTON

University of Notre Dame (emerita) / University of Victoria

kkerby@nd.edu

Mary Raschko. *The Politics of Middle English Parables: Fiction, Theology, and Social Practice*. Manchester: Manchester University Press, 2019. Pp. ix + 255.

One of the more abiding misconceptions about medieval literature is the presumptive equivalence between Christian piety and textual stability. The long history of this presumption may offer the most obvious explanation for it, but that does not make its continuing persistence any less puzzling. There is simply no reason to assume piety needs or even wants an unambiguous, univalent literary signifier anchoring and foreshortening its own possibilities of literary expression. Yet the presumption persists, even though every piece of medieval literature of any note at all belies it. For yet further evidence, we may now turn to Mary Raschko's elegant, robustly documented, crisply argued *Politics of Middle English Parables: Fiction, Theology, and Social Practice*. The parable, as Raschko rightly notes in her opening sentence, is 'among the most dynamic, yet routinely neglected, literary forms in the corpus of Middle English texts' (p. 1). Raschko's ample demonstration of the form's dynamism should go a long way to remedying some of this routine neglect.

Raschko analyses five of the 'most commonly retold' parables (p. 14): the Laborers in the Vineyard (Matthew 20. 1–16); the Prodigal Son (Luke 15. 11–32); Dives and Lazarus (Luke 16. 19–31); the Good Samaritan (Luke 10. 25–37); and the Wedding Feast (Luke 14. 7–14). She devotes a chapter to each of these. Her discussion of the Wedding Feast includes the parable of the Great Supper (Matthew 22. 1–14; Luke 14. 15–24), as the two were sometimes paired in Middle English discussions. The book also includes briefer discussions of Parables of the Kingdom (that is, parables such as the Pearl of Great Price, which begin with a direct comparison to the kingdom of heaven). Raschko anchors each chapter with an analysis of the deployment of the parable in question in a well-known text, four of them of major poems: *Pearl*, the *Confessio Amantis*, *Piers Plowman*, and *Cleanness*. The fifth such text, in the second chapter, is *Book to a Mother*. As one would expect, Raschko's larger archive is somewhat eclectic, dictated in each case by the particular parable. It includes sermons, liturgical

The Yearbook of Langland Studies, 34 (2020), 235–238   BREPOLS ✺ PUBLISHERS   10.1484/J.YLS.5.121097

readings, pastoralia, biblical paraphrases, hagiography, and the occasional conduct book. The relation Raschko adumbrates between each anchoring text and the wider cultural context also varies. Typically, what she finds is that the major text amplifies ambiguities and ambivalences already evident in the treatment of the parable in question in the culture at large.

Raschko makes very little fuss about this aspect of her method. But I found it to be one of the volume's most attractive features. It strikes me as an instance of the best of kind of literary historicism. That is, it treats cultural context neither as a foil for the oppositional genius of the great poet, nor — which is even worse — as a strict hermeneutical limit foreclosing ostensibly anachronistic interpretations. Instead, analyses like Raschko's offer a much more organic conception of the relation between text and context. The canonical poet becomes a particularly thoughtful, particularly well-informed native informant, an authoritative guide to the cultural materials out of which their poems arise. This book should be of interest to anyone with a decent literary interest in Middle English poetry and culture, and it will undoubtedly be of most interest to those most interested in didacticism and in the relation between poetry and religiosity. But because of her subtle and nuanced approach to the relation of poem to culture it should also appeal to those of a more formalist bent as well.

Raschko also situates her discussion in relation to the huge tradition of modern biblical scholarship on the parables, which she cites judiciously and weaves into her readings unobtrusively. Noting the notorious difficulties confronting an attempt at genre analysis of medieval writing, she proposes to follow Nicolette Zeeman's rightly celebrated notion of 'imaginative literary theory', pursuing the generic expectations shaping the use of parables in Middle English as those expectations are revealed in the retellings themselves. What she says of treatments of Dives and Lazarus holds for the genre as a whole: the relation between 'instructional narrative and moral narrative' is 'generative, not restrictive' (p. 107). In the case of the Laborers in the Vineyard, she finds that in homiletic and liturgical contexts the emphasis is on the spiritual value of work as opposed to the ineffability of grace. Both Mirk and Thomas Wimbledon are so committed to this value that they truncate their versions of the narrative to leave out the moment of payment entirely. The *Pearl* poet retains this interest in the social conditions of labour animating his contemporaries, but he does so mainly to heighten the tension already implicit in the parable, in the interests of dramatizing the radically paradoxical, radically inhuman power of grace: 'while human conventions cannot guarantee salvation neither can they constrain the gratuitous gift of grace' (p. 51). In the second chapter, Raschko notes that Middle English versions rewrite the return of the Prodigal Son as an explicitly confessional scene, with the son asking for forgiveness from his father as if his father were a confessor. She finds the fullest expression of this tendency in *Book to a Mother*. Paradoxically, since she accepts Fiona Somerset's conclusion that *Book to a Mother* is a Wycliffite text, she finds it to contain 'the only Middle English retelling to articulate a full threefold process of penance [that is, contrition, confession, satisfaction]' (p. 67).

There was one aspect of this chapter I did not find convincing: Raschko's account of the relation between penitential tradition and *Book to Mother*. She begins by disavowing 'the predominant Foucaldian narrative that describes medieval penance as a site of invasive ecclesiastical power' (p. 66). The problem is that this view certainly did not originate with Foucault. The name Henry Charles Lea comes to mind, not to mention John Calvin, or John Wyclif, for that matter. One reason Foucault has had such noticeable influence on recent scholarship is that his pungent formulations reflect back to the field some of its deepest historiographical predispositions, even if they do so in ways that make some scholars uncomfortable. These predispositions ultimately originate in Reformation polemic and failure to confront that fact renders any attempt to see late medieval penance on its own terms futile. I could not help noticing that Raschko will go on to claim that *Book to a Mother* 'inverts normal ecclesiastical hierarchies' (p. 83), thus repeating one of the terms of the Foucauldian metanarrative she has just disavowed. To be clear: I am convinced by her argument that vernacular retellings of the Prodigal Son reflect the influence of Lateran IV, and I also found convincing the substance of her reading of the *Book*. But when she brings the two together so as to suggest a complexity or flexibility in vernacular adumbrations of penitential doctrine not present in their Latin models, I think she is chasing a will o' the wisp. The *Book*'s investment in confession is surprising only if one expects a full-bore, puritan-style anti-prelacy *avant la lettre*. The *Book*'s ideal of spiritual perfection is one that originated in ancient monasticism; the ritual of confession had its roots in the practice of self-examination guided by more senior monks. When Raschko rightly notes that the *Book* describes 'penance as an interim stage on an ambitious path to spiritual perfection' (p. 85), that description might be better understood as a recuperation rather than a break, and a recuperation facilitated by the papal initiative that was Lateran IV.

In her third chapter, Raschko finds a complexity in the Middle English reception of the parable of Dives and Lazarus that puts it into a slightly oblique relation to the parable's obvious hostility to material wealth. Concentrating on Robert Mannyng's *Handlyng Synne* and Peter Idley's *Instructions to his Son*, as well as the *Confessio Amantis*, Raschko notes a modulation toward the social responsibilities of wealth, and away from its spiritual vacancy, which results in interpreting the parable as a warning against gluttony. In Gower, she finds the fullest expression of this tendency. Centring his retelling on the spiritual needs of Dives, he makes it 'a cautionary tale against personal misrule' (p. 130), viewing reformation of those in power as essential to society as a whole. (It might be noted parenthetically that the modulation from greed to gluttony is not quite as unprecedented as Raschko treats it. In his brief taxonomy of the deadly sins toward the end of *De planctu Naturae*, Alain de Lille presents both as related forms of idolatry, an association Jean de Meun preserves in *Le roman de la rose*. Mannyng's knowledge of this tradition is unclear, but Idley probably would have been aware of it, and Gower certainly was.)

Raschko's fourth and fifth chapters are the most powerful in the book. In each her analysis of a parable's deployment produces compelling new readings of the larger work. William Langland turns to the Good Samaritan in *Piers Plowman* at a particularly climactic moment in the poem; interpretations of this moment have played important role in the poem's modern critical history, from Robertson and Huppé to David Aers. Like Aers, she views Langland's treatment of the parable as

Christological. In contrast to Aers, however, she argues that Langland's Christology establishes an innate connection between human kindness and divine love, showing 'the necessity of human kindness in the ultimate figure of divine love, the Trinity' (p. 162). She demonstrates that Langland scholarship has construed the parable too narrowly, concentrating solely on its allegorical significance, while ignoring its 'moral' or literal implications. Her survey of its broader Middle English reception shows that the latter was as important to the culture at large as the former, especially the recognition of the Samaritan's otherness in the original historical moment of Christ's Jerusalem. Langland responds to this broader context by transforming the ideal of the *imitatio Christi* the parable was often read as affirming to a notion of 'participation' in Christ and the human community His grace enables.

The Parable of the Wedding Feast has played an even greater role in the modern critical reception of *Cleanness* than has the Good Samaritan in that of *Piers Plowman*. Raschko rightly observes that most modern scholars 'regard the parable' as simply 'a negative exemplum concerned with how to be saved' (p. 179). I would add that the scholarship has come to this conclusion somewhat reluctantly, for it pretty much requires abandoning the ways that the poem encourages identification with the plight of the unfortunate guest. Recognizing the inevitability of the ineffability of divine grace leaves the reader with the stark opposition between an angry god and the suffering of the damned without much insight as to how the two relate. Moreover, this dilemma holds for the poem as a whole. Raschko finds a compelling way out with two imaginative interpretive manoeuvres, one of them with some precedent in previous scholarship and one of them brand-new. The first is to note that the poem actually conflates its recounting of the Wedding Feast with the parable of the Great Supper, which treats the problem of Grace in more positive terms. *Cleanness* scholarship has long recognized this conflation, but until now no one has ever made much of it. Raschko's second move is to compare the poem's treatment of these parables with that of the *Glossed Gospels*. Her purpose is not to uncover some Wycliffite leaning in the poem. Instead, she uses the *Glossed Gospels* for the same reason that some of its original readership used it: that is, access in the vernacular to the traditions of scriptural commentary. Rashko argues that the poem 'invites audiences to scrutinize not only their own conduct but also the very nature of God' (p. 179) and that it 'holds up paradox to theology, as what people encounter when they strive to understand God' (p. 190). Her parting observation about *Cleanness* admirably sums up the book as a whole: the poem 'affirms scriptural multiplicity: the stories are both true and contradictory because divine revelation says more than human readers can hope to comprehend' (p. 204). Her conclusion calls for a fuller appreciation of the parable's influence on Middle English literature as a whole; this excellent book should make such appreciation likely.

Larry Scanlon
Rutgers University
lscanlon@english.rutgers.edu

Thomas A. Goodmann, ed. *Approaches to Teaching Langland's 'Piers Plowman'*. New York: Modern Language Association, 2018. Pp. xiv + 266.

At long last instructors have a rich and varied resource to support our work with students at all levels in the study of *Piers Plowman*! The twenty-four scholar-teachers who have contributed their expertise to this volume provide new teachers of Langland with encouragement and tools while offering seasoned veterans inspiration and a range of fresh ideas. There is pedagogical food for thought here for any teacher of *Piers*, in any setting, with any (or no) amount of prior classroom experience. The volume includes specific lesson plans ready for adoption as-is or creative adaptation.

The first part of the book ('Materials') is a descriptive guide to a wide array of currently available resources useful to *Piers Plowman* teachers. These include student-friendly Middle English editions of the A, B, and C texts as well as scholarly editions, electronic editions, early print editions, print facsimiles, and translations. The discussion of available primary texts is accompanied by information about guides to the poem that are suitable for students at various levels. Sections titled 'Aids to Teaching and Advanced Study' and 'The Instructor's Library' follow, which provide descriptions of many additional resources that instructors can use in the classroom or while preparing lessons, or that we might teach students themselves to use.

The second and much longer section of the book ('Approaches') consists of individually authored essays by *Piers Plowman* instructors that model specific lessons, offer practical pedagogical suggestions, and theorize more broadly about *why* we should teach *Piers Plowman* now, in the twenty-first century, in a wide range of contexts. The essays in this section are arranged into groups around shared topics. They're preceded by an introduction written by the editor, Thomas A. Goodmann, and an initial essay by David Lawton, a prologue of sorts that considers a major way Langland's poetry differs from the standard fare offered in our literature courses. *Piers Plowman* has a unique formal openness that is a by-product of Langland's eclectic combination of literary and extraliterary strategies. As Lawton puts it, 'by not withdrawing into a form other than its own, it remains in the fair field, which is our world of discourse' (p. 43). As the essays that follow in this volume testify, that fact renders it useful in a wide range of pedagogical contexts.

The first cluster of essays in the 'Approaches' section falls under the heading 'Practices of Reading'. Ralph Hanna's contribution, following nicely upon Lawton's, models a class on the Prologue that helps students discover that the complexity of Langland's poetry is a necessary effect of its discursive multiplicity. C. David Benson likewise focuses on Langland's 'difficult, cunning, early postmodern poetry' (p. 58) to promote a pedagogy that emphasizes 'tensions, contradictions, and irresolutions' as reflections of Langland's 'deliberate attempts to represent the complexity of his themes' (p. 57). But we're soon reminded that thematic reading is only one pedagogical possibility. Ian Cornelius's essay illustrates with clear and specific examples the ways

The Yearbook of Langland Studies, 34 (2020), 239–242   BREPOLS ❧ PUBLISHERS   10.1484/J.YLS.5.121098

that teaching metrical analysis can provoke questions distinct from those generated by thematic reading, thus differently enriching students' understanding of *Piers Plowman*. William E. Rogers promotes a combination of 'dramatic' and 'recursive' reading (p. 68) in a pedagogy that draws an analogy between students' struggles to understand *Piers* and the poet's struggles to make sense of his world.

The second cluster of essays, 'History and Historicism: Contexts Then and Now', opens with an offering by Thomas A. Prendergast that focuses on using *Piers* to teach students indoctrinated in reading literally that 'all textualities ultimately require interpretation' and that any approach to a text is itself 'a choice that they make freely' (p. 78). Nicholas Watson's essay also proposes using *Piers* as a way to open up questions and discussion of issues much larger than *Piers*: in a secular university context the teaching of *Piers* can help debunk students' commonly held misconceptions about religious societies, helping them learn 'to reflect critically on the status of the secular West in its narrative of progress' (p. 79). Even more important, perhaps, the journey of the narrator Will can be taught 'as a quest to live in the present with urgency' (p. 86), obviously of relevance to college students in today's complicated world. The teaching of *Piers* in relation to history becomes more specific in the cluster's final two essays. Madonna Hettinger teaches the Hunger episode to history students as a way of simultaneously illuminating the complexity of the medieval worldview and inviting comparative thinking about malnutrition, then and now. Gina Brandolino concludes the cluster with an innovative lesson that draws a productive analogy between the figure of Piers and Superman as he appeared in World War II-era comic book covers, where he is illustrated fighting Axis powers.

The next cluster, '*Piers Plowman* in Literary Dialogue', considers how to approach teaching *Piers* in conjunction with other texts. Lawrence Warner's essay reveals that *Piers* and Dante's *Commedia* share certain features that are handled remarkably differently by their respective poets. Teaching Langland with Dante thus 'sharpens our understanding of some central characteristics of *Piers Plowman*' (p. 104). Lawrence M. Clopper's essay makes an analogous case for the utility of teaching Langland's Prologue with Chaucer's, a contrast that highlights Langland's distinction 'between workers and wanderers in all of the estates' (p. 119). Sarah A. Kelen approaches literary dialogue through the lens of the early modern reception of *Piers*, a pedagogy that not only teaches students about the literary culture of early modern England but also opens opportunities for consideration of the historically situated forces that shape literary judgements and influence canon formation. Judith H. Anderson's consideration of the use of Langland in teaching allegory 'as a mode of thought and an organization of experience' (p. 126) concludes this cluster with suggestions of fruitful pairings: *Piers* with *Pearl*, Julian of Norwich's *Showings*, *The Dream of the Rood*, the York *Crucifixion*, Malory, and, especially, the first book of Spenser's *Faerie Queene*.

A cluster on 'Topics and Tropes' comes next and ranges widely across thematic, theoretical, and linguistic approaches to teaching Langland. Stephanie Trigg's essay suggests that among the many thematic threads in *Piers* 'the relation between minstrelsy, poetry, and work is one that promises to engage students' (p. 132) while providing a good example of Langland's 'flexible symbolic method' (p. 141). Emily Steiner's contribution offers ways to emphasize the poem's commitment to social reform so as to allow students to engage contemporary issues 'such as immigration, incarceration, minimum wage, and religious diversity' (p. 144). Langland's use of gender is Elizabeth Robertson's focus. She offers specific teachable examples with abundant references to scholarship that can be put to pedagogical use. Goodmann, the editor, concludes the cluster with a contribution of his own that shows how translation itself can be the focus of teaching *Piers*, through comparative analysis of different translations of the Middle English texts or through acts of translation undertaken by students.

'Curricular Contexts' more broadly conceived organizes the next cluster, which opens with an offering by Sr. Mary Clemente Davlin, OP that reveals the usefulness of *Piers* both in academic settings and also for Christian spiritual retreats, due to its rich poetic 'investigation of the great mysteries of the Christian faith' that 'cannot be explained or understood logically' (p. 176). Richard K. Emmerson takes us out of discipline-specific contexts with several examples of how *Piers* can work well in interdisciplinary courses on topics ranging from Apocalypticism to Medieval London to Monasticism and the Arts, appealing to students in literature, history, art history, and religious studies. Dramatic enactment is the pedagogy Andrew Galloway's contribution promotes. He observes that much of *Piers*'s generic and formal variety can in fact be traced to performative genres in the London of Langland's day, and that 'performance, in raw amateur or highly professional forms, helps us encounter the poem's obsession with learning by experience, in a way that interpretation alone cannot' (p. 195). Kate Crassons promotes a different sort of learning by experience by incorporating the teaching of *Piers Plowman* into a course on poverty with a strong service learning component. Crassons's students volunteer at a local soup kitchen, a Head Start classroom, or a homework club for children from low-income families. She reports that studying Langland better enables these students to work in these ways with their neighbors, and working in the community likewise makes them more empathetic readers of *Piers Plowman* who are better equipped to understand the complexity of poverty in Langland's world.

The 'Approaches' section of the book concludes with a final cluster, 'Beyond the B-Text'. Míceál F. Vaughan outlines practical reasons to teach the A version of *Piers*, noting that 'its reception provides unambiguous testimony of its importance to contemporaries' (p. 215). And Kathryn Kerby-Fulton argues in favour of teaching the C version as 'the poet's last surviving word' (p. 217).

The volume is then capped off with two appendices: Axton Crolley offers a student-friendly introduction to Langland's South-West Midlands dialect that is intended to accompany Derek Pearsall's edition of the C text. Clopper provides an equally student-friendly 'Sketch of the Clerical Orders', both regular and secular, with an explanation of the duties associated with various offices.

The great strength of this volume is the wide range of pedagogical approaches that are represented. Even with such diversity, however, the collection has some common threads and refrains that reveal widely shared attitudes toward teaching *Piers Plowman* today. The contributors share the view that the complexity of Langland's texts is an asset, not a hindrance; that the best pedagogy is oriented around discussion, not lecture; that our duty as instructors is to guide our students toward questions, not answers. As a *Piers* instructor myself, I wholeheartedly endorse these commitments. I also share a view that emerges again and again across the pages of this volume, which is that by teaching *Piers* we offer our students something more than just an encounter with some of the most astonishingly brilliant poetry written in English, and more than just that plus knowledge of fourteenth-century theology, philosophy, politics, and economics. Even more important, engaging with *Piers* also teaches students that intellectual work is never separate from ethics. Like Will, today's students live in a bafflingly complex and troubling world in which the discernment of how to live well is not easy. Teaching *Piers* gives us one endlessly interesting way to open up a conversation with our students about what it might mean for us too, in our world, to do well, better, and best.

Jennifer L. Sisk
University of Vermont
jennifer.sisk@uvm.edu

C. David Benson. *Imagined Romes: The Ancient City and its Stories in Middle English Poetry*. University Park, PA: Penn State University Press, 2019. Pp. xi + 201.

C. David Benson begins *Imagined Romes* with the assertion that 'Rome and Romans have been hiding in plain sight in Middle English poetry, waiting to be recognized as an important topic of study' (p. 1). At the most basic level, Benson's book makes a compelling case for Rome as a coherent subject of Middle English literature, and thus Middle English literary criticism. That is to say, Benson presents diverse representations of Rome and Romans found in the works of Geoffrey Chaucer, John Gower, William Langland, John Lydgate, and two other anonymous poets as part of a larger, more expansive, and hitherto unexplored vernacular conversation about Rome and Roman-ness. What he does not do, however, is formulate any sort of unified theory of a 'Middle English Rome' and its particular significance as opposed to, say, Troy — the subject of Benson's 1980 monograph *The History of Troy in Middle English Literature*. Rather, Benson offers a series of, in his words, 'close readings' (p. 7) aimed at demonstrating the range of possible Romes available to Middle English poets.

The book's brief introduction defines the scope of Benson's inquiries — Middle English poems about ancient Rome and Romans — and outlines his methodology. Though he promises to 'pay attention to late medieval English contexts when appropriate', Benson declares that his project is neither a history nor motived by or related to the contemporary English experience of Rome (p. 7). Instead of historicizing English Romes, Benson relies on the tools of a more traditional aesthetic criticism.

These choices of topic and method have real consequences. For example, severing 'ancient' from 'medieval' and poetry from historical context allows Benson to insulate Langland's Trajan from the anti-Roman vitriol aimed at late medieval Rome that animates large swathes of *Piers Plowman* (chapter 5). Likewise, limiting the scope of his study to Middle English poetry enables Benson to exclude texts like the most famous Anglo-Latin account of Roman topography, Master Gregorius's *De mirabilibus urbis Romae*; all three Middle English translations of the single most popular history of Rome, Martinus Polonus's *Chronicon Pontificum et Imperatorum*; John Capgrave's *Solace of Pilgrims*; and Margery Kemp's reflections on her experience as a pilgrim in Rome. These lacunae do not, however, compromise the integrity of Benson's basic argument. In fact, pointing out that *Imagined Romes* omits other possible Romes only reaffirms Benson's core thesis that Middle English representations of Rome are 'an important topic of study' (p. 1). Moreover, Benson makes it clear that he views his book as a beginning rather than an end. In lieu of a conclusion, he invites his readers to imagine new and different Middle English Romes.

The body of *Imagined Romes* is divided in half: part one, 'Ancient Rome and its Objects', focuses on two anonymous topographic poems, and part two, 'Narratives of Ancient Romans', addresses the representation of ancient Rome in the poetry of Gower, Chaucer, Langland, and Lydgate. Chapter 1, 'The Relics of Rome: Christian Mercy and the *Stacions of Rome*', begins with a cheerfully optimistic reading of the *Stacions of Rome*, a poem Benson views as 'express[ing] the yearning for universal salvation found in many Middle English religious writers' (p. 31). In his view, the *Stacions* imagines Rome as a 'sacred place of holy martyrs and pious popes' overflowing with 'infinite pardons' available to all — even those who simply read the *Stacions* (pp. 31–32). While Chapter 2, 'The Ruins of Rome: Pagan Marvels and the *Metrical Mirabilia*', returns to Roman topography, the *Metrical Mirabilia* is a very different type of poem from the *Stacions*. Unlike the free-standing *Stacions*, which survives in nine fourteenth- and fifteenth-century manuscripts, the *Metrical Mirabilia* is, in fact, a lengthy interpolation into the single witness of the *Metrical Version of Mandeville's Travels*. Where chapter 1 was devoted to a recuperative reading of the *Stacions* aimed at ameliorating the harsh judgements of critics as diverse as Frederick J. Furnivall and Eamon Duffy, a substantial part of chapter 2 is dedicated to recovering the actual text of the *Metrical Mirabilia* and reconstructing its history. Indeed, Benson's firm commitment to Middle English poetry leads him to downplay one of the most substantial achievements of his book: the identification of a previously unrecognized version of the Latin *Mirabilia* particularly popular in later medieval England, his 'Hybrid Version' (pp. 41–42). Hopefully, a fuller presentation and edition of this discovery is forthcoming. Nevertheless, despite its brevity, Benson's treatment of the Latin *Mirabilia* and, by extension, the *Metrical Mirabilia* is some of the best work in *Imagined Romes* precisely because it locates a Middle English poem about Rome within a textual, historical, and literary context that extends beyond the poem itself. It is this more inclusive context that enables Benson to conclude that the *Metrical Mirabilia* rejects the celebratory representation of pagan ruins found in the Latin tradition and turns instead towards the view of Rome in the *Stacions* as a locus of pardon and grace (p. 54).

Chapter 3, 'Civic Romans in Gower's *Confessio Amantis*', focuses on the politics of Gower's Rome. Benson's readings of the Roman stories that punctuate Gower's *Confessio Amantis* are lively and convincing, but this chapter is, by and large, an expansion and reaffirmation of Winthrop Wetherbee's earlier argument that ancient Rome has a stable signification throughout the *Confessio*: 'it is associated with wise government [...] and stable institutions' (cited by Benson, pp. 60–61). Or, as Benson concludes, ancient Rome is Gower's 'principal model of civic responsibility and cooperation', and though it 'is not a substitute for the lost golden age [...] it does offer a workable system of human governance' (p. 78). Conversely, Benson claims that Chaucer's Rome 'is a place of unrelenting oppression' (p. 79). More specifically, chapter 4, 'Heroic (Women) Romans in Chaucer's *Canterbury Tales* and the *Legend of Good Women*', argues that stories like the *Legend of Lucrece*, the *Physician's Tale*, the *Second Nun's Tale*, and the *Man of Law's Tale* 'feminize' Roman heroism and critique the politics of the ancient city by depicting its power hierarchies as masculine, violent, corrupt, and ultimately ineffective. Indeed, Benson goes so far as to conclude that Chaucer's 'unremitting hostility to the ancient city [...] has no parallel in the work of any other Ricardian poet' (p. 99). While Benson's argument is convincing, it is, like the previous chapter, a modest addition to a relatively conventional conclusion regarding Chaucer's sympathetic representation of women. Moreover, given Benson's sympathetic reading of Chaucer's Roman women, additional engagement with recent feminist and postcolonial accounts of gender and the idea of empire would have been very welcome.

Chapter 5, 'Virtuous Romans in *Piers Plowman*', returns to a question akin to those which animated the *Metrical Mirabilia*, i.e., the spiritual potential of pre-Christian Romans. In this chapter, Benson offers a daring new reading of the Trajan episode from *Piers Plowman* B.11. Specifically, Benson contends that previous debates regarding the nature and meaning of Trajan's salvation have 'diverted attention from the emperor's behavior while on earth and his relationship with Gregory, which are what Langland emphasizes in *Piers*' (p. 111). For Benson, each of these ancient Romans embodies 'a specific virtue appropriate to his own historical period: the emperor's pagan *truthe* and the pope's Christian *love*' (p. 111). Building on Richard Firth Green's influential understanding of *truthe* in later medieval England (*A Crisis of Truth: Literature and Law in Ricardian England* (Philadelphia: University of Pennsylvania Press, 1998)), Benson presents Langland's Trajan as the epitome of such *truthe* and as a model to contemporary leaders. But Trajan's *truthe* is, in Benson's eyes, more than a political or ethical concept. Rather, he reads the B text's commentary on Trajan's speech in 11.161–69 as equating Trajan's Roman *truthe* with 'divine Truth itself', that, in 11.163, is the kind of 'truthe that so brak helle yates' (p. 115). As Benson points out, Langland's Trajan is not delivered by Gregory's papal prayers but rather his own 'leel love and lyvvng in truthe' (11.161). For Benson, the relationship between Gregory and Trajan is one of mutual respect rooted in shared Roman virtues rather than a hierarchical power dynamic in which the emperor is saved by the pope. Nor does Benson view the Trajan episode as anomalous within *Piers*'s broader spiritual economy. Instead, he argues that Trajan 'is a *figura* of the brotherhood and blood relationship that Christ says he shares with all his human kindred', and the reconciliation of pagan *truthe* and

Christian love is an idealized image of Rome's twin legacy — a premonition of the heavenly city of God (pp. 119–20). Rome, in Benson's reading of this episode, is the ground of mutual relation through which justice and love will find their eventual reconciliation beyond the horizon of history. Benson's method means, however, that his insights are applied only to Langland's Trajan, and he does not attempt to situate this reading of Rome in conversation with other medieval conceptions of Roman exemplarity.

Chapter 6, 'Tragic Romans in Lydgate's *Fall of Princes*', doubles as Benson's conclusion. In this chapter, Benson presents Lydgate as a transitional figure. On one hand, Lydgate's Lucretia 'looks back to the patristic thought of Augustine', yet on the other, her 'psychological depths and inner divisions' anticipate 'the great English dramatic tragedies to come' (p. 144). Compared to the relatively static Romes of Chaucer and Gower, Benson's evocation of Lydgate's complex and layered Rome marks a welcome methodological return to his more richly contextual approach to the *Metrical Mirabilia* in chapter 2. Likewise, just as that chapter grappled with textual issues, so too this chapter adopts a comparative approach that reads Lydgate in relation to his sources, namely Laurent de Premierfait's *Des cas des nobles hommes et femmes* and, in the case of Lucretia, Lydgate's own earlier treatment of her within the *Fall*. Reading Lydgate's two versions of Lucretia against each other, Benson argues that the *Fall of Princes* abjures both the sort of 'practical' ethical teaching requested by the Duke of Gloucester and the 'straightforward sympathy for oppressed women' of Chaucer's Rome (p. 143).

From Lydgate's Lucretia, Benson pivots outward to offer a truncated conclusion that is separated from the rest of chapter 6, though it lacks a section title (pp. 144–45). This long paragraph begins with an ambiguous medieval/early modern periodization organized around the representation of Rome combined with a plea for scholars to pay more attention to the Middle English Rome. On that last count, Benson succeeds. At the very least, *Imagined Romes* starts a much-appreciated conversation. One hopes, however, that this conversation might grow to include prose texts and medieval Rome, situate these texts in a more wide-ranging interest in the social, political, religious, and cultural ties between England and Rome in the later Middle Ages, and engage with more recent theoretical discourses, particularly those regarding gender, empire, and race. Nevertheless, Benson's book is valuable on its own and merits a close reading. Benson not only locates and recovers an overlooked topic of Middle English literature, he also pursues this topic in a way that opens vastly more doors than it closes. Reading *Imagined Romes* will enable future critics to imagine the possibility of even more Romes.

ZACHARY STONE
McGill University
zachary.stone@mail.mcgill.ca

Arvind Thomas. *'Piers Plowman' and the Reinvention of Church Law in the Late Middle Ages.* Toronto: University of Toronto Press, 2019. Pp. xiv + 267.

In this erudite and incisive study of Langland's active engagement with canon law, Arvind Thomas takes seriously the 'reinvention' of his title. His book throughout relies on its two senses — finding ('inventio') and founding ('invention') — to persuasively show that Langland challenged and reformulated canon law maxims and, in turn, that Langland's poetic experiments shaped the understanding and reception of those maxims. Thus, rather than merely show that Langland cites canon law, Thomas depicts 'the art of poetry as sharing in the craft of law making' and argues for Langland 'as a penitential legislator in a world shaped by both poetry and law' (pp. 5–6).

Contributing to ongoing law-and-literature discussions in Langland studies — John Alford, Emily Steiner, and Nicholas Gray are among those Thomas explicitly cites — this book demonstrates that the field is far from tapped when it comes to *Piers*. This study distinguishes itself from those discussions in two contradictory ways: on one hand, it is very specific, sticking not just to canon law but more particularly to a few maxims that focus on penitential practice and its requirements. On the other hand, however, it more capaciously addresses the interrelationship between legal practice and poetic form, analysing how 'law is produced from within the poem' (p. 15). By examining this interrelationship closely and actively, Thomas can recognize canon law not as a static set of rules but rather as a dynamic, open, and hermeneutically stretchy method of constituting norms in the face of specific and complex circumstances.

Thomas organizes his book by penitential practice, moving through contrition, confession, restitution, and satisfaction. This unusual organization provides a structural sturdiness that permits him to move nimbly throughout both the B- and C-texts. Thus, rather than bring readers chronologically through the poem or show how a theme develops over its course, Thomas instead pinpoints specific passages that most overtly express Langland's canonistic thought without necessarily formulating direct connections between them. As a result, he offers readings of the poem that avoid flattening it out to fit his overall argument.

Indeed, his interpretations often rely on precise grammatical surgery. For example, when reading Reason's citation of the *nullum malum* maxim during Wrong's trial (B.4 / C.4), Thomas methodically shows how Reason moves slowly, almost imperceptibly, from the indicative mode to the canonistic subjective mode. Such focused readings might remain trapped in pedantry but for the fact that Thomas always lifts up to articulate their larger stakes; in this case, the move from indicative to subjunctive shifts 'a justification of punishing Wrong on personal grounds to a broader ecclesiastical reflection on penances to be interpreted and imposed by confessors' (p. 178). This is a teacherly book, one that throughout shows deep research and hermeneutic skill but always strives to explain why understanding Langland's interpretation and transformation of canon law matters for thinking about poetic process.

The Yearbook of Langland Studies, 34 (2020), 246–249   BREPOLS ❧ PUBLISHERS   10.1484/J.YLS.5.121100

Chapter 1 focuses on contrition in Meed's and Contricion's confessions, tracking the ways these confessions both deploy and critique the canonistic set of procedures designed to produce and judge remorse. On one hand, Thomas argues that Langland 'stages a performative but canonistically orthodox recuperation of contrition from those Wycliffite followers who rejected oral confession or even the entire ecclesiastical institution of penance on the grounds that heartfelt remorse alone remits sin' (pp. 34–35). Langland follows such canonists as Raymond of Peñafort and William of Rennes, who insist that contrition is both sign and thing and thus requires oral expression, solicited by a confessor who can draw it out with gentle admonitions. But on the other hand, Thomas shows that Langland does not merely rehearse such canonistic semiotics. Rather, the scene of Meed's confession (B.3 / C.3) inverts canonistic norms; there, the confessor uses the mild speech of consolation not to elicit a genuine expression of remorse but to extract money and gifts from Meed. Moreover, the C text emphasizes Meed's lack of contrition by depicting her laughter, a complicated sign that the confessor must try to read. Thomas argues that Meed's laughter signifies a mockery of canonistic signs of contrition, but I would have liked to have seen a broader, more complex account of Meed's laughter. Might we read her laughter not as mockery, but as humiliation, anger, or coyness? How does canonistic thought or Langland (or both) conceptualize non-verbal signs such as gestures, laughter, or tears within a theatre of contrition?

Chapters 2 stays with Meed to read her controversial gift-giving through the canonistic injunctions against usury. Noting that the canonistic maxims that deal with usury are quoted in B but absent in C, Thomas reads Conscience's refutation of Meed's apology as an invention of a corrective model of spiritual usury: that is, as a way of thinking about gift-giving and usurious relationships as descriptive not only of those between God and penitent, but of those between earthly lords and vassals. For Langland, then, usury becomes a way to conceptualize ethical human relationships as well as a moral relationship with the divine. Canonists such as Gratian and Hostiensis developed complex theories around risk and doubt to accommodate profit-driven transactions, and Langland uses those categories to understand loans and interest as potentially solidifying a 'relacioun rect' between labourer and lord. In other words, Meed's material gifts can become, in Conscience's ideal, ethical and moral gifts that charge interest in the form of love and good works, and which in turn operate in the service of communal and spiritual harmony.

In chapter 3, Thomas maps the canonistic grounds upon which the poem formulates a horizontal vision of restorative justice. Coveitise's confession (B.5 / C.6) focuses on Repentance's distinction between 'rule' and 'law' to universalize law for everyone (including the pope) and thus, more broadly, to explore the limits of the papal lawmaker. Whereas such canonists as Dynus Muxellanus and Johannes Andreae emphasized the necessity of discretionary application of canon rules (that is, by a pope or priest), Langland argues that the restitutive requirement of penance should be applied without contingency. Langland thus depicts the confessor as a mere middle ground between penitent and doctrine, such that the priest himself becomes subject to restitution. For Langland, then, restitutive justice requires a horizontally oriented penitential system, in which its operators are as subject to it as its participants.

At this point in the book, Thomas has developed an argumentative arc that sees in penitential practice an opportunity for ethical revision, which Langland promotes by imagining specific scenarios in which penitential method can be challenged, reframed, or extended. This arc specifically develops a thesis around Langland's depictions of penitential mediators (including confessors, bishops, and popes); Langland repeatedly formulates them as neglectful in their duties and, more crucially, as beholden to penitential practice and evaluation rather than above it. Accordingly, Langland suggests a capacious, even egalitarian model of penance that can dismantle earthly hierarchies or at least pierce the bubble of false authority. Thomas does not go so far as to make this claim, and, indeed, it does not seem that Langland is so bold or radical. But I found myself wanting more clarity about the overall purpose of Langland's experiments with canon law. Do his revisions add up to a broader theological, ethical, or poetic program? How far does Langland take the ethical potential of canon law?

The second part of the book — chapters 4 and 5 — more overtly addresses specific intersections of canonistic thought and figurative language, focusing on satisfaction. These final chapters are the most intricate and challenging of the book, as well as the longest. Chapter 4 looks at satisfaction through the lens of metaphor (Thomas relies on Paul Ricoeur) to show the mechanics of Langland's translation of satisfaction from law into work. Noting Reason's citation of the *nullum malum impunitum …* *nullum bonum irremuneratum* maxim ('no evil unpunished … no good unrewarded') in Wrong's trial, the chapter argues that Langland explicitly and atypically imagines satisfaction as field labour. In doing so, Langland mobilizes the relational work of metaphor to emphasize the dual sense of satisfaction as both matter (that is, what work must be performed by the penitent) and manner (that is, the approach the confessor must take in assigning appropriate penitential labour).

To assert Langland's metaphorical equation of penitential satisfaction and labour, Thomas notes that C differs from B in that it states that the confessors have interpreted the *nullum malum* maxim 'kyndeliche', a term on which Thomas puts quite a bit of pressure. Reading how Langland uses the term throughout the poem, Thomas ultimately argues that here *kyndeliche* denotes charitability, such that satisfaction must balance justice with mercy. Again, this reading suggests that Langland seems to advance a horizontal model of penance that emphasizes communal harmony over individual rectitude, but Thomas does not quite make that argument explicitly.

The book's fifth and final chapter argues that allegory helps explain Langland's depictions of the relationship between individual, private penance and the Church's penitential system, and, moreover, that Langland envisions allegory as the appropriate mode for regulating the relationship between penitent and God. Locating such mediatory semiotics with Peter Lombard, this chapter turns to Patience's sermon (B.14 / C.16) to address a shift from a 'patente' in B to a 'chartre' in C. Thomas argues that the shift from patent to charter signals a shift from penance as Christological and individual to penance as institutional, such that C relies on a canonistic understanding of penance as a semiotic mediation between inner contrition and divine remission.

Yet again, Langland does not merely rehearse penitential theory. Rather, he challenges and reformulates the system of penitential signs developed by Thomas of Chobham and Peñafort. 'Whereas for Thomas or Raymond, the confessor typically resolves the difference between the penitent's signs of contrition and the referent remission at the conclusion of every confession', Thomas explains, Patience puts off such resolution 'until "domesday"' (p. 230). Such deferral takes us to Paul de Man, who situates allegory within the temporal divide between sign and referent. Via de Man, Thomas argues that Patience's patent in B works like a symbol, in which the patent can be easily and immediately identified with both the document and Christ's body. In contrast, Patience's charter in C links the triadic system of Dowel, Dobet, and Dobest to contrition, confession, and satisfaction. In doing so, it formulates an allegorical — that is, temporally deferred — relationship between penitential sign and divine restitution. In C, penance is rendered provisional and, as such, requires institutional advocacy and support.

The short epilogue meditates on how momentary Langland's call for institutional advocacy was. As Thomas says, 'The poem's innovations within the terms of canon law become increasingly strange and unintelligible to readers to whom the church's legal institution no longer represented an open dialectical process but a closed dogmatic system of jurisprudence' (p. 238). Thomas has captured a moment in English literary and legal history, and as a result, he offers a foundational lens for anyone looking backward or forward to think about the parallel, intersecting, and contentious lives of legal and literary modes of thought in England.

This book is certainly crucial reading for Langlandians interested in the poem's canonistic investments, but it will also be more broadly foundational for anyone thinking about how form operates dialectically between 'rule' and 'invention'. Moreover, although the book is quite contained in its object of analysis — keeping specifically focused on moments in B and C — its historical and theoretical underpinnings will be illuminating for anyone thinking forward toward the theological, legal, and philosophical turbulence of the sixteenth century. Elegantly written and persuasively argued, this book merits persistent return for its suggestive insights and careful attention to Langland's intricate poetic experiments.

JAMIE K. TAYLOR
Bryn Mawr College
jktaylor@brynmawr.edu

CHASE PADUSNIAK

Annual Bibliography, 2019

The annual bibliography attempts to cover the year's work on *Piers Plowman* and other didactic or allegorical poems in the alliterative tradition (e.g., *Winner and Waster*, *Parliament of the Three Ages*, *Death and Life*, *Mum and the Sothsegger*, *Pierce the Ploughman's Crede*, *Richard the Redeless*, and *The Crowned King*) but not alliterative romances or the works of the *Gawain*-poet. The bibliography may occasionally include a selection of books and articles of more general interest to *YLS* readers. Authors should send abstracts of their books (*c.* 600–800 words) and articles (250–400 words) and details of doctoral dissertations and reviews to Chase J. Padusniak, at chasejp@princeton.edu.

1. 'Annual Bibliography, 2019', *Yearbook of Langland Studies*, 34 (2020), 287–325.

Sixty entries, comprising thirty-four annotated studies and a catalogue of reviews of thirty-seven books.

2. Aers, David, 'What Is Charity? William Langland Answers with Some Diachronic Questions', *Religions*, 10.8 (2019), 458–69.

Charity turns out to be the virtue which is both the root and the fruit of salvation in L's *PPl*, a late fourteenth-century poem, the greatest theological poem in English. It takes time, suffering and error upon error for Wille, the central protagonist in *PPl*, to grasp Charity. Wille is both a figure of the poet and a power of the soul, *voluntas*, the subject of charity. L's poem offers a profound and beautiful exploration of Charity and the impediments to Charity, one in which individual and collective life are inextricably bound together. This exploration is characteristic of late medieval Christianity. As such it is also an illuminating work in helping one identify and understand what happened to this virtue in the Reformation. Only through diachronic studies which engage seriously with medieval writing and culture can scholars hope to develop an adequate grasp of the outcomes of the Reformation in theology, ethics and politics, and the remakings of what we understand by 'person' in these outcomes. Although this essay concentrates on one long and extremely complex medieval work, it actually belongs to a diachronic inquiry. This will only be explicit in some observations on Calvin, in which Aers considers L's treatment of Christ's crucifixion, and in some concluding suggestions about the history of this virtue. (DA)

The Yearbook of Langland Studies, 34 (2020), 251–272   BREPOLS ❧ PUBLISHERS   10.1484/J.YLS.5.121101

3. Albin, Andrew, *Richard Rolle's Melody of Love: A Study and Translation with Manuscript and Musical Contexts* (Toronto: PIMS, 2019).

Excepting Nicholas Watson's magisterial *Richard Rolle and the Invention of Authority* (Cambridge, 1991), it is Rolle's vernacular works, and those of his Latin works translated into Middle English in the 1430s, that have received nearly all modern scholarly attention. This has led to the neglect of some of the hermit's most singular texts, chiefly his autobiographical sequence of biblical postils in alliterative, rhythmic Latin prose, the *Melos amoris*. Albin aims to redress this neglect in this comprehensive study of the *Melos amoris*, which also contains the first full translation of the text into English in alliterative prose that mirrors the Latin original, and a series of appendices providing access to key aspects of the work's manuscript contexts. The book is accompanied by a website, offering enlarged versions of these resources. Albin seeks to prompt a re-evaluation of the *Melos amoris* as Rolle's 'crowning literary achievement, an unmatched mannerist experiment whose matter is as profound as its language is pyrotechnic' (xvi).

The book's opening study identifies ten critical pathways for approaching Rolle's *Melos*. The first three sections of the study focus on the Latin text proper. Section I assesses the *Melos*'s form and content. Section II reflects on the work's rhetorical and alliterative style. Albin resolves that the text does not stand in genetic relationship to prose *cursus* or to the Alliterative Revival and refutes the standard interpretations of the *Melos*'s alliteration as mimetic of Rollean mystical song, instead terming it 'a playful work of late medieval English sound art' (36). Section III traces textual citations, allusions, and broader literary sources and influences. The next section inventories surviving, fragmentary, and attested *Melos amoris* manuscripts, some newly identified, providing detailed descriptions for each witness and observations on ownership and circulation. Section IV provides historical and biographical background on Rolle's Yorkshire heritage, education, eremitic practices, and notoriously idiosyncratic lifestyle. The next four sections offer sustained studies of Rolle's anthropology and angelology, his embeddedness in late medieval musical practice, and the entwined relationship he constructs between the *Melos amoris* and Scripture. In the final section, Albin comments on the ethos informing his translation of Rolle's Latin text. His translation of the fifty-eight chapters of Rolle's *Melos amoris* follows, amply footnoted to trace references, highlight interpretive cruxes, and supply the original Latin for challenging passages.

The five appendices with which Albin's book concludes invite readers to return to the *Melos amoris*'s manuscript contexts. Appendix I edits and translates a spurious fifty-ninth chapter, pastiched from Rolle's *Incendium amoris*, as it appears in three witnesses. The second and third transcribe lengthy marginal annotations and music from a gathering of fifteenth-century sacred polyphony found in one outstanding manuscript witness, Lincoln College MS Latin 89. Appendix IV supplies texts and translations for an audio recording based on MS Latin 89's music. The final appendix lists unusual or specialized Latin terms Rolle employs in his text. *Richard Rolle's Melody of Love*'s companion website (https://pims.ca/article/melos-amoris) expands on these appendices with the aforementioned audio recording and semi-diplomatic transcriptions of the entirety of MS Latin 89, text and music. The site promises open-access publication of Albin's translation soon. (AA)

4. Benson, C. David, *Imagined Romes: The Ancient City and its Stories in Middle English Poetry* (University Park: Pennsylvania State University Press, 2019).

This volume explores the conflicting representations of ancient Rome — one of the most important European cities in the medieval imagination — in late Middle English poetry.

Once the capital of a great pagan empire whose ruined monuments still inspired awe in the Middle Ages, Rome, the seat of the pope, became a site of Christian pilgrimage owing to the fame of its early martyrs, whose relics sanctified the city and whose help was sought by pilgrims to their shrines. Benson analyses the variety of ways that Rome and its citizens, both pre-Christian and Christian, are presented in a range of Middle English poems, from lesser-known, anonymous works, to the poetry of Gower, Chaucer, L, and Lydgate. Benson discusses how these poets conceive of ancient Rome and its citizens — especially the women of Rome — as well as why this matters to their works. *Imagined Romes* addresses a crucial lacuna in the scholarship of Rome in the medieval imaginary and provides fresh perspectives on the work of four of the most prominent Middle English poets. (Adapted from the publisher's abstract)

5. Bude, Tekla, 'Wet Feet, Dirty Coats, and the Agency of Things: Thinking Personification through New Materialism' *Yearbook of Langland Studies*, 33 (2019), 205–09.

This article considers *PPl's* construction of personifications in light of New Materialism, arguing that the poem is particularly receptive to the ways in which matter plays on language even as language seeks to contain and police the material world. Specifically, it argues that personification involves an inversion of animacy hierarchies (the assignation of relative liveness, sentience, or humanness to objects in the material world that has an effect both on how these objects are interpreted in the world and on how they operate as grammatical constructs). In this, it borrows from Mel Y. Chen's articulation of the notion of animacy. As Chen and other sociolinguists argue, hierarchizing language practices shape our view of reality and the likelihood with which we view any given noun — or object — as being 'animate' or 'inanimate', but this language is in turn shaped by human interactions with the material world. By placing abstract concepts in human bodies, *PPl* creates a momentary poetic inversion of animacy hierarchies; personification can be thought of as a material act. The article concludes by considering a particularly difficult problem of personification in the poem, which is its reliance not on visual metaphors to imagine the embodied forms that people the poem's landscape but instead focuses on sound. The materiality of the sound, Bude argues, becomes an animating principle in the poem — one that has important ramifications for the way the *persona* is understood. (TB)

6. Cady, Diane. *The Gender of Money in Middle English Literature: Value and Economy in Late Medieval England* (**London: Palgrave Macmillan, 2019**).

This book explores the vital and under-examined role that gender plays in the conceptualization of money and value in a period that precedes and shapes what we now recognize as the discipline of political economy. Through readings of a range of late Middle English texts, including *PPl*, this monograph demonstrates the ways in which gender ideology provided a vocabulary for articulating fears and fantasies about money and value in the late Middle Ages. These ideas inform beliefs about money and value in the West, particularly in realms that are often seen as outside the sphere of economy, such as friendship, love and poetry. Exploring the gender of money helps readers to better understand late medieval notions of economy, and to recognize the ways in which gender ideology continues to haunt our understanding of money and value, albeit often in occluded ways. (Adapted from the publisher's abstract)

7. Chenlin, Shou, 'Ideal of the Imitatio Christi in Chivalric Works in Late Medieval England: A Case Study' (unpublished doctoral thesis, University of Edinburgh, 2019), abstract in DAI-C 81/6(E) (2019), 27746257. Abstract available through ProQuest; abstract and full text at https://era.ed.ac.uk/handle/1842/35744.

8. Cordell, Jacqueline, 'Historicising Corpus Stylistics: Keywords and Collocation in William Langland's *Piers Plowman*' (unpublished doctoral thesis, University of Nottingham, 2019). Abstract and full text available through the British Library Ethos service (uk.bl.ethos.791439) and at http://eprints.nottingham.ac.uk/56152.

9. Cornelius, Ian, '*The Lay Folk's Catechism*, Alliterative Verse, and *Cursus*', *Review of English Studies*, **70.293 (2019), 14–36.**

The Lay Folks' Catechism is an English rendering of injunctions issued in 1357 by John Thoresby, Archbishop of York, setting forth the elements of Christian belief. Ever since W. W. Skeat's treatments, the *Catechism* has been placed in the general orbit of alliterative verse, yet closer identifications have proved elusive. The text is now recorded in both *The Index of Middle English Verse* and *The Index of Middle English Prose*; the principal stylistic study proposes that John Gaytryge, the author of the English text, may have been influenced by the system of Latin prose rhythm known as cursus. Renewed treatment must begin by establishing an accurate and authoritative text. Collation of the two best copies, York, Borthwick Institute, MS Abp Reg 11 and Oxford, Bodleian Library, MS Don.c. 13, confirms the general authority of the York copy. Recent studies of alliterative metre allow Gaytryge's composition to be distinguished with confidence from that English verse form. Affiliations to Latin *cursus* are more difficult to assess, but doubtful: more likely influences are the Latin of the Creed, *Pater noster*, and other *pastoralia*, and the plain style that preachers were instructed to adopt in preaching to the laity. The form of the *Catechism* may have been a deliberate innovation: a new plain style in the vernacular, aiming to embody the priorities of pastoral instruction. (IC)

10. Craun, Ed, 'A Taciturn Will', *Yearbook of Langland Studies*, 33 (2019), 43–67.

Taciturnity, the inclination to silence, comes to matter for Will in the final episode of the third dream, when his 'out of mesure' rebuke of Reason, responsible, as Will sees it, for human reckless conduct, results in the loss of his revelatory inner dream. This essay argues that thirteenth- and fourteenth-century discourse on taciturnity in moral texts informs the entire episode, from the end of Recklessness's diatribe. Rooted in a Roman ethic of cautionary self-interest and in Hebrew wisdom literature, this sapiential discourse is consequentialist: to act against human limitations and the nature of the world as humans have observed it over time is pointless and leads to painful consequences, while acting in accordance with both yields a productive life. L employs this discourse to develop the painful consequences of Will's uncontrolled, adversarial speech, a dimension of reckless conduct. While Reason harps on Will's limitations as a critic of the natural order, Imaginatif develops how Will may embrace taciturnity not only as a prudent way of protecting himself from self-inflicted injury, but also as a means of listening attentively and receptively in order to learn what he desires to know. This essay focuses on the C text, where revisions, additions, and excisions link Will's rebuke to Recklessness's diatribes and to intemperate sexual conduct and explore more fully the causes and painful consequences of Will's speech. In the opening of C.14, a major addition and excision make it clear that Will adopts taciturnity at the end of the third dream as a result of his experience and in light of moral discourse on the benefits of silence. (EC)

11. Crocker, Holly A., 'Feminism without Gender: *Piers Plowman*, "Mede the Mayde", and Late Medieval Literary Studies', *Exemplaria* 31.2 (2019), 93–104.

This article argues that an emphasis on gender has dampened the insights and energies of feminism in analyses of L's *PPl*. Inquiries into gender as a social construction of power have long highlighted women's dispossession, even erasure, in medieval representations. But such inquiries also have the potential to reinforce, or even naturalize, social conditions that privilege elite masculinity in those same medieval representations. Crocker proposes that we focus less on binarist notions of gender, and more on women's vulnerability in L's poem. As the shifting representation of 'Mede the Mayde' affirms, women's vulnerability is a constitutive social force in its own right: women's lives were shaped by vulnerability, and the vulnerability of women's lives critiqued social inequities. L's emphasis on vulnerability, and his focus on modes of agency and expression traditionally associated with women — submission and compassion, for instance — shifts the grounds of ethics in this poem, thereby rendering an interventionist, feminist version of the human that is not defined by domination and governance, but by forbearance and endurance. (HAC)

12. Desaillan-Olsen, Timothy Nodin, 'Vilifying Vermin: Creation of a Noxious "Kinde", 1300–1625' (unpublished doctoral thesis, University of Colorado at Boulder, 2019), abstract in DAI-A 81/3(E) (2019), 22592418. Abstract and full text available through ProQuest.

13. Flannery, Mary, 'Response: Langlandian Personification', *Yearbook of Langland Studies*, 33 (2019), 231–38.

This paper examines some of the characteristics of Langlandian personification. It begins with a brief look at the interpolations in the copy of Chaucer's *Cook's Tale* found in Oxford, Bodleian Library, MS Bodley 686. As a number of scholars have noted, these alliterative and allegorical interpolations seem much more immediately reminiscent of L's poetry than they do of Chaucer's. This paper argues that this is not simply because these interpolations are alliterative and allegorical, but because of the way they mimic L's distinctive style of personification. It goes on to link these interpolations with the themes considered in this issue's cluster of essays on 'Personification'. As this paper shows, the essay cluster's attention to L's treatment of both nonhuman materiality and embodied knowledge sheds new light on the notable lack of visual description that L provides for the personifications in *PPl*, as well as his reliance on sound and voice for bringing his personifications to life. (MF)

14. Fonzo, Kimberly, 'William Langland's Uncertain Apocalyptic Prophecy of the Davidic King', in *Catastrophes and the Apocalyptic in the Middle Ages and the Renaissance*, ed. by Robert Bjork (Turnhout: Brepols, 2019), pp. 53–64.

This chapter explores the content and meaning of Conscience's apocalyptic prophecy in Passus 3 of the B-Text. Fonzo notes that that some critics, notably Morton Bloomfield and Kathryn Kerby-Fulton, have linked this discourse with texts and ideas ultimately stemming from Joachim of Fiore and his eschatological tradition. By contrast, others, like David Aers and Robert Adams, have read Conscience's speech as a derivation from the writings of St Augustine and St Jerome. She shirks both interpretations, contending that this prophecy is a critique of the self-serving motivations often implicitly expressed in apocalyptic — and political — pronouncements. She points to several propaganda poems written during the Hundred Years War; these works connect the notion of an anointed, Davidic king — an image found in Conscience's prophecy — with the French crown. The English, the true heirs of the *translatio imperii* — or so the argument goes — have the real claim to power over and against the French pretenders. In certain cases, these works were written for war profiteers. *The Prophecy of John Bridlington* was, for example, produced for the notable war profiteer Humphrey de Bohun. Having observed these resonances, Fonzo notes that Conscience's speech appears during an argument with Lady Mede, the personification of greed and pecuniary power. They debate the merits of the 1360 Treaty Brétigny, with Mede contending that the English ought to have stayed in the war because then they would have further enriched themselves. Conscience retorts by reminding Mede of Saul and David. Coming right before the Davidic prophecy, this section implies, according to Fonzo, a critique of Edward III, who, like Saul, trusted bad counsel and put profiteering first. Seen in this light, Fonzo argues that L uses Conscience to show the need for penitence, rather than wars and get-rich-quick schemes. This passage thus becomes a mode of political critique, not an Augustinian or Joachimite prophecy. (CP)

15. Goodrich, Micah James, 'Lolling and the Suspension of Salvation in *Piers Plowman*', *Yearbook of Langland Studies*, 33 (2019), 13–42.

This essay considers the temporality of salvation in *PPl* through the mechanics of lolling and hanging — modes of temporal and somatic suspension that disrupt the teleological operations of redemption. Bringing Elizabeth Freeman's discussion of chrononormative time — the temporal arrangements that have dominion over life — into the soteriology of *PPl*, this article sees the temporal manoeuvre of lolling as a confrontation to a salvific system built on waiting. It is the asynchrony of waiting that produces precariousness and this temporal pause shows its effects on the body. Those who depend on — literally hang and loll on — Christ's return must wait in expectation of his coming, but have no promise, only hope, of a salvific future. This essay suggests that the temporal schematics of lolling and hanging reveal the inequities of salvific politics and expose the precariousness of temporally-bound subjects that institutional powers benefit from. As a temporal marker, lolling can stand for a variety of suspended actions: an imitation of Christ's suffering on the cross, an idle worker, a hanged felon, or a retroactive redemption, to name a few. The poem identifies the suspended pause of lolling as both necessary for and an obstruction to Christ's return. In this way, lolling makes manifest the asynchronicity that a quest for Truth requires because not all who loll and hang can access salvation. *PPl* takes seriously the precariousness of lolling subjects and questions how those who are suspended in time can *dowel* and secure a spot in a salvific future. (MG)

16. Grossman, Joel, '*Piers Plowman*' in '*Middle English*', *The Year's Work in English Studies*, 98 (2019), 201–66 (224–31).
A qualitative bibliographical review of work on *PPl* published in 2017.

17. Hamman, Grace E., 'Matter of Meekness: Reading Humility in Late Medieval England' (unpublished doctoral thesis, Duke University, 2019), abstract in DAI-A 80/11(E) (2019), 13806343. Abstract available through ProQuest.

18. Hanna, Ralph, 'Put the Load Right on Me': Langland on The Incarnation (With Apologies to the Band)', *Notes and Queries*, 66.2 (2019), 197–201.

Hanna comments on a possible source for image of the plant of peace at *PPl* B.1.153–56, originally suggested by Anne Middleton. Scholars have often considered these lines particularly ethereal, and even mysterious. Middleton traces this section to a commonplace textbook for schoolboys, the *Ecloga Theoduli*. Considering this a helpful insight, Hanna remarks how easily we forget these everyday sources, texts and traditions that carry little weight or prestige in modern critical discourse. He further notes that one can find echoes of L's lines in a well-documented sermon by the fourteenth-century Augustinian friar and Oxford theologian, John Waldeby. In doing so, Hanna clarifies that he is not merely interested in providing a possible genealogy for this part of the poem; rather, he takes the opportunity to comment on the habits of reading *PPl* so many medievalists have developed. Following Morton W. Bloomfield in seeing the poem as a commentary on some unknown mystery, critics seek out literary sources. Medievalists, trained by tracing Chaucer's allusions to Boccaccio, Jean de Meun, and other medieval *literati*, miss the ways in which so much of *PPl* has its basis in commonplaces and truisms endemic to the later middle ages. This work thus seems so mysterious, in part, because its references to various common traditions, texts, and even school exercises remain unexplored. Responding to Galloway, Hanna suggests that, to truly learn to read L's poem, we must be open to these sources, rather than obsessed with tracking down high-culture analogues. In this sense, *PPl* offers critics an opportunity to practice a new mode of source criticism, one geared at reading schoolrooms and sermons rather than canonical texts. (CP)

19. Horobin, Simon, 'John But and the Ending of the A Version of *Piers Plowman*', *Yearbook of Langland Studies*, 33 (2019), 127–42.

This article reconsiders the conclusion to the A version of *PPl* attributed to John But, reassessing how much of it can be attributed to But and how much to L himself. Where previous critics have sought to identify the historical John But on the assumption that this will shed light on the biography of L, the article adopts a more sceptical stance. It begins by deconstructing Edith Rickert's claims to have identified John But with a royal messenger of that name, showing how this is based on a number of baseless assumptions that have not been questioned by subsequent scholarship. The article goes on to consider other John Buts that have been proposed as possible candidates for the continuator, including the Norfolk family associated with the Rokele family discussed by Robert Adams and argued to have been a close associate. But instead of attempting to identify John But with a historical individual, the article questions the reasons for assuming a connection between continuator and poet. Rather than seeing But's conclusion as an attempt by a friend and admirer to claim the work as L's, the continuation is viewed alongside other scribal attempts to provide a satisfactory ending for L's unfinished work. When compared with other scribal attempts to impose closure upon the A version, John But's decision to name himself does not appear unusual, since several copyists include their names in scribal colophons. Instead of considering John But as a member of L's coterie, the article suggests that his knowledge of the author may have been entirely derived from reading his work. Analysis of the text composed by But and comparison with other scribally composed lines leads to the suggestion that But may have been familiar with L's poem from having copied it. (SH)

20. Jager, Katharine, ed., *Vernacular Aesthetics in the Later Middle Ages: Politics, Performativity, and Reception from Literature to Music* (London: Palgrave Macmillan, 2019).

This collection of essays explores the formal composition, public performance, and popular reception of vernacular poetry, music, and prose within late medieval

French and English cultures. This collection of essays considers the extra-literary and extra-textual methods by which vernacular forms and genres were obtained and examines the roles that performance and orality play in the reception and dissemination of those genres, arguing that late medieval vernacular forms can be used to delineate the interests and perspectives of the subaltern. Via an interdisciplinary approach, contributors use theories of multimodality, translation, manuscript studies, sound studies, gender studies, and activist New Formalism to address how and for whom popular, vernacular medieval forms were made. *PPl* is among the texts so explored. (Adapted from the publisher's abstract)

21. Johnston, Mike, 'The Clerical Career of William Rokele', *Yearbook of Langland Studies*, 33 (2019), 111–25.

In this essay, Johnston expands upon an earlier article about the life of William Rokele ('William Langland and John Ball', *Yearbook of Langland Studies*, 30 [2016], 29–74), who has been suggested as the author of *PPl*. He details new evidence from manorial court rolls that specifically narrows down the window in which this Rokele held his first two benefices. Johnston show that he held his first benefice, at Easthorpe, from the early 1350s until 1354–1355, following which he held the benefice of Redgrave until 1363–64. These dates align with recent suggestions by others that this same Rokele was priest at Newton from 1363 until 1368–1369. After surveying the evidence for Rokele's clerical career, Johnston then turns to evidence about the poem's dates and connections to London, arguing that Rokele's biography fits with this evidence. If Rokele were the poem's author, much of the A text would have been written while he was a rural priest. Nothing in the poem itself would contradict authorship by such a person, for only the B and C texts are definitively the products of a London poet. If Rokele is the author, then he had to have moved to London before beginning his expansion of the poem into B — again, the dates would allow this. In particular, the B text's reference to the mayoralty of Chichester in 1370 marks the time when he began expanding A into B. Since 1368–1369 is when the trail of Rokele's clerical career goes cold, if he is the author it would have to have been in these years that he relocated to London. This dating would explain why the B and C texts are so much more London-centric than A was. Johnston's argument is ultimately *not* that he thinks we have discovered who wrote *PPl*; rather, he intends that this new information demonstrate that Rokele's candidacy is reasonable and is the best case we currently have for *PPl*'s authorship. (MJ)

22. Lears, Adin E., 'On Bells and Rebellion: The Auditory Imagination and Social Reform, Medieval and Modern', in *Vernacular Aesthetics in the Later Middle Ages: Politics, Performativity, and Reception from Literature to Music*, ed. by Katharine Jager (London: Palgrave Macmillan, 2019), pp. 87–115.

Contrasting elite and lay forms of aural understanding, Lears turns to T. S. Eliot's coinage for a deeply felt, affective form of listening — the 'auditory imagination' (88). Texts associated with the cacophonous unrest of 1381 had to concern themselves with the sounds of the mob — were they wild and untamed or part of the embodied understanding of everyday people? While authors such as Gower distrusted and policed the squawks and howls — the empty sounds — of the crowd, using terms like 'vox fera' ('wild voice') and 'ore sonus' ('sounding voice' or 'sounding mouth') (88) to describe them, Lears argues that this alternate, lay mode of understanding operates in both the *Rebel Letters* and *PPl*. Turning to the former epistles, she contends that the *sound* of these texts 'made meaning at the material level' (90). They 'invite rhythmic and physical engagement' (90–91) from their readers, offer scholars an opportunity to glimpse the affective hearing of late-medieval people. Then, turning to *PPl*, Lears connects these ideas to the rat parliament, the belling of the cat, and these scenes' transition to the ambient noise of the medieval cityscape. In her view, L shares some of Gower's suspicion but also invites the physical engagement through hearing found in the *Rebel Letters*. Finally, she traces these strands through Victorian medievalists, especially William Morris. His *A Dream of John Ball* imagines the middle ages as a time more susceptible to immediate experience than his own, a fact that leads him to connect this mythologized past and its mode of being with his own utopian socialist vision. (CP)

23. McTurk, Rory, 'Contrapuntal Alliteration in *Piers Plowman* and Skaldic Poetry', in *Crossing Borders in the Insular Middle Ages*, ed. by Aisling Byrne and Victoria Flood (Turnhout: Brepols, 2019), pp. 113–32.

In this chapter, McTurk compares various forms of alliteration in both *PPl* and skaldic poetry. 'Contrapuntal alliteration', the most prominent form detected by the author and itself a term borrowed from A. V. C. Schmidt, refers to when a 'spare' alliterative syllable creates an 'interweaving effect' (113). L's normal metrical pattern is *aa/ax* (where 'a' refers to an alliterating stressed syllable and where 'x' signifies a non-alliterating stressed syllable). Contrapuntal alliteration, by contrast, creates either an *aab/ab* pattern or, alternatively, an *aba/ab* one, in which two different alliterating sounds are combined to produce a contrasting, interwoven effect. Schmidt calls the former form 'standard' and the latter one 'inverse'. McTurk, explaining these insights and then drawing upon them, shows that similar patterns may be found in a variety of Old Norse, skaldic poetry. Although these are organized into couplets, and thus are essentially different from L's single-line alliterative units, he fruitfully demonstrates that understanding how skalds created patterns may help us improve our understanding of meter and alliteration in *PPl*. McTurk further investigates 'liaisonal alliteration', a process by which an alliterating consonant occurs not at the beginning of a word, but rather at its end, resulting in its elision into the vowel that follows it. For example, he cites B.III.303 to this end: 'That **M**oyses or **M**essie // be **c**ome into this erthe' (116). While evidence for this form of alliteration is scarcer in *PPl*, McTurk adeptly demonstrates that these poetic approaches help to shed new light on L's poem, suggesting that, should another scholar wish to take such comparisons up, much could be learned about the ins-and-outs of alliteration and line-building in this seminal work of medieval poetry. (CP)

24. Orlemanski, Julie, 'Langland's Poetics of Animation: Body, Soul, Personification',
Yearbook of Langland Studies, 33 (2019), 159–84.

In medieval homiletic writings, body and soul were less often objects of explicit
theorization than they were representational devices, deployed to make subjectivity
thinkable and malleable in new ways. The fractious pairing of body and soul asked
medieval Christians to make a distinction not self-evident in living creatures — between
animating principle and material substrate, between what is immortal and what is
perishable, between spirit and flesh. Body and soul together acted like a conceptual
machine, churning through portrayals of human life to introduce difference and, so,
occasions for that difference's management. As this essay observes, the incision between
body and soul opened a field of representational invention, where what exactly the two
terms designated — and so the topology of the Christian subject — were mediated
through interminable circuits of distinction and analogy, metaphor and metonymy.
At several points in *PPl*, L sets the protean meanings of body and soul at odds with
the operations of personification. Their misalignment creates dizzying effects in part
because personification and the 'body-soul machine' share a similar structure: each
presumes a conceptual incision, a cut, distinguishing between matter and spirit (that
is, between literal and figurative senses, body and soul), and each generates its own
restless movement by refining and mediating that division. *PPl*'s poetics of animation
emerges from the distinctive manner in which the poem entangles the logics of
corporeal and allegorical animation, to drive itself toward crisis. The present essay
draws on the idea of the metaphoric and metonymic axes, formulated by Roman
Jakobson, to analyse this effect. The fraught Langlandian interplay of body and soul
can be seen in the confessions of the sins, in the contradictory personifications of the
vices; in the exchange between Haukyn and Patience, which troubles the structuring
analogy between religious language and food; and in the infiltration of the Barn
of Unity, which ironizes the metaphors organized around *Christus medicus*. The
clashing of literal and allegorical levels in these scenes stages the poem's profound
ambivalence about the legitimacy of bodily need, the resources of personification,
and the possibility of doing well in a fallen world, of which the human body is the
most immediate concretization. (JO)

25. Rigby, Stephen H., ed., with Sîan Echard, *Historians on John Gower* **(Cambridge:**
D. S. Brewer, 2019).

The late fourteenth century was the age of the Black Death, the Peasants' Revolt, the
Hundred Years War, the deposition of Richard II, the papal schism and the emergence
of the heretical doctrines of John Wyclif and the Lollards. These social, political and
religious crises and conflicts were addressed not only by preachers and by those involved
in public affairs but also by poets including Chaucer and L. Above all, though, it is in
the verse of John Gower that we find the most direct engagement with contemporary
events. Yet, surprisingly, few historians have examined Gower's responses to these
events or have studied the broader moral and philosophical outlook which he used
to make sense of them. In this volume, a number of eminent medievalists seek to
demonstrate what historians can add to our understanding of Gower's poetry, of his

life and of his ideas about society, the church, gender, politics and science. Whilst it would be a mistake to take Gower's works as merely straightforward *reportage*, it remains crucial to acknowledge how Gower addressed the issues of his day: because Gower's work includes such overt political and social commentary, an understanding of the period in which his work was rooted is particularly important. The aim of this volume is to enable a group of historians to bring their specialist expertise to bear on Gower's poetry and to show what a detailed knowledge of England in the late fourteenth and early fifteenth centuries can add to our understanding of his work. By examining the ideological frameworks which were available to Gower and his contemporaries, by determining the social, religious and political issues which his works tackled, and by ascertaining the assumptions and expectations of his original audience, historians can, it is to be hoped, contribute to the project of helping modern readers to arrive at a greater appreciation of the meanings of his texts.

The book begins with Martha Carlin's chapter, offering an important reassessment of Gower's biography which is based on newly-discovered primary sources and which lists all known Gower life-records. On society, David Green examines Gower's views on the nobility and chivalry. Mark Bailey discusses his attitudes toward the peasantry and the 1381 revolt. James Davis explores how the poet's views on trade were linked with contemporary London politics, whilst Anthony Musson reassesses his engagement with the law and his use of legal discourses. On the neglected topic of Gower and the church, David Lepine shows how Gower's poetry relates to contemporary debates about the papacy, secular clergy and Lollardy. Martine Heale asks how Gower's critique of contemporary monasticism was compatible with his own personal piety, whilst Jens Röhrkasten locates Gower's work in the context of medieval anti-fraternalism. On gender, Katherine Lewis looks at the possible reception of Gower's work by female owners of the *Confessio Amantis*; Christopher Fletcher offers a detailed linguistic analysis to illuminate Gower's understanding of masculinity. With regard to politics, Stephen Rigby asks why Gower's political theory has been open to such contradictory interpretations by modern critics. At the same time, Michael Bennett shows how Gower's personal connections may have influenced his shifting political positions. Finally, on science, Seb Falk identifies some new sources for Gower's use of astronomy. Whilst much modern study has focused on Gower's Middle English *Confessio Amantis*, the contributors to this volume also examine his works in French and Latin including the *Mirour de l'Omme*, *Vox Clamantis* and *Cronica Tripertita*.

Although the contributors to this volume emphasise the importance of historical context for an understanding of Gower's poetry, they do not seek to reduce his works simply to the status of vehicles for ideas, values, discourses and ideologies which originated outside them. Rather, the exchanges between history and literature documented in these pages are a two-way street. The historical explications on offer are often matched by these scholars' recognition of the rewards made available for historians from a close engagement with literary texts and with the work of literary scholars. The volume thus seeks not only to throw new light on Gower's work but, more generally, to encourage historians to engage with the debates which literary scholars have initiated about how we should locate medieval literature in its contemporary context. (SHR)

26. Steiner, Emily, 'William Langland', in *The Cambridge Companion to Medieval English Law and Literature*, ed. by Candace Barrington and Sebastian Sobecki (Cambridge: Cambridge University Press, 2019), pp. 121–34.

In this chapter, Steiner theorizes the various ways in which L imagines laws, lawful bodies, and legal frameworks in *PPl*. She argues that, for L, 'law is a language-making machine' (p. 127). Steiner begins by noting that 'law' in the middle ages ran through a variety of disciplines now thought to be distinct: theology, ethics, political theory, and aesthetics, *inter alia*. In reading *PPl*, therefore, we must be attentive to the variety of intersections and overlaps historically attached to this concept. The most obvious of these, according to Steiner, is the way in which L explores, and at times skewers, the corruption of the legal system in his own time. Lady Mede expresses, for example, how easily money can complicate and even poison everything from clerical power to personal relationships to just rule by the king. In addressing this issue, L downplays the role of legal bodies such as parliaments; he does not offer us a mirror for princes, concerning himself instead with the individual responsibility each person has for choosing the good. Using this observation as a springboard, Steiner then interrogates how L's understanding of salvation is necessarily caught up in legal concepts and metaphors. The poet, she argues, asks people to imagine themselves as legal entities who can sue or be sued, enter into contracts, and pay back debts. Turning to concepts like inheritance and mainprise, Steiner shows how inextricably L links such legal ideas with Christians' 'inheritance' of the kingdom of heaven. These observations return Steiner to an explication of how wonderfully elastic legal metaphors are when placed in L's hands. In B.11.129–36, for example, the dreamer imagines baptism as 'a contract of unfreedom between a lord and a churl' (p. 128). This image shocks the reader into faith, tying together spiritual fears about the soul and salvation with earthly fears about villeinage and legal bondage. According to Steiner, however, L's exploration of the law is not limited to such grimness; he imagines a variety of exceptions, feeling out the limits of medieval legal frameworks, most especially in cases where canon and common law rubbed up against each other. Steiner, in laying out this variety of modes of engagement, showcases how deftly L handles this series of interrelated frameworks — their abuttals, controversies, and stakes. (CP)

27. (Addendum to the 2018 annual bibliography.) Stevenson, Kath, '"Ther are Bokes Ynowe": Texts and the Ambiguities of Knowledge in *Piers Plowman*', in *Aspects of Knowledge: Preserving and Reinventing Traditions of Knowledge in the Middle Ages*, ed. by Marilina Cesario and Hugh Magennis (Manchester: Manchester University Press, 2018), pp. 163–81.

Traditions of Christian knowledge are an abiding preoccupation in *PPl*, where L explores fundamental questions about the pre-eminence or otherwise of abstract learning, textually mediated and transmitted ('clergie'), over experiential knowledge ('kynde knowing'), and about the role of learning in Christian salvation. What good is knowledge? In an age of abstruse academic discourse in which L himself was deeply versed, L's protagonist Will searches urgently for the knowledge that is truly valuable, that is, the knowledge that will enable him to save his soul. In this chapter,

Stevenson locates the ambivalence concerning the efficacy of textually mediated learning within the wider contexts of vernacular authority in the late fourteenth and fifteenth centuries and in particular shows L's treatment of the Passion in the central passus of his poem to be informed by the developing traditions of affective piety. For L, the Passion can function as a site in which textual and experiential knowledge are united, with abstract intellectual knowledge becoming transfigured as it is fused with 'kynde knowing'. (Adapted from the editors' introduction).

28. Stone, Zachary E., 'Towards a Vernacular Ecclesiology: Revising the *Mirour de l'Omme*, *Vox Clamantis*, and *Piers Plowman* During the Western Schism', *Yearbook of Langland Studies*, 33 (2019), 69–109.

This article triangulates John Gower's revisions to the *Mirour de l'Omme* and *Vox Clamantis*, L's revisions to *PPl*, and English representations of the early years of the Western Schism (1378–1414). In the *Mirour*, Gower appended a brief allusion to the Schism at the end of his discussion of the papacy. Likewise, changing ecclesiological landscape forced Gower to rework beginning of book III and, to a lesser extent, the end of book IV of the *Vox* twice. The first part of this article argues that we can date the references to the Schism in the *Mirour* and the *Vox*, and thus Gower's revisions to those poems, to specific moments between the outbreak of the crisis in Rome in the summer of 1378 and the aftermath of Bishop Henry Despenser's Flemish Crusade (*c.* 1382/3). The second half of the article situates Gower's revisions to the *Mirour* and the *Vox* in relation to L's potential references to the Schism in the B and C texts of *PPl*, especially the last two passus (B.19–20/C.21–22). Unlike Gower, L does not make clear, datable, references to the Schism. Nevertheless, his depiction of the papacy in the B and C texts resonates with Gower's account of the papacy during the Schism as well as a much broader cultural discourse regarding the basic shape, history, and possible future of the Roman church. Recovering Gower's and L's representations of the Schism not only brings these two contemporary poets into direct dialogue, but it also illuminates an undertheorized set of religious, political, and imaginative discourses centred on the institutional nature and shape of the Church. This article concludes by suggesting that scholars understand these discourses as a loose but recognizable 'vernacular ecclesiology' common to both the poetic works of L and Gower as well as much broader spectrum of later medieval literature. (ZES)

29. Thomas, Arvind, *Piers Plowman and the Reinvention of Church Law in the Late Middle Ages* (Toronto: University of Toronto Press, 2019).

This book discovers a mutually productive interaction between literary and normative 'makyngs' in *PPl*. It argues that L's poetic art is shaped by ecclesiastical procedures and principles and, reciprocally, shapes an understanding of them. Thomas focuses on *PPl*'s preoccupation with sin and its juridical correction, reading the poem in relation to treatises that were written to 'handle' sinners according to the rules ('canons') of ecclesiastical jurisprudence. In the poem's representations of trials, confessions, penalties and pardons, there is a resourceful interaction with the core digests of, and commentaries on, canon law (such as Gratian's *Decretum*, Pope

Gregory's *Decretals*, Hostiensis' *Summa aurea*, and Boniface VIII's *Sext*), as well as confessors' manuals. Throughout the book, Thomas explores the extent to which characteristics we understand as 'literary' inform and transform those we would distinguish as 'legal'. Specifically, he uncovers the ways in which the poem's narrative voice, metaphor, syntax and style not only reflect but also act upon properties of canon law such as penitential procedure, authoritative maxim, and decretist or decretalist gloss. L's mobilization or modification of juridical terms and concepts, Thomas contends, not only engenders a poetics informed by canonist thought but also expresses a vision of canon law alternative to that offered by medieval jurists or by contemporary medievalists.

Ever since Walter Skeat's famous edition of the three versions of the poem over a hundred years ago, L scholarship has sought to identify their borrowings from penitential and legal traditions. But despite amassing a wealth of knowledge of the poet's debts to legislative sources, we still know little about how the poem's versions themselves contribute to an understanding of the discourse of medieval Church law. For the most part, scholars tend to treat *PPl*'s recourse to authoritative texts as passive — as one of derivation or reflection, rather than of re-creation or co-production. This book challenges this mode of reading and spotlights a juridical agency indigenous to the poem itself and, hence, meaningful to both literary critics and legal historians. In essence, Thomas argues that the places in *PPl* where one detects an indebtedness to normative treatises are, at the same time, sites of poetic re-envisioning and re-founding Church law. In such places, the words of the poet invoke and impact the world of the lawyer. Nowhere is this twofold sense of poetic-legal invention more evident in *PPl* than in the differences between the B and C versions of the poem. By attending to the various additions, excisions, and interpolations that differentiate the two versions, Thomas tracks the shaping of Church law in and across *both* B and C versions of *PPl*. Acutely aware of the current scholarly dissension over the nature, number and authorship of the poem's versions, this study treats B and C as exemplifying a range of approaches to Church law rather than as illustrating stages in the development of a single poet or poem.

Composed of five chapters along with an epilogue, *Piers Plowman and the Reinvention of Church Law in the Late Middle Ages*, is structured around the stages of handling sin in the Church's forum of penance: confession, contrition, restitution, and satisfaction. In each chapter Thomas tells three stories. The first is a story aimed at any reader curious about the creative interdependence between poetry and law in the late medieval period. The second is a story for historians interested in the construction of Church law in fictional compositions. The third is a story for L scholars invested in the poem's versions and their interrelations. Together, these readings describe a poetic-legal state of affairs that remains relevant up until the closing of the Middle Ages. In the epilogue, Thomas casts a retrospective glance at *PPl* and ecclesiastical jurisprudence from the perspective of Martin Luther's burning of papal law books. He does so in order to suggest why we may have lost sight of L's legal makings: they belong to a historical moment that flickers and fades forever in the wake of the Reformation when Church law ceased to hold the institutional power and imaginative potential that once allowed for its shaping by poets and thence beyond in the world of lawyers. *Piers Plowman and the Reinvention of Church Law in the Late Middle Ages seeks to* recover that moment and to make it visible at a time when the legislative role of ecclesiastical institutions remains a deeply relevant issue in the Anglo-American world. (AT)

30. Ward, Jessica D., 'Penitentials to Poetry: The Literary Critique of Avarice in Fourteenth-Century England' (unpublished doctoral thesis, University of North Carolina at Greensboro, 2019), abstract in DAI-A 81/1(E) (2019), 13806650. Abstract available through ProQuest.

31. Warner, Lawrence, 'The Ilchester Prologue, the Penultimate Passus of Corpus 201 (F), and a New School of *Piers Plowman* Textual Studies', *Journal of English and Germanic Philology*, 118.4 (2019), 486–516.

Ralph Hanna and Sarah Wood simultaneously published near-identical essays mocking those many textual scholars who consider it likely that loose sheets of revision material found their way into the B archetype and the manuscript behind the Ilchester Prologue. The first part of this essay shows that the mockery is not justified, as the supposed counter-evidence does not exist and no other explanation of Ilchester's text makes any sense. It argues Wendy Scase's 1987 argument was correct, and that those parts of D. Vance Smith's recent essay that stand up accord with Scase's argument. (Smith putatively argues against Scase on the basis of his miscounting of the number of lines in the passages at issue.) In the second part of the essay, Warner addresses Hanna's claim that he had failed to recognize that MS F of B follows C rather than B in its penultimate passus. At stake here is F's role in a much bigger argument that Hanna is keen to undermine without having to confront it head-on. Warner points out that Hanna offers no evidence for his own proposal, which is not surprising since all available evidence is against it. He reaffirms that F follows B, despite the willingness of many critics to accept Hanna's proposal. Their mutual willingness to reject coincident variation and the logic of textual studies at large in the service of mocking fellow scholars identifies Hanna and Wood as members of a new school of *PPl* textual studies. This essay explicitly urges a return to common sense in our approach to such matters and implicitly urges abandonment of the rhetoric of mockery that pervade Hanna's and Wood's textual work on these issues. (LW)

32. Waters, Claire, 'The Voice of the Sluggard: Demi-Personification in the *Manuel des pechiez*', *Yearbook of Langland Studies*, 33 (2019), 185–204.

William of Wadington's *Manuel des pechiez* offers lay and clerical audiences ways to recognize sin in themselves and reform their hearts. Personification might seem to be a valuable tool in this effort, but William very seldom uses it, famously preferring to resort to lively exempla. His depiction of sloth, however, presents a miniature dramatization of the sin through the figure of a semi-personified, semi-exemplary figure, *le perecous* or the sluggard. The *Manuel* works to show how sloth's varied names, shifting boundaries, and primarily negative expression make it difficult to recognize. At the same time, sloth can be seen as a 'special vice' that William consistently associates with 'unnaturalness' and dehumanization. The conjunction of sloth's danger and its slipperiness make it especially urgent to represent it effectively. The *Manuel's* section on sloth launches, after a brief list of characteristic behaviours, into a lengthy passage that begins with the sluggard lying in bed rather than going to church and proceeds to follow his actions (or inaction) as he progresses through his day. The setting and the depiction of various internal and external voices that the sluggard hears create a sense of quotidian plausibility that leads into a scene of mortal failure, as the sluggard finds himself singing, 'Now it is too late', an evocation of popular song that intermingles the voices of sluggard and preacher and shows how the everyday and the eternal fold into one another. Neither a fully human individual nor a fully allegorical personification, William's sluggard helps to convey the divided self created by sin and recalls the variety of figures used to represent sin in *PPl*, from embodied personifications to collective identities to faulty individuals. William's sluggard, unlike L's Sleuthe, combines this variety in one body and urges readers to imagine themselves in his place. He also evokes a realistic soundscape that returns in the figure of Will listening to the church bells and calling to his family; Will, rather than Sleuthe, is the true descendant of William's sluggard. (CW)

33. Weiskott, Eric, 'A Sixteenth-Century Political Prophecy Inspired by *Piers Plowman*', *Notes and Queries*, 66.2 (2019), 217–19.

This note discusses 'When wealth is walked away', a sixteenth-century English political prophecy that shows a remarkable affinity for *PPl*. The poem, whose dystopian vision probably reflects opposition to enclosure, includes characters, allegorical motifs, and political provocations characteristic of L's writing. 'When wealth is walked away' constitutes yet another direct connection between *Piers Plowman* and the genre of political prophecy in sixteenth-century literary culture. The note includes a complete edited text of 'When wealth is walked away'. (EW)

34. Weiskott, Eric, 'William Langland's First First Word', *Notes and Queries*, 66.4 (2019), 509–10.

PPl is known for its depictions of social upheaval, its theological discourse, textuality, and its visionary poetics, less so for the invention of literary English. Yet although Chaucer now has the clearer claim to have initiated a literary language, L has the prior claim. This note examines the first word that Langland was, evidently, first to use in the first version of *Piers Plowman*, composed *c.* 1370. This word is *iaperis*, 'jesters' (A.Prol.35). In line 35 and elsewhere in the prologue to the A version, Langland discovers categorizations for social malpractice, categorizations he never left behind in the process of rewriting his life's work. (EW)

Advance online access was available in 2019 to Andrew Galloway, 'Langland and the Reinvention of Array in Late-Medieval England', *Review of English Studies* <https://doi-org/10.1093/res/hgz123>, and Benjamin D Weber, 'The Chains of Charity: *Piers Plowman* B.5.607 and Hosea 11:4, *Notes and Queries* <https://doi-org/10.1093/notesj/gjz167>.

Book Reviews

35. Aers, David, *Beyond Reformation?: An Essay on William Langland's Piers Plowman* (Notre Dame: University of Notre Dame Press, 2015). Rev. by Larry Scanlon, *Journal of English and Germanic Philology*, 118.2 (2019), 276–80.

36. Atkin, Tamara, and Francis Leneghan, eds, *The Psalms and Medieval English Literature: From the Conversion to the Reformation* (Cambridge: D. S. Brewer, 2017). Rev. by Emma Knowles, *Parergon*, 36.1 (2019), 180–82; Hannah Piercy, *Medium Ævum*, 88.1 (2019), 196.

37. Barney, Stephen A., *The Penn Commentary on Piers Plowman, 5: C Passūs 20–2; B Passūs 18–20* (Philadelphia: University of Pennsylvania Press, 2006). Rev. by Michael Baker, *Medium Ævum*, 88.2 (2019), 409–411.

38. Burrow, John A., and Thorlac Turville-Petre. *Piers Plowman: The B-Version Archetype (Bx)* (Raleigh: The Society for Early English and Norse Electronic Texts, 2018). Rev. by Lawrence Warner, *Journal of English and Germanic Philology*, 118.4 (2019), 590–92.

39. Calabrese, Michael, *An Introduction to Piers Plowman* (Gainesville: University Press of Florida, 2019). Rev. by Thomas Goodmann, *Modern Philology*, 117.4 (2019), E233–E236; Rosemary Neill, *Arthuriana*, 29.2 (2019), 117–19.

40. Cervone, Cristina Maria, and D. Vance Smith, eds, *Readings in Medieval Textuality: Essays in Honour of A. C. Spearing* (Cambridge: D. S. Brewer, 2016). Rev. by Holly A. Crocker, *Journal of English and Germanic Philology*, 118.1 (2019), 145–47.

41. Connolly, Margaret, and Raluca Radulescu, eds, *Editing and Interpretation of Middle English Texts: Essays in Honour of William Marx* (Turnhout: Brepols, 2018). Rev. by Alexandra Barratt, *Parergon*, 36.1 (2019), 237–38.

42. Cornelius, Ian, *Reconstructing Alliterative Verse: The Pursuit of a Medieval Meter* (Cambridge: Cambridge University Press, 2017). Rev. by Andrew Galloway, *Arthuriana* 29.4 (2019), 76–78; Geoffrey Russom, *Journal of English and Germanic Philology*, 118.4 (2019), 583–86; Thorlac Turville-Petre, *Medium Ævum*, 88.1 (2019), 160–61.

43. Critten, Roy G., *Author, Scribe, and Book in Late Medieval English Literature* (Rochester: Boydell & Brewer, 2018). Rev. by Alastair Minnis, *Medium Ævum*, 88.1 (2019), 164–66.

44. Davis, Rebecca, *Piers Plowman and the Books of Nature* (Oxford: Oxford University Press, 2016). Rev. by Michael Baker, *Medium Ævum*, 88.2 (2019), 411–412; Ian Cornelius, *Journal of English and Germanic Philology*, 118.1 (2019), 151–54; Kellie Robertson, *Speculum* 94.2 (2019), 523–24.

45. Deskis, Susan E., *Alliterative Proverbs in Medieval England: Language Choice and Literary Meaning* (Columbus: The Ohio State University Press, 2016). Rev. by Ian Cornelius, *Medium Ævum*, 88.1 (2019), 159–60.

46. Escobedo, Andrew, *Volition's Face: Personification and the Will in Renaissance Literature* (Notre Dame: University of Notre Dame Press, 2019). Rev. by Sarah Tolmie, *Yearbook of Langland Studies*, 33 (2019), 239–42.

47. Galloway, Andrew. *The Penn Commentary on Piers Plowman, 1: C Prologue – Passus 4; B Prologue Passus 4; A Prologue – Passus 4* (Philadelphia: University of Pennsylvania Press, 2006). Rev. by Michael Baker, *Medium Ævum*, 88.2 (2019), 409–411.

48. Garrison, Jennifer, *Challenging Communion: The Eucharist and Middle English Literature* (Columbus: The Ohio State University Press, 2017). Rev. by Kerilyn Harkaway-Krieger, *Journal of Medieval Religious Cultures*, 45.1 (2019), 81–83; Natalie Jones, *Medium Ævum*, 88.1 (2019), 163–64.

49. Goodmann, Thomas A., *Approaches to Teaching Langland's 'Piers Plowman'* (New York: Modern Language Association of America, 2018). Rev. by Katie Little, *Journal of British Studies*, 58.4 (2019), 813–14; Mary Raschko, *Medieval Review* (2019), 19.11.18.

50. Gruenler, Curtis A., *Piers Plowman and the Poetics of Enigma: Riddles, Rhetoric, and Theology* (Notre Dame: University of Notre Dame Press, 2019). Rev. by Alastair Bennett, *Speculum*, 94.4 (2019), 1161–62; Jennifer Garrison, *Journal of English and Germanic Philology*, 118.3 (2019), 430–432.

51. Hanna, Ralph. *Patient Reading / Reading Patience: Oxford Essays on Medieval English Literature* (Liverpool: Liverpool University Press, 2017). Rev. by Alastair Bennett, *Modern Philology*, 117.4 (2019), E237–E240; Michael Calabrese, *Yearbook of Langland Studies*, 33 (2019), 243–46; Sarah Noonan, *Journal of English and Germanic Philology*, 118.4 (2019), 587–89; Robin Waugh, *Journal of British Studies*, 58.3 (2019), 620–621.

52. Hanna, Ralph. *The Penn Commentary on 'Piers Plowman', Volume 2: C Passūs 5–9; B Passūs 5–7; A Passūs 5–8* (Philadelphia: University of Pennsylvania Press, 2017). Rev. by Michael Baker, *Medium Ævum*, 88.2 (2019), 409–411; Ian Cornelius, *Medium Ævum*, 88.2 (2019), 412–414.

53. Horobin, Simon, and Aditi Nafde, eds, *Pursuing Middle English Manuscripts and Their Texts: Essays in Honour of Ralph Hanna* (Turnhout: Brepols, 2017). Rev. by Michael Johnston, *Yearbook of Langland Studies*, 33 (2019), 247–49; Jenna Mead, *Parergon*, 36.1 (2019), 204–06; Stephen H. A. Shepherd, *Studies in the Age of Chaucer*, 41 (2019), 377–83; Sebastian Sobecki, *Speculum*, 94.3 (2019), 844–45; Leah Tether, *Medieval Review* (2019), 19.06.05

54. Johnson, Eleanor, *Staging Contemplation: Participatory Theology in Middle English Prose, Verse, and Drama* (Chicago: University of Chicago Press, 2018). Rev. by Jessica Brantley, *Studies in the Age of Chaucer*, 41 (2019), 383–87; Michael P. Kuczynski, *Modern Philology*, 117.2 (2019), E85–E87; Barbara Newman, *Yearbook of Langland Studies*, 33 (2019), 250–53; Luke Penkett, *Comitatus*, 50 (2019), 223–24.

55. Knox, Philip, Jonathan Morton, and Daniel Reeve, eds, *Medieval Thought Experiments: Poetry, Hypothesis, and Experience in the European Middle Ages* (Turnhout: Brepols, 2018). Rev. by R. D. Perry, *Medieval Review*, 19.12.17.

56. Lawler, Traugott, *The Penn Commentary on Piers Plowman, Vol. 4: C Passūs 15–19; B Passūs 13–17* (Philadelphia: University of Pennsylvania Press, 2018). Rev. by Michael Baker, *Medium Ævum*, 88.2 (2019), 409–411; Alastair Bennett, *The Library*, 20.4 (2019), 559–62; Michael Calabrese, *Medieval Review* (2019),

19.03.09; Ian Cornelius, *Anglia*, 137.3 (2019), 502–06; Lawrence Warner, *Yearbook of Langland Studies*, 33 (2019), 253–57.

57. Lawton, David, *Voices in Later Medieval Literature: Public Interiorities* (Oxford: Oxford University Press, 2017). Rev. by Katherine Zieman, *Yearbook of Langland Studies* 33 (2019), 258–60; Julie Orlemanski, *Modern Philology*, 116.3 (2019), E151–E154.

58. Lochrie, Karma, *Nowhere in the Middle Ages* (Philadelphia: University of Pennsylvania Press, 2016). Rev. by Theresa Tinkle, *Journal of English and Germanic Philology*, 118.1 (2019), 149–51.

59. Lenzi, Sarah E., *The Stations of the Cross: The Placelessness of Medieval Christian Piety* (Turnhout: Brepols, 2016). Rev. by John Munns, *Speculum*, 94.3 (2019), 855–56.

60. Meyer-Lee, Robert J., and Catherine Sanok, eds, *The Medieval Literary: Beyond Form* (Cambridge: D. S. Brewer, 2018). Rev. by Katharine Breen, *Studies in the Age of Chaucer*, 41 (2019), 387–91.

61. Raschko, Mary, *The Politics of Middle English Parables: Fiction, Theology, and Social Practice* (Manchester: Manchester University Press, 2018). Rev. by David Lavinsky, *Studies in the Age of Chaucer*, 41 (2019), 405–408.

62. Robertson, Kellie, *Nature Speaks: Medieval Literature and Aristotelian Philosophy* (Philadelphia: University of Pennsylvania Press, 2018). Rev. by Rebecca Davis, *Yearbook of Langland Studies*, 33 (2019), 260–65; Carles Gutiérrez-Sanfeliu, *Parergon*, 36.2 (2019), 241–42.

63. Russom, Geoffrey, *The Evolution of Verse Structure in Old and Middle English Poetry: From the Earliest Alliterative Poems to Iambic Pentameter* (Cambridge: Cambridge University Press, 2017). Rev. by Ian Cornelius, *Arthuriana*, 29.4 (2019), 82–85; David O'Neil, *Medium Ævum*, 88.1 (2019), 155–56.

64. Schrock, Chad D., *Medieval Narrative: Augustinian Authority and Open Form* (New York: Palgrave Macmillan, 2015). Rev. by Theresa Tinkle, *Yearbook of Langland Studies*, 33 (2019), 266–69.

65. Sidhu, Nicole Nolan, *Indecent Exposure: Gender, Politics, and Obscene Comedy in Middle English Literature* (Philadelphia: University of Pennsylvania Press, 2016). Rev. by Suzanne M. Edwards, *Yearbook of Langland Studies*, 33 (2019), 269–72.

66. Strong, David, *The Philosophy of Piers Plowman: The Ethics and Epistemology of Love in Late Medieval Thought* (New York: Palgrave Macmillan, 2017). Rev. by Jessica Rosenfeld, *Yearbook of Langland Studies*, 33 (2019), 272–74; Cheryl Taylor, *Parergon*, 36.1 (2019), 224–26.

67. Thomas, Arvind, *Piers Plowman and the Reinvention of Church Law in the Late Middle Ages* (Toronto: University of Toronto Press, 2019). Rev. by Conrad van Dijk, *Studies in the Age of Chaucer*, 41 (2019), 419–423.

68. Turville-Petre, Thorlac, *Description and Narrative in Middle English Alliterative Poetry* (Liverpool: Liverpool University Press, 2018). Rev. by Stephen A. Barney, *Yearbook of Langland Studies*, 33 (2019), 274–77; Ian Cornelius, *Anglia*, 137.3 (2019), 488–495; Richard Moll, *Medieval Review* (2019), 19.12.09; Alex Mueller, *Review of English Studies*, 70.296 (2019), 754–56; Eric Weiskott, *Modern Philology*, 117.1 (2019), E26–E28.

69. Walter, Katie L., *Middle English Mouths: Late Medieval Medical, Religious and Literary Traditions* (Cambridge: Cambridge University Press, 2018). Rev. by Katherine Harvey, *Medieval Review* (2019), 19.12.13; Mary Hayes, *Yearbook of Langland Studies*, 33 (2019), 277–81; Michael Leahy, *Nottingham Medieval Studies*, 63 (2019), 218–21; Daniel McCann, *Review of English Studies*, 70.294 (2019), 358–60; Sarah Star, *Medium Ævum*, 88.2 (2019), 418–419.

70. Warner, Lawrence, *Chaucer's Scribes: London Textual Production, 1384–1432* (Cambridge: University of Cambridge Press, 2018). Rev. by Julia Boffey, *The Library*, 20.3 (2019), 397–99; Michael Calabrese, *Modern Philology*, 117.3 (2019), E167–E169; Neil Cartlidge, *Medium Ævum*, 88.2 (2019), 414–415; Noelle Phillips, *Studies in the Age of Chaucer*, 41 (2019), 432–436; David Raybin, *Yearbook of Langland Studies*, 33 (2019), 281–86.

71. Weiskott, Eric, *English Alliterative Verse: Poetic Tradition and Literary History* (Cambridge: Cambridge University Press, 2018). Rev. by Anna Helene Feulner, *Anglia*, 137.4 (2019), 670–678; Judith A. Jefferson, *Journal of English and Germanic Philology*, 118.2 (2019), 266–68.